The Federal Communications Commission

THE FEDERAL COMMUNICATIONS COMMISSION

☆ ★ ☆

Front Line in the Culture and Regulation Wars

Kimberly A. Zarkin and Michael J. Zarkin

Understanding Our Government

Greenwood Press
Westport, Connecticut • London

Library of Congress Cataloging-in-Publication Data

Zarkin, Kimberly.
    The Federal Communications Commission : front line in the culture and
regulation wars / Kimberly A. Zarkin and Michael J. Zarkin.
       p.   cm.—(Understanding our government, ISSN 1556–8512)
    Includes bibliographical references and index.
    ISBN 0–313–33416–1 (alk. paper)
    1. United States. Federal Communications Commission. 2. Telecommunication policy—United
States—History. 3. Telecommunication—Law and legislation—United States. I. Zarkin,
Michael J. II. Title. III. Series.
    HE7781.Z367   2006
    384.0973—dc22   2005033759

British Library Cataloguing in Publication Data is available.

Library of Congress Catalog Card Number: 2005033759
ISBN: 0–313–33416–1
ISSN: 1556–8512

First published in 2006

Greenwood Press, 88 Post Road West, Westport, CT 06881
An imprint of Greenwood Publishing Group, Inc.
www.greenwood.com

Printed in the United States of America

The paper used in this book complies with the
Permanent Paper Standard issued by the National
Information Standards Organization (Z39.48–1984).

10 9 8 7 6 5 4 3 2 1

Teachers are created by the hard work of the dedicated people who taught them. We have both been blessed with wonderful teachers throughout our educations, but there are two special ones to whom we wish to dedicate this volume:

Mary Leahy, Rockland High School

William Chamberlin, Ph.D., University of Florida

Contents

Series Foreword

Since the founding of our country in 1776, the U.S. government has transformed significantly. Changing societies and events, both domestic and international, have greatly affected the actions and development of our country. The Industrial Revolution, World War II, the civil rights movement, and the more recent "war on terrorism" are just a few of the events that have changed our government and its functions. Depending on the needs of our country at any given time, agencies are developed or terminated, their size and/or budget increased or decreased, or even transferred to another department within the government, in order to meet policy makers' objectives. Whether an independent agency or part of the fifteen executive branch departments overseen by the president and the cabinet, each is given specific responsibilities and all are formed to fulfill an important role for the country and its people.

The Understanding Our Government series was developed to offer an in-depth view of the most powerful, controversial, and misunderstood agencies of the U.S. government and how they have changed American society and, in some cases, the world. Well-known agencies frequently in the media spotlight, such as the Central Intelligence Agency and the National Aeronautics and Space Administration, are included, as well as lesser-known, but important, agencies such as the Bureau of Indian Affairs and the Forest Service. Written by experts on the particular agencies, including former employees or advisory committee members, each volume provides a historical overview of an agency and includes narrative chapters describing such aspects as organization, programs, significant events, controversies, key people, and influence on society, as well as additional topics tailored to the particular agency. Subjects vary greatly among the different titles. Depending on readers' interests or needs, some will be able to find information including the Central Intelligence Agency's role in the Cuban missile crisis, as well as its history of covert operations, while others may be interested in the Environmental Protection Agency's response to environmental disasters such as the *Exxon Valdez* oil spill and the Three Mile Island nuclear accident. Still others may be curious to learn about the Federal Communication Commission's role in communications policy and regulation of the media, and the fine line between censorship and freedom of speech, or the Drug Enforcement Administration's enforcement of drug laws and methods of combating drug trafficking, and how the legalization of certain illegal drugs would affect the agency and the country in general.

Whether readers are students conducting research on a specific agency for a high school or college assignment, or just want to learn more about one or how the government works, our hope is that each will gain further knowledge about the U.S. government and its employees. We want readers to comprehend our nation's significant achievements, yet also understand its failures and how we can learn from them. Over the years, our country has performed great feats, from creating lifesaving drugs to space exploration, but it has also experienced tragedies including environmental catastrophes and terrorist attacks. Readers will learn of how such events shape legislation and public policy, and how they affect everyday life for the citizens of this country. While many agencies have been portrayed in certain ways in newspapers, on television, and in films, such representations have not always been realistic or impartial. As a result, this series attempts to offer fair, objective views of U.S. government agencies, and to allow readers to think about them and form their own opinions.

Steven Vetrano
Greenwood Press

Preface

The writing of this volume took place during a sixteen-month interval running from the spring of 2004 to the late summer of 2005. In reality, however, this volume represents more than twenty years of research on the part of the authors. Although this is a reference volume aimed mainly at cataloging information, we did have a theme in mind as we wrote. We believe that any thorough discussion of the FCC (and perhaps any other administrative agency, for that matter) should include four interrelated components: people, policy, politics, and procedures. With these themes in mind, the volume has been organized into the following eight chapters:

- Chapter 1 provides a broad introduction to the FCC, including a discussion of its political origins, history, statutory authority, and regulatory activities.
- Chapter 2 provides an overview of the FCC's organization and procedures, including a discussion of its major administrative units and offices, as well as a discussion of the agency's decision-making procedures and the means through which the public can obtain information regarding agency activities.
- Chapter 3 contains a broad discussion of the FCC's political environment, including its relations with the president, Congress, the courts, and various interest groups throughout its history.
- Chapter 4 provides a historical overview of the Commission's major policy initiatives in the area of common carrier regulation, including such matters as the development of competition in the telephone industry, the development of data communications services, the breakup of AT&T, and policy changes contained in the Telecommunications Act of 1996.

- Chapter 5 provides a historical account of the Commission's major policy initiatives in the areas of broadcasting and cable regulation, including the Fairness Doctrine, the regulation of indecency on broadcasting and cable, and must-carry rules.
- Chapter 6 provides biographical sketches of all of the commissioners who have ever served at the FCC.
- Chapter 7 contains an annotated list of Supreme Court cases to which the Commission and its predecessor, the Federal Radio Commission, were a party. (Appendix 1 is a list of all cases heard at the intermediate appellate level to which the FCC was a party.)
- Chapter 8 is a chronology of key events.

A volume as vast and lengthy as this one requires the assistance of many people. The authors wish to thank Westminster College and the Gore family for a generous faculty development grant that helped pay for research assistance and the acquisition of photographs. Miranda Taft provided much-needed assistance with locating and categorizing the cases in Appendix 1. In addition, the following people provided assistance in locating the photographs contained in this volume: Dave Massey, Stan Schreier, D. Bowden (AP/Wide World), Karen Wheeless (FCC History Project), Chip Larkin (AT&T Archives), Holly Reed (National Archives and Records Administration), Rose Jeffrey (Republic Properties), and Judy Davis (Hoachlander-Davis Photography).

Introduction

The U.S. Federal Communications Commission (FCC) came into existence with the passage of the Communications Act of 1934, which also provided the agency with its core statutory authority. The authority vested in the FCC under this statute was substantial but by no means novel. As a practical matter, the Communications Act simply consolidated the authority previously possessed by the Interstate Commerce Commission and the Federal Radio Commission. While the Communications Act continues to serve as the legal backbone of federal communications regulation, subsequent enactments such as the Cable Acts of 1984 and 1992 and the Telecommunications Act of 1996 have significantly amended the Commission's powers.

Since the very beginning, the FCC has confronted the challenge of regulating a technologically diverse industry. Communications has never been a single, unified industry, but rather a series of "niches" organized around different technologies. These distinct technological niches have frequently required their own distinct form of regulation. For instance, early in the FCC's history the two main niches were telephony and broadcasting. By 1934, it had been established through precedent that telephony should be regulated as a public utility much like the railroads. Broadcasting, by contrast, had for several years been subject to a different model of "public interest" regulation pioneered by the Federal Radio Commission. Implementing these distinct models of regulation has at times caused conflict within the FCC as commissioners have argued about the appropriate amount of time, resources, and personnel to devote to each industry. As new technologies such as cable television, data communications, and cellular telephony have come under the FCC's jurisdiction, these matters have only grown more complicated. Not surprisingly, the FCC has gone through numerous internal reorganizations over the years in an effort to grapple with changes in its responsibilities.

Nevertheless, a survey of the FCC's major activities over its more than seven decades of existence reveals that issues relating to telephony and broadcasting have occupied most of the agency's time and attention. With respect to these two technologies, the FCC has for most of its history operated almost as two separate agencies. The formulation of telephone regulation has been handled by the FCC's Common Carrier (now called Wireline Competition) Bureau, while broadcast policy has been dealt with by the Broadcasting (now called Media) Bureau. These policymaking bureaus each contain their own professional staff who report to a bureau chief. All policy recommendations are passed from the bureau chief directly to the full Commission, generally with little or no input from the other bureaus. The political environment surrounding these two areas of policy has also been somewhat distinct. The policy case studies contained in Chapters 4 and 5 of this volume demonstrate that the FCC's regulation of the telephone industry has generated only intermittent political controversy, while broadcast regulation has been the subject of ongoing scrutiny by Congress, the courts, and a range of interest groups.

While the FCC has generally treated telephony and broadcasting as separate regulatory issues, a review of its major policy initiatives across time reveals that the Commission does operate under a fairly consistent regulatory philosophy. For the first four decades of its history, the FCC remained committed to a philosophy of extensive government management of the communications industry. Since the 1970s, however, the FCC has adopted deregulation as its core regulatory philosophy. In virtually every sector of the communications industry, the FCC has sought to fashion policies aimed at increasing marketplace competition and reducing regulation. The one exception to this pattern has been the regulation of indecent communication over the broadcast medium. In this area, the FCC's overall commitment to regulation has increased in recent decades.

Deregulation, however, has meant a change in focus for the FCC, not a reduction in its workload. The FCC in recent years has continued to work on a whole host of key policy initiatives including the implementation of the Telecommunications Act of 1996, the implementation of spectrum auctions, issues relating to media consolidation, and the regulation of certain areas of broadcast content. Given the highly dynamic nature of the communications industry and its central place in the economy and social life of an information age society, it is reasonable to expect that the FCC will continue to shape our communications policy for many years to come.

☆ 1 ☆

The FCC: The Origins and Purpose of an Agency

The U.S. Federal Communications Commission (FCC) took up formal operations on July 11, 1934. Established by the Communications Act of 1934, the agency took on the challenge of regulating two divergent industries—common carrier communications (telegraph and telephone) and broadcast communications (radio and later television). The FCC was not the first regulatory agency to possess authority over these industries. Prior to 1934, regulatory authority over common carriers was exercised by the U.S. Post Office and later the Interstate Commerce Commission. Broadcasting was regulated first by the U.S. Department of Commerce and later by the Federal Radio Commission. By the time the FCC began operations, two quite different models of regulation had developed in response to the divergent technological realities of these two industries. In many respects, the FCC's regulatory activities since that time have been influenced by these early precedents. Thus, to fully comprehend the nature of the FCC as a regulatory agency, some knowledge of the historical development of the common carrier and broadcast models of regulation must be possessed.

COMMON CARRIER REGULATION

A common carrier is essentially a kind of neutral transportation conduit for people, goods, and messages. Thus, railroads and trucking companies could be described as common carriers because they transport goods manufactured by other companies from one location to another. Likewise, telegraph and telephone companies are common carriers because they transport messages between two parties. Many common carrier industries possess unique economic and technological characteristics that make them good candidates for government regulation. A brief review of the history of communications

1

The Portals II Building in Washington, D.C., is the headquarters of the Federal Communications Commission. (Judy Davis/Hoachlander Davis Photography)

common carriers helps to better illustrate the nature of these industries and the types of government regulation that are traditionally applied to them.

Electronic communication was first made possible in 1835 when Samuel F. B. Morse invented the telegraph. In 1841 Morse received a federal grant to construct a telegraph system between Washington and Baltimore. By the early 1860s the Western Union Company was constructing a transcontinental telegraph line and, within a few years, underwater cables were used to create the beginnings of a transatlantic system.

Common carrier communication took a technological step forward in 1876 with the invention of the telephone. Patented in that year by Alexander Graham Bell, telephone lines were being constructed a year later between Boston and Somerville, Massachusetts. In 1885, the initial Bell companies were incorporated as the American Telephone and Telegraph Co. (AT&T), which would emerge after the turn of the twentieth century as the holding company for a vast telephone empire.

By the final decades of the nineteenth century, federal regulators were beginning to believe that common carriers like the railroad, telegraph, and telephone industries would function best if they were regulated by the government. The need for government regulation of these industries seemed to stem from two related factors. First, these industries were judged by many economists of the era to be natural monopolies—industries in which goods or services were most efficiently provided by a single firm. Second, these industries were characterized as public utilities—industries so central to the economic ordering of society that they needed to be made available to the public without discrimination and at reasonable rates.

Modern public utility regulation developed as a response to these two considerations. Public utility regulation consists of two main activities—setting rates and creating barriers to market entry. Rates are set through a process that involves the valuation of the firm's capital assets and the creation of an approved set of prices for individual services. Second, out of recognition of the natural monopoly status of these industries, barriers to entry are set up to limit the entry of new firms into these markets. Historically, the authority to carry out these regulatory activities has been granted to an independent regulatory commission—a type of government agency designed to handle highly technical regulatory matters with minimal outside political interference. As will be discussed further in Chapter 2, the FCC is a prime example of an independent regulatory commission.

The need to apply public utility regulation to communications common carriers became evident to Congress within a few decades of the creation of these industries. As early as 1866, Congress granted the postmaster general the authority to set rates for certain types of telegraph services used by the government. In 1910, Congress granted the now defunct Interstate Commerce Commission (ICC) full regulatory authority over communications common carriers. This proved to be a mistake, however, because the ICC was originally set up to deal with the railroads and had little experience with the unique technological characteristics of electronic communications. Given virtually no additional resources, the ICC made little effort to regulate communications common carriers in the nearly twenty-four years it held authority over these industries. By the 1930s President Roosevelt and many members of Congress believed it was time to set up a new regulatory agency to deal exclusively with communications matters.

BROADCAST REGULATION

A very different style of regulation developed in response to the unique technological characteristics of broadcasting. Broadcasting, like other forms of radio communication, operates without a physical connection between the transmitters and receivers. Instead, messages are carried over the air via radio waves—electromagnetic currents that move through the atmosphere in a manner similar to light waves. Radio waves were first postulated in the 1860s by the Scottish physicist James Maxwell and demonstrated in practice in 1886 by German physicist Heinrich Hertz. The potential of radio waves as a communications device, however, did not become apparent until 1902 when Italian inventor Guglielmo Marconi sent the first transatlantic wireless telegraph signal.

Initially, radio technology served primarily as an alternate means of sending telegraph and telephone messages. Perhaps the first significant use of the technology was as a communications device aboard ships. In 1910, Congress passed the Wireless Ship Act, requiring the installation of radio equipment aboard large passenger ships. As more operators began using the airwaves to communicate, it became clear that radio frequencies were a scarce commodity that needed to be better coordinated if they were going to be used without technical interference. In response to this consideration, Congress passed the Radio Act of 1912, requiring the secretary of commerce to license frequencies to radio operators.

The need for further government control over the airwaves became apparent with the advent of broadcasting. Unlike the telephones and telegraphs, which were neutral common carriers, broadcasters were more like newspapers in the sense that they created as well as delivered content. However, unlike newspapers, which were potentially unlimited in number, broadcast viewpoints were limited to the number of content providers that could gain access to scarce spectrum resources. Furthermore, the growing demand for broadcast spectrum only exacerbated the problem of interference over the airwaves. By the early 1920s, the need to preserve order and fairness led Secretary of Commerce Herbert Hoover and many other prominent government officials to conclude that a more elaborate regulatory regime was necessary.

Hoover in particular believed that further regulation was justified because broadcasting was an industry vested with a "public interest." From Hoover's perspective, the airwaves were a public resource, the use of which bestowed upon broadcasters certain public obligations. By using the airwaves, broadcasters entered into a public trust that obligated them to supply informative political and social content. As Hoover noted in his opening address at the First National Radio Conference in 1922:

> [T]he wireless telephone has one definite field, and that is for the spread of certain pre-determined material of public interest from central stations. This material must be limited to news, to education, to entertainment, and the communication of such commercial matters as are of importance to large groups of the community at the same time. It is therefore primarily a question of broadcasting, and it is of primary public interest to say who is to do the broadcasting, under what circumstances, and with what type of material.[1]

Thus, by 1922, Hoover had described the rationale for a system of broadcast regulation, one in which the special nature of the industry necessitated not only government control over the spectrum, but also a certain amount of control over broadcast content to serve the public interest. This basic philosophy would guide Congress several years later when it passed the Radio Act of 1927, the first major piece of legislation dealing with broadcasting.

The Radio Act provided that no broadcaster could stake "any claim to the use of any particular frequency or wavelength ... as against the regulatory power of the United States because of the previous use of the same, whether by license or otherwise." Here, Congress sought to reinforce the notion that the airwaves were a public resources and not the property of individual broadcasters. The law also created the Federal Radio Commission (FRC), an independent regulatory commission empowered to grant use of the spectrum based in the "public interest, convenience, and necessity." While the exact meaning of this phrase was debatable, early regulators at the FRC (and later at the FCC) interpreted it in terms that closely reflected Secretary Hoover's vision—broadcasters served the "public interest" by providing their audience with informative content.

THE FEDERAL COMMUNICATIONS COMMISSION

In February 1934, President Franklin Roosevelt sent a message to Congress advocating the creation of a new agency to be called the Federal Communications Commission that would possess all regulatory authority held at that time by the ICC and the FRC. While the president's message did not lay out a clear rationale for the reorganization, the matter was discussed further in a study of the communications industry submitted to Congress by an interdepartmental committee. The committee noted in its report that the "scattering of the regulatory power of the government has not been in the interest of the most economical or efficient service." Testimony in Congressional hearings by the chairman of the ICC and others seemed to buttress this opinion.

The interdepartmental committee was adamant in its view that Congress should create a brand new agency rather than simply transferring regulatory authority over common carriers to the FRC. This opinion was based in part on the nearly twenty-five-year history of common carrier regulation at the ICC. As noted above, the ICC during this time had done very little to regulate common carrier communications. The ICC frequently treated the communications industry as an afterthought, dedicating no administrative units and few personnel to its regulation. Even Joseph B. Eastman, chairman of the ICC in the early 1930s, noted in testimony before Congress that "the supervision of the communications companies by one commission would be preferable to the present method of divided control." The FRC at that time, however, was no better equipped in terms of personnel to handle common carrier communications than the ICC. Instead, members of Congress concurred with the committee that an entirely new agency, comprised at the outset of a more diverse array of personnel, would be better suited to the task of regulating the communications industry as a whole.

Acting quickly on these recommendations, Congress passed the Communications Act on June 14, 1934. The Communications Act folded existing regulatory authority into the hands of the newly created FCC, which officially began operations on July 11 of that year.

Early FCC Activity, 1934–1960

The FCC's first two and a half decades of operation can best be characterized as a time of adjustment to a complex technological and political environment. There were a few stumbling blocks along the way, including a fifteen-year debate over how best to organize the Commission's staff. Throughout this time the FCC was embroiled in a series of broadcasting controversies that included the chain broadcasting rules, the development of a public interest standard for licensees, and the quiz show scandals. During this time, the FCC also struggled to accommodate the growing demand for non-broadcast spectrum.

With respect to common carrier regulation, very few major controversies emerged prior to 1960. Perhaps the most important thing the FCC did during this period was to develop a method for determining long distance telephone rates. The FCC also gradually started to respond to changes in technology, including the development of microwave-based communications and new forms of communications equipment. While there was very little political controversy surrounding these early common carrier decisions, they did raise the specter that technological change might someday force the FCC to confront competition within the telephone industry.

An Era of Incrementalism, 1960–1978

During the period running from roughly 1960 to 1978, the FCC sought to gradually respond to technological innovation in the communications industry while forestalling any major changes in policy. In the realm of broadcasting, the FCC generally affirmed its commitment to the public interest standard. Much more of the FCC's time during this period was devoted to figuring out how best to regulate the emerging cable television industry.

Within the realm of common carrier regulation, the FCC faced the daunting challenge of how to deal with the growing technological integration of telephones and computers. As businesses sought new and more flexible ways to transmit voice and data communications, a new category of specialized communications providers came onto the scene, seeking to compete with some of AT&T's more traditional offerings. Fearing the consequences of bringing competition to the telephone industry too quickly, the FCC sought to limit the activities of these new firms to only very specialized types of communications offerings. Ultimately, however, new technological innovations combined with political pressure for policy change forced the FCC to fully confront the issue of competition by the end of the 1970s.

The Era of Competition, 1979–Present

Since roughly 1979, the FCC has generally pursued a strategy of introducing the principles of free market competition into communications regulation whenever possible. The first major step in the direction of competition in broadcasting came in the 1979 Deregulation of Radio Inquiry, when the FCC sought to reconsider some aspects of the public interest standard for radio, noting that "the public interest is best served by reducing [government] involvements in programming decisions in broadcast radio and substituting the public will through the workings of marketplace forces."[2] During this time, some within the agency also began advocating the licensing of broadcast spectrum through auctions, much the same way that people "bid" for other commodities. Even as the FCC has withdrawn regulation of many aspects of broadcasting, it has at least sporadically continued to regulate the content of broadcast messages that fall within the realm of "indecency."

The use of competitive principles in common carrier regulation began at the FCC in 1980, when it allowed increased competition between telephone companies and data communications firms. In addition, over the next ten years the FCC would also deregulate the manufacture of telephone equipment and begin to loosen price regulation of long distance telephone providers. In 1992, the FCC also issued a decision in which it sought to foster competition between telephone companies and cable television providers in the provision of video programming services. As the FCC has confronted new technologies and statutory requirements since that time, it has continued to work out the details of competition.

THE FCC'S STATUTORY AUTHORITY

The FCC's regulatory authority over the communications industry today is drawn from a variety of statutes. While the Communications Act of 1934 (P.L. 73-416) still provides the basic framework for federal communications regulation, it has been amended over the years, with the most recent and important additions provided by the Cable Acts of 1984 and 1992, and the Telecommunications Act of 1996. The Telecom Act, discussed at greater length in subsequent chapters, generally directed the FCC to move further in the direction of competition in virtually all areas of the communications industry. The following is a summary of the major provisions of the Communications Act as amended.

Title I: General Provisions

Title I, section 1 of the Communications Act begins by stating the purposes of the law, which include:

President Bill Clinton and Vice President Al Gore at the signing of the Telecommunications Act of 1996. The Telecommunications Act ushered in sweeping changes in U.S. communications law. (AP/Wide World Photos)

[R]egulating interstate and foreign commerce in communication by wire and radio so as to make available, so far as possible, to all the people of the United States, without discrimination on the basis of race, color, religion, national origin, or sex, a rapid, efficient, nationwide and world-wide wire and radio communication service with adequate facilities at reasonable charges, for the purpose of the national defense, for the purpose of promoting safety of life and property through the use of wire and radio communication, and for the purpose of securing a more effective execution of this policy by centralizing authority heretofore granted by law to several agencies and by granting additional authority with respect to interstate and foreign commerce to wire and radio communication, there is hereby created a commission to be known as the "Federal Communications Commission," which shall be constituted as hereinafter provided, and which shall execute and enforce the provisions of this Act.

Following the purposes stated in section 1:

- Section 2 provides for the general geographical jurisdiction of the FCC.

- Section 3 provides definitions for important statutory terms.

- Section 4 contains provisions relating to the Commission, including the number of commissioners and the qualifications and compensation for commissioners.

- Section 5 deals with the organization of the Commission. This section specifies the duties of the chairman of the FCC and mandates that the agency staff be organized around a series of bureaus structured around the Commission's "principal work load operations." This section also details the procedures for judicial review of a Commission action.

- Section 6 deals with the authorization of appropriations to the Commission.

- Section 7 states that "[i]t shall be the policy of the United States to encourage the provision of new technologies and services to the public" and authorizes the Commission to determine whether any new proposed technology or service is in the public interest.

- Section 8 sets application fees for those seeking spectrum licenses and authorizes the Commission to adjust them from time to time in response to inflation.

- Section 9 sets regulatory fees for the recovery of costs incurred by the Commission in the conduct of its enforcement, policy and rulemaking, and other regulatory activities. The Commission is authorized to adjust the schedule of fees from time to time.

- Section 10, added by the passage of the Telecommunications Act of 1996, is intended to reinforce the general policy of encouraging competition in the communications industry. It specifies that the Commission "shall forebear from applying any regulation or any provision of this Act" if it determines that it is not necessary to ensure that the charges and practices of telecommunications carriers are just and reasonable, protect consumers, or otherwise serve the public interest. The Commission is also generally required to consider the impact of new regulations on competition.

- Section 11 requires the Commission to conduct a biennial review of each of its regulations to determine whether or not they continue to serve the public interest.

Title II: Common Carriers

Title II of the Communications Act as amended by the Telecommunications Act of 1996 is generally divided up into three parts: common carrier regulation (sections 101–231), provisions pertaining to competition (sections 251–261), and provisions pertaining to the Bell Operating Companies (sections 271–276). Key portions of title II, particularly those added by the Telecommunications Act, are discussed in more detail in Chapter 4.

- Section 201 deals with common carrier services and charges. All common carriers engaged in interstate or foreign communication must provide their services upon reasonable request in accordance with rules established by the Commission. This section also authorizes the Commission to determine whether the "charges, practices, classifications, or regulations for and in connection with such communications services" are just and reasonable.

- Section 202 outlaws any unjust or unreasonable discrimination in "charges, practices, classifications, regulations, facilities, or services for or in connection with" common carrier offerings. The Commission is authorized to collect fines for the violation of this provision.

- Section 203 requires common carriers to file with the Commission and make available to the public a schedule of the rates and charges for its services. This section also requires carriers to file changes in their rate schedules, service offerings, and policies 120 days before they go into effect.

- Section 204 authorizes the FCC to call a hearing on proposed new rate schedules or services to determine their lawfulness. With the passage of the Telecommunications Act of 1996, the FCC now has only seven days to review a rate reduction and fifteen days to review a rate increase if it intends to call a hearing.

- Section 205 authorizes the Commission to prescribe "just and reasonable" rates for common carriers following an appropriate hearing and investigation.

- Section 206 states the liability of carriers for monetary injuries caused by unlawful actions. Section 207 allows for the recovery of damages through a complaint to the Commission.

- Section 208 outlines the process by which individuals and governments can file complaints against common carriers with the FCC. Legally, the Commission is required to investigate complaints and issue an order in the matter within five months. Section 209 states that the Commission may issue an order directing a carrier to pay damages to the complainant if indicated by the investigation.

- Section 210 states that carriers are free to exchange franks and passes for use by their officers, agents, employees, and their families.

This section also allows common carriers to provide free service to the government for purposes relating to national defense.

- Section 211 requires carriers subject to the Act to file copies of all contracts, agreements, or arrangements with other carriers with the Commission.

- Section 212 prohibits individuals from serving as an officer or director of more than one carrier subject to the Act under most circumstances.

- Section 213 authorizes the Commission to conduct valuations of carrier property and to require carriers to file inventories of all owned property and its original cost.

- Section 214 deals with the extension of new common carrier lines. No carrier may build a new interstate line or extend a line without first obtaining a certificate of "public convenience and necessity" from the Commission. Amendments to this section by the Telecom Act authorize state public utility commissions to designate "eligible telecommunications carriers" for the extension of lines to unserved rural areas. These carriers are eligible to receive "universal service" support under section 254(c) of the Act and may be ordered to extend lines to unserved areas if the state commission deems it to be in the public interest.

- Section 215 authorizes the Commission to investigate financial transactions made by carriers that might impact rates.

- Section 216 states that the provisions of the Act apply to all receivers and operating trustees of carriers to the same extent that they apply to the carriers themselves.

- Section 217 states that carriers are liable for the actions of their agents and employees.

- Section 218 authorizes the Commission to inquire into the management activities of any carrier subject to the Act.

- Section 219 authorizes the Commission to require all carriers subject to the Act to submit annual reports providing information about their personnel and finances.

- Section 220 authorizes the Commission to prescribe methods of accounting and record keeping for carriers subject to the Act. The Commission retains the right to examine these records and accounts and conduct audits from time to time.

- Section 221 contains special provisions closely limiting the Commission's authority over the telephone industry to only those matters of rate setting and property valuation that clearly relate to interstate operations.

- Section 222, added by the Telecommunications Act, requires carriers to protect the privacy of customer information in their business dealings.
- Section 223, amended by the Telecommunications Act, provides for criminal proceedings against individuals who make obscene, lewd, lascivious, indecent, or harassing communications over interstate lines or within the District of Columbia.
- Section 224 authorizes the Commission to make regulations and hear disputes regarding access to public utility poles by interstate telecommunications carriers.
- Section 225 requires the Commission to make and enforce regulations pertaining to telecommunications services for the hearing and speech impaired.
- Section 226 sets the legal obligations of carriers providing telephone operator services and authorizes the Commission to make and enforce additional regulations pertaining to these provisions.
- Section 227 establishes restrictions on the use of automated telephone equipment, sets technical and procedural standards for the use of fax machines, and authorizes rules pertaining to the protection of telephone customers from unwanted solicitations.
- Section 228 authorizes the Commission to make and enforce rules pertaining to pay telephone services.
- Section 229 authorizes the prescription of rules to implement the Communications Assistance for Law Enforcement Act. These provisions are designed to aid law enforcement officials in the interception of evidence through communications media when legally appropriate.
- Section 230, added with the passage of the Telecommunications Act, is aimed at promoting the development and use of Internet blocking and screening software.
- Section 231 requires that access to commercial communications distributed over the World Wide Web that are deemed "harmful to minors" be restricted to adults.
- Sections 251–261, added by the Telecommunications Act, establish a set of general guidelines for the development of competition in local telephone service markets and new programs for the extension of telecommunications services to rural areas and to healthcare and educational facilities.
- Sections 271–276 provide a set of procedures and requirements for the Bell Operating Companies to move beyond their local telephone monopolies by entering previously restricted markets, such as long distance telephone service, information services, and equipment manufacturing.

Title III: Provisions Relating to Radio

Title III sets the Commission's powers with respect to the licensing and operation of "radio" communications services: services utilizing the electromagnetic spectrum. These include broadcast radio and television, spectrum used by ships and aircrafts, cellular telephone providers, and radio communication by public safety officials. Sections 301–336 relate to general matters, sections 351–386 deal with radio services aboard ships, and sections 390–399 are concerned with public telecommunications facilities. The major provisions of title III can be summarized as follows:

- Section 301 states generally that transmission of communication over the electromagnetic spectrum requires a license issued by the federal government.
- Section 302 authorizes the Commission to regulate devices that interfere with radio communications.
- Section 303 outlines the general powers of the Commission relating to the licensing and regulation of radio services. This includes the power to set up classifications of radio services, establish geographical zones to be served by radio services, assign call letters for broadcasters, and require record keeping by providers of radio services. This section also gives the Commission the authority to suspend the licenses of radio operators for violating treaties, failing to carry out lawful orders, broadcasting profane or obscene language, sending false or deceptive signals or communications, willfully interfering with another operator's frequency, or providing the Commission with fraudulent information. As discussed further in Chapter 2 of this volume, operators who have had their license suspended are entitled to a fair hearing. Provisions added to this section under the Telecommunications Act empower the Commission to regulate direct-to-home satellite services.
- Section 304 requires radio service licensees to waive any claim to ownership of their frequency.
- Section 305 provides that radio stations belonging to and operated by the government are to be licensed by the president of the United States and are not subject to the requirements of sections 301–303. Section 306 states that the requirements of 301 do not apply to communications sent from a foreign ship residing within the jurisdiction of the United States.
- Section 307 sets the terms of licenses for radio services. Amendments to this section added under the Telecommunications Act lengthened the term of a license to a maximum of eight years and reduced the amount of paperwork that had to be submitted at license renewal time.

- Section 308 further elaborates the contents for an application for a radio license.

- Section 309 outlines the procedural requirements the Commission must follow in taking action on a radio license application. For most types of licenses, the Commission must determine within thirty days of providing public notice on an application whether or not to grant the license. The application review process is discussed further in Chapter 2.

- Section 310 places limits on the ability of foreign governments and individuals to hold licenses and provides procedural requirements for the transfer of licenses between parties.

- Section 311 outlines a number of special requirements for the licensing of broadcast stations.

- Section 312 states the circumstances under which the Commission may revoke a license or construction permit. See Chapter 2 for a further discussion of this section.

- Section 313 provides for the revocation of licenses for violations of the antitrust laws.

- Section 314 provides for the preservation of competition by placing limits on the ability of commercial radio operators to enter other areas of the communications business.

- Section 315 requires broadcasters to provide equal time to candidates for public office.

- Section 316 allows the Commission to modify station licenses or construction permits if it determines that it is in the public interest, convenience, and necessity to do so. Broadcasters are entitled to a hearing on the matter if they desire.

- Section 317 provides that broadcasters must announce the names of persons or organizations that have paid for broadcast time.

- Section 318 generally provides that the transmitting apparatus in any radio station may only be operated by the licensee.

- Section 319 states that a construction permit issued by the Commission is a precondition for receiving a radio license. This section also sets out the requirements for obtaining a construction permit.

- Section 320 authorizes the Commission to designate radio stations liable to interfere with the distress signals of ships.

- Section 321 authorizes ships to send high-powered distress signals and requires radio stations to give priority to these signals. Radio stations must also cease operations temporarily if their broadcasts are likely to interfere with distress signals.

- Section 322 states that all land stations open to public service between the coast and vessels or aircraft at sea must exchange radio communications with ships and aircrafts.

- Section 323 states that private or commercial radio stations on land that interfere with government radio stations must cease operations for the first fifteen minutes of each hour.

- Section 324 mandates that, with the exception of vessels sending distress signals, all radio stations must use the minimum amount of power necessary to carry out communications.

- Section 325 prohibits false distress signals, places limits on the ability of a cable system or other multichannel video programming distributor to retransmit the signal of a broadcasting station, and prohibits the sending of radio transmissions to foreign broadcast studios.

- Section 326 states that nothing in the Act gives the Commission the power of censorship over radio communications.

- Section 327 authorizes the reception of commercial and press messages over frequencies operated by the Navy.

- Section 329 authorizes the Commission to designate officers of other federal government departments to administer the Act within U.S. territories and possessions.

- Section 330 prohibits the shipment or importation of televisions with decoding (closed caption) and blocking apparatus that do not comply with FCC standards.

- Section 331 establishes that the Commission must allocate very high frequency (VHF) television stations in such a manner that at least one is present in each state whenever feasible. This section also establishes provisions to promote the development of full-time AM radio stations throughout the country.

- Section 332 sets parameters for the allocation of spectrum to private mobile radio services.

- Section 333 prohibits willful or malicious interference with radio communication.

- Section 334 limits the authority of the Commission to revise regulations concerning equal employment opportunity in television broadcasting.

- Section 335 authorizes the Commission to make rules concerning the rates, facilities, and programming of direct broadcast satellite service providers.

- Section 336, added by the Telecom Act, authorizes the Commission to distribute spectrum for digital broadcasting services to incumbent television broadcasters. In the future, when broadcasters take over the "digital" spectrum, they are required to surrender the analog frequencies on which they were originally licensed to operate.

- Section 337 provides for the allocation and assignment of certain frequencies for commercial and public safety services by the Commission.

- Section 338 requires carriage of local television signals by satellite carriers under regulations issued by the Commission.

- Section 339 places limits on the ability of satellite carriers to carry the signals of network affiliates from outside the viewing area.

- Sections 351–386 deal with radio equipment and radio operators on board ships. Large passenger ships, cargo ships, and ships operated by the government on the open sea must be licensed to operate a radio frequency. Large ships are also required to carry radio officers and a radiotelegraph station. With the passage of the Telecommunications Act, some ships are exempt from this requirement if they carry automated distress and safety systems. Passenger ships for hire are required by these sections to have radio telephone equipment. The Commission has the authority in some instances to set technical standards and operating requirements.

- Sections 390–393a set up a program of matching grants for the construction, planning, and operation of public telecommunications facilities to be administered by the secretary of commerce. This portion of the Act also creates criteria for the approval of grants by the secretary and obligations for the recipients of the funds, and it requires long-range planning in the use of these appropriations.

- Section 394 sets up a National Endowment for Children's Educational Television to be administered by the secretary of commerce.

- Section 395 authorizes the secretary of commerce to make grants and enter into contracts to carry out demonstrations of nonbroadcast telecommunications facilities and services aimed at assisting communication in the fields of health, education, and public and social services.

- Sections 396–399b create the Corporation for Public Broadcasting and set requirements for the operation of noncommercial educational television stations.

Title IV: Procedural and Administrative Provisions

Title IV deals with questions of due process in Commission decisionmaking.

- Section 401 states that Commission orders and decisions may be enforced by the district courts of the United States through a judicial order.

- Section 402 provides that proceedings to enjoin, set aside, annul, or suspend an order of the Commission must be taken before the U.S. Court of Appeals for the District of Columbia Circuit. Appeals of Commission decisions are further discussed in Chapter 2.

- Section 403 authorizes the Commission to undertake investigations on its own initiative in response to complaints or in enforcement of any of the provisions of the Act. Section 404 provides that the Commission must conclude its investigations with a report stating its findings and any order that follows.

- Section 405 allows aggrieved parties to file a petition for reconsideration of any Commission decision.

- Section 406 gives jurisdiction to the U.S. district courts to issue orders of compliance to carriers who have refused to furnish interstate communications facilities upon petition from a complainant.

- Section 407 allows parties who have won a monetary settlement against a carrier in a Commission proceeding to seek an order of enforcement from a U.S. district court.

- Section 408 states that all orders of the Commission other than those involving payment of money will take effect thirty days following the date of notice of the order.

- Section 409 establishes procedures for presenting evidence in hearings and adjudicatory proceedings before the Commission.

- Section 410 authorizes the Commission to establish joint boards to discuss and resolve regulatory matters that require cooperation between the federal and state governments.

- Section 411 authorizes the inclusion of all persons interested in or affected by a regulatory action as parties to a Commission proceeding or plaintiffs in a court action.

- Section 412 states that documents filed as part of a Commission proceeding must be preserved as public records.

- Section 413 requires that all carriers subject to the Act must designate an agent to formally interact with the Commission in official proceedings and litigation.

- Section 414 states that none of the remedies provided in this section should be understood to abridge or alter those available at common law.

- Section 415 sets some general limitations as to the timeframes and circumstances under which some legal actions may be taken before the Commission.

- Section 416 states that Commission orders affecting a carrier must be served on its agent designated under section 413 of this Act.

Title V: Penal Provisions

Title V of the Act establishes a range of civil and criminal penalties for violation of the Communications Act as amended.

- Section 501 establishes the maximum fines and terms of imprisonment for persons who violate provisions of the Act.
- Section 502 establishes fines for persons who violate the rules and regulations of the Commission.
- Section 503 establishes additional penalties for those who accept unlawful rebates or offsets against scheduled rates and charges.
- Section 504 states that all monetary forfeitures accruing from penalties are to be paid to the U.S. Treasury. The U.S. Attorney General, working through the federal courts, has the duty to prosecute for the recovery of these forfeitures.
- Section 505 states that all prosecutions shall be undertaken in the district in which the offense was committed. Offenses committed on the high seas will be prosecuted in the district in which the individual is found or first brought upon return to land.
- Section 506 establishes maximum civil penalties for violation of the Great Lakes Agreement.
- Section 507 requires the disclosure of sums of money paid to broadcasters for the production and/or broadcast of certain materials and states criminal penalties for the violation of the provisions of this section.
- Section 508 establishes criminal penalties for dishonest or deceptive practices relating to game shows.
- Section 510 authorizes the seizure by the government of any radio device not authorized in accordance with sections 301 and 302 of this Act.

Title VI: Cable Communications

Title VI consists largely of amendments that were added with the passage of the Cable Communications Act of 1984 and the Cable Television Consumer Protection and Competition Act of 1992. The most recent major additions came with the passage of the Telecommunications Act of 1996. Sections 601–602 contain general provisions, sections 611–617 deal with the use of channels and cable ownership, sections 621–629 concern franchising and regulation, sections 631–641 contain miscellaneous provisions, and sections 651–653 relate to video programming services provided by telephone companies.

- Section 601 states the general purposes of the cable provisions and Section 602 provides statutory definitions.

- Section 611 authorizes franchising authorities to require cable providers to supply channels for public, educational, or governmental use as a part of their franchising agreement.

- Section 612 requires larger cable systems to set aside a certain portion of their channels for commercial use by unaffiliated persons. The Commission has the authority to enforce this provision and to set rates for the leasing of these channels.

- Section 613 prohibits cable operators from providing certain other types of video programming services within their cable franchising area unless they are already subject to "effective competition" as determined by the Commission. This section also limits the ability of state franchising authorities to restrict ownership of cable systems within their jurisdictions.

- Section 614 requires cable operators of a certain size to carry the signals of local commercial broadcast television stations and qualified low power stations. The Commission is empowered to determine the "viewing area" of local stations if necessary.

- Section 615 requires cable operators of a certain size to carry any qualified local noncommercial educational television station requesting carriage. The Commission is empowered to enforce these provisions through appropriate remedies.

- Section 616 requires the Commission to maintain regulations governing the carriage agreements between cable operators and other video program distributors and vendors.

- Section 617 states that franchising authorities, when authorized to, may take no more than 120 days to act upon a request for approval of the sale of a cable system. In doing so, the franchising authority must act in accordance with Commission regulations.

- Section 621 reiterates that all cable franchises must be written in accordance with the requirements of the Act as amended, and prohibits franchising authorities from awarding exclusive franchises. Provisions added to this section by the Telecommunications Act also prohibit the franchising authority from regulating telephone or other telecommunications services provided by the cable operator.

- Section 622 authorizes franchising authorities to require cable operators to pay franchising fees not to exceed 5 percent of the operator's gross revenues from providing cable service during a twelve-month period.

- Section 623 authorizes franchising authorities to regulate cable rates if there is not effective competition within its jurisdiction. The Commission is also empowered under this section to regulate the rates of basic tier cable service.

- Section 624 prohibits franchising authorities from regulating the services, facilities, and equipment provided by a cable operator. This section does recognize the exception of obscene communication and also requires cable operators to provide subscribers, upon request, with a device to block programming that is sexually explicit. In addition, this section requires the Commission to maintain regulations regarding the minimum technical standards of operation and signal quality for cable operators.

- Section 624[a] requires the Commission to make and periodically review and modify regulations regarding the compatibility of televisions, video cassette recorders, and cable systems.

- Section 625 states that cable operators may obtain modifications to their franchising agreements with respect to certain matters of programming if they can demonstrate that these requirements are no longer practicable.

- Section 626 sets up standard proceedings for the renewal of franchises that require public notice and participation. This section also provides for a right of appeal in the federal district courts for cable operators whose franchise renewal has been denied.

- Section 627 establishes conditions for the sale or transfer of cable systems in the event that a franchising agreement is not renewed or revoked.

- Section 628 seeks to promote competition and diversity in video programming by requiring the Commission to make and enforce regulations prohibiting unfair methods of competition relating to the prices, terms and conditions of service.

- Section 629, added with the passage of the Telecommunications Act, requires the FCC to adopt regulations to assure that consumers can purchase on a commercial basis cable television converters and types of equipment used to obtain video programming services.

- Section 631 relates to the protection of subscriber privacy. Under this section, cable operators must disclose to consumers their methods of collecting and distributing personal information. This section also states the circumstances under which a cable operator may disclose the personal information of subscribers to third parties and prescribes civil remedies for the failure to comply with these provisions.

- Section 632 pertains to the regulation of customer service requirements for cable operators. The Act, as amended in 1992, requires the commission to establish standards by which cable operators may fulfill their customer service requirements. The matters covered by these standards include cable operator office hours and telephone availability to consumers, service calls, and communications between the cable operator and the subscriber.

- Section 633 outlaws and provides criminal and civil penalties for the unauthorized reception of cable services.

- Section 634 requires cable system operators to maintain an equal employment opportunity program in accordance with regulations established by the Commission.

- Section 635 further spells out the procedures for the judicial appeal of a franchising authority decision.

- Section 635a prohibits the awarding of monetary damages as a part of the judicial proceedings spelled out in section 635.

- Section 636 reiterates the general authority of state governments over cable franchising matters and further states that nothing in this title should be understood to interfere with the sovereign powers of state governments regarding matters of public health, safety, and welfare.

- Section 637 states that all franchises that are in effect are subject to the provisions of this title at its time of passage.

- Section 638 states that nothing in this title should be construed to alter the criminal or civil liability of cable operators under federal, state, and local laws pertaining to libel, slander, obscenity, incitement, invasion of privacy, or false or misleading advertising.

- Section 639 states specifically that the federal laws pertaining to obscene communication apply to cable operators.

- Section 640 requires cable operators to block or scramble signals for all channels to which an individual customer does not subscribe upon his request.

- Section 641 states that a cable provider must fully scramble or block the signals of sexually explicit adult programming.

- Section 651 exempts telephone companies that provide video programming services from most of the provisions of title VI.

- Section 652 establishes the terms and conditions under which cable television operators and local telephone companies can enter joint ventures or purchase one another.

- Section 653 orders the Commission to make rules and regulations for the provision of cable television service by telephone companies through open video systems.

Title VII: Miscellaneous Provisions

Sections 701–714 contain a host of miscellaneous provisions pertaining to Commission powers and the regulation of the communications industry. Section 701 transfers to the Commission certain duties, powers, and functions under existing law previously held by the ICC and the postmaster general. Section 705 contains provisions relating to the unauthorized publication of communications, and Section 706 grants emergency powers to the president to suspend certain Commission regulations during times of war. Section 707 establishes July 1, 1934, as the effective date of the Act, Section 708 contains a "separability" clause, and section 709 provides that the Act should be referred to as the Communications Act of 1934. Sections 710–714 contain additional regulatory provisions:

- Section 710 requires the Commission to establish regulations to provide for reasonable access to telephone services by the hearing impaired.
- Section 711 requires closed captioning for public service announcements.
- Section 712 requires the Commission to make syndicated exclusivity rules for the delivery of syndicated programming for transmission by satellite of broadcast station signals.
- Section 713, added by the Telecommunications Act, required the Commission to undertake a study and report to Congress regarding the extent of closed captioning in cable television as well as the availability of video descriptions for the visually impaired.
- Section 714 establishes a telecommunications development fund to promote access to capital for small businesses, promote technological development, and support universal service.

FCC RULES AND REGULATIONS

From the above discussion of the Communications Act, it should be evident that the FCC's statutory delegation of authority is quite far reaching. In carrying out its statutory mandates, the Commission has written a vast range of administrative rules over the years. Administrative rules are quasi-legislative statements of policy written and passed under the authority granted by a statute. In making rules, the FCC generally follows the procedural requirements stated in the federal Administrative Procedures Act of 1946 (discussed in greater detail in Chapter 2). FCC rules, once passed, are codified in title 47 of the Code of Federal Regulations. The following is a general summary of title 47 broken down by parts:

- Part 0 deals with Commission organization. In general, this part spells out the duties of the chairman, the responsibilities of the major offices and bureaus housed within the Commission, and information about Commission rules, proceedings, and facilities.

- Part 1 covers the formal practices and procedures followed by the Commission as it carries out its statutory authority.

- Part 2 contains rules pertaining to the allocation of spectrum frequencies for different purposes by separating them into "bands." This section also outlines the Commission's table of frequency allocations and states general requirements pertaining to radio stations and radio equipment.

- Part 3 is where the FCC delineates its responsibilities in the certification and monitoring of the accounting authorities that settle accounts due to messages transmitted to foreign administrations at sea by or between maritime mobile radio stations.

- Part 5 rules prescribe the procedures through which frequencies are made available by the Commission for experimental radio services pursuant to title III of the Communications Act.

- Part 6 contains rules intended to ensure that telephones and telecommunications equipment are designed and produced in a manner that makes them accessible to persons with disabilities.

- Part 7 contains rules intended to ensure improved access to voicemail and interactive menu services and equipment by persons with disabilities.

- Part 11 sets up the technical standards and operating requirements for the Emergency Alert System for AM and FM radio, broadcast television, cable television, and other participating entities.

- Part 13 rules prescribe the manner and conditions for the licensing of commercial radio operators.

- Part 15 contains rules by which an intentional, unintentional, or incidental radiator of a radio signal may operate without a license.

- Part 17 rules provide guidelines for the construction, marking, and lighting of radio antennas.

- Part 18 sets forth the conditions under which industrial, scientific, and medical equipment may be operated without undue interference with authorized radio services.

- Part 19 contains rules prescribing appropriate standards of conduct for Commission employees pursuant to the Uniform Standards of Ethical Conduct contained in the Code of Federal Regulations.

- Part 20 sets out requirements and conditions for providers of commercial mobile radio services.

- Part 21 prescribes procedures for making portions of the spectrum available to common carriers and multipoint distribution service operators who require such transmitting facilities.

- Part 22 sets out the requirements and conditions for licensing common carrier radio stations for the provision of public mobile radio services.

- Part 23 sets out the requirements and conditions for the licensing and operation of international fixed public radio-telecommunications services.

- Part 24 contains rules relating to the licensing and operation of personal communications services.

- Part 25 contains rules relating to the licensing and operation of satellite communications.

- Part 27 contains rules relating to the licensing and operation of miscellaneous wireless communications services.

- Part 32 sets up a uniform system of accounts for telecommunications carriers.

- Part 36 contains the procedures for separating a telecommunications carrier's property costs, revenues, expenses, taxes, and reserves for the purposes of delineating federal and state regulatory jurisdictions.

- Part 42 contains rules pertaining to the preservation of common carrier accounts, records, memoranda, documents, papers and correspondence, including those obtained through mergers and acquisitions.

- Part 43 contains guidelines for the submission of reports by common carriers to the Commission regarding their financial dealings.

- Part 51 rules authorize state regulators to approve agreements between common carriers for the interconnection of their lines and facilities.

- Part 52 rules establish the requirements and conditions for the administration and use of telephone/telecommunications numbers.

- Part 53 rules implement sections 271–272 of the Communications Act pertaining to the entry of the Bell Operating Companies into long distance telecommunications services.
- Part 54 rules implement the universal service provisions of section 254 of the Communications Act, as amended.
- Part 59 rules require local telephone companies to share their infrastructure and facilities with competitors under certain circumstances.
- Part 61 contains rules pertaining to the initial filing and revision of tariffs for the setting of charges and the provision of services.
- Part 63 rules concern the extension of lines by common carriers under section 214 of the Communications Act, as amended.
- Part 64 contains miscellaneous other rules pertaining to common carriers.
- Part 65 rules relate to the regulation of rates for interstate telecommunications services.
- Part 68 rules set standards for the attachment of terminal equipment to telecommunications networks and the compatibility of hearing aids and telephones.
- Part 69 sets up the rules by which access charges are to be paid to local telephone companies by long distance companies to compensate them for the use of their infrastructure.
- Part 73 contains rules relating to the classification, assignment, and operation of AM radio frequencies and stations.
- Part 74 contains rules relating to the licensing and operation of experimental, auxiliary, and special broadcast and other program distribution services.
- Part 76 rules pertain to the operation of multichannel video and cable television services. These provisions include requirements for the certification of cable television systems as well as rules and standards for their operation pursuant to title VI of the Communications Act, as amended.
- Part 78 rules pertain to the licensing and operation of cable television relay service stations.
- Part 79 contains rules relating to closed captioning and video description in video programming.
- Part 80 rules implement the Commission's authority to license and regulate radio stations in the maritime service.
- Part 87 rules implement the Commission's authority to license and regulate radio stations for aviation service.

- Part 90 rules provide for the licensing and regulation of stations for private land mobile radio services such as public safety services and industrial/business radio pool.

- Part 95 contains rules pertaining to the licensing and operation of general mobile radio services.

- Part 97 contains rules pertaining to the licensing and operation of an amateur radio service.

- Part 101 contains rules pertaining to the allocation and licensing of frequencies for fixed microwave communications services.

THE FCC: PROFILING AN ORGANIZATION

As should be clear by now, the FCC's expansive legislative mandate makes the agency the principal policymaking organization in the realm of federal communications regulation. In spite of its seemingly endless list of provisions and requirements, the Communications Act mainly provides a basic legal framework that authorizes the FCC to use its broad rulemaking powers to regulate the communications industry. Over the decades, the FCC has used this broad delegation of authority to do such far-reaching things as limiting and expanding competition in the telephone industry, constructing and later doing away with public interest requirements for broadcasters, introducing new technologies into the marketplace, and making rules concerning the broadcast of indecent messages over the airwaves.

Like any policymaking organization, the FCC and its policies are shaped by (1) the people that work within the organization, (2) its political environment, (3) and the procedures and institutional arrangements that structure policymaking. The purpose of this volume is to provide a broad reference to the FCC's major policy initiatives and the people, political environment, and institutional arrangements that have shaped them.

NOTES

1. Quoted in Marvin R. Bensman, *The Beginning of Broadcast Regulation in the Twentieth Century* (Jefferson, NC: McFarland, 2000), 50.
2. *In the Matter of Deregulation of Radio*, 73 FCC 2d 457 (1979).

☆ 2 ☆

Organization and Procedures

Scholars of public bureaucracy have long noted that the nature of an agency's organization and procedures impacts decision-making outcomes. How an agency organizes the conduct of work through its bureaus and offices as well as its procedures for making rules, issuing administrative orders, and appealing decisions to the federal courts can determine whether or not discretionary authority is carried out in a fair and efficient manner. Furthermore, agency organization and procedures can also have political implications. For example, in writing the Communications Act of 1934, Congress put some thought into determining who would have the right to challenge an FCC broadcast licensing decision and under what circumstances. In making decisions such as these, Congress and administrative agencies may be able to empower some interest groups at the expense of others in the bureaucratic decision-making process.

The purpose of this chapter is to describe in detail the organization and procedures of the Federal Communications Commission. The first part of the chapter provides an in-depth description of the FCC's major administrative components and officers. The second part of the chapter provides a discussion of procedures for rulemaking, broadcast licensing, judicial review of agency decisions, and mechanisms through which the public can obtain information regarding Commission activities.

ORGANIZATION OF THE COMMISSION

Perhaps the most important organizational decision made by Congress in writing the Communications Act of 1934 was to make the FCC an independent regulatory commission. Independent regulatory commissions differ from traditional government agencies in that they do not report directly to the

FIGURE 2.1. Organization Chart of the FCC, August 2005

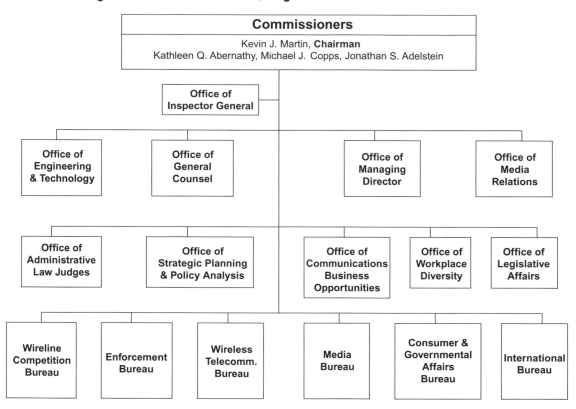

president. While the president does nominate the agency heads—or commissioners, as they are called—they then sit on the Commission for lengthy fixed terms and cannot be fired for reasons other than corruption or serious misconduct. Furthermore, independent regulatory commissions, unlike most other types of public agencies, have plural chief executives consisting of three to seven commissioners who make policy decisions as a collegial body. Commissions are typically also bipartisan, with no more than a simple majority of their members coming from any single political party. All of these structural considerations are intended to make commissions somewhat independent from traditional electoral politics and enable them to make the most reasoned, technically correct decisions they possible can. This is not to say, however, that independent regulatory commissions are not highly political entities. Commissioners are appointed by elected officials and bring their own political preferences into the decision-making process. This is just as true of the FCC as any other commission.

From an organizational standpoint, the FCC can be broken down into three major components: (1) the Commission itself, (2) the six policymaking bureaus, and (3) the various staff offices within the agency. The description of

Commission organization that follows distinguishes between these major components of the agency.

The Commission

The FCC today consists of five commissioners who are appointed by the president subject to confirmation by the Senate. The normal terms of commissioners are fixed at five years, with one commissioner appointed or reappointed each year. No more than three of the five commissioners may be members of the same political party. Commissioners are full-time political appointees who are prohibited from retaining any other employment or receiving honoraria for speeches or holding any financial interests in any sector of the communications industry. Beyond these considerations there is no standard career path for becoming a commissioner. The Communications Act does not list any specific qualifications for being a commissioner, though most have been lawyers and many have had prior experience as state-level utility commissioners or at the FCC.

The president holds the authority to designate one member of the Commission to serve as chairman. The chairman serves as the chief executive officer of the agency, which includes such responsibilities as presiding over all meetings and sessions of the Commission, representing the Commission before Congress and other governmental bodies, appointing bureau and office heads subject to the approval of the whole Commission, and generally coordinating the work of the agency. When a new president comes into office, it is his prerogative to designate a new chair from among the sitting commissioners. Technically, dismissal as chair does not mean dismissal as a commissioner, since the appointment is a fixed term. As a practical matter, however, chairmen facing dismissal have traditionally resigned their seat on the Commission and allowed the president to fill the vacancy with a commissioner of his choosing. In the event that the Commission is lacking a chair due to a vacancy, the sitting commissioners may designate from among themselves an acting chairman.

In addition, one commissioner out of the five is designated to serve as the Defense Commissioner. Among other things it is the job of the Defense Commissioner to keep the Commission informed regarding matters relating to emergency preparedness and defense activities and to represent the Commission in national defense matters requiring conferences with other governmental entities. In addition, the Defense Commissioner works with the staff in each of the policy bureaus to develop preparedness programs for the telecommunications industry. Finally, in the event of an enemy attack or imminent threat in which the entire Commission is unable to function at its Washington, D.C., offices, the Defense Commissioner is empowered to temporarily assume the duties and powers of the full Commission and chairman.

Kevin Martin, current chairman of the Federal Communications Commission. (Courtesy of the FCC)

The work of the Commission is primarily done as a collegial body. The Commission holds the final say within the agency on all policy matters, though some decision-making authority may be delegated to bureau chiefs and professional staff. Commission decisions are made in weekly meetings, which normally require a quorum of at least three commissioners in order for formal actions to be taken. The agenda for formal meetings is set by the chairman, who provides each commissioner with a list of agenda items at least a week in advance. Commissioners prepare for the meetings with the assistance of their personal staff by gathering information and evaluating the agenda items. The consideration of agenda items in meetings typically involves testimony by staff members in the various bureaus and offices of the agency who were involved in preparing the items for Commission consideration. Commissioners are then given the opportunity to question those testifying and to have open discussion among themselves before taking a final vote on the matter. Under the federal Sunshine Act, most formal Commission meetings are open to the public.

Some types of Commission decisions are made through mechanisms other than formal meetings. For instance, in the event that a quorum cannot be obtained, either because of absences or vacancies on the Commission, the chairman may convene a "board of commissioners" consisting of all commissioners present and able to act. A board of commissioners, however, may not act on major policy initiatives. Some fairly routine matters, such as certain types of hearings, may also be handled by individual commissioners acting on behalf of the Commission. On some occasions, Commission business is also done through a process called "circulation" in which a document or agenda item is circulated among the commissioners and approval or rejection is submitted to the chair outside of a formal meeting.

The Policymaking Bureaus

Below the Commission itself are a host of different staff offices, including the six policymaking bureaus. Sometimes functioning like self-contained bureaucracies, each bureau consists of a series of offices and professional staff that work to identify and act upon the major policy matters of the day. The bureau system of organization was started in 1949 as a way to better coordinate staff work relating to specific types of telecommunications policy problems. Prior to that time, staff members were organized around professional affiliations—accounting, engineering, and law. This system of organization posed at least two problems for the Commission. First, staff members were functioning as generalists, never really developing expertise in a specific sector of the telecommunications industry. Second, the three main staff offices largely worked independently of one another. Thus, commissioners could get three very different viewpoints with respect to a policy problem depending on who they asked. In an effort to obtain more unified opinions on policy matters, staff members were organized into bureaus in which professionals from the different fields worked together on specific policy issues.

A major component of the bureau system of organization today is the maintenance of a bureau for each main sector of the telecommunications industry. Thus, there is a Wireline Competition Bureau to regulate the telephone industry, a Media Bureau to regulate broadcasting and cable television, a Wireless Bureau to handle spectrum matters, and an International Bureau to handle international telecommunications issues. In addition, the Commission has established an Enforcement Bureau and a Consumer and Governmental Affairs Bureau. Each bureau is headed by a bureau chief who serves as the principal executive, coordinating the work of the staff. Through authority delegated by the commissioners, the bureaus write rules, undertakes adjudicatory proceedings, and take other policy actions on behalf of the Commission, taking what amounts to final action on many matters. The significance of many of these bureaus cannot be understated. Because they are staffed by career civil servants who become technical experts in the matters they deal with, it is frequently the bureaus, rather than the Commission itself, that sets the regulatory agenda for the agency.

Wireline Competition Bureau

Originally called the Common Carrier Bureau, the Wireline Competition Bureau is principally charged with carrying out regulatory responsibilities relating to the telephone industry. As specified in section 47 of the Code of Federal Regulations, the main responsibilities of the Wireline Competition Bureau include:

1. Developing and recommending policy goals, objectives, programs, and plans for the Commission in rulemaking and adjudicatory matters concerning wireline telecommunications. Overall objectives include meeting the present and future wireline telecommunications needs of the nation; fostering economic growth; ensuring choice, opportunity, and fairness in the development of wireline

telecommunications; promoting investment in wireline telecommunications infrastructure; promoting the development and widespread availability of wireline telecommunications services; and developing deregulatory initiatives where appropriate.

2. Administering the provisions of the Communications Act requiring that the charges, practices, classifications, and regulations of communications common carriers providing interstate and foreign services are just and reasonable.

3. Acting on applications for the provision of wireline telecommunications services and the construction of wireline telecommunications facilities.

4. Interacting with local, state, and other governmental agencies, the public, and industry groups on wireline telecommunications regulation and related matters.

5. Assisting the Consumer and Governmental Affairs Bureau on issues involving informal consumer complaints and other general inquiries by consumers.

6. Reviewing and coordinating orders, programs, and actions initiated by other bureaus and offices in matters affecting wireline telecommunications to ensure consistency with overall Commission policy.

Because of the technical nature of the matters it deals with, the Commission has historically given a great deal of deference to this bureau and its staff. Over the course of several decades, this deference has allowed the Wireline Competition Bureau to exert significant influence over the direction of telephone regulation. Under the direction of Chief Bernard Strassburg (1964–1974), the bureau fashioned policies that furthered the development of new technologies such as data communications and gradually opened the door for competition in the long distance telephone industry. This tradition was continued in the 1970s and 1980s under the direction of chiefs such as Phillip Verveer, Albert Halprin, and Gerald Brock, who also took steps to further competition.

The Wireline Competition Bureau is further broken down into several divisions, which include a Competition Policy Division that handles the creation of rules and policies dealing with the local competition and long distance competition provisions of the Telecommunications Act of 1996. The Industry Analysis and Technology Division conducts economic, financial, and technical analyses of telecommunications markets in support of the bureau's activities. The Pricing Policy Division deals with policies and rules pertaining to the rates of long distance telephone service providers. Finally, the Telecommunications Access Policy Division works to advance the universal service goals contained in the various portions of the Telecommunications Act.

Media Bureau

According to section 47 of the U.S. Code of Federal Regulations, the Media Bureau "develops, recommends, and administers the policy and licensing programs for the regulation of media, including cable television, broadcast television, and radio and satellite services in the United States and its territories." Specifically, the Media Bureau's duties include:

1. Processing applications for authorization, assignment, transfer, and renewal of broadcast radio and television station licenses.

2. Conducting comprehensive studies and rulemakings relating to the legal, engineering, and economic aspects of media service.

3. Administering and enforcing rules and policies pertaining to political programming.

4. Administering and enforcing rules pertaining to cable television systems, including those relating to rates, technical standards, and customer service.

5. Assisting the Consumer and Governmental Affairs Bureau on issues involving informal consumer complaints and other general inquiries by consumers.

The Media Bureau is further broken down into eight divisions and offices. The Office of Broadcast License Policy develops, recommends, and administers policies and programs for the regulation of broadcast services. The Audio and Video Divisions handle the licensing of radio and television stations. The Policy Division conducts rulemakings and other proceedings relating to various aspects of broadcasting, cable, and satellite services. The Industry Analysis Division conducts economic research on media ownership and other issues relating to the media industry. The Engineering Division conducts technical analyses of media related matters. Finally, the Office of Communications and Industry Information works with the Office of Legislative Affairs to keep bureau staff apprised of Congressional concerns relating to media regulation.

Wireless Bureau

The Wireless Bureau maintains the authority to make rules and undertake adjudications pertaining to wireless telecommunications services, most prominent among which are cellular telephone, Personal Communications Services, pagers, and two-way radios. A major function of the Wireless Bureau is to manage and license spectrum for these services as well as for use by businesses and state and local governments. The Wireless Bureau is broken down into five major divisions. The Auctions and Spectrum Access Division handles procedural issues relating to spectrum auctions and licensing. The Broadband Division works to facilitate the widespread deployment of wireless broadband services. The Mobility Division makes rules and handles the licensing of various mobile radio services. The Public Safety and Critical Infrastructure Division handles regulatory issues relating to mobile radio services used by public safety authorities. The Spectrum and Competition Policy Division formulates policies aimed at promoting competition and innovation in the use of spectrum and wireless infrastructure. Finally, the Spectrum Management Resources and Technologies Division manages the Bureau's information technology and outreach programs.

International Bureau

The purpose of the International Bureau is to develop and recommend policies and rules pertaining to international telecommunications services. The International Bureau advises the Commission on matters of international telecommunications policy and represents the Commission on international telecommunications matters at conferences and meetings. The bureau also conducts policy analyses and provides advice and technical assistance to U.S. trade officials in the negotiation and implementation of telecommunications trade agreements. It is also charged with interacting with Congress and other executive agencies on international telecommunications matters.

The International Bureau consists of three divisions—Policy, Satellite, and Strategic Analysis and Negotiations. The Policy Division works to formulate international spectrum policy and license international telecommunications facilities. Other important components of the division's work include working to lower rates for international telephone service and providing assistance in trade negotiations. The Satellite Division undertakes policies aimed at developing competitive and innovative telecommunications services through the fast and efficient deployment of satellite services. The Strategic Analysis and Negotiations Division conducts research and participates in international telecommunications conferences and negotiations.

Consumer and Governmental Affairs Bureau

In 2002, the FCC's Consumer Information Bureau was reorganized as the Consumer and Governmental Affairs Bureau. In a press release describing the organization, the Commission stated that a major purpose of the revitalized bureau was to "engage consumers, states, other governmental organizations and the industry in an ongoing discussion, with one objective being to better inform and educate consumers and to enable them to make smart choices in the increasingly competitive telecom marketplace."

More specifically, the jobs of the bureau include advising the Commission on matters pertaining to consumer and governmental affairs, collecting and analyzing data on consumer inquiries and complaints, developing and distributing materials to inform the public, and providing informal mediation and resolution of consumer inquiries and complaints. The Consumer and Governmental Affairs Bureau contains a Policy Division that is responsible for consumer-related rulemakings, orders, and analysis of consumer complaints. The Disability Rights Office handles policy matters pertaining to the impact of telecommunications policy on the disabled community. The Consumer Affairs and Outreach Division works to increase awareness of the FCC as a consumer resource. Consumer centers in Washington, D.C., respond to consumer inquiries and resolve informal complaints, including those pertaining to cable service matters. The Information Access and Privacy Office reviews matters arising under the Freedom of Information Act. Finally, the Consumer and Governmental Affairs Bureau houses the Reference Information Center, which works with anyone wishing to obtain FCC records and documents.

Enforcement Bureau

The Enforcement Bureau holds the responsibility of enforcing the communications laws and Commission rules through the resolution of formal complaints and other actions. The Investigations and Hearings Division handles a wide range of enforcement activities, including those relating to broadcast indecency, telephone company violation of competition and universal service rules, and telephone company auditing. It also enforces rules pertaining to collusion and misrepresentation in nonbroadcast spectrum auctions. The Market Disputes Resolution Division generally investigates and takes action on complaints brought by competitors against dominant telephone carriers. The Office of Homeland Security assists the bureau chief and Defense Commissioner in rulemakings and proceedings relating to the Emergency Alert System and operates the Communication and Crisis Management Center, which handles a variety of secure and nonsecure official communications for the federal government. The Spectrum Enforcement Division enforces a variety of technical rules and requirements pertaining to the provision of radio services. The Telecommunications Consumers Division enforces legal provisions aimed at protecting consumers from fraudulent practices undertaken by telephone companies. Finally, the Enforcement Bureau maintains three regional offices, sixteen district offices, and nine resident agents around the country to conduct on-site inspections, investigations, and audits.

The Staff Offices

In addition to the six bureaus, there are numerous staff offices assisting the Commission in the fulfillment of its policy, procedural, and administrative responsibilities.

Office of the Managing Director

The managing director acts as the FCC's chief operating officer and executive official. The duties of the managing director and his deputies include preparing the FCC's budget, developing and overseeing personnel policies and procedures, and managing a wide range of agency resources, including telecommunications services, physical space, and security. Through the Office of the Secretary, the managing director also coordinates the FCC's meeting schedule and handles the distribution of public documents. The Office of the Managing Director also maintains a special officer to handle public requests for documents and information under the Freedom of Information Act.

Office of the General Counsel

The General Counsel acts as the official legal advisor to the FCC and its staff and represents the agency before the federal courts. The Office of the General Counsel contains three divisions—Administrative Law, Litigation, and the Transactions Team. The Administrative Law Division assists the Commission and the various bureaus in drafting rules and orders and provides procedural advice on matters relating to the Administrative Procedures Act, the Freedom of Information Act, and other federal statutes that frame the agency's regulatory discretion. The Litigation Division represents the Commission before the federal courts. The Transactions Team provides legal analysis of proposed economic transactions such as the transfer of spectrum licenses and telecommunications mergers.

Office of Administrative Law Judges

The Office of Administrative Law Judges conducts adjudicatory proceedings ordered by the Commission in relation to investigations, rulemakings, and orders. All proceedings are presided over by an administrative law judge—a legal professional employed by the agency who conducts the adjudicatory proceeding similar to a trial with sworn testimony and the cross-examination of witnesses. Decisions handed down by the Office of Administrative Law Judges are subject to appeal to the full Commission.

Office of the Inspector General

Since 1989, the FCC has had an inspector general to help prevent waste, fraud, and abuse within the agency. Specifically, the inspector general holds the responsibility of conducting audits and investigations relating to the programs and operations of the agency and its employees. In many instances, these investigations are motivated by allegations brought by FCC employees, citizens, and other interested parties. In addition, the Inspector General reviews proposed and existing programs and makes recommendations regarding how they could more efficiently be administered. The Office of the Inspector General submits semiannual reports to the chairman detailing its activities.

Office of Engineering and Technology

The Office of Engineering and Technology is the principal advisory body to the Commission on scientific matters. It conducts scientific and engineering studies and advises the Commission and bureaus on matters relating to spectrum management and frequency allocations. The Office maintains contacts with other governmental entities and the public on matters relating to communications technology and represents the Commission at national conferences and meetings dealing with technology and standards. Finally, the Office of Engineering and Technology is also actively involved in making legislative recommendations and participating in rulemaking proceedings throughout the FCC administrative structure.

Office of Strategic Planning and Policy Analysis

Originally called the Office of Plans and Policy, the Office of Strategic Planning and Policy Analysis was created in the early 1970s to assist the Commission and its bureaus in the identification of significant communications policy problems and the development of solutions consistent with agency objectives. The Office of Strategic Planning and Policy Analysis presents its ideas through a series of working papers published periodically by the Commission. The working papers are available to the public and the most recent ones have been placed on the FCC web site. Numerous working papers have been cited prominently in Commission proceedings and academic writings, and several have been very influential in shaping major Commission policies. For example, one particularly influential working paper published in 1987 recommended that the FCC replace traditional telephone rate regulation with a method known as price caps implemented in Britain a few years earlier. When Dennis Patrick became Chairman of the FCC later that year, he moved forward with the price caps proposal and it eventually became national policy in 1989. Staff in this office also wrote several influential working papers during the 1980s arguing that spectrum licensing proceedings should be conducted through competitive auctions. Spectrum auctions were eventually authorized by Congress in 1993.

Office of Legislative Affairs

The Office of Legislative Affairs is the FCC's official liaison to Congress. Its responsibilities include advising and making recommendations to the Commission regarding proposed legislation, responding to requests for information on Commission policies by members of Congress, and preparing members of the FCC and its staff to testify.

Office of Media Relations

The Office of Media Relations is responsible for the dissemination of information on FCC policies and procedures to the news media. The Office of Media Relations also manages the FCC web site and audio/visual support services, maintains contacts with outside parties regarding the broadcast of Commission proceedings, and works with the Consumer and Governmental Affairs Bureau on media issues concerning complaints and other consumer issues.

Office of Workplace Diversity

The Office of Workplace Diversity addresses matters relating to equal employment opportunity and affirmative action within the agency. The Office advises the Commission and its various administrative entities regarding their equal employment responsibilities under the federal civil rights laws and conducts independent analyses of FCC policies and practices to make sure they are in line with those goals. The Office also works with the FCC and its staff offices to formulate policies and foster an environment that values diversity.

Office of Communications Business Opportunities

The Office of Communications Business Opportunities works to promote ownership, employment, and other business opportunities for women and minorities. The Office of Communications Business Opportunities acts as the Commission's official advisor in proceedings that impact women and minorities and works to increase awareness of Commission policies and activities among these groups.

FCC DECISIONMAKING PROCESSES

As noted in Chapter 1, the FCC's statutory authority under the Communications Act of 1934 provides it with the ability to make a wide range of discretionary decisions. Two major types of decisions—rulemakings and broadcast licensing proceedings—are discussed below.

Rulemaking

Rulemaking proceedings at the FCC follow the general guidelines provided in the federal Administrative Procedures Act of 1946 (APA) as amended. Most rulemakings undertaken at the FCC are of the "notice and comment" variety in which there is no formal trial-type proceeding. Rather, the proposed rules are published in the *Federal Register* and the public is given the opportunity to comment on them before they go into effect. Most FCC rulemakings have been initiated at the discretion of the agency within the fairly broad limits of its statutory authority. The impetus for rules, however, may come from a variety of sources. Many of the FCC's most recent rulemakings were mandated by the Telecommunications Act of 1996. The judicial branch can also mandate new rulemakings when it overturns existing rules. Other government agencies, citizens, and other nongovernmental entities can also influence the Commission from time to time by suggesting proposed rules.

The formal process of making a rule is initiated by staff at the FCC within the six major bureaus. A rulemaking is identified by its "docket" number, which contains the abbreviations of the name of the originating bureau, the last two digits of the year, and a specific reference number for the proceeding in question (for instance, a 2004 rulemaking at the Wireline Competition Bureau might be labeled WC #04-132). The rulemaking process generally proceeds with some combination of the following actions by the FCC and the public:

Petition for Rulemaking

While most FCC rulemakings originate with the commissioners and agency staff, members of the public can also initiate a proceeding by submitting a petition for rulemaking. The petition generally contains a discussion of the reasons for the rule as well as the specific wording of the rule that is being requested. Petitions are printed on a weekly basis in the FCC's *Filings* newsletter and the public is given thirty days to comment on their merits. Following the comment period, the FCC may choose to simply dispose of the decision if there is little public interest in the matter. If the agency decides to move forward, however, the next step is either a Notice of Inquiry or a Notice of Proposed Rulemaking.

Notices of Inquiry and Proposed Rulemaking

A Notice of Inquiry (NOI) is issued to solicit comments on some broad topic or issue without formally proposing a rule at that time. By contrast, a Notice of Proposed Rulemaking (NPRM) solicits comments on a specific rule the Commission seeks to adopt. Either an NOI or an NPRM may be used as the first formal step in a rulemaking proceeding. In some instances, however, an NPRM may follow an NOI after a more specific proposal has been generated. In either case, the issuance of an NOI or an NPRM marks the beginning of a formal rulemaking proceeding. Both types of documents are printed in the *Federal Register* as well as in the FCC's weekly newsletter, *Open Proceedings*. Once released, the public is given thirty days or more to comment on NOIs and NPRMs. Following the comment period, written comments are evaluated by the staff in the issuing bureau before further action is taken. Sometimes public comments reveal things that the Commission staff had not originally taken into consideration, such as new facts or possible unintended consequences that might be brought about by the proposed rule. In these instances the FCC will frequently issue a Further Notice of Proposed Rulemaking (FNPRM) in which the rule is amended or further public comment is sought on more specific issues. In some instances, several FNPRMs may be necessary to fully clarify all relevant issues.

Report and Order

After considering the comments submitted in response to the NPRM and FNPRMs, a Report and Order (R&O) is issued in which the Commission publishes its final decision. In the R&O, the Commission might choose to adopt the original rule, adopt an amended rule in response to the public comments, or drop the matter altogether. In any instance, however, the FCC is careful to detail the reasons for its actions. R&Os typically include a description of the adopted regulations and a summary of the major public comments and the FCC's responses to them. If the FCC chooses to side with a particular party or ignore all parties, it explains its reasoning in detail to avoid charges that its decision was "arbitrary and capricious" and, thus, subject to a possible court challenge. A summary of the R&O is published in the *Federal Register* for public review. In many instances, however, the R&O isn't the end of the process. There may still be additional regulatory issues to clarify and the R&O may be accompanied by an additional FNPRM.

Petition for Reconsideration

Parties that are not satisfied with the outcome of the rulemaking process may file a Petition for Reconsideration within thirty days after the appearance of the R&O in the *Federal Register*. Once the Petition for Reconsideration has been fully investigated by the Commission, a Memorandum Opinion and Order is issued in which the rules are either amended or the reconsideration is denied. In either case, the FCC once again provides an explanation for its actions.

Judicial Review of FCC Rules

Under the Administrative Procedures Act, interested parties are allowed to challenge FCC orders in the federal courts unless otherwise precluded by the Communications Act as amended. Challenges to FCC rules go directly to the U.S. Court of Appeals for the District of Columbia Circuit. Parties challenging FCC rules must have standing, meaning that they must in some way have suffered a legal wrong as a result of the rule, although the simple fact that a plaintiff has suffered monetary harm by no means guarantees relief. Parties challenging a rule in court must be able to demonstrate that the agency violated their constitutional rights, did not follow proper procedure, went beyond the authority delegated to it by statute, or acted in an arbitrary and capricious manner by failing to consider all relevant facts, considering facts that were not relevant, or rendering an implausible interpretation of those facts. A judicial decision overturning an FCC rule can force the agency to drop the matter altogether or rewrite the rule to meet court mandates.

Broadcast Licensing

As noted in Chapter 1, the FCC possesses the statutory authority to license all major users of the electromagnetic spectrum, including commercial and noncommercial broadcasters. Although the commissioners hold the ultimate authority to grant, deny, or revoke a license, initial decisions in these matters are rendered by the agency's Media Bureau. While the demand for licenses may vary from year to year, there is very little frequency space available to new broadcasters and the submission of an application is no guarantee of success.

TABLE 2.1. Total Broadcast Stations Licensed as of June 30, 2005

AM Stations	4,759
FM Commercial	6,213
FM Educational	2,585
Total	**13,557**
UHF Commercial TV	779
VHF Commercial TV	589
UHF Educational TV	253
VHF Educational TV	126
Total	**1,747**
Class A UHF Stations	489
Class A VHF Stations	109
Total	**598**
FM Translators & Boosters	3,906
UHF Translators	2,669
VHF Translators	1,822
Total	**8,397**
UHF Low Power TV	1,604
VHF Low Power TV	494
Total	**2,098**
Low Power FM	498
Total	**498**
Total Broadcast Stations	**26,895**

Source: FCC.

Furthermore, the application process can be difficult and expensive, requiring the submission of extensive information relating to financial, legal, and technical matters. For these reasons, applicants frequently retain the assistance of legal counsel and broadcast engineering consultants. In addition, most types of applications require payment of a fee to cover regulatory costs. Thus, applying for a broadcast license is not something that is done on a whim.

The first step in obtaining a license is locating an available frequency. For those seeking to start an AM station, a frequency search must be conducted within the community to be served. The applicant must locate an available frequency between 540 and 1700 kHz and be able to demonstrate that the unused frequency will not interfere with other stations or receive interference. Applicants for FM radio and television licenses search for a frequency in the FCC's table of allotments—a list of frequencies assigned to different communities. If no allotted frequency exists, FM radio and television applicants may petition to add an available frequency to the table. To do this, the applicant must conduct an engineering study to demonstrate the existence of a nonassigned frequency that will not cause or receive interference. At this time no new applications for television stations are being accepted by the FCC until the conversion is made to digital television.

Once a frequency has been located, the proper forms must be filled out and submitted to the Commission. The proper forms are available on the FCC's web site or can be obtained by contacting the FCC Forms Distribution Center. Many FCC filings will only be accepted electronically now, so access to a computer is essential. Applicants seeking permission to construct a commercial broadcast station are required to complete Form 301, while noncommercial applicants must file Form 340. The application must be accompanied by information that demonstrates the legal qualifications of the applicant, including proof of sufficient financial resources to construct and begin operation of the station according to established standards. In addition, the applicant must provide engineering specifications, the type of program format that will be employed, and an explanation of how it meets the needs of the local community.

Once the proper applications and filing fees have been submitted, all applicants, with the exception of those applying for a low power FM license, must give local notice in a newspaper of general circulation in the proposed community of service. Copies of the application must be kept on file in some accessible location, such as a public library or post office, where they may be accessed by members of the community. At this stage, the public has the opportunity to file comments with the FCC regarding the application. This same local notice procedure must also be followed by stations seeking a license renewal.

Applications that have been formally accepted by the FCC are publicized in a public notice, thus opening up a thirty-day window during which competing applications may be filed. During this time, interested parties may also file petitions to deny the application. Petitions to deny must be served on the applicant and must provide evidence that approval of the application is not in the public interest, convenience, or necessity as spelled out in the Communications Act of 1934.

Assuming that there are no competing applications or petitions to deny filed within the thirty-day window, the FCC moves forward with the application. Depending on the backlog at any given time, processing the application may take several months or more. Assuming the application is complete and free of defects, approval for construction is given. If the application is deemed problematic in some way, it may be returned to the applicant for correction. However, if either the application itself or pleadings filed in relation to the matter raises substantial questions of fact that must be resolved before a license can be granted, the Commission may call a formal hearing before an administrative law judge. Once an application has been designated for a hearing, all interested parties must be notified and provided with a summary of the reasons for the action. Following the formal hearing, the application is either accepted or rejected. Whether approved or not, the disposition of the application is publicized in a public notice and thirty days are allowed for the filing of Petitions for Reconsideration. In the event that there are multiple competing applications for a single frequency, the FCC may in some instances call for competitive bid auctions in which the highest bidder is awarded the license.

License Renewal

Licenses are currently granted for terms of up to eight years, though the FCC has the authority to grant shorter licenses at its discretion. When a licensee's term is set to expire, they must file an application for renewal with Form 303-S. Renewal applicants must certify that they are in compliance with a variety of federal laws and regulations, including those relating to foreign ownership, equal opportunity, criminal activity, and environmental impact. As with the initial license application, those seeking renewal must file local notice and provide the public with the opportunity to scrutinize the filing and make public comments regarding whether or not the station has operated in a manner consistent with the public interest. Assuming no violations or important questions of fact are raised, renewals are routinely granted.

Suspension/Revocation of Licenses

Under the Communications Act the FCC holds the authority to suspend or revoke licenses for a variety of reasons including: (1) false statements made during the application process; (2) willful or repeated failure to operate as set forth in the license; (3) failure to abide by federal statutes, treaties and regulations; (4) violation of a cease and desist order issued by the Commission; or (5) willful or repeated failure to allow candidates for federal office to purchase reasonable amounts of air time. The FCC may suspend the license of a station that violates federal laws and regulations, including those regarding the broadcast of obscene and indecent communication. If a station broadcasts false or deceptive signals or communications, or willfully or maliciously interferes with any other radio communication or signals, its license can also be revoked. Finally, if a licensee fails to broadcast for a period of twelve consecutive months, its license automatically expires at the end of that period.

Before a license can be revoked, the FCC must serve upon the licensee an order showing the cause for the action. The licensee must then appear before the Commission within thirty days to present evidence refuting the charges. If the evidence presented in the hearing is deemed insufficient, the Commission may then issue an order of revocation stating the reasons for the action and specifying the effective date of the termination. In all hearings pertaining to the revocation of licenses, the burden of proof lies with the Commission.

Appeal of Licensing Decisions

Licensing decisions that go against an applicant may be subject to numerous appeals. Initial adverse decisions by the Media Bureau may be appealed to the full Commission. Final Commission decisions may then be appealed to the U.S. Court of Appeals for the District of Columbia Circuit. Appeals may be made by the applicant or any other aggrieved party whose interests have been adversely affected by the decision. Appeals must be made within thirty days following public notice of the decision. Upon filing, the appellant must provide a statement of the reasons for the appeal and the evidence upon which the appellant wishes to rely. Interested parties wishing to intervene and participate in the action must file with the court and the Commission a notice of intention to intervene stating the nature of their interest in the matter within thirty days following the notice of appeal. If the FCC's decision is overturned by the Court, the matter is then remanded back to the Commission to carry out the judgment of the court. U.S. Court of Appeals decisions may further be appealed to the U.S. Supreme Court.

THE FCC AND THE PUBLIC

There are a number of ways in which the public can participate in or obtain information regarding FCC activities. Many of them have been mentioned briefly in earlier sections of this chapter. This section elaborates on some of the ways the public can keep up on FCC activities.

FCC Public Documents

The FCC releases a range of official documents, reports, and notices that are available for public scrutiny. The most important among these are:

The FCC Record

The *FCC Record* is the official compilation of agency rulemaking documents and all other agency actions, including those previously published in the *Federal Register*. The *FCC Record* is published every two weeks and is paginated by volume. Official legal citations from the current *FCC Record* contain the volume number, abbreviated name of the publication, and page number of the citation followed by the year in parentheses (thus, a document appearing in volume 7, page 5781 of the record in the year 1992 would be cited as 7 FCC Rcd. 5781 (1992)). The *FCC Record* is available through the U.S. Government Printing Office and is subscribed to by law libraries and university research libraries throughout the country.

Annual Performance Reports

Under the Communications Act as amended the FCC is required to submit an annual report to Congress detailing its activities during the previous fiscal year. The FCC is broadly required to report on current policy matters before the agency, the adequacy of current agency resources for meeting these challenges, and the potential need for new legislation. As a practical matter, however, the content of the Annual Reports has varied over the years. Most have started off with a summary of the Commission's organization and procedures, including any changes made during the previous year. Most of the report is then dedicated to the activities of the individual bureaus, including new and ongoing rulemaking dockets and adjudicatory proceedings. Renamed the *Annual Performance Report* in 1999, more recent reports have focused on performance and the achievement of strategic and policy goals set forth by the Commission and the communications laws. For the communications policy consumer, the *Annual Performance Report* can be a good way to keep updated on current FCC activities.

Public Notices and News Releases

The FCC issues Public Notices with information regarding upcoming meetings and legal actions. News Releases publicize events and inform the press regarding FCC activities. Both items are disseminated through the FCC's Office of Media Relations and are published on the FCC web site (www.fcc.gov) regularly.

Daily Digest

The *FCC Daily Digest* is perhaps the quickest and easiest way for those interested in communications policy to stay updated regarding Commission activities. The *Digest* contains a summary of all Commission speeches, official actions, public notices, and news releases. The *Daily Digest* is coordinated by the Office of Media Relations and can be viewed through a link on its homepage. A free e-mail subscription to the *Digest* may also be obtained through a link on the homepage of the FCC web site.

Consumer's Guide

The FCC puts out a twenty-six page booklet entitled *About the FCC: A Consumer's Guide to Our Organization, Functions, and Procedures*. The pamphlet contains a concise and accessible description of the major organizational units of the FCC, the rulemaking process, methods of public participation and information gathering, and key contacts within the agency. The pamphlet can be obtained directly from the FCC or downloaded at the web site in PDF format.

Public Participation and Information Requests

Any member of the public may participate in FCC decisionmaking by attending meetings of the Commission, filing comments in a rulemaking docket, or filing a formal complaint with the agency. In addition, publicly available documents may be obtained through Freedom of Information Act (FOIA) requests. The remainder of this section describes the processes for undertaking these activities:

Commission Meetings

Under the federal Sunshine Laws, most meetings of the FCC are publicized and open to the public. The dates and times of Commission meetings are published in the *Federal Register* and the FCC's *Daily Digest* at least one week in advance. Meeting times and agendas can also be obtained from the FCC's Web site or by calling the Commission directly.

Submitting Public Comments

Public comments may be submitted by anyone so long as they are in writing and comply with established timetables. Comments may be filed electronically over the FCC web site or be hand-delivered or mailed to the Commission. Comments submitted in general rulemaking proceedings require the submission of one original and four copies (nine if you want the commissioners to receive them). Comments must be typed in 10- or 12-point font or legibly written, contain contact information (name, address, telephone number), be clearly labeled with the docket number for the proceeding, and be signed by the commenter above their printed name. Hand-delivered comments must be delivered to the Commission's secretary. Comments sent via the U.S. mail may be sent directly to the Commission at the Portals II building.

Filing Complaints

Complaints are handled either by the FCC's Consumer and Governmental Affairs Bureau or the Enforcement Bureau (depending on the type) and may be submitted in paper form via the U.S. Mail or filed over the telephone or electronically over the FCC's web site. The FCC currently processes three categories of complaints: general, slamming, and indecency/obscenity.

General complaints include those relating to the service offerings or billing practices of a telecommunications or cable television provider. General complaints may be submitted to the FCC by calling the FCC directly, sending a complaint letter, or filing form 475 electronically through the Commission's web site. In any event, the complaining party should be prepared to supply his or her name, address, and telephone number, specific information about the complaint, the steps that have been taken to resolve the complaint, names and telephone numbers of the company employees spoken with, the dates on which the party talked to them, copies of bills listing any disputed charges, and the relief being requesting. Complaints sent through the U.S. mail should be addressed to the Consumer and Governmental Affairs Bureau, Consumer Inquiries and Complaints Division.

The FCC currently maintains a separate process for submitting "slamming" complaints. Slamming occurs when a telephone company switches your service without your authorization. Slamming complaints should be filed in writing (either on paper or electronically) using form 501. When not using this form, complaints must include your name, address, and telephone number, the name of the telephone company that allegedly slammed you, your authorized local and long distance providers, and a statement of the facts. All complaints should also be accompanied by copies of phone bills displaying the name of the unauthorized carrier and the disputed charges. Slamming complaints should be addressed to the Consumer and Governmental Affairs Bureau, Slam Team.

Finally, the FCC has a separate complaint process for those who have heard or viewed indecent, profane, or obscene radio or television broadcasts (see Chapter 5 for a description of obscenity and indecency). An obscenity/profanity/indecency complaint must be accompanied by information detailing what was said or depicted during the alleged broadcast (a full or partial excerpt of the program in question or a transcript containing the alleged violation is ideal). Obscenity/profanity/indecency complaints may be filed directly with the FCC's Enforcement Bureau, Investigations and Hearings Division.

Libraries and Reference Rooms

The FCC maintains an extensive array of records that are easily accessed by the public through its library and numerous reference rooms. The FCC Library, located in the Portals II building, houses a wide range of information and publications dealing with telecommunications-related subjects. The library's legal collection contains federal and statutory histories, reference works, treatises, and cross-indexed legislative histories dating back to the beginning of communications law. Government documents contained in the library include title 47 of the Code of Federal Regulations (FCC rules), FCC Annual Reports, FCC Federal Court Briefs, the FCC Record, Federal Radio Commission Annual Reports, the *Federal Register* since 1934, as well as proposed and enacted statutes pertaining to communications, administrative procedures, and independent agency regulations.

In addition to the library, there are a number of reference rooms affiliated with different administrative components of the FCC. The Reference Information Center in the Consumer and Governmental Affairs Bureau maintains files containing the records of all rulemakings, license applications for broadcast stations, and various other types of applications and documents submitted to the FCC by broadcasters and telecommunications providers. The Reference Information Center should probably be regarded by members of the public as the first stop in seeking out official regulatory documents relating to communications companies. However, additional documents may in some instances be cataloged by reference rooms contained in the individual policymaking bureaus. Title 47, section 0.453 of the U.S. Code of Regulations provides further information regarding where publicly available FCC documents can be found.

FOIA Requests

In the event that a member of the public wishes to view documents not normally available to the public, a request may need to be filed under the

Freedom of Information Act (FOIA). Originally passed by Congress in 1966, FOIA guarantees Americans reasonable access to nonclassified public records and documents. Under current FCC regulations, members of the public may submit an electronic FOIA request through the FCC web site or by sending a written request to the FOIA officer in the Office of the Managing Director. The FCC asks that those submitting written requests write or type "Freedom of Information Act Request" on the letter and envelope and supply their name, mailing address, telephone number, and as much information as possible with respect to the documents in question. Because the FCC has the right to charge for the location and reproduction of all documents requested under FOIA, be sure to also specify a maximum search fee you are willing to pay.

The FCC may deny a FOIA request if it determines that the requested documents either do not exist or are exempted from disclosure. Under FOIA, documents may be exempted from disclosure if they contain: (1) national defense or foreign policy secrets; (2) internal personnel rules or agency practices; (3) information exempted from disclosure by another statute; (4) trade secrets and commercial or financial information that is confidential; (5) inter- or intra-agency memos that would not be available to a party in litigation with the agency; (6) personnel or medical files that might constitute an invasion of individual privacy; (7) records compiled for law enforcement purposes; (8) records relating to the examination, operation, or conditions of financial institutions; or (9) oil well data. In some instances, the FCC might choose to release an exempted document, depending on the circumstances and the type of exemption in question.

Under FOIA, the FCC is required to respond to all written requests within twenty business days of their receipt. If the FCC determines that it cannot respond within that timeframe, it may write the requester and establish a response date of no more than ten days after the initial twenty-day deadline. If this ten-day extension will prove insufficient, the FCC must either ask you to modify your request or arrange a timeframe with you in which your request can be processed.

In the event that a FOIA request is denied by the FCC the applicant has the right to appeal by filing an administrative application for review under Code of Federal Regulations Title 47, section 0.461(j). The envelope containing the application should be labeled "Application for Administrative Review" and mailed to the Office of the General Counsel at the FCC. All applications for administrative review must be filed within thirty days of the date of the FCC's initial denial. If the application for administrative review is denied in whole or in part, the party may seek a judicial ruling in a U.S. District Court.

☆ 3 ☆

The Political Environment

The Federal Communications Commission is an independent regulatory commission that was created to act as an "expert" agency, one that would be able to work "outside" the political environment. The reality, however, is that the FCC is an organization that is particularly open to interference by outside forces. According to the definitive book on the matter, *The Politics of Broadcast Regulation* by Erwin G. Krasnow, Lawrence D. Longley, and Herbert A. Terry, there are six determiners of regulatory policy. The FCC is, of course, at the center, but it is surrounded by Congress, the White House, the courts, citizen groups and members of the public, and the regulated industries. According to Krasnow, Longley, and Terry, the FCC, Congress, and the regulated industries make up the primary forces in broadcast regulation. The other actors, while important, exert less influence.

The model of FCC policymaking depicted in Figure 3.1 is adapted from the model presented by Krasnow, Longley, and Terry. It demonstrates that Congress and the regulated industries are of primary political importance when looking at FCC decisionmaking. The White House, the courts, and citizen groups and members of the public are often of secondary importance. The three less powerful actors often succeed only when supported by one of the primary actors.

CONGRESS

Congress has considerable influence over the Commission for many reasons. The Senate maintains advice and consent power over the president's choice for commissioners. Congress holds the purse strings of all federal agencies because of its constitutional budget powers. The House Committee

FIGURE 3.1. A Schematic Illustration of the FCC's Political Environment

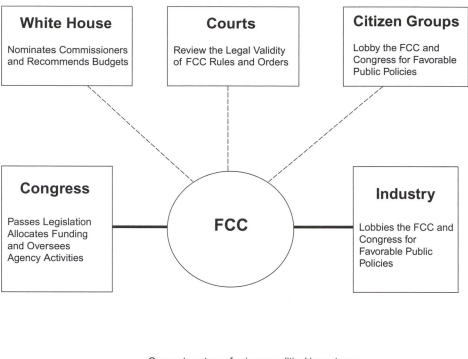

| Connects actors of primary political importance
| Connects actors of secondary political importance

Source: Based on the "systems" model of broadcast regulation developed by Erwin Krasnow, Lawrence Longley, and Herbert Terry in their book *The Politics of Broadcast Regulation*.

on Energy and Commerce and the Senate Committee on Commerce, Science, and Transportation, along with the associated subcommittees, maintain oversight of all agency activities. Congressional committees can also hold hearings on issues related to the business of the Commission. Finally, Congress can threaten or pass legislation that can direct the Commission to do or not to do something. Newton Minow tells the story that shortly after he became chair of the Commission, House Speaker Sam Rayburn put his arm around Minow's shoulder and said, "Just remember one thing, son. Your agency is an arm of the Congress; you belong to us. Remember that and you'll be all right."[1] That sentiment often leads commissioners to do the things that they believe powerful members of Congress would like them to do.

An example of the influence of Congress through nomination hearings can be seen in 1991. When the Senate Commerce Committee held hearings regarding the nominations of Al Sikes, Andrew Barrett, and Sherrie Marshall, a number of senators expressed deep concern about indecent broadcast programming. In particular, Senators Al Gore and Daniel Inouye questioned the future commissioners extensively on their feelings about the FCC's regulation of indecency. When the question first came up during the hearing, all three nominees expressed the opinion that the First Amendment did not allow the Commission to regulate nonobscene, sexually explicit material such as that performed by "shock jock" Howard Stern. Gore and Inouye repeatedly asked the nominees their opinions on the matter and expressed their own opinions that indecency not only could, but should, be regulated. By the end of the hearings, the nominees had all changed their positions and advocated for increased regulation. The nominees also wrote letters to the committee after the hearing affirming their beliefs in indecency regulation. It was a surprise to no one that when Sikes, Barrett, and Marshall took office later that year, the new Commission's first major action was to issue significant fines to Infinity Broadcasting for the *Howard Stern Show*.

Congress can also use its budgetary power to influence the Commission's activities. In 1978, Senator Lowell Weicker added $750,000 and five staff positions to the FCC's budget for a study comparing UHF and VHF television. In the 1980 budget, Senator Ernest Hollings added $440,000 for a study of AM radio allocation. Congress will also include "suggestions" to an agency like the FCC in the reports that go along with appropriations bills. In 1974, Congress "warned" the FCC that it was not happy with its lack of enforcement of the broadcast indecency standard and ordered the Commission to make a study of the matter. Shortly thereafter, the FCC took action against Pacifica Foundation station WBAI in the George Carlin case and laid out a new definition of indecency that was then sent to Congress.

Congress holds hearings on issues of concern whenever its members feel the Commission is not being responsive enough. Examples of this tactic can be seen in the numerous hearings on television violence that have been held periodically since the 1950s. The FCC has no authority to regulate violence, but that does not stop Congress from holding hearings and taking the Commission to task. Another example was when the quiz show scandals broke in the 1950s. Members of the Commission, particularly Chairman John Doerfer, believed that rigged quiz shows, while unsavory, were not against the law. Members of Congress disagreed and subpoenaed a number of past contestants to look into the matter. Not long after those hearings, the FCC began considering rules regarding the "honesty" of game shows.

As the legislative branch of the federal government, Congress proposes and passes legislation that can impact the Commission. A good example can be seen in the passage of the Telecommunications Act of 1996. In that legislation, Congress ordered the Commission to do a biennial review of the ownership regulations on the broadcast industry. The review is supposed to determine whether the regulations are still serving the public interest. The every-two-year review process is going on almost constantly at the Commission, since two years is a short time for the Commission to do much of anything. Congress has also statutorily ordered the Commission to regulate,

FCC officials testifying at a congressional hearing on telephone competition, February 20, 2003. Congress holds regular hearings to keep updated on FCC activities. (AP/Wide World Photos)

then deregulate, then regulate, and finally deregulate cable rates over the years, regardless of the commissioners' positions on the matter.

Personalities can often influence the relationship between Congress and the Commission. Republican Chairman Mark Fowler was considered arrogant by many of the Democratic Congressmen on the House and Senate Commerce Committees, and it is believed that this hostile relationship damaged Fowler's ability to move forward on his deregulatory agenda. Fowler's successor, Dennis Patrick, was also unpopular on the Hill and thus did not achieve as much as he would have liked. Chairman Alfred Sikes, who was much more conciliatory toward the Democratic Congressmen, is considered to have achieved much more deregulation because of that positive relationship. In addition to the interparty hostility, particular members of Congress have often clashed with particular commissioners. Representative Eugene Cox was extremely hostile toward Chairman James Lawrence Fly and held numerous hearings in which he publicly berated Fly for incompetence.

But Congressional power and influence do have their limits. Congress does not always get what it wants. For example, in 1987 the FCC decided to end the Fairness Doctrine. Democrats in Congress were furious and immediately passed legislation reinstating the rules. The bill was vetoed by President Ronald Reagan and there were not enough votes to overturn the veto.

REGULATED INDUSTRIES

The FCC regulates telephone, broadcasting, cable, and satellite and thus spends much of its time dealing with representatives from those industries. The commissioners speak at conventions and meet with industry members and lobbyists on a regular basis. At the staff level, that relationship is often even closer. It would be impossible for the Commission to regulate the industries without talking to them. This brings up the notion that the Commission is "captured" and that because of proximity, commissioners and staff sympathize more than regulate.

The regulated industries influence the Commission in two ways, directly and indirectly. They directly influence by working with and lobbying the commissioners and staff. They also indirectly influence the Commission through their lobbying of Congress. In fact, the regulated industries are second in influence only to Congress. Much of their influence comes through influence exerted on members of Congress. Lobbyists for telephone, broadcasting, cable, and satellite blanket the Hill on a regular basis and often drive the regulatory agenda. Many in the public interest sector believe that industry lobbyists basically wrote the Telecom Act to move their agendas forward.

It is important to remember, however, that the regulated industries rarely speak with one voice. Telephone and cable are frequently in conflict over entry into each other's fields. Even within industries there is disagreement. The broadcast networks often want different things from small station owners. When the Chain Broadcasting Rules were handed down in 1941, Mutual Broadcasting supported everything the Commission was doing. CBS objected mostly to the option time requirements and did not care about the ownership restrictions. NBC, on the other hand, felt option time was not an issue but did not want to sell either its stations or its second network. Thus, the Commission is often at the center of a battle between and within industries.

Another example of the FCC being caught between regulated industries can be seen in the issue of must carry for digital television. When cable first began to gain significant penetration, broadcast stations were concerned that the systems would import distant TV signals and thus put local broadcasters out of business. As a result, the FCC created the must carry rules. When the Telecom Act mandated the transition to digital television, there was no explanation of how that would impact must carry. A station broadcasting in analog offers only one channel of programming. But when the switch to digital happens, broadcast stations could suddenly begin offering multiple programming channels. The question of the cable companies' carriage of those signals has been a point of contention for close to a decade. Thus, while the regulated industries can be enormously influential over the actions of the Commission, when industries conflict, the power is diluted.

When a regulated industry calls on its allies in Congress, however, the FCC is often completely at its mercy. A classic example of an industry ganging up on the Commission with Congress came after the FCC's publication of the *Blue Book*. Throughout the early years of the Commission, Congress regularly excoriated the Commission for not doing anything about the overcommercialization of radio. But when Chairman James Lawrence Fly took action and released the new rules, the industry drove the response. The relationship between members of Congress and local broadcast stations has always been close. Broadcasting is the most effective way for a member of Congress to talk to constituents. So when local broadcasters call on their Representatives and Senators, they listen. The broadcasters were deeply unhappy with the *Blue Book* and suddenly, the same people who berated the Commission for inaction were berating it for acting. With pressure from both the industry and Congress, it is not surprising that the *Blue Book* was never enforced.

The regulation of cable demonstrates that industry actors are not all-powerful. The Cable Act of 1984 was passed at the urging of the cable industry, which was tired of rate regulation and punishing franchise agreements. In response to these concerns, Congress deregulated rates and put limits on what cities could ask for in franchise contracts. By 1992, however, the public was fed up with outrageous rates and poor customer service. Congress responded to the public outcry with the Cable Act of 1992. In 1996, the Telecom Act again deregulated rates at the behest of the industry. Thus, even when the industry is not being challenged by another industry, other factors, such as public pressure, can come into play during the regulatory process.

THE WHITE HOUSE

The president of the United States nominates an FCC commissioner whenever an open seat is available, but the nominee is not always a member of the president's party. Only three commissioners from the president's political party can serve at any time; two must nominally be from the other party. The president also designates the chair, who is almost always a member of his party. In fact, tradition dictates that the FCC chair resign if his party is not reelected. This power of nomination is the White House's real source of influence, although budgets are suggested by the president.

While all presidents nominate FCC commissioners, not all presidents are that interested in the business of the Commission. Franklin Roosevelt was, of course, deeply involved with the creation and first years of the FCC. Harry Truman, however, was not all that interested. Lyndon Johnson's family owned broadcast stations and some viewed his influence at the Commission as improper. Technology was a major policy concern of Bill Clinton's and he was very focused on the Commission. George W. Bush, on the other hand, left seats from his own party open for months without making a nomination.

The relationship between the chairs and the White House is also important when considering the influence of the president. James Lawrence Fly was a personal friend of Roosevelt and that relationship helped set the FCC's agenda. E. William Henry was close to President Kennedy but did not have the same relationship with Johnson and thus was considered to have lost power after Johnson become president. In addition to personal friendships, a number of commissioners have actually worked at the White House before joining the Commission, such as Dennis Patrick and Margita White. Chairman Dean Burch was very close to President Richard Nixon, who often tried to use to the Commission to punish enemies in the press. For example, during Watergate, *The Washington Post* found that its television license renewals were suspiciously delayed. Chairmen Reed Hundt went to prep school with Vice President Al Gore and law school with President and Mrs. Clinton. It is said that during Hundt's tenure, the Commission was virtually run out of Gore's office.

Presidents are sometimes surprised by the actions of those they nominate. A good example of that can be seen when Nicholas Johnson was appointed by Lyndon Johnson. The president soon regretted the nomination when Commissioner Johnson began to advocate for public involvement in broadcasting against the wishes of station owners like the president's family.

THE COURTS

The judicial branch of the federal government is charged with ruling on decisions made by independent regulatory commissions like the FCC. Many FCC actions, especially those related to media, are appealed to the U.S. Court of Appeals for the District of Columbia Circuit. Some cases, particularly those involving the telephone companies, come up through the other appellate courts. A number of cases involving the FCC have made their way to the Supreme Court, the highest court in the land.

The courts rule on both the process by which the Commission makes rules and decisions and the constitutionality of the results. The courts also frequently rule on whether the Commission has the statutory authority to carry out a particular action. In the Broadcast Flag decision, the D.C. Circuit ruled that the FCC did not have the authority to require television manufacturers to install the copyright technology. In that case, like many others that have come before, the court did say that Congress could grant new powers to the Commission but that the FCC could not do something that Congress had not mandated.

When Congress writes communication legislation, it often proposes sweeping policies but leaves the specific rules for the Commission to develop. Many industry players challenge the laws, the rules, and the process by which the rules were made. The courts are often asked to determine whether the Commission acted in an arbitrary and capricious manner, meaning that the rules were not justified by the evidence in the record. Since the passage of the Telecom Act, the telephone companies have undertaken almost constant litigation over how the Commission interpreted the will of Congress.

The FCC knows that its decisions are subject to review by the courts and takes this factor into consideration when it acts. Thus, although few FCC actions result in litigation, the influence of the courts is always there. The Commission sometimes even seeks out the court's opinions. When considering a new definition of indecency in the 1970s, the Commission deliberately sought out a test case. The FCC looked for a station that would appeal so that a judicial ruling on the First Amendment issues could be obtained.

Because of the nature of the U.S. government, the courts have the final say over the constitutionality of the actions of the executive and legislative branches. In the 1980s, Congress repeatedly tried to ban indecent programming from broadcasting. The Supreme Court had established in *FCC v. Pacifica* (1978) that adults had a right to access sexually explicit, nonobscene programming at times of day when children would not be in the audience. Known as the safe harbor, indecent programming can be aired between the hours of 10:00 P.M. and 6:00 A.M. In 1987, and without much explanation, the FCC moved the safe harbor to midnight and the U.S. Court of Appeals for the District of Columbia Circuit said it was arbitrary and capricious and ordered the old safe harbor reinstated. Around the same time, Congress attempted to alter the safe harbor twice, including a complete ban on broadcast indecency. The D.C. Circuit ruled twice that the new safe harbor violated the First Amendment. After ten years of litigation over the parameters of the safe harbor, the final court decision returned it to 10:00 P.M. to 6:00 A.M. So it is evident that while Congress is usually a greater influence on the Commission's actions, the courts do get the final say.

CITIZEN GROUPS AND MEMBERS OF THE PUBLIC

Members of the general public, whether acting independently or in an organized group, can influence both the Commission and Congress to act. Individual citizens can provide comments on a Notice of Inquiry or a Notice of Proposed Rule Making and can also initiate rulemakings, as was the case with low power FM. They can also file complaints about specific programming or other industry actions. While the power of the public is limited in communications policy, there are times when public sentiment has prevailed.

The United Church of Christ case in the 1960s changed the relationship between the public and the Commission. For the first time, the public was granted standing, the legal right to challenge a station's license. Following that decision by the U.S. Court of Appeals for the District of Columbia Circuit, many citizen groups were empowered to act. This was encouraged by Commissioner Nicholas Johnson and the late 1960s and early 1970s are considered the highwater mark for civic involvement at the Commission.

For the most part, however, citizen groups have found that their concerns go unheeded. After the UCC case, many groups sought to bring the issue of format change to the Commission's attention. These groups wanted the FCC to forbid radio stations from changing formats when no other station in the market was playing that kind of music. In another example, groups from the Religious Right have worked to remove indecent programming from radio and television since the 1960s. Groups like Morality in Media and the American Family Association have worked for years to get stations fined and, more importantly, get licenses pulled. While they have had some success with getting inappropriate material fined, the Commission has never revoked a license or refused to allow a company to grow because of sexually explicit programming.

In the age of the Internet, the FCC is closer, in some ways, to the citizens and citizen groups. E-mail allows almost instantaneous connection between people across the country who are concerned about a particular issue. Following the 2004 Superbowl appearance of Janet Jackson's breast, more than 500,000 complaints poured into the Commission. The Commission seemed overwhelmed by the public response and issued a record fine. The FCC justified the fine by commenting on the number of complaints it received. But when more than a million and a half complaints were filed on the media ownership issue, the Commission did and said nothing.

The public has had moments of success in influencing Commission policy over the years. But those successes have come only when the agenda of the citizen group or individual has matched the agenda of another, more powerful, actor. When Morality in Media had an ally in Senator Al Gore, its concerns were made part of the nomination hearings for new commissioners. When the same group wanted Infinity Broadcasting to lose its licenses because of Howard Stern, nothing happened. The public is the weakest actor in the policymaking universe, having impact only for moments instead of the sustained influence of Congress and the regulated industries.

In *How to Talk Back to Your Television Set*, Commissioner Nicholas Johnson wrote that the FCC doesn't just respond to pressure from the broadcast industry, it "responds to pressure from anybody."[2] The interplay of the relationships between the Commission and the other five actors is also influenced by the environment in which they all exist. The 2004 presidential election focused attention on issues of "values" and it was in that environment that record indecency fines were issued. In the 1960s, when citizen activism was changing the face of America, the United Church of Christ was successful in gaining access to the FCC's processes. So in addition to particular actors, the times can also be a factor in which influence wins out.

Finally, past and future employment of both commissioners and staff can influence who is influential. Former commissioners often become powerful forces for the regulated industries. Even staff with FCC experience are much desired by the lobbying firms and the industries with business before the Commission. Law firms like former chairman Richard Wiley's Wiley Rein, and Fielding see many future and past FCC employees on its roster. Many commissioners come to the FCC from congressional staff positions, and thus have deep loyalties to members of Congress who oversee the Commission. A few commissioners even move to the public interest sector and use their influence to further the agenda of citizen groups. This "revolving door" is often seen as a major source of influence on how the Commission as a whole makes decisions.

NOTES

1. Erwin G. Krasnow, Lawrence D. Longley, and Herbert A. Terry, *The Politics of Broadcast Regulation,* 3rd ed. (New York: St. Martin's Press, 1982), 89.

2. Nicholas Johnson, *How to Talk Back to Your Television Set* (New York: Little, Brown & Co., 1979), 163.

★ ④ ★

Notable Controversies in Telephone Regulation

For nearly twenty-five years after the creation of the FCC the regulation of the telephone industry was a secondary consideration. Members of Congress and FCC commissioners devoted most of their time to issues relating to broadcasting. Indicative of this early emphasis on broadcasting is an anecdote related by Fred Henck and Bernard Strassburg in their book *The Slippery Slope*. The story goes that an FCC commissioner had just delivered a lengthy statement on telephone regulation to a congressional committee. At the end of the statement, a senior member of the committee, barely containing his boredom, responds by saying, "All right, so much for that. Now let's get back to the important subject—radio stations."[1]

What explains this early emphasis on broadcasting at the expense of common carrier issues? The potential answers are numerous. For members of Congress, telephone regulation was probably viewed as a very technical matter that was best left up to the "experts" at the FCC. Furthermore, since the FCC's jurisdiction mainly included the regulation of long distance telephone services (which were used only sparingly by the average American during this time period), members of Congress probably saw little advantage in devoting time to these issues on behalf of their constituents. For the FCC commissioners, there was little controversy relating to the telephone industry that required a regulatory response. The most politically controversial issue that the FCC had to confront during this time was the setting of long distance rates. Since AT&T rarely asked for a rate increase, rate controversies were generally resolved informally and with little fanfare.

Beginning in the late 1950s, however, regulatory controversies relating to the telephone industry came to occupy more of the Commission's time. The FCC found itself in the midst of a host of new controversies, including an ongoing rate dispute and a series of new technologies that had not existed when the Communications Act was written in 1934. This chapter examines some of these telephone-related regulatory controversies in detail.

THE TELEPHONE INVESTIGATION AND *UNITED STATES V. WESTERN ELECTRIC*

One of the very first actions taken by the FCC with respect to the telephone industry was an investigation authorized by Congress under the Communications Act of 1934. The investigation was chaired by Paul Walker, the only FCC commissioner at the time with experience as a telephone regulator. The initial version of the report, issued in 1938, strongly criticized the relationship between AT&T and its manufacturing arm, Western Electric. The report charged financial impropriety, among other things. Communications equipment manufacturing was not a natural monopoly, but AT&T insisted that it needed to manufacture its own equipment to maintain the integrity of the telephone network. According to the report, however, by manufacturing its own equipment, AT&T significantly curtailed competition within the industry. This allowed the firm to charge artificially high prices. The initial version of the report provoked outrage from AT&T's supporters in Congress and so the final version, issued in 1939, was toned down significantly.

Nearly a decade later, the report served as the basis of a Department of Justice antitrust action taken against AT&T in the case of *United States v. Western Electric*. Interestingly enough, the case against AT&T was prepared by Holmes Baldridge, who had worked on the report as a staff member at the FCC. Justice wanted to force AT&T to divest itself of Western Electric and divide its manufacturing plants into three competing independent entities. Ultimately, however, the case received little support from the Eisenhower Administration or members of the FCC serving during the 1950s, who argued that a divestiture of Western Electric could lead to higher prices for local telephone service. As a result, Justice abandoned the suit in 1956 in favor of a consent decree in which AT&T agreed to what seemed like fairly minor sanctions at the time, such as restricting itself to manufacturing only communications-related equipment and staying out of the computer business.

THE SEPARATIONS CONTROVERSY

In *Smith v. Illinois Bell* (1930), the U.S. Supreme Court ruled that because the local telephone network is used in the delivery of both local and long distance telephone service, some of the costs of the local network needed to be paid through long distance revenues. This decision required the institution of a practice known as separations, through which telephone company expenses were separated into categories and allocated to either intrastate or interstate service. Because telephone rate regulation has historically been based on estimations of the firm's profits (see rates discussion below), the separation of telephone company costs in this manner was essential to determining federal versus state regulatory jurisdiction.

Between the 1940s and the 1970s, federal and state regulators made numerous adjustments in the separations formulas, gradually allocating more of the costs of telephone service to interstate business. The act of attributing greater costs to interstate business had the effect of keeping long distance telephone rates higher and local rates lower because AT&T's long distance department had to absorb a greater portion of the overall costs of telephone service. As a result, high-volume users of long distance services (mainly business customers) were subsidizing the costs of residential local telephone services. Higher long distance rates and lower local rates fit with the overall philosophy of public utility regulation, which was aimed at making "essential" services widely available. At the same time, however, such a rate scheme was politically popular with the average consumer who used long distance services only sparingly during much of this period.

THE TELEPHONE EQUIPMENT CONTROVERSIES

Since 1913, AT&T had maintained a strict policy against the attachment to its telephone network of communications devices that were not manufactured by Western Electric. As noted earlier, the policy existed to prevent any kind of interference with the quality of telephone service. At times, however, this policy was taken to extremes. For instance, AT&T once refused to allow a customer to put a cover on the telephone directory as this constituted a foreign attachment. The ban on foreign attachments was generally backed by the FCC, but some doubted that AT&T really had a strong rationale for the policy.

In the 1950s and 1960s, the FCC was involved in two controversial decisions—the Hush-A-Phone and Carterfone decisions—in which AT&T's policy on foreign attachments was challenged. It could be argued that these decisions, while relatively minor in scope, represent two of the earliest attempts to authorize competition in the telephone industry.

The Hush-A-Phone Controversy

The Hush-A-Phone was a plastic device that attached to the telephone receiver to provide the speaker with greater privacy. In 1948, Harold Tuttle, inventor of the Hush-A-Phone, petitioned the FCC to overturn AT&T's foreign attachments policy, but his request was denied in 1951 and again in a final decision issued in 1955. Recognizing that the Hush-A-Phone posed little risk to the integrity of the telephone network, the FCC staff chose to stick by AT&T, fearing that even a small exception would open the door for future challenges to the policy. Through a court appeal, however, Tuttle won and

The Carterfone was the first electronic "foreign attachment" that the FCC allowed to be attached to the telephone network. (Photograph by Stan Schreier)

the FCC was forced to amend the policy to exempt devices that did not involve direct electrical connection or otherwise interfere with telephone service.

The Carterfone Decision

Shortly after the Hush-A-Phone controversy was resolved in 1955, the Carter Electronics Corporation sought approval to sell a device called the Carterfone. The Carterfone was a device that made it possible to connect the telephone network to a land mobile radio system without establishing an electronic connection between the two. Carter Electronics argued that because the device did not make an electronic connection, it was similar in character to the Hush-A-Phone and should be approved under existing policies. Under pressure from AT&T, however, the FCC refused to approve the device initially and Carter Electronics moved to file an antitrust suit against AT&T.

Eventually, the matter was passed back to the FCC where a thorough investigation of the Carterfone was undertaken in 1966. By that time, Common Carrier Bureau Chief Bernard Strassburg was interested in moving the terminal equipment policy in a new direction. The Carterfone inquiry was used as the basis for completely reassessing AT&T's policies on network attachments. Ultimately, the Commission ruled that only devices that caused "actual harm" to the network could be prohibited. Thus, the final decision in the Carterfone inquiry made it possible to attach a range of new electronic devices to the telephone network.

LONG DISTANCE COMPETITION

The microwave controversies (1956–1977) marked the beginning of competition in the long distance telephone industry. The decisions were necessitated by the development of microwave technology as a medium for commercial communications and the subsequent efforts by entrepreneurs to use this technology to compete with AT&T. Microwave technology utilized high-frequency radio waves capable of transmitting large amounts of information over long distances. Microwave technology allowed for a much higher carrying capacity than standard copper telephone wires, making it possible to transmit voice, video, or data services. Furthermore, microwave technology, unlike traditional, wire-based telephony, was not a natural monopoly. Thus, the commercial development of microwaves by the end of the 1950s created the possibility that long distance telephone service might some day be opened to competition. Over the course of more than two decades, four decisions relating to microwave technology gradually opened the door for long distance telephone competition: (1) the "Above 890" decision; (2) the MCI decision; (3) the Specialized Common Carrier decision; and (4) the Execunet Decision.

The Above 890 Decision

To many business entrepreneurs, AT&T was an inflexible monopoly. Thus, the prospect of competition from microwave technology was an exciting alternative to AT&T. This was particularly true at a time when the computer industry was developing and entrepreneurs in this field were looking for flexible new communications channels for the transmission of data. For the FCC, however, microwaves represented an untested technology that needed to be approached with caution. Would microwave technology be an adequate substitute for traditional long distance telephone service? Would competition for these services really be possible? For the FCC, only time and experience would provide the answers to these questions.

For this reason, the FCC chose to tread lightly in authorizing the use of microwave technology as a substitute to traditional long distance telephone service. In 1959, the Commission issued its Above 890 decision, through which it began authorizing companies to build and operate their own "private line" microwave systems using frequencies above 890 mc. This meant that a company could, for example, build a microwave system connecting its offices in two different cities for its own private use. This was at best an incremental step, as there were really no commercial providers of microwave services in direct competition with AT&T at the time.

The MCI Decision

The Above 890 decision did not authorize the licensing of microwave common carriers. In 1964, however, Jack Goeken, head of a fledgling company called Microwave Communications Incorporated (later known as MCI Telecommunications), went before the FCC and asked for permission to build a common-carrier microwave system for the provision of service between Chicago and St. Louis. FCC officials were reluctant to grant this authorization because it would put MCI in direct competition with AT&T, something that was understood by regulators at that time to be unthinkable. For that reason, MCI's application was delayed for several years while regulators deliberated. Ultimately, the MCI application proposed to provide only a limited range of services, mainly communications services for businesses in a narrow geographical area. Recognizing the need to foster the commercial development of new technologies, the FCC finally approved MCI's application in 1969.

The Specialized Common Carrier Decision

After the MCI decision, the FCC was inundated with applications from firms seeking to start common carrier microwave enterprises for the provision of specialized communications services similar to those being offered by MCI. For instance, a firm called the Data Transmission Company (DATRAN) proposed to build a thirty-five-city digital network for the transmission of computer data. Recognizing the need to keep up with changing marketplace demands, in 1971 the FCC issued its Specialized Common Carrier decision in which it outlined a standard set of rules by which these new communications companies could apply for and receive authorization to utilize microwave frequencies. Thus, by the early 1970s, it seemed as if the door was beginning to open for competition in the telephone business, if only in limited ways.

The Execunet Decision

The FCC's Execunet decision in 1976 touched off a controversy that ultimately resulted in the full deregulation of the long distance telephone industry. The controversy began when MCI notified the FCC in 1974 that it was introducing a new microwave service called Execunet that would allow customers in fifteen different cities to communicate with one another. Unlike previous services introduced by MCI, which were mainly private line services for business customers, Execunet appeared to allow for a much more public type of communication that directly rivaled AT&T's standard long distance services. Believing that a service such as Execunet went too far in the direction of full long distance competition, the FCC turned down MCI's application.

MCI appealed the decision before the U.S. Court of Appeals for the District of Columbia Circuit and won. The decision was historic in that it had the effect of casting aside the decades-old AT&T monopoly in long distance telephone service and forcing the FCC to open the door to competition. The court concluded that since the FCC had never ruled in any formal proceeding that a monopoly in long distance telephony was in the public interest, it could not simply restrict competition without a more systematic justification. In writing for the court, Judge J. Skelly Wright noted that:

> The Commission must be ever mindful that, just as it is not free to create competition for competition's sake, it is not free to propagate monopoly for monopoly's sake. The ultimate test of industry structure

in the communications common carrier field must be the public interest, not the private financial interests of those who have until now enjoyed the fruits of defacto monopoly.

The implication of the court's ruling was clear—the era of monopoly in long distance telephony was now over and the Commission needed to begin focusing its regulatory activities on how best to facilitate competition within the industry.

BREAKUP OF THE BELL SYSTEM

One of the most important governmental actions to shape the telephone industry in the last thirty years was the antitrust consent decree that broke up AT&T into eight separate companies on January 1, 1984. The breakup of AT&T was undertaken to spur competition in the telephone industry. While the FCC was not directly a party to the antitrust suit, the resolution of this case set the agenda for the Commission's regulatory activities for the next decade.

United States v. AT&T

By the early 1970s, AT&T was facing competition in the long distance telephone business from a growing number of small firms. AT&T's acceptance of this new competition, however, did not come quickly or easily. Competitors charged that AT&T was actively engaging in anticompetitive behavior. To be able to adequately compete, these new firms needed to be able to interconnect their networks with AT&T's land lines for the purposes of delivering their services to customers. For years, AT&T actively resisted interconnection, claiming that they were under no legal obligation to do so. With the FCC largely backing them up on this prior to the Execunet decision, AT&T was able to drag its feet on the interconnection issue. To competitors like MCI, however, refusal to interconnect constituted a conspiracy to monopolize under the antitrust laws. It was primarily the interconnection controversy that motivated the Nixon Administration Justice Department to file an antitrust suit against AT&T in 1974.

Over the next seven years the government would build up an impressive case against AT&T that included several major antitrust violations. The Justice Department argued that AT&T not only discriminated against its competitors by refusing to interconnect them to the network, but it also eliminated any hope of competition in the market for telecommunications equipment by requiring its twenty-two local telephone companies to purchase all equipment from Western Electric. Furthermore, Justice argued that AT&T had engaged in pricing without regard to cost with respect to many of its services. This latter charge emanated from earlier FCC rate controversies where it was demonstrated that AT&T made a habit of under-pricing in markets where it faced competition while charging artificially high prices in its monopoly markets.

Ultimately, the case was resolved in 1982 when AT&T agreed to a consent decree that divided the company into eight separate corporate entities. AT&T agreed to spin off its twenty-two local telephone companies into seven Regional Bell Operating Companies (RBOCs). Because of their status as local telephone service monopolists, the RBOCs were restricted from participating in three key telecommunications markets—long distance service, equipment manufacturing, and "information services," which, broadly defined, included cable television and a host of computer-based data communications services. In exchange for agreeing to this massive corporate restructuring, AT&T was allowed to continue participating in these latter three markets, two of which—equipment manufacturing and information services—were considered essential to its ability to remain competitive.

The consent decree and the decision to break up AT&T were shaped not only by AT&T's corporate interests, but also by the regulatory philosophy of William Baxter, the Assistant Attorney General for Antitrust under the Reagan Administration. As a disciple of free market economics, Baxter believed that regulated firms could not compete in competitive markets. Thus, from his perspective, the full structural separation of the monopoly local telephone companies from the now competitive long distance portion of the business was necessary to facilitate competition. With both the government and AT&T ready to sign off on the restructuring, the consent decree took effect January 1, 1984.

The Access Charge Decision

The breakup of AT&T was billed as a necessary step to promote competition in the telephone industry. It also ignited new regulatory controversies, including the need to devise a system of access charges. As noted above, AT&T had kept its long distance telephone rates artificially high for many decades in order to provide lower local rates to residential customers. With the breakup of the Bell System, however, this arrangement would no longer exist and local telephone rates would likely go up. Furthermore, AT&T and its competitors would still need to be able to interconnect with local telephone lines to deliver their calls to residential customers, which meant that some new compensation mechanism was necessary. In order to maintain low local rates and defray the replacement costs for local telephone lines, a new mechanism needed to be devised through which the long distance companies and their customers would pay for access to the RBOC's infrastructure.

In response, the FCC issued an order in 1982 mandating that the RBOCs be able to collect access charges to cover the costs associated with usage of the local telephone network for long distance communication. The decision was controversial because it proposed to collect the access charges in part through

Assistant Attorney General William Baxter (left) and AT&T Chairman and CEO Charles L. Brown (right) shake hands following the announcement of the 1982 consent decree that broke up the telecommunications giant. (Courtesy of AT&T)

a flat monthly fee imposed on individual telephone subscribers. Recognizing that the telephone bills of their constituents would go up, members of Congress quickly became alarmed and took actions aimed at stopping the FCC. In spite of all the controversy, the FCC ultimately moved forward with access charges immediately following the official breakup of AT&T in 1984.

RATE REGULATION

One of the FCC's greatest struggles throughout its more than seventy years of existence has been the regulation of rates for long distance telecommunications services. Traditional public utility rate regulation, sometimes referred to as "rate-of-return" regulation, involves figuring out the total expenditures or "rate base" of the firm and prescribing an appropriate profit ceiling. Once this is accomplished, prices are then set for individual services. While this may sound simple in principle, the accounting practices of a firm as large as AT&T could be quite complicated to sort through, requiring numerous trained accountants and other professionals and countless man-hours. Lacking the time and resources to thoroughly review a firm's accounts, regulatory commissions such as the FCC tended to shy away from formal rate investigations, opting instead for negotiations and other informal mechanisms for setting rates. Throughout its history, the FCC has employed three main mechanisms of rate-setting: (1) continuing surveillance; (2) formal rate-of-return investigations; and (3) price caps regulation.

Continuing Surveillance, 1934–1964

From 1934 until 1964, the FCC set long distance rates through negotiations rather than formal proceedings. At the FCC, the terminology used to describe this process was "continuing surveillance." Under continuing surveillance, FCC staff analyzed AT&T's records and maintained ongoing conversations with company officials regarding financial matters. When overall profit levels were deemed unsatisfactory by either party, rate changes for individual services were implemented through negotiations. While continuing surveillance lacked the rigor of a formal rate investigation, it was less costly and time consuming. Furthermore, all but one negotiation during this time resulted in a rate reduction. Given these realities, both the FCC and AT&T were satisfied with making rate adjustments through informal cooperation. With no political pressure to do otherwise, the FCC saw no need to formally confront AT&T on its pricing and accounting practices.

Formal Rate Investigations, 1965–1989

The FCC abandoned continuing surveillance in the mid 1960s in favor of more formal rate investigations. The decision to exercise more systematic control over AT&T's prices and profits was motivated by the discovery that the firm was charging excessive amounts for some of its services. The realization came following the 1959 decision to authorize private line microwave systems discussed above. Following that decision, AT&T significantly reduced its prices for microwave services, raising suspicions that its charges had been excessive in the past. A more thorough investigation of AT&T's accounts led to the discovery that the firm appeared to be undercharging for its microwave services in an effort to undercut competitors. Regulators soon began to suspect that AT&T was allocating its profits and structuring its prices in a manner that was intended to prevent competition from developing.

As a result, the FCC undertook a protracted effort to make sense out of AT&T's accounts and prescribe more rigorous rates beginning in 1965. The result of this process was more rigorous rate regulation and an effort to develop a cost allocation manual and a more uniform system of accounts to assist regulators in making sense of AT&T's corporate operations. Ultimately, however, the FCC's efforts to regulate AT&T's rates proved a failure as charges of anticompetitive behavior escalated throughout the 1970s. The failure of the FCC to more adequately prevent anticompetitive abuses through rate regulation was a major point of contention in the court battle to break up AT&T in the late 1970s and early 1980s.

Price Caps Regulation, 1989–Present

In 1987, the FCC needed to reconsider its policies and rules for setting long distance telephone rates. The breakup of AT&T in 1984 meant that the firm would now only be participating in competitive markets, theoretically eliminating the need for rate regulation. At the same time, however, AT&T continued to control nearly 70 percent of the long distance telephone service market, making it a virtual monopoly. As long as AT&T continued to dominate long distance markets, regulators needed to employ some sort of rate regulation as a safeguard to insure that anticompetitive behavior did not continue to occur. At the same time, however, traditional forms of public utility rate regulation were falling out of favor at the Commission. Those who approached communications policy from the standpoint of economic analysis tended to believe that profit-based "rate-of-return" regulation was difficult to apply to firms that participated in competitive markets. Thus, by the late 1980s, FCC officials were casting about for alternative methods of rate regulation.

Ultimately, the Commission settled on a method proposed in 1987 by economists in the Office of Plans and Policy known as "price caps" regulation. Much as its name suggests, price caps regulation focused on capping prices for specific services rather than profits levels, as was the case with rate-of-return regulation. Prices were capped at modest but competitive levels and allowed to rise each year at intervals that were slightly less that the rate of inflation. For AT&T, price caps provided an incentive to be more efficient and reduce costs in order to maintain high profit margins. At the same time, however, regulatory safeguards were put in place to make sure that AT&T did not undercut their competitors. Competing firms like MCI and SPRINT would also be forced to become competitive in their pricing over time to maintain their market share. Following a rulemaking that lasted nearly two years, price caps regulation of long distance rates was officially adopted in 1989.

The price caps inquiry did not proceed without controversy. Hearings were held by Congress in which the FCC's decision to implement price caps was questioned. Nevertheless, history has demonstrated that the move toward price caps regulation was one of the FCC's most successful major policy decisions during the 1980s and has been adopted in various forms by several states since that time to regulate local telephone rates.

THE COMPUTER INQUIRIES

Between 1965 and 1986, the FCC labored to find a workable approach to the regulation of data communications services that integrated computer and telephone technologies. The prospect that monopoly telephone companies might seek to enter the data communications business created a new regulatory problem the FCC could not avoid. AT&T was forbidden from entering the computer business by the 1956 antitrust consent decree. The smaller independent telephone companies, however, might try to provide data communications services and use their market power as regulated monopolies to offer artificially lower prices that would drive competitors out of business. As the FCC struggled to find a workable solution to the computer dilemma, its efforts were continually frustrated by rapid technological change. During this period, the FCC issued three computer decisions.

Computer I

By the mid 1960s, the gradual technological integration of computers and telephones was making the two industries more difficult to distinguish. AT&T developed computerized telephone switches to make the routing of calls faster and easier. Devices known as modulator-demodulators (modems) allowed the transmission of computer data over the telephone lines. A line of increasingly sophisticated "dial-up" services was confusing things even further. For instance, the Bunker-Ramo Corporation developed a service called Telequote IV, which allowed subscribers to obtain up-to-date information on the stock market and communicate with each other through a centralized computing system. In essence, under Telequote IV the Bunker-Ramo computer system was acting as a telephone switch, raising the prospect that telephone companies and data communications firms might soon be crossing over into each other's business.

To stave off this possibility, in 1971 the FCC handed down the final decision in what has come to be known as its Computer I inquiry. In Computer I the FCC adopted a *maximum separation policy* for the provision of data communications services. This meant that telephone companies could only offer certain types of data communications services through a fully separate subsidiary—a separate corporate entity that maintained its own personnel, equipment, and accounts. It was hoped that this more discrete regulatory division between telephony and data communications would minimize the possibility of anti-competitive behavior by telephone companies.

Computer II

By the mid 1970s, the maximum separation policy handed down by the FCC in Computer I was becoming unworkable amid changing technologies. An important component of this changing technological environment was the development of "smart terminals" and other types of smaller computers that served as the forerunner to modern personal computers. These new devices both processed data and served as a piece of telecommunications

70

equipment that could connect to the telephone line, making it even more difficult to draw a distinction between telecommunications and data communications services. Furthermore, some telephone companies were arguing that the maximum separation policy produced inefficiencies by forcing them to incur the costs of fully separate personnel and equipment for the provision of data communications services. Finally, telephone companies further argued that more innovative services could be developed if data communications operations could be more fully integrated with traditional telephone services. For these reasons, the FCC began an inquiry to reconsider the maximum separation policy in 1976.

The result of this inquiry was the landmark Computer II decision of 1980 in which the FCC fully embraced competition as a goal of telecommunications policy. Computer II made three major changes in existing policies. First, AT&T was allowed to compete in the data communications business through a separate subsidiary for the first time. Second, telephone companies other

FCC Chairman Charles Ferris (1977–1981) presided over the FCC's landmark 1980 Computer II decision. (Courtesy of the National Archives)

than AT&T were given more freedom to integrate data communications and traditional telephone services than they had under the maximum separation policy. Finally, Computer II had the effect of fully deregulating the market for terminal telecommunications equipment, making it easier for both telephone and computer companies to invent and market innovative new communications devices.

Computer III

In 1986, the FCC moved further in the direction of competition in data communications when it handed down its Computer III decision. The Computer III rules allowed AT&T and other telephone companies to enter data communications markets without creating a fully separate subsidiary as long as they provided their competitors with equal access to the various components of their networks.

The FCC proposed to implement this "non-structural" approach to regulation in two phases. The first was a transitional mechanism called Comparably Efficient Interconnection (CEI) through which telephone companies would make components of their network available to competitors on a service-by-service basis. During the second phase called Open Network Architecture (ONA), the FCC envisioned a more drastic reconfiguration of the telephone networks to provide for easier access to the network elements by competitors. The long-term plan under Computer III was to gradually free telephone companies from the subsidiary requirements as they complied with their CEI and ONA obligations. While the ambitious goals of Computer III have never been fully implemented, the basic framework continues to guide the regulation of data communications services.

TELEPHONE-CABLE COMPETITION

Yet another major common carrier issue that the FCC has grappled with over the decades is the potential for competition between telephone and cable television companies. As was the case with the development of long distance competition and the computer inquiries, the FCC found it necessary to respond to changing technologies and marketplace developments in the area of telephone-cable competition.

The Telephone-Cable Cross-Ownership Ban

Cable television involves the delivery of video programming into the home via a coaxial cable—a broadband technology that offers a wire-based alternative to traditional over-the-air delivery of video programming. Initially, cable was mainly a way to deliver broadcast programming to rural areas lacking stations of their own. In this sense, it could be argued that cable television was little more than a "common carrier" of video programming much in the same way that the telephone carried private voice conversations. Small independent cable television systems were slowly emerging around the country to provide this service but telephone companies also sought to get into the business, viewing it as a logical next step beyond common carrier voice services.

Fearing that the telephone companies would try to monopolize the cable television business, fledgling cable companies implored the FCC to draw a regulatory line between the two markets. In response to these concerns, the FCC issued what came to be known as the "telco-cable" cross-ownership ban in 1970. This prohibited telephone companies from owning cable systems in their service markets. In cases where telephone companies did own cable television systems, a fully separate subsidiary of the kind required for data communications services was mandated. The telco-cable cross-ownership ban was later codified in statute by Congress in the early 1980s.

The Video Dial-Tone Decision

In 1987, the FCC undertook an inquiry to partially reconsider the telco-cable cross-ownership ban. Although the ban had been codified by Congress several years earlier, Chairman Dennis Patrick and some of the FCC staff believed the rule had become an impediment to competition and innovation within the industry. Since 1971, when the ban was initially put in place, cable television had grown from a fledgling ancillary to broadcasting into a bur-geoning sector of the communications industry. Regulators at the FCC held out hope that cable companies might some day be a source of competition for telephone companies because they brought a second wire into the home. Telephone companies, for their part, argued that access to cable television markets provided them with an incentive to more rapidly invest in the de-velopment of a fiber optic telecommunications infrastructure to replace the old copper wire lines. Fiber optics would allow the high-speed delivery of voice, video, and data content into the home or office, theoretically making a wide range of new and innovative services possible and better preparing the nation's infrastructure for the economic realities of the information age. With these considerations in mind, the FCC solicited comments regarding whether or not recommendations should be made to Congress that the telco-cable cross-ownership ban be repealed.

In 1989, however, a change in leadership within the agency caused the inquiry to take a new turn. At that time Alfred Sikes became the chairman and brought with him an agenda for telecommunications policy reform of his own that had been formulated during his years as Assistant Secretary of Commerce for Telecommunications and Information under President Reagan. With respect to telephone-cable competition, Sikes envisioned a transition step through which telephone companies, rather than owning cable systems out-right, might serve as a kind of "video common carrier" by bringing the video content of competing cable providers into the homes of customers over a fiber optic infrastructure. This concept, known as "video dial-tone," was appealing to regulators because it was viewed as a way to encourage video competition and investment in fiber optics in the short run while Congress considered the more drastic step of formally repealing the cross-ownership rules.

Formally authorized by the FCC in 1992, video dial-tone proved unsuc-cessful as an effort to encourage telephone company involvement in the provision of video entertainment. For one thing, it was a very vague concept that left open such questions as what types of programming should be offered and how they should be delivered. Ultimately, however, telephone companies found it unprofitable to invest significant amounts of capital to develop in-frastructure for video delivery when they themselves could not formally enter the cable television business. Nevertheless, the inquiry to consider repeal of the telco-cable cross-ownership rules was significant in that it identified in-frastructure development as an important goal of telecommunications policy that would become a prominent topic of discussion during the debates over the Telecommunications Act of 1996.

THE TELECOMMUNICATIONS ACT OF 1996

Without question, the Telecommunications Act of 1996 was the single most important piece of legislation to impact federal policy in this area since the passage of the Communications Act of 1934. The Telecom Act not only ushered in significant policy changes aimed at making the telecommunications industry more competitive, but it also created a range of new administrative and policymaking responsibilities for the FCC.

By the end of the 1980s, the regulatory reforms of the previous decade had significantly altered the terms of debate over telecommunications policy in Washington. The move toward competition, while painful at first, caused telecommunications companies to restructure their business practices. Before long, formerly entrenched monopolies sought opportunities to compete in new markets. Furthermore, technological advances such as fiber optics and digital technology promised to make possible formerly unheard of new "information age" services that combined voice, video, and data communication in innovative new ways. For many industry players, the only obstacles standing in the way of these economic realities were regulatory barriers to competition.

It was within this context that several members of Congress, including Rep. Edward Markey and Senators Ernest Hollings and Conrad Burns began actively considering proposals for policy reform. A particularly important topic between 1989 and 1993 was the need to maintain competitiveness in the information age. Numerous legislative hearings in the late 1980s and early 1990s revealed that the United States might be falling behind other industrialized nations in the realm of telecommunications. France, for example, was making public investments in information services, while Japan was investing billions of dollars in the construction of a fiber optic telecommunications infrastructure. With rising federal budget deficits and a general bias against large-scale industrial policy ventures in the United States, public investment in telecommunications infrastructure seemed infeasible. Nevertheless, policymakers found themselves casting about for ways to remain globally competitive as the nation entered the information age.

In the eyes of many, the solution to this dilemma seemed to be increased competition within the telecommunications industry. In many of these legislative debates, the RBOCs continued to advance the argument that the ability to openly compete in high-tech telecommunications markets would provide them with the incentive to invest in information services and rapidly deploy a fiber optic infrastructure. By that time, their claims were backed up by several government reports that highlighted the need for a more proactive telecommunications policy. From a rhetorical standpoint, the idea of using competition to promote infrastructure development worked perfectly—it was easily understood by legislators, promised results without public investment, and fit neatly with an already established trend of competition and deregulation in U.S. telecommunications policy.

With the newly elected Clinton administration promising to make the "information superhighway" a top priority, telecommunications policy reform emerged as a prominent issue on the Congressional agenda in 1993. Legislation was introduced both in the House and Senate to allow local telephone, long distance telephone, and cable television companies to openly compete with one another. While the House bills both passed in June of 1994, Senate Republicans and Democrats were unable to reach a compromise and no legislation was passed that year.

Throughout 1995 Congress gradually pieced together the compromise that would become the Telecommunications Act of 1996. The stated goal of the new law was to establish "a pro-competitive, de-regulatory national policy framework" in order to make available to all Americans "advanced telecommunications and information technologies and services by opening all telecommunications markets to competition."

Telephone Industry Competition

Perhaps the most important set of regulatory changes under the Telecom Act were the various provisions dealing with telephone industry competition. One of the most important things the new law did was to preempt state barriers to entry by those seeking to compete in intrastate telephone service. For many decades it had been the prerogative of state public utility commissions to determine whether or not there should be telephone competition within state boundaries. Thus, by the 1980s, virtually every state in the union had granted monopoly status to local telephone companies. Under section 253, these protectionist policies were preempted, opening the door for long distance telephone companies, cable television companies, and other willing providers to get into the local telephone business. State regulatory commissions would still have to approve their entry into local markets, but would be limited to ruling on such things as service quality standards, public safety standards, and a few other specific considerations.

The Telecom Act also opened the door for the RBOCs to participate in formerly restricted lines of business upon FCC approval. Sections 271–275 opened the door for the RBOCs to participate in long distance telephone markets, equipment manufacturing, and information services such as electronic publishing and alarm monitoring. To provide long distance services within their local service region, however, RBOCs must receive permission from the FCC after satisfying a fourteen-point "competitive checklist" designed to insure that they will provide local service competitors with interconnection and equal access. The major points of the checklist include:

- Nondiscriminatory access to various components of the RBOC telephone network, including telephone poles, ducts, conduits, and rights of way. Competitors must also be allowed to interconnect with the various elements of the RBOC network. These nondiscriminatory access requirements are intended to prevent the problems encountered with long distance competition in the 1970s by insuring that competing firms will be able to deliver calls to their customers by utilizing the existing physical infrastructure.

- Unbundling of the lines, transport, and switching functions of the RBOCs for resale to competitors. These provisions reflect the realization that many fledgling local telephone competitors will not be able to build an entirely new telephone network consisting of all the lines, switches, and infrastructure components necessary to transport calls within a particular geographical area. Unbundling allows competitors to purchase access to components of the RBOC infrastructure on a wholesale basis.

- Nondiscriminatory access to various other elements of the telephone network, including 911 services, telephone directories, telephone number databases, and other features essential to the provision of complete telephone service.

The implementation of these provisions has required extensive FCC rulemaking, some components of which continue to this day. In particular, the FCC's rules with respect to the unbundling of network elements continue in the wake of several court challenges that have forced the agency to go back to the drawing board.

Telephone-Cable Competition

The Telecom Act also provided a number of opportunities for telephone companies to enter video programming markets. The new law terminated the FCC's video dial-tone rules, replacing them with a concept known as "open video systems." The open video systems concept was vaguely defined at best in the new law, but can be described as a modified version of video dial-tone. The major difference was that telephone companies operating open video systems were given some discretion to select programming content (rather than serving solely as a common carrier) and were freed from equal access requirements and some other regulations that were viewed as burdensome. The FCC was required under the Telecom Act to begin rulemaking proceedings almost immediately to implement this portion of the law. The new law also repealed the telco-cable cross-ownership ban, allowing telephone companies to formally own and operate their own cable systems.

Universal Service

Universal service is the notion that common carrier communications services should be made widely available to the public on a nondiscriminatory basis. This has been a long-standing principle of telephone regulation. In the Telecom Act, Congress sought to redefine universal service as an evolving concept that would apply to advanced telecommunications technologies such as information services and internet access. Integral to the expanding notion of universal service was the extension of traditional and advanced telecommunications services to lower income citizens, schools, libraries, rural health care providers, and the disabled. The FCC was ordered to assemble a federal-state joint universal service board to consider the types of telecommunications services that should be subject to universal service requirements. Once the joint board's recommendations were made, the FCC undertook a rulemaking to implement the universal service requirements. In 1997, the FCC issued an order that extended a federal Universal Service Fee to all providers of interstate communications, including wireless services. The extension of the fee helped to provide more than two and a half billion dollars in subsidies, which assisted schools, libraries, and rural healthcare facilities in gaining access to advanced telecommunications technologies.

NOTE

1. Fred Henck and Bernard Strassburg, *The Slippery Slope: The Long Road to the Breakup of AT&T* (Westport, CT: Greenwood Press, 1988), 1.

Notable Controversies in Mass Media Regulation

Radio, followed by television, cable, and satellite, came into the nation's homes and brought the world. The mass media industries regulated by the Commission represent the first national media in the United States. With the birth of the radio networks, the whole country, for the first time, was experiencing exactly the same thing at exactly the same time. It is not possible to overestimate the impact of the introduction of the mass media on the social, cultural, and political life of the United States.

With industries that powerful, it is not surprising that there have been controversies. The regulation of the mass media truly began with the Radio Act of 1927 and the creation of the Federal Radio Commission. That was followed quickly by the Communications Act of 1934 and the establishment of the Federal Communications Commission. Since that time, the Commission has faced issues with both the industries and audiences.

The controversies discussed in this chapter are listed in alphabetical order. Cross-references to related topics within the chapter are noted in parentheses when applicable.

AM STEREO

In the beginning, radio was all on the AM band and all in mono. In 1961, FM stereo broadcasting was authorized. At the same time, engineers were also developing AM stereo. But since FM was in it infancy and struggling to gain listeners, the FCC held off authorizing any AM stereo broadcasts in an effort to boost the new band. The introduction of the higher fidelity of FM stereo broadcasts coincided with the rise of rock and roll recording in stereo, and as music became the dominant form of radio programming, FM became the dominant band.

The FCC began investigating AM stereo in 1977 by issuing a Notice of Inquiry seeking to gauge interest in the technology and a technical standard for the new service. Five different systems were proposed. All were compatible with current radio receivers but none were compatible with each other. In April 1980, the FCC stated that it would be in the public interest to choose a single system and revealed that the Commission engineers had settled on the Magnavox system as technically superior. Almost immediately, and before the FCC staff could finish the Report and Order that would implement the choice, complaints flooded into the Commission, many spurred by Magnavox's competitors. In September 1980, the Commission asked for additional technical information about all five of the proposed systems.

In November 1980, Ronald Reagan was elected president and his appointment of four deregulatory-minded commissioners changed the future of AM stereo. Chairman Mark Fowler believed that the market was a better regulator than the Commission and in 1982 announced that the FCC would not choose a technical standard. Fowler argued that the public should be allowed to choose the superior design, which would lead to price competition and technological innovation. The FCC final rule set only minimum technical standards and by November 1982, four systems were competing in the marketplace.

Despite Fowler's belief that the market was better able to choose the best system, reality did not quite work that way. The four competing systems were not compatible, thus a station broadcasting with one could not be picked up by listeners with a receiver built for another. Stations were hesitant to invest tens of thousands dollars in a system that its listeners very likely would not be able to pick up. Radio listeners did not buy the receivers because stations were not broadcasting in AM stereo. Receivers were eventually developed that picked up all the systems, but they were expensive. It soon became clear that the FCC's decision to not decide was a disaster.

In 1993, Congress directed the FCC to designate a single standard. The Commission finally choose the Motorola C-Quam system, which was the standard in other parts of the world. By this time, however, the dominant formats on the AM band were news and talk radio, programming that was not enhanced in any way by stereo broadcasting. Although there are hundreds of stations broadcasting in AM stereo around the world, the technology has never caught on in any significant way in the United States.

ANTI-ABORTION POLITICAL ADVERTISING

In the early 1990s, Michael Bailey was the founder of the Christian Media Ministries and a fervent anti-abortion activist. In the lead up to the 1992 election, Bailey discovered that federal law prevented stations from editing certain political advertisements. He saw this as an opportunity to spread his anti-abortion message and filed to run for Congress from Indiana.

Bailey had discovered Section 312(a)(7) and Section 315 of the Communications Act. Section 312(a)(7) requires broadcast stations to make reasonable amounts of time (by gift or sale) available to candidates for federal office. Section 315 requires that candidates for federal office be provided equal opportunity. Section 315, which is often called the Equal Time provision, states that if a station sells a prime time ad to one candidate for X dollars, the station must give other candidates for that office the opportunity to buy the same time at the same price. Section 315 also bans stations from censoring any political advertising.

Bailey's ads included video footage of dead fetuses, dismembered body parts, and bloody uterine fluid. He acknowledged that he ran for Congress solely to air these ads. He admitted the ads were disturbing but felt the message was something to be disturbed about. He also made the footage available to other anti-abortion candidates around the country who were pursuing the same strategy. The Commission received a number of complaints about the graphic nature of the ads, and stations around the country were concerned about their audience and their liability in carrying the ads, which some found indecent. Many stations asked the Commission for clarification of their ability to possibly channel the ads to a time when children were less likely to be in the audience.

At the same time, another anti-abortion activist named Daniel Becker was running for a Congressional seat in Georgia. In July, he ran an ad on WAGA-TV that contained pictures of dead fetuses. The station received complaints about the graphic ad and asked the FCC if it could channel any future political ads to a safe harbor if it believed the ads were indecent or unsuitable for children. The Commission determined that the Becker ad was not indecent and that Sections 312 and 315 barred any such channeling.

In October, Becker went back to WAGA-TV and asked to buy thirty minutes for a program called *Abortion in America: The Real Story*. He wanted it to air on November 1, between 4:00 P.M. and 5:00 P.M., immediately following a football game. The program contained footage of an actual abortion. The station responded that it believed the program was indecent and it would only run it between midnight and 6:00 A.M. Becker complained to the Commission.

The FCC sought comments from the public on the matter and told Becker that the station was acting within the law by choosing to air the program during the safe harbor until the Commission made a ruling. In November 1994, the FCC announced that nothing in the Communications Act barred a station from channeling ads that it felt were inappropriate to a time when children would not be in the audience. Stations around the country either channeled or refused to carry candidate ads that contained graphic abortion imagery.

Becker appealed the FCC's ruling to the U.S. Court of Appeals for the District of Columbia Circuit. In *Becker v. FCC* (1996), the court ruled that any channeling of political advertisements violated both Sections 312(a)(7) and 315 and is therefore illegal. Following the case, graphic anti-abortion imagery continued to appear on television stations around the country.

ASCERTAINMENT

The Radio Act of 1927 established the notion that broadcast licensees must serve the public interest, convenience, and necessity without giving much concrete direction as to how broadcasters could accomplish and measure that service. During the 1960s and 1970s, the FCC explored the issue of ascertainment as one way to measure a station's service to the local community.

Formal ascertainment was introduced in the *1960 Programming Policy Statement*, which proposed that future license applications and renewal forms ask: "(1) the measures he [the broadcaster] has taken and the effort he has made to determine the tastes, needs, and desires of his community or service area, and (2) the manner in which he proposed to meet those needs and desires." Broadcasters responded by asking a few community leaders what kinds of programming they would like to see and including a brief description of their usually vague answers on the renewal form.

Throughout the 1960s, the FCC tried to clarify the ascertainment requirements, asking stations for detailed demographic studies of their service areas and providing stations with specific procedures for interviewing community leaders. In 1968, the Commission issued a document entitled *Ascertainment of Community Needs by Broadcast Applicants*, which provided more guidelines to stations and a more formalized ascertainment process. Broadcasters were increasingly confused and unhappy with the situation and a little more than a year later, the Commission issued a Notice of Inquiry on the matter. In 1971, the FCC released the result of the NOI in the form of the *Primer on Ascertainment of Community Problems by Broadcast Applicants*.

The 1971 *Primer* required that all commercial broadcasters determine the demographic make-up of their service areas. Management-level employees were then supposed to interview community leaders in the six months prior to the application. At the same time, a general survey of the public was to be done. The stations were then required to create a list of the major concerns in the community, identify the issues that could be dealt with by the station, and compile a list of programming that could focus on the issues. The broadcast industry overwhelmingly rejected the new requirements as unfair and unduly burdensome. The FCC again had to issue a number of inquiries to develop the appropriate methodology for stations to ascertain community needs and concerns.

In 1975, a revised *Primer* that greatly lessened the ascertainment burden was released by the Commission. Instead of asking stations to do its ascertainment in the six months prior to applying for its license renewal, stations would now be expected to maintain a public file with information gathered on a continuous basis. General demographic information and a "reasonable" number of community interviews were expected. A list of community problems was to be kept in the public file with a list of programs that discussed those problems.

Broadcasters mostly welcomed the 1975 *Primer* as an acceptable ascertainment requirement.

Deregulation of the communications industry came in the 1980s and the ascertainment rules were among the first to fall. In 1981, the formal ascertainment requirements for radio stations were removed. The television rules followed in 1984. Many stations, particularly public radio and television stations, continue to formally ascertain the concerns and problems in their communities and design programming to fill those needs. The majority of commercial stations, however, abandoned the process when the FCC stopped making it a requirement.

BLUE BOOK

By the 1940s, the FCC generally renewed station licenses on the basis of engineering reports. If stations had no technical violations, the renewals were automatic. Commissioner Clifford Durr was disturbed by the FCC's lack of consideration for programming and began to abstain from renewal votes. When an engineering report on WBAL, a Baltimore radio station owned by the Hearst group, stated that the station had missed a required hourly call letter announcement because of a five-minute sales talk, Durr asked for an investigation.

He found that during a sample week in 1944, WBAL aired no sustaining (unsponsored) programming. It aired the NBC-sponsored shows but mostly failed to carry the network's public affairs programming. During the same week, the station aired sixteen commercials in one forty-five-minute period. It carried ten hours of religious broadcasting, but most of that had been sold at the commercial rate. Durr's staff looked further and discovered that WBAL was not alone. For example, KMAC in San Antonio aired 2,215 commercial spots in 133 hours of programming, averaging out to 16.7 commercial spots per hour.

In March 1945, Chairman Paul Porter made a speech at the NAB convention where he said that station promises about programming would now be compared to actual programming before renewal. Durr and his staff put together a report of the so-called promise and performance data on twenty-two stations up for renewal that April. The data showed that stations across the board were failing to live up to their promises and the Commission issued temporary licenses to all twenty-two. More temporary renewals followed and the Commission decided that it needed to issue a report that detailed the state of the industry and the standards the Commission would now use to judge whether a station had served the public interest. Edward Brecher, an FCC staff member, was drafted to compile and write the report with consultant Charles Siepmann and FCC statistician Dallas Smythe.

The report, called *Public Service Responsibility of Broadcast Licenses*, was released in early 1946 and became known as the *Blue Book* because the cover of the report was blue. The *Blue Book* reported that although the industry was recording record profits, programming was substandard. The biggest concern was excessive advertising. The Commission documented egregious examples of stations essentially interrupting a series of ads with occasional programming. The FCC also found that few stations were fulfilling the promises made on their renewal applications.

The Commission then set out to present clear guidelines on what it meant for a station to serve the public interest. The *Blue Book* guidelines cautioned stations against excessive advertising. It also suggested stations allocate time to sustaining programming, live local programming, and discussion of important issues of the day. When the *Blue Book* was first released, it drew praise from many as an acceptable way to improve the quality of broadcasting.

Then NAB president Justin Miller took the position that the FCC had absolutely no authority over programming and that the idea that the public owned the airwaves was "hooey and nonsense."[1] *Broadcasting* magazine, which had initially editorialized that the *Blue Book* was "nothing to get alarmed about,"[2] took up Miller's attacks. In the months following the release of the *Blue Book*, *Broadcasting* referred to staff and commissioners as socialists, fascists, and communists. References to Hitler and Goering were also made. Additional criticism came from members of Congress who, used to getting considerable free airtime from stations back home, were looking for cheap programming. Interestingly enough, none of the attacks centered on the actual content of the *Blue Book*, but instead focused on the temerity of the Commission in telling broadcasters they were not living up to their license obligations.

Just before the *Blue Book* was released, Charles Denny took over as Chairman from Paul Porter. Although Denny initially said that the *Blue Book* would not be "bleached," it soon became clear that the Commission was not willing to revoke station licenses for failing to live up to the newly defined public interest standards. One example can be seen when WBAL, the station whose overcommercialization started the whole process, was given a television license in the summer of 1946 without even a hearing. When another group challenged the renewal of WBAL radio, the FCC, in the form of Commissioner Rosel Hyde, stated that Hearst should keep the station on the basis of "demonstrated competence."[3]

By the end of 1946, it was clear that FCC would not use the *Blue Book* to guide its license renewal decisions. Chairman Denny told the *New York Times* that it was up to the local audience to demand better programming from stations.[4] While the *Blue Book* was never officially disavowed, it never became official Commission policy.

BROADCAST FLAGS

As the country moved into the digital age, many in the film and television community were increasingly worried about piracy. Many believed that file sharing on the internet was cutting deeply into the profits of the music industry. As more and more people got high-speed internet connections and as the switch to digital television loomed, producers feared that mass file swapping of video programming was bound to cost the film and television industries millions.

The Broadcast Discussion Working Group, a gathering of approximately 230 movie, television, computer, and electronics executives, released a report in 2002 citing a technology known as the broadcast flag as the way to maintain copyright integrity in the digital age. The flag was a small bit of data embedded in the broadcast signal that would tell receivers and copying equipment how many, if any, copies could be made of a program and whether that program could be retransmitted over the internet. House and Senate leaders then asked the FCC to develop rules regarding the flag.

The Commission adopted the broadcast flag rule in 2003. The flag was to be embedded in whatever digital television signals the broadcasters chose. All devices capable of receiving digital television signals manufactured after July 1, 2005, were required to have the technology necessary to read the flag and limit or block recording and copying. Parties on both sides of the issue were vocal. Many public interest groups claimed it would interfere in a host of legal uses, including home copying of programming for personal use. Some technology companies opposed the broadcast flag on the grounds that it might limit technological innovation. Movie companies threatened not to sell newer movies to television and CBS said it would stop high definition broadcasts altogether if the technology was not implemented. There was much public debate and confusion over exactly what uses the flag would limit and what uses the flag would allow.

Public interest groups, including the American Library Association, turned to the U.S. Court of Appeals for the District of Columbia Circuit. The court ruled in May 2005 that the FCC did not have the authority to order the makers of television sets and other receivers to do anything. The court also said that Congress could grant the Commission such authority, but as of summer 2005, it had not done so.

CABLE AND A LA CARTE PROGRAMMING TIERS

Cable has long sold its services in program bundles called tiers. Channels are grouped together based on interest or popularity or contractual obligations as each cable system sees fit. The advent of digital cable has also brought special digital tiers of programming. Although premium channels like HBO and Showtime are still sold on an individual basis, very few other channels are sold that way.

In recent years, however, many interest groups and their allies in Congress have raised the issue of a la carte cable. This would mean that cable systems would allow subscribers to select only those channels they want, rather than having to buy tiers that include channels they do not want. The push came from both the right and the left of the political spectrum. Groups like the Parents Television Council, with their concern about "decency," want families to be able to avoid channels like MTV that air programming containing both sex and profanity. Groups on the left, like the Consumers Union, look to a la carte as a way for people to gain better control over cable rates.

The cable industry trade group, National Cable and Telecommunications Association (NCTA), vehemently opposes any move toward mandatory a la carte pricing. The NCTA claims that a la carte would dramatically increase the price of cable. It also maintains that small channels would disappear and that new channels would not be created if the tier structure were to go away. But smaller cable systems, represented by the American Cable Association, have endorsed a la carte.

Powerful senators like John McCain and Ted Stevens have publicly advocated a la carte as a way to control both the content and cost of cable. In 2004, the House Commerce Committee asked the FCC to investigate whether rates would indeed go down if a la carte was mandated. The Commission found that if subscribers chose nine or fewer channels, they would save money. If customers choose more than nine channels, however, their cable bills would increase under a la carte pricing. Chairman Kevin Martin has publicly supported a "kid-friendly" tier that would be sold on an a la carte basis. Despite these rumbles from Congress and the Commission, nothing has been done to require that cable systems offer channels a la carte.

CABLE AND COPYRIGHT

One early criticism of cable involved accusing systems of copyright violations. Broadcasters and program producers maintained that cable systems were stealing programming when they carried television stations, whether distant or local. Cable systems said that once a television station sent its signal into the air, it was free. In the cases of *Fortnightly Corp. v. United Artists Television* (1968) and *Teleprompter Corp. v. Columbia Broadcasting System* (1974), the Supreme Court said that cable systems were not violating copyright law and that cable was merely an extension of people's antennas.

In 1976, Congress completely revised U.S. copyright law, in part to deal with new technologies like television and cable. The new law said that cable owed no copyright fees to local television stations. If a cable system imported a distant signal, it would be responsible for some fees. That money would be paid to the U.S. Copyright Office for distribution to the appropriate copyright owners. In practice, most of that money has gone to feature film producers.

With the proliferation of digital programming and delivery systems, concerns about piracy are growing in the cable community. The FCC has ruled that cable operators can insist that all set-top cable boxes contain anti-piracy technology (*see* Broadcast Flags).

CABLE ANTI-SIPHONING RULES

Cable networks began to appear with the development of satellites. Broadcasters were immediately concerned that new channels like HBO would steal programming away from their stations. One of the biggest worries was that newer movies would air first on HBO instead of the broadcast networks. The FCC issued rules in 1975 that aimed to protect broadcasters from having their programming siphoned away by the new cable networks. The FCC's rules barred cable networks from the following kinds of programming:

- feature films that were between three and ten years old;
- individual sporting events like the World Series that had been shown on broadcast television within the previous five years;
- most regular season sporting events that had been previously broadcast on television (only a limited number were allowed); and
- series programming, anything with recurring characters of continuing plots.

Cable networks were also limited in the number of hours that could be devoted to sports and films and barred from showing commercials on channels that were paid for by subscribers. The FCC eventually removed the series programming restriction. The Commission claimed the other rules were necessary because pay channels could offer producers more money than the advertiser-funded TV stations. Thus, programming like movies and sports would all end up on cable, where only the few wealthy subscribers would have access.

The U.S. Court of Appeals for the District of Columbia Circuit struck down the antisiphoning rules in *HBO v. FCC* (1977). The court held that not only did the Commission exceed its authority in these rules, there was no justification for them.

CABLE EXCLUSIVITY AND NON-DUPLICATION RULES

When cable systems import distant television signals, there is a possibility that programming appearing on a local station will be duplicated. Such duplication could cost the local station advertisers and thus revenue. The FCC created the Exclusivity and Non-duplication rules in 1972 in order to protect local broadcasters.

There are two kinds of syndicated programming. The first is reruns of off-network shows like *Friends* or *Everybody Loves Raymond* that have run for at least five seasons and are sold to individual stations for airing even while new episodes are being produced. The second kind of syndicated programming is called first-run, and it is made up of programs like *Wheel of Fortune* or *Jeopardy* that are produced specifically to be sold to individual stations. Syndicated programming is usually sold on an exclusive basis, with only one station in each market carrying the program. If a cable system is importing a station that carries the same syndicated programming as a local station, that local station can ask the cable system to black out the specific show or shows. The Exclusivity rule was rescinded in 1980 and reinstated in 1988. In 1989, the U.S. Court of Appeals for the District of Columbia Circuit upheld the rules in *United Video, Inc. v. FCC* (1989).

The Non-duplication rule refers to broadcast network programming. If a cable system imports a distant station that is affiliated with the same network as a local station, the local station can ask the cable system to black out all network programming on the distant station.

Blackouts can also be requested for sporting events shown on cable systems in the local market if the games are not sold out.

CABLE FRANCHISING

Cable systems use public rights-of-way, meaning the wires carrying cable are hung on utility poles or placed underground. Thus a system cannot be built without the permission of the local government. This permission comes in the form of the franchise agreement. Franchise agreements evolved with cable and were officially required by the FCC in 1972. The need for a franchise agreement was reaffirmed by Congress with the Cable Act of 1984.

Franchise agreements are contracts between a cable company and the government of the area it serves. In some states, franchises are granted at the state level. In most places, however, it is granted by a local municipal government. The franchise agreement generally outlines the number and kind of channels to be offered, including the number and kind of access channels that will be provided for public use. The agreement usually mandates that the companies make cable available to all homes in the franchise area. It also generally sets forth the rate structure, the length of the contract (usually fifteen years), and the franchise fee. The franchise fee is money paid to the franchising authority every year because of the company's use of public rights-of-way. In the early years of cable, the fee could run as high as 36 percent of a system's revenues. In 1972, the FCC placed some limits on what fee could be demanded by the municipality. The Cable Act of 1984 capped the franchise fee at 5 percent of the system's gross revenues.

Cable exploded in the 1980s and systems were being built everywhere. There was much competition between companies for choice locations. When a municipality announced it was ready for cable, systems would place bids outlining the service they would provide the locale. Companies began to make extravagant promises in exchange for the franchise. These included such things as impossibly high channel capacities, two-way communication, multiple access channels, and facilities to produce the access programming. The bid also usually included the rate structure and generous franchise fees. Bids grew more and more outlandish. An early 1980s bid by Sammon Communications for the Fort Worth, Texas, franchise demonstrates how much a company would promise for the right to build a system. The Sammon bid included a multi-million dollar community access package that included three mobile television vans, $50,000 for student internship programs, $175,000 annual budget for the access channels, and $100,000 to modernize educational buildings and studios.[5]

Cable companies sometimes made promises in the franchise agreement that they could not or would not deliver. Municipalities sometimes made outrageous and impossible demands on cable companies in exchange for the franchise. Litigation over broken promises, unreasonable contracts, and rising rates was common. In an effort to protect the struggling cable industry, Congress passed the Cable Act of 1984, which capped the franchise fee and made it more difficult for municipalities to change companies at the end of the franchise agreement.

In the beginning, most municipalities offered exclusive franchises, since the construction of a cable system can be disruptive to a locality's life. When more than one company is granted the right to build a cable system, that is called overbuilding. The issue of granting an exclusive franchise does have First Amendment implications. When choosing one cable system over another, a municipality often chooses what content cable subscribers will get to see. The Supreme Court concluded in *City of Los Angeles v. Preferred Communications, Inc.* (1986) that unless there is a physical reason why another company cannot build in an area, then an exclusive franchise should not be granted. If there is room on the utility poles, there is room for another cable company. The Cable Act of 1992 went even further and forbade municipalities from offering exclusive franchise agreements. Despite this mandate for overbuilding, only a tiny percentage of homes have more than one cable system to choose from.

CABLE IMPORTATION OF DISTANT BROADCAST SIGNALS

Cable began in the 1940s, when various people around the country built big antennas to pull distant television signals into rural and mountainous areas that were without television stations. As cable spread to places with stations, the local broadcasters grew concerned that no one would watch the local stations if big city stations were an alternative. Local broadcasters complained to the FCC, but in 1956 the Commission held that cable was outside its jurisdiction.

But early cable was not completely out of the FCC's regulatory reach. Cable systems used microwave technology to bring in the distant television signals. The FCC controlled microwave licenses because they required spectrum. Until 1962, the Commission granted the licenses based on spectrum availability and whether the system would cause any interference with existing spectrum users. But in 1962, the FCC decided that it could deny a license based on whether the cable system would cause economic harm to a local broadcast station. The Commission denied the application of Carter Mountain Transmission, which wanted to bring signals from Denver to Riverton, Wyoming. The Commission stated that this would cause economic harm to the local station, KWRB-TV. In *Carter Mountain Transmission Corp. v. FCC* (1963), the U.S. Court of Appeals for the District of Columbia Circuit ruled that the FCC did have the authority to regulate the importation of distance broadcast signals based on the economic impact on local television stations.

In 1964, this issue became front page news when the FCC refused to allow an Austin, Texas, cable system to import a distant signal. The local television station had protested and the FCC sided with the station. The owner of the television station in question was the family of President Lyndon Johnson.

During this time, the National Community Television Association, the cable trade group, was in negotiations with the National Association of Broadcasters over the issue of distant signals. Although a compromise appeared close on a number of occasions, no agreement was ever reached. Then cable companies began to announce plans to build systems in big cities like New York. While the larger stations and, by extension, the networks, had not cared about cable in smaller towns and rural areas, this move to build in their backyards sparked action. In 1964, ABC formally asked the FCC to regulate cable. This was the first policy position taken by a broadcast network on cable. In early 1965, the Association of Maximum Service Telecasters (a group of 150 big market stations) asked the Commission to ban cable systems from importing distant signals.

At that point, it became a public relations battle between the cable and broadcast industries. Broadcasters were successful in painting the cable operators as thieves stealing the hard work of TV. Television had great support in Congress, where Senators and Representatives knew that the broadcasters controlled access to their constituents. Cable, on the other hand, had little to offer the politicians, since it did not have local programming of its own. Despite the fact that the NCTA hired former FCC Commissioner Frederick Ford to be its president, cable did not have the lobbying power of the broadcast industry. As part of this PR campaign, the NAB spent $25,000 on a study that "proved" that cable was bad for TV. Television stations ran anti-cable advertising to sway public opinion. In the end, cable was viewed by most in Washington and around the country as an unscrupulous business from which television needed protection.

In 1965, the Commission issued the first cable rules, calling it an ancillary service to broadcasting. Among other things, the rules forbade the importation of distant signals that duplicated any material available from local broadcast stations and introduced the concept of must carry. The industry challenged the rules and in *United States v. Southwestern Cable* (1968), the Supreme Court upheld the Commission's stance that cable was within the jurisdiction of the

Commission. Shortly after the ruling, the Commission created rules that banned the importation of distant signals into the top 100 television markets completely. After that, the battle between broadcasters and cable systems focused on must carry (*see* Must Carry and Retransmission Consent).

CABLE PROGRAMMING AND LOCAL ORIGINATION REQUIREMENTS

When cable first started, it served only as a conduit for broadcast television stations and offered no programming of its own. In 1972, the FCC began to require larger cable systems (3,500+ subscribers) to produce local programming. The Commission said that if the cable system did not create this local programming it would be barred from carrying *any* television signals. This rule was upheld by the Supreme Court in *United States v. Midwest Video Corp.* (1972) as an appropriate regulation of cable as an ancillary service to broadcasting. Despite the Court's affirmation, the FCC removed the local origination requirement shortly thereafter.

CABLE RATE REGULATION

Because of the expense of building and maintaining a cable system, cable was viewed as a natural monopoly in the early days. Public policy has long been that a monopoly requires rate regulation. Many early franchise agreements set the rates that cable systems could charge. In 1971, the FCC prohibited municipalities from regulating the rates for pay-per-view services but said nothing about other programming.

To encourage the growth of cable, Congress passed the Cable Act of 1984. The act declared that municipalities could only regulate rates if there was not effective competition. At that time, effective competition was defined as three or more over-the-air broadcast signals available throughout the franchise area. This meant that very few systems were regulated.

Following the 1984 Cable Act, cable rates skyrocketed and the public complained to Congress and the Commission. Rate regulation was reinstated with the Cable Act of 1992. The rates for the basic service tier, which includes broadcast stations and public access channels, were now regulated by the franchising authority. The rates for the basic cable tier, which often includes channels like CNN, ESPN, and MTV, were now regulated by the FCC. Rates for premium channels like HBO remained unregulated.

Congress removed the FCC's authority over cable rates with the Telecommunications Act of 1996. The FCC's basic cable rate regulation ended on March 31, 1999. Local franchise authorities are still allowed to regulate the rates of the basic service tier. But certain small cable systems and ones that face effective competition are not subject to any rate regulation. The definition of effective competition is now dependent on how many people within the cable system's service area are subscribers. If fewer than 30 percent of the households in the franchise area have cable, the system is considered to have effective competition.

CHAIN BROADCASTING

As far back as 1922, there was concern about monopoly control over radio. Throughout the 1930s, NBC and CBS were growing in power. The third network, Mutual Broadcasting, was having difficultly expanding nationally since so many stations were locked into air-tight contracts with the two bigger networks. Congress berated the Commission at every turn for not sufficiently or appropriately regulating the industry. The FCC was growing increasingly concerned about the negative effects of the domination of the networks, which were outside its regulatory authority.

In 1938, the FCC announced it would investigate the matter. The Commission held six months of hearings, and in 1940 it issued a report that criticized the networks but offered no solutions. The White House and Congress were deeply dissatisfied with the Commission and there was much discussion regarding reorganization. In late 1939, President Franklin Roosevelt appointed James Lawrence Fly as the new FCC Chairman. Fly, who was deeply suspicious of the growing concentration of ownership in radio, took the lead in developing specific rules regarding the networks.

In 1941, the FCC issued the *Report on Chain Broadcasting*. Chairman Fly knew that the only way the Commission could do anything about network domination was to regulate the kinds of contracts that individual stations could make. Thus the *Report* stated that the Commission would not renew the license of any station that entered into a network affiliate contract that included any of the following eight practices.

1. Networks could not require that a station affiliate exclusively with one network.
2. Stations could not require that they be an exclusive outlet for a particular network.
3. Contracts could be only for one year, instead of the usual five.
4. Networks could no longer exercise option time, the practice of networks demanding that stations preempt local programming if the network wanted to air a program.
5. Networks could no longer force stations to carry programming that it did not want.
6. Networks could no longer own two stations in the same market.
7. Networks were not allowed to own more than one network with the same coverage area.

8. Networks could not demand money from stations if the local station sold advertising time for less that the network's rates.

The Commission also promised to give "continuing attention"[6] to issues like the network-owned artist bureaus. The FCC maintained that no performer could get a fair deal when they were being represented by the people with whom they were negotiating. Both networks quickly divested themselves of their artist bureaus.

Stations were given ninety days to bring their contracts into compliance with the new rules. CBS and NBC reacted badly, with CBS's William Paley prophesizing the ultimate destruction of broadcasting. The National Association of Broadcasters (NAB), which held its annual convention two weeks after the release of the *Report*, also vehemently criticized the new regulations. CBS was most opposed to the option time rule. NBC, which owned both NBC-Red and NBC-Blue, was most opposed to the divorcement order that required it to sell off four stations as well as one entire network. Fly himself was a target for an heretofore unseen amount of venom from both the industry and its allies in Congress. The House Commerce Committee even began hearings on a bill to reverse the FCC's new rules. Fly eventually softened some of the rules, including allowing contracts to be two years in length.

Both networks appealed all the way to the U.S. Supreme Court. In *National Broadcasting Co., Inc. v. United States* (1943), the Court not only upheld the Chain Broadcasting rules, but it also stated that because of the scarce nature of radio, the FCC was authorized to regulate more than just the technical aspects of broadcasting. The Commission was responsible for seeing that stations operated in the public interest, convenience, and necessity. As a result of this case, NBC sold off one of its networks and the ABC network was born.

CHILDREN'S TELEVISION ACT OF 1990

Studies show that children watch an average of three hours of television every day. Congress passed the Children's Television Act of 1990 as an attempt to require broadcasters to serve the educational and informational needs of children. Congress left it to the FCC to write the specific rules regarding how television stations would serve those needs. At first, the Commission wrote very general rules that resulted in an uneven amount of programming for children. After Reed Hundt was appointed chair, he began to campaign for rules mandating a specific number of hours of children's programming. This was controversial and opposed by many in the industry and within the Commission itself, including Commissioner James Quello.

On August 8, 1996, the FCC issued a Report and Order with new rules for children's television. The rules came about as a compromise between the Commission and the industry after years of debate. Each television station would be required to provide at least three hours per week of what was called "core" programming. Core programming was defined as regularly scheduled, weekly shows aimed at serving the educational and informational needs of children under sixteen that were at least thirty minutes in length and aired between 7:00 A.M. and 10:00 P.M.

Congress also sought to limit the amount of advertising that children see. The FCC's rules for children's television limit commercial material to ten and a half minutes per hour on weekends and twelve minutes per hour on weekdays. These limits apply to programming aimed at children twelve and younger. The Commission also requires that licensees keep very detailed records of commercial material during children's programming in their public file (see Public File). Commercial material can include more than just traditional spot advertising. If an ad includes references to or offers of products related to the program during which the ad is being aired, that program becomes an illegal program-length commercial. Thus, the entire program will be counted as commercial material under the Children's Television Act. Another advertising restriction bans "host-selling." The FCC maintains that character endorsement of a product during that character's program could confuse a young viewer and is thus unacceptable.

CIGARETTE ADVERTISING

Cigarette advertising was a mainstay of broadcasting from the very beginning. Many of the most popular shows on radio and later television were sponsored by tobacco companies, including the *Jack Benny Show* (Lucky Strikes) and *I Love Lucy* (Philip Morris). At the same time that Philip Morris was bringing America the adventures of Lucy, Ricky, Ethel, and Fred, evidence concerning the link between smoking and cancer began to surface. In 1964, the Surgeon General's Office officially linked smoking with lung cancer.

In December 1966, a lawyer named John F. Banzhaf III asked WCBS-TV in New York to provide free time to anti-smoking activists under the Fairness Doctrine. Banzhaf claimed that pro-smoking views were implicit in cigarette commercials and that since smoking was an issue of controversy, free time to respond was required under the law. WCBS responded that it had provided ample coverage of the anti-smoking position in its news programming and in the public service announcements (PSAs) from the American Cancer Society it broadcast free of charge. In addition, WCBS maintained that content of paid advertising could not trigger the Fairness Doctrine.

Banzhaf then went to the FCC. In a letter dated June 2, 1967, the Commission agreed that cigarette commercials presented smoking as "socially acceptable and desirable, manly, and a necessary part of a rich full life,"[7] and, thus invoked the Fairness Doctrine. The Commission refused to mandate equal time, but did state that stations airing tobacco advertising were obliged under the Fairness Doctrine to devote a significant amount of time to the anti-smoking message. The Commission encouraged stations to fulfill this obligation by broadcasting anti-smoking PSAs on a regular basis. The Commission strictly limited this decision to the advertisement of cigarettes only.

Over the next few months, many appeals were made to the Commission from both sides of the issue. The FCC stuck by the original ruling and many of the interested parties went to the U.S. Court of Appeals for the District of Columbia Circuit for relief. In the case of *Banzhaf v. FCC* (1968), the court sided with the FCC and mandated that the antismoking advocates be given reasonable time to respond to claims made by cigarette advertising.

The *Banzhaf* decision became moot in 1971, when the congressional ban of all broadcast cigarette advertising took effect. Advertisements for other tobacco products were banned shortly thereafter. Concerns remain, however, about the presence of cigarettes on television in the form of tobacco companies' sponsorship of professional sporting events and individual athletes.

CLOSED CAPTIONING

Closed captioning is an assistive technology designed to give people with hearing disabilities access to television programming. Closed-captioned programs display the audio as text on the screen, similar to subtitles. Congress first considered requiring that televisions be caption-ready in 1991 and ordered that any television set larger than thirteen inches manufactured after July 1993 include the technology.

The Telecommunications Act of 1996 included a directive to the Commission to order video program distributors (cable operators, broadcasters, satellite distributors, and other multichannel video programming distributors) to begin captioning many of their television programs. The FCC has a schedule by which these producers will continue to expand captioning until all programming is available to those with hearing impairment. Any programming first aired after January 1, 1998, is supposed to be captioned. By 2006, all programming aired must be captioned, no matter when it initially aired. The Commission has also created a second schedule for Spanish-language programming, with full captioning completed by 2010.

There are exceptions to the captioning rule. The following programs are not required to be captioned:

- most programs that are shown between 2:00 A.M. and 6:00 A.M. local time;
- locally produced and distributed non-news programming with no repeat value (e.g., parades and school sports);
- commercials that are no more than five minutes long;
- instructional programming that is locally produced by public television stations for use in grades K–12 and post secondary schools

(only covers programming narrowly distributed to individual educational institutions);

- programs in languages other than English or Spanish;

- programs shown on new networks for the first four years of the network's operations;

- public service announcements and promotional announcements that are shorter than ten minutes, unless they are federally funded or produced; and

- programming provided by program providers with annual gross revenues less than $3 million (although such programmers must pass through video programming that has already been captioned).[8]

Captioning is considered important not only because it aids those with hearing loss, but because it has also been shown to improve language comprehension and fluency for those individuals for whom English is not their first language. Captioning has also been shown to help children learn to read.

COLOR TELEVISION

Experimental work on color television happened largely at the same time as the development of black and white television. Although a number of companies were working on color television in the 1930s and 1940s, the main rivalry was between CBS and RCA. CBS developed what was known as a mechanical color television, with spinning wheels of red, blue, and green that created the color picture. The CBS system was not compatible with existing televisions and the color receivers would not be able to pick up black and white programs. At the same time, RCA was developing an electronic color television that was compatible with existing sets.

In 1946, CBS demonstrated its color television to the FCC, but the Commission declared that it was not ready for the market. At the same time, RCA was selling its black and white televisions that were not compatible with the CBS system as well as further developing its own compatible color system. In November 1950, the FCC announced that the CBS system would be the standard for all color television. The introduction of color was delayed while RCA and other manufacturers challenged the decision all the way to the Supreme Court. In *Radio Corp. of America v. United States* (1951), the Court eventually upheld the FCC's right to choose the CBS standard. Color television was again delayed by the Korean War freeze on the production of sets. The freeze was lifted in 1953.

By this time, the RCA system had been perfected and in 1953 the FCC approved the RCA electronic color television as the national standard. Color televisions were extremely expensive when they were introduced: $1,000 in 1954. RCA predicted that it would sell 75,000 sets that year, but reported selling only 5,000. Of those 5,000 sets, it is estimated that only 1,000 were actually sold to the public. The others were either sold to RCA employees at a discount or donated to schools. *Time* magazine called color TV "the most resounding industrial flop of 1956."[9]

It took a long time for color television to become the standard. The first experimental color television broadcast using the RCA system was an August 1953 episode of *Kukla, Fran and Ollie*. NBC debuted *Bonanza* in 1959 as the first regularly scheduled color television program. The 1966–1967 television season was the first when all three networks were airing full color schedules. By 1969, one-third of all television homes had a color set.

COMMUNISM AND THE FCC

Communism in the broadcast industry and in the Commission itself was an ongoing concern for the FCC. In 1936, Chairman Anning Prall forced a Pittsburgh radio station to carry the speech of the presidential candidate from the communist party under the Equal Time provisions of the Fairness Doctrine. But this concern for "fairness" to communists did not last long. Like many government agencies, the FCC got caught up in the Red Scare of the 1940s and 1950s.

In 1941, two FCC employees, Dr. Goodwin Watson and Dr. William E. Dodd, Jr., were accused of being communists by the House Un-American Activities Committee. Although Committee Chairman Martin Dies demanded that the two be fired and even attached amendments to appropriations bill barring the use of federal money to pay their salaries, FCC Chairman James Lawrence Fly and Commissioner Clifford Durr refused to dismiss them.

Commissioner Durr continued to fight against the escalating war on communism. In 1947, he publicly criticized FBI Director J. Edgar Hoover for sending unsolicited reports on the political loyalties of radio personalities to the Commission. Out of fear of Hoover's power, as well as a growing concern about communism among the other commissioners, the FCC drafted a letter distancing the Commission from Durr's comments and welcoming Hoover's investigations into radio. Durr later refused reappointment to the Commission in 1948 because of his opposition to the loyalty oaths being required by the Truman Administration.

When another Commission employee was accused of being a communist in 1948, the swing to the right by the Commission became obvious. Walter Gee was investigated by the FBI for being a communist. When the report was turned over to the Commission, Gee was asked to explain the charges and the Internal Loyalty Board of the FCC cleared him. Just four years later, Gee again came under investigation (with virtually the same information). This time, however, he was suspended from the Commission. Gee then resigned without responding to the charges. This demonstrates that within a few short years, the Commission had become much more concerned about rooting out communism from its own ranks as well as the broadcasting industry as a whole.

This period of time also saw a number of broadcast licensees accused of communist sympathies. While no one lost a license during this time, several stations faced renewal trouble. For example, the Commission began to investigate the political loyalties of the owners of WLOA in 1951. The matter was complicated by the fact that the Department of Justice refused to allow the FBI evidence to be used in an open hearing. Without the open hearing, the Commission could not deny the renewal. In another case, Edward Lamb, the owner of a number of television stations in Pennsylvania and Ohio, faced charges that he was a communist sympathizer. When one of his station's licenses came up for renewal in 1953, it was held up for more than a year while the Commission investigated his political beliefs.

The height of the anti-communism fervor at the Commission can be seen with the inception of what *Broadcasting* magazine referred to as the Anti-Red Rule. In 1952, a man named Nicholas Garland applied to renew his first-class radiotelephone operators license. Garland was on an FBI list of suspected communists who were "capable of clandestine radio communications."[10] The Commission sent a questionnaire to Garland asking if he was now or had ever been a member of the communist party. Waiting for Garland's response, the Commission faced a quandary. There was nothing in the Communications Act that justified denying a license merely for membership in the communist party. However, if Garland refused to answer, the Commission could deny the license based on the fact that he didn't respond to a Commission request, which was legal grounds for refusal. Garland chose not to answer and the FCC denied his license renewal. The lawyers at the Commission knew, however, that a policy against granting amateur and commercial radiotelephone operators licenses to communists had to be developed.

The Commission's first move in this direction was to create a policy that allowed them to send the communism questionnaire to all applicants. The next step was to propose a rule that barred anyone with a history of communist membership from holding a radiotelephone operators license. The constitutionality of the rule was questioned during a short 1955 hearing and no further word about the anti-communist policy was heard until 1962. In that year, the Commission announced that it would not be in the public interest to adopt the rule.

That long silence did not mean, however, that the anti-communism policy was never enforced. In ten cases, the FCC received license applications or renewals from men on an FBI list. Four applications were granted because the Commission could not confirm the evidence of communism. Two applications were denied because they failed to return the communism questionnaire. The other four applicants challenged the Commission's authority to even ask about political affiliations. While the applicants fought the issue at the Commission and the courts, the FCC denied the licenses on other legal grounds. Thus while the Anti-Red rule never became official Commission policy, there is evidence that in the years leading up to the 1962 denouncement of the rule the Commission pursued an agenda of preventing communists from getting radiotelephone operators licenses.

COPYRIGHT, RECORDED MUSIC, AND RADIO

From the early days of radio, the use of phonographic records as a source of programming material stirred up controversy. Under the 1909 copyright law, copyrighted music could not be performed in public for profit without the permission of the copyright holder. The American Society of Composers, Authors, and Publishers (ASCAP) was formed in 1914 and focused on gathering fees for performance rights, holding that composers should be compensated for any public performance of his or her work.

The government also weighed in on the matter of recorded music and the new technology of radio. In 1922, Secretary of Commerce Herbert Hoover banned large stations from using recorded music. In 1924, Senator Clarence Dill introduced a bill that would exempt musical broadcasts from U.S. copyright law. Although the bill never passed, Dill became a leading figure in radio regulation and helped author the Radio Act of 1927. An early rule created by the Federal Radio Commission said that stations had to identify when a "mechanical recording" was played, for fear that people would think it was a live band.

In the very early days of radio, ASCAP gave cheap or free licenses to stations to encourage the growth of the medium. But by 1922, ASCAP wanted broadcasters to pay for the use of recorded music. ASCAP first went after WEAF in New York and demanded $1,000 a year for a license to play ASCAP-controlled music. WEAF countered with an offer of $500 and ASCAP accepted. When ASCAP asked WJZ, Newark, for a license fee, the station announced that it would no longer play ASCAP music.

ASCAP then began monitoring WOR, Newark and heard an ASCAP song called "Mother Machree." WOR maintained that since the station was not profitable and operated merely as a way to promote the Bamberger department stores, the performance was not "for profit," as defined by copyright law. In *Witmark v. Bamberger* (1923), a federal district court in New Jersey ruled that all radio play was, in fact, a for-profit use under copyright law. After that decision, many stations agreed to pay ASCAP an annual license fee, which generally began at $250. As a result, the networks banned recorded music, preferring to focus on live bands. The National Association of Broadcasters was organized in 1923 largely as a way for broadcasters to fight ASCAP.

In 1932, ASCAP negotiated an agreement with the radio industry that established fees based on a percentage of advertising sales. By the mid-1930s, more than half of all radio programming was music. By 1936, the fee was set at slightly more than 2 percent of a station's advertising revenue. Between 1931 and 1939, ASCAP payments went from $960,000 to $4.3 million. The last agreement between the radio industry and ASCAP was signed in 1935. In 1937, ASCAP began to talk about sharply increasing the license fees after 1939. As a response, Broadcast Music, Inc. (BMI) was organized in 1939 by the industry as a way to buffer radio stations from ASCAP's demands. BMI came to represent many of the young songwriters who had hit songs but who were not allowed to join ASCAP. In March 1940, ASCAP wanted a 100 percent rate increase from the previous year and most of the industry turned to BMI. By 1941, 660 stations out of 796 signed on with BMI. The year 1941 was also when the radio industry boycotted ASCAP and only played music controlled by BMI or songs that were in the public domain. The year was known as the era of "Jeannie with the Light Brown Hair," a Stephen Foster tune that was played endlessly because it was in the public domain.

Eventually, the industry and ASCAP settled their differences when ASCAP reduced their demands. But then the American Federation of Musicians (AFM) voted to stop making records, claiming that movies and radio were putting musicians out of work. In 1943 and 1944, the major record labels yielded to AFM demands for a welfare fund for unemployed musicians.

With the introduction of television, recorded music became the dominant programming on radio. The conflicts between industry and ASCAP were eventually settled and copyright fees are currently negotiated between all-industry representatives and both ASCAP and BMI. Most radio stations purchase a blanket license, rather than a per-program license.

DIGITAL AND HIGH DEFINITION TELEVISION

As early as 1970, the Japanese were working on what was called high definition television (HDTV). HDTV promised far better pictures and a screen ratio that looked more like the rectangular movie screen than the square television set. In 1981, the Japanese "Muse" system of analog HDTV was demonstrated in Washington, D.C., for members of the Commission and others. The United States began to move toward HDTV a few years later.

The Advisory Committee on Advanced Television Service (ACATS) was appointed by the FCC in 1987. Former FCC Chairman Richard Wiley was named chair and the group was charged with reviewing, testing, and recommending a technical standard for HDTV. ACATS was supposed to make a report to the Commission by the second quarter of 1993. The Committee considered more than twenty technical proposals and narrowed it down to nine by 1990. At that time, all the proposals were based on an analog system. Then General Instrument proposed a digital HDTV system and everything changed. The FCC had always supported choosing an HDTV system that would function on the existing channels allocated to television. But in 1992, the Commission announced that broadcasters would be given additional spectrum for HDTV with the expectation that the old analog channels would be returned after the switch to all-digital broadcasting.

Just before ACATS was to have made its final recommendation, the companies involved in the development of these technologies asked for time to make improvements. Four systems were eventually identified as being possible standards for U.S. broadcasting. Those four groups, AT&T/Zenith, General Instrument, DSRC/Thompson/Philips, and the Massachusetts Institute of Technology, then decided to form what was called the Grand Alliance to work together to develop a "super" HDTV system, which would include the best of each. Technical parameters were finally set and the Grand Alliance successfully tested the new system.

In the Spring of 1995, FCC Chairman Reed Hundt asked ACATS to include standard definition television as well as HDTV in the digital plan. ACATS made its recommendation to the Commission on November 28, 1995. The computer industry then got involved in the digital television debate and the question of the scanning formats to be used for digital was again up in the air. After reaching a compromise between all parties, the final standard was approved by the Commission on December 24, 1996.

In the Fifth Report and Order on digital television, the FCC required that affiliates of ABC, CBS, FOX, and NBC in the top ten largest markets have a digital signal on the air by May 1, 1999. Affiliates in markets eleven through thirty were supposed to have a digital signal by November 1, 1999. The Commission set a target date of 2006 for the return of the analog channels. While all this was going on, Congress reinforced the move toward digital and mandated the 2006 date for the return of the analog spectrum in the Telecommunications Act of 1996.

The 2006 date to return the spectrum was to be based on whether 85 percent of the population was able to receive digital signals. Although Chairman Michael Powell and others looked to tie measurement of digital penetration to cable and DBS subscription levels, by the spring of 2005 it did not look as though the country would be ready for all-digital television. Very few people had purchased the new digital sets on account of high cost, lack of awareness, and lack of programming. Many in Congress were concerned about the millions of people who do not subscribe to cable or DBS services and thus would need a new set, or at least a converter box, in order to continue to receive television. As a result, Congress began to debate a new deadline as well as whether it would allocate money for converter boxes for the people who would be left without television.

On October 26, 2005, the House Commerce Committee approved the Digital Television Transition Act of 2005, setting December 31, 2008, as the end of analog television broadcasts in the United States. On November 3, 2005, the full Senate approved the Digital Transition and Public Safety Act of 2005 that set a hard date of April 7, 2009, as the end of analog television broadcasting in the United States. The two bills also conflict over the amount of money being set aside to help the estimated 21 million homes without cable or satellite service buy the needed set top digital converter box. With the differences between the legislation, it will be up to a conference committee to iron out what, if any, legislation will be acted on sometime in 2006.

Digital television will likely take many forms. Technology allows a broadcaster to air a single high definition program or multiple programming streams, known as multicasting. Using the digital signal, stations can send programming at a variety of quality levels.

- *Standard Definition TV (SDTV)*: SDTV is the basic level of quality display and resolution for both analog and digital. Transmission of SDTV may be in either the traditional (4:3) or widescreen (16:9) format.

- *Enhanced Definition TV (EDTV)*: EDTV is a step up from Analog Television. EDTV comes in 480p widescreen (16:9) or traditional (4:3) format and provides better picture quality than SDTV, but not as high as HDTV.

- *High Definition TV (HDTV)*: HDTV in widescreen format (16:9) provides the highest resolution and picture quality of all digital broadcast formats. Combined with digitally enhanced sound technology, HDTV sets new standards for sound and picture quality in television. (Note: HDTV and digital TV are not the same thing—HDTV is one format of digital TV.)[11]

The quality of the signal will likely depend on how many programming streams the broadcaster chooses to send. This issue of multicasting has caused significant debate over the future shape of cable and satellite must carry (*see* Must Carry and Retransmission Consent).

The transition to digital television has also raised many questions about how digital broadcasters will serve the public interest, convenience, and necessity. In March 1997, the Clinton Administration established the Advisory Committee on the Pubic Interest Obligations of Digital Television Broadcasters to study the issue. After fifteen months, the committee made a number of recommendations to the White House, including a return to community ascertainment and a minimum requirement for public affairs programming. Most controversial, however, was the recommendation that political candidates be given five minutes of free airtime each night during the thirty days before an election.

Chairman William Kennard wanted to issue a Notice of Proposed Rule Making (NPRM) on the free airtime proposal, but Congress threatened to cut the FCC's budget if it did. Instead, the Commission issued a general Notice of Inquiry (NOI) on the public interest obligations of digital broadcasters in 1999. The NOI eventually led to a NPRM on the children's television obligations of digital broadcasters. On January 18, 2001, Chairman Kennard had one day left in office. He delivered the *Report to Congress on the Public Interest Obligations of Television Broadcasters as They Transition to Digital Television*, which included recommendations for a public affairs programming requirement, reinstatement of ascertainment requirements, and the free airtime proposal.

On November 23, 2004, the Commission released a Report and Order and a Further Notice of Proposed Rule Making on the matter of Children's Television Obligations of Digital Television Broadcasters. The Commission essentially carried forward the existing programming and advertising requirements (*see* Children's Television Act of 1990). The Further NPRM asked for comments on the use of direct, interactive links to commercial content in children's programming.

EQUAL EMPLOYMENT OPPORTUNITIES

Since the 1960s, there has been concern about the representation of women and minorities on the broadcast media. One way of addressing that concern has been to make sure that women and minorities have the opportunity to work at radio and television stations. Since 1964, the FCC has required that broadcasters not discriminate on the basis of race, gender, religion, color, or national origin in hiring, promoting, or firing.

The struggle to define an Equal Employment Opportunities (EEO) policy has not been easy. In the 1990s, the Commission required broadcasters to take a number of affirmative steps to increase minority participation in broadcasting. Among other things, broadcasters were expected to publicize job openings with minority and women's organizations and make a concerted effort to hire women and minorities. They were also required to file reports on their employment practices with the Commission. In *Lutheran Church-Missouri Synod v. FCC* (1998), the U.S. Court of Appeals for the District of Columbia Circuit declared the rules unconstitutional, saying the goal of diversity in programming was too abstract. In 2002, the FCC adopted new EEO rules. Stations were to widely publicize any job openings and then report the race and gender of applicants to the Commission. In *MD/DC/DE Broadcasters Association v. FCC* (2001), the Court of Appeals again struck down the rules.

In response to the D.C. Circuit, the FCC issued yet another set of EEO rules on November 7, 2002. These rules required broadcasters to:

1. widely disseminate information concerning each full-time (thirty hours or more) job vacancy, except for vacancies filled in exigent circumstances;

2. provide notice of each full-time job vacancy to recruitment organizations that have requested such notice; and

3. complete two (for broadcast employment units with five to ten full-time employees or that are located in smaller markets) or four (for employment units with more than ten full-time employees located in larger markets) longer-term recruitment initiatives within a two-year period. These include, for example, job fairs, scholarship and internship programs, and other community events designed to inform the public of employment opportunities in broadcasting.

The Commission also adopted a number of rules that required broadcasters to keep detailed records for each job search, including copies of any ads or announcements, types of outreach, number of interviewees, and the date on which the job was filled. These files would be reviewed at renewal time and through random audits throughout the year. Although many broadcasters remained unhappy with the EEO requirements and asked the Commission to reconsider, the 2002 EEO policy is currently being enforced.

FAIRNESS DOCTRINE

In 1939, the license for WAAB, Boston, was set to expire. Mayflower Broadcasting wanted to build a new station to air on WAAB's frequency. The Commission held hearings to determine who would get the license. WAAB's license was eventually renewed, but the Commission used the announcement to criticize WAAB for editorializing. In a document called *In the Matter of Mayflower Broadcasting Corporation and the Yankee Network, Inc.* (1941), the FCC wrote that "the broadcaster cannot be an advocate."[12] This ruling against editorializing became known as the Mayflower Doctrine.

The Mayflower Doctrine was overturned in 1949 by the FCC document, *In the Matter of Editorializing by Broadcast Licensees*. The Commission said that the right of the public to be informed was more important than the right of a station to air only the licensee's opinion. The Commission said that licensees were required to devote a reasonable amount of time to the discussion of controversial issues of public importance and give reasonable opportunity for the presentation of opposing viewpoints on those issues. This became known as the Fairness Doctrine.

Part of the Fairness Doctrine was the Personal Attack rule, which said that if a broadcast attacks someone's honesty, character, or integrity, that person has a right to airtime to respond. In 1964, Reverend Billy James Hargis attacked a man named Fred J. Cook during a broadcast on WGCB, a station licensed to Red Lion Broadcasting. Among other accusation, Hargis said that Cook had worked for a Communist publication and had been fired for lying about a public official. Cook asked WGCB for time to reply to the broadcast and WGCB sent him a rate card and told him he could buy advertising time if he wanted to defend himself. Cook then complained to the Commission and the FCC ordered WGCB to give Cook airtime to respond to the attack. WGCB's owner, Red Lion Broadcasting, appealed the Commission's decision.

While all this was happening, the FCC created formal rules explaining both the Personal Attack and the Political Editorial sections of the Fairness Doctrine. In 1967, the FCC established that any person whose honesty, character, or integrity was attacked during a broadcast on a controversial issue had the right to reply on the air. The rule stated that the station was obligated to notify that person that he or she had been attacked and provide that person with time within one week of the original broadcast to respond. The Political Editorial rule said that if a station editorialized for or against a candidate, the station was obligated to notify all candidates for that office and allow them a reasonable opportunity to reply.

Red Lion took its case all the way to the Supreme Court. The Court consolidated the Red Lion case with a lawsuit filed by the Radio and Television News Directors Association (RTNDA). The RTNDA wanted the Court to throw out the 1967 rules as a violation of the First Amendment. In 1969, the Supreme Court upheld the Fairness Doctrine in general and the 1967 rules specifically in *Red Lion Broadcasting v. FCC*. The Court ruled that the Fairness Doctrine served the public interest because radio was a scarce resource. The Court said that because of this scarcity, the rights of the listeners and viewers to hear information were more important than the rights of the broadcast licensees to speak.

In 1974, the FCC said that a station's observance of the Fairness Doctrine was the most important issue at renewal time. Then Ronald Reagan became president and Mark Fowler became the chair of the FCC. Chairman Fowler was vocal in his opposition to the Fairness Doctrine. In 1985, the Commission released its *Report Concerning General Fairness Obligations of Broadcast Licensees*, which said that much had changed since the Supreme Court's ruling in Red Lion. The Fowler FCC maintained that scarcity was no longer an issue and that the Fairness Doctrine actually discouraged broadcasters from covering issues of controversy.

The U.S. Court of Appeals for the District of Columbia Circuit also began to rule against the Fairness Doctrine. In *Telecommunications Research and Action Center v. FCC* (1986), the court ruled that the doctrine was not a statutory obligation, but merely an FCC rule that the Commission could choose to enforce or not. In *Radio-Television News Directors Ass'n v. FCC* (1987), the court ruled that the Commission was obligated by its *1985 Fairness Report* to hold a rulemaking to eliminate or alter the Fairness Doctrine. After the Commission decided that Syracuse television station WTVH violated the Fairness Doctrine by airing commercials in support of a new nuclear plant without allowing for presentation of the antinuclear side, the court ruled in *Meredith Corp. v. FCC* (1987) that the FCC must consider the constitutionality of the Fairness Doctrine.

The FCC abolished the Fairness Doctrine with its 1987 *Syracuse Peace Council* decision. The Commission maintained that the scarcity that existed during the time of *Red Lion* no longer existed in the age of cable. In *Syracuse Peace Council v. FCC* (1989), the U.S. Court of Appeals for the District of Columbia Circuit upheld the Commission's right to determine that the Fairness Doctrine was no longer in the public interest. The court did not, however, rule on the matter of the Fairness Doctrine and the First Amendment.

Shortly after the Commission removed the Fairness Doctrine, Congress voted to reinstate it. President Reagan vetoed the bill and there were not enough votes to overturn the veto. Fairness Doctrine legislation again passed Congress during the presidency of George H. W. Bush and again it was vetoed.

The Commission did leave the Personal Attack and Political Editorial rules in effect after the *Syracuse Peace Council* decision. The RTNDA continued to ask the courts and the Commission to remove the rules, as it had in the *Red Lion* case. After much back and forth between the courts and the Commission and several tied votes at the Commission, the rules were finally suspended in October 2000.

In 2004, Representative Maurice Hinchey of New York introduced the Media Ownership Reform Act of 2004, which would have reinstated the Fairness Doctrine. It was never voted on.

A hearing held by the FCC on the Fairness Doctrine. Amid tremendous public controversy, the Fairness Doctrine was repealed in 1987. (Courtesy of the National Archives)

FAMILY VIEWING HOUR

In 1974, Congress asked the Commission to take action on what was perceived as excessive sex, crime, and violence on television. Early the next year, Chairman Richard Wiley made a report to Congress detailing Commission involvement in a series of discussions with the television networks and the National Association of Broadcasters over the creation of a Family Viewing Hour and program content advisories. The report also included the initial FCC regulatory action against the Pacifica Foundation broadcast of George Carlin's "Seven Words You Can Never Say on Television."

Chairman Wiley was known as a consensus-builder who liked to hammer out policies in private. In fact, during his time as chair, the public Commission votes tended to be 7–0. The Family Viewing Hour was a result of a number of phone calls and five private meetings. Wiley had called together the networks to discuss how they could best reduce the amount of sex and violence on television without government regulation. The conclusion was the Family Viewing Hour.

Out of fear of accusations of collusion between the networks, it was decided that the Family Viewing Hour would be added to the NAB Television Code. According the NAB, "entertainment programming inappropriate for viewing by a general family audience should not be broadcast during the first hour of network entertainment."[13] The Family Viewing Hour was controversial from the beginning. On the one hand, the citizen groups who were interested in "cleaning up" television felt the rule did not go far enough. On the other, program producers like Norman Lear objected, saying the rule was too restrictive and suppressed artistic freedom.

Lear and many other writers and producers, as well as the Writers Guild of America, the Directors Guild of America, and the Screen Actor's Guild, brought suit against the FCC, claiming it has infringed on the First Amendment and inappropriately colluded with the networks (*Writers Guild of America, West, Inc. v. FCC* (1976)). The lawsuit maintained that since the policymaking process in this instance was completely different from normal FCC rulemaking, it was unconstitutional.

The district court judge agreed with the Writers Guild and said that although the Family Viewing Hour might be a good idea, the way the policy was created was deeply flawed. The judge said that if the networks had come up with the policy on their own, or even if the NAB had come up with the policy on its own, there would not be a problem. However, since Chairman Wiley was involved, the policy evolved under the threat of government sanction and this brought the First Amendment into play. As a result of the case, the NAB removed the Family Viewing Hour from its Television Code.

The U.S. Court of Appeals for the Ninth Circuit eventually threw out the lower court's ruling in 1979. The Writers Guild appealed to the Supreme Court, but the Court would not take the case. The NAB never reinstated the Family Viewing Hour.

FINANCIAL INTEREST AND SYNDICATION RULES (FIN-SYN)

If a television show is produced by an independent company, the network pays a flat fee for the show and sells advertising to make money. That flat fee often does not cover the cost of production and the producers of prime time television often lose money when first airing a program on a broadcast network. The real money is made when the program goes into syndication. When a network show runs for five or more seasons, it is then sold on a market-by-market basis to be shown on local stations. Syndicated off-network programming is usually shown in strips, or five days a week, and in the hours immediately before or after prime time. In the early decades of television, the broadcast networks often owned all or part of most of the shows they aired. The FCC saw this as a potential limit on creativity and diversity and decided to limit the financial involvement of the networks in the creation and syndication of programming.

The Financial Interest and Syndication Rules were created in 1970 as a way to limit the power of the networks and increase program diversity. The Financial Interest rule barred networks from having any financial stake in the programs after they ran for the first time on the network. The Syndication rule barred the networks from having in-house syndication arms that managed the sale of programming they aired. In 1977, the rules were reinforced by a Consent Decree that resulted from an antitrust suit brought against the networks by the Justice Department. The Consent Decree also placed limits on the amount of programming the networks could produce in-house.

The FCC was worried about vertical integration and wanted to separate production from distribution. At this time, NBC, CBS, and ABC drew in more than 95 percent of the television audience on any given night. The Commission also wanted to lessen the incentives for the networks to produce programming, hoping to allow more independent producers access to the large network prime time audiences. The Commission believed that if independent producers were able to reap the financial benefits of syndication without having to give a share to the networks, it would lead to a wider variety of programming. In addition, if the networks were not involved in syndication, they could not favor their own affiliates when selling popular shows. This would help independent television stations to buy programming that would attract an audience.

The Fin-Syn rules faced immediate and vocal opposition from almost everyone in the television community. Critics said that the only people helped by the Fin-Syn rules were the large Hollywood studios that became the main producers of television shows. Few independent companies could afford to run a program at a deficit for the five years before syndication kicked in. Once the networks were removed from the equation, only the studios had that kind of equity.

In 1983, the FCC considered repealing the rules as part of the larger deregulation of broadcasting. There was massive opposition from the Hollywood studios. The studios' opposition to the repeal of the rules was supported by a former actor now in Washington, President Ronald Reagan. With the president on their side, the studios were able to convince the FCC to keep the rules in place.

In the early 1990s, television itself had changed. The networks were no longer the only players. The prime time network audience had shrunk to approximately 60 percent, with cable taking up the rest. Another player that helped edge the Commission toward repealing the rules was FOX. In 1991, FOX wanted to become a full-fledged network, but it owned a number of its own programs. Many at the Commission and in Congress wanted to see FOX dilute the power of the Big Three and were supportive of repealing the rules. FOX received a one-year waiver and then the FCC relaxed the Fin-Syn rules. The U.S. Court of Appeals for the Seventh Circuit said the Commission had not justified the changes and ordered it to review them again. In 1993, the Commission finally voted to repeal the rules, but the Consent Decree remained in effect. In November 1995, the rules fully disappeared.

The biggest immediate impact of the repeal of the Fin-Syn rules came in the form of mergers. The biggest merger: Disney's purchase of ABC. The removal of the Fin-Syn rules also opened up the way for the WB and UPN networks, both arms of production houses.

Fin-Syn has not completely disappeared, however. Independent producers, the Hollywood production companies, and media activists continue to call for the reinstatement of the rules. When Michael Powell was chair of the Commission, he said that the FCC would not bring back the rules without direction from Congress. In 2004, Representative Maurice Hinchey of New York included reinstating Fin-Syn as part of a larger bill aimed at rolling back the deregulation of broadcasting. The Media Ownership Reform Act of 2004 was never voted on.

FM

From a technical perspective, FM, or frequency modulation, differs from AM, or amplitude modulation, in a number of ways. FM waves can be adjusted to remove static but AM cannot. AM can travel great distances, whereas FM is restricted to line of sight. FM signals can even be interrupted by tall buildings. At night, AM signals can bounce off the ionosphere and travel for thousands of miles, even around the curvature of the earth. That is why some AM stations are authorized for daytime hours only. FM signals use more spectrum space than AM, which leads to a corresponding ability of FM to produce higher-fidelity stereo broadcasts.

The history of FM broadcasting is an interesting one. FM broadcasting was invented by Edwin Howard Armstrong in 1933. Working with RCA, Armstrong installed FM transmitter equipment in the Empire State Building and placed the receiver seventy miles away on Long Island. On June 16, 1934, the system was tested and the results were phenomenal. The static, which many believed to be a permanent part of radio, was gone. After the successful test, Armstrong waited to hear from RCA. Instead, he was asked, by letter, to remove his transmitter from the Empire State Building. RCA soon announced that it would spend $1 million on television and made no mention of FM. Armstrong decided to take his invention public and in November 1935 presented a paper on FM to the Institute of Radio Engineers. He also made the first public demonstration of the new technology.

Armstrong then turned to the FCC for spectrum for FM. At the same time, RCA was lobbying heavily for the same spectrum to be given to television. Armstrong asked the Commission for a license for an experimental FM station, and after an initial rejection, he got permission to build a station in Alpine, New Jersey. The station began operating at full power in 1939. Armstrong contracted with General Electric to build FM sets for demonstrations. GE was so impressed that it prepared to manufacture FM radios. Another station was built in Massachusetts and by the end of the year, the FCC had 150 applications for FM stations.

But the Commission had not allocated enough spectrum to FM to meet the growing demand. Despite opposition from RCA, the FCC stripped channel one from the television allocation. More manufacturers began to make FM radios and in 1940, commercial broadcasting on FM was authorized. The Commission also decided that television should have FM sound. Even RCA began to express interest in FM, although the negotiations over royalties were strained, at best. World War II halted this initial development spree and Armstrong, a World War I veteran, made the FM technology available to the military for free. FM became the communications backbone of the Allied effort.

After the war, the FCC, under pressure from RCA and the broadcast networks, moved FM radio to other spectrum space, making all pre-war FM transmitters and receivers useless. The rush to move forward on television continued. The battle between RCA and CBS over the future of color television also impacted FM, with CBS encouraging its affiliates to apply for FM licenses instead of television licenses. The FCC further damaged FM when it announced that AM-FM combination stations could simulcast programming.

At the same time, RCA had been using the FM technology for its televisions for years without paying Armstrong a cent. By 1948, negotiations had broken down completely and Armstrong sued. The suit dragged on for years. By 1953, Armstrong was a broken man, estranged from his friends and family and in poor health. He was finally ready to authorize a settlement and then on January 31, 1954, he put on his hat, coat, and scarf and walked out of the window of his thirteenth-floor apartment.

FM did not stop with Armstrong's death, however. His widow eventually won a settlement from RCA and the technology continued to flourish. FM was key to the development of educational radio. When the Commission moved

FM to its new spectrum, channels were reserved for noncommercial, educational use. In 1961, the FCC authorized FM stations to broadcast in stereo. In 1963, the FCC reversed the rule allowing AM-FM combinations to broadcast the same programming, thus sending many stations looking for a new format. Many programmers took advantage of the higher fidelity by turning to recorded popular music. At the same time, rock and roll was on the rise and was perfectly suited to the sound quality of the new medium. By 1970, FM stations were considered competitive with AM. By 1979, FM had surpassed AM for the first time and began the domination of radio that persists to the present.

FORMATS

While television aims to attract a broad audience, radio is driven by formats that attract narrow audiences. In many markets, there are only a few types of music that are available from commercial radio stations. There are many formats, like classical and jazz, that are offered by only one station in a market, if at all. When a station like that proposes to change from the unique format to something more popular and more commonly available, listeners often complain. This has been particularly true when the format change came as a result of the sale of a station.

In the early 1970s, the power of citizen groups with the FCC was at its highest point (see UUC). Many listeners began organized protests to the Commission when local stations changed formats. The FCC's long-held position was that the choice of entertainment programming belonged solely to the licensee. The decision could be based on any factors the licensee chose, from market forces to personal preference. The Commission maintained that competition between radio stations would lead to providing the formats desired by the audience and the issue of the public interest standard did not apply to format choices.

The citizens groups then turned to the courts for relief. The U.S. Circuit Court of Appeals for the District of Columbia heard a series of cases in the early 1970s involving license transfers that were going to result in format changes. Through cases like *Citizens Committee to Preserve the Voice of the Arts in Atlanta v. FCC* (1970) *and Citizens Committee to Save WEFM v. FCC* (1973), the court began to develop a set of criteria for determining when the FCC was required by the public interest standard to hold a hearing regarding the sale of a station that involved a format change. The court stated that a hearing was not needed if the following were true:

1. There was no significant public complaint about the change.
2. The listening audience for the type of music was too small to be accommodated by the number of stations in the area.
3. There was an adequate substitute for the format available in the listening area.

4. The format was not economically feasible even with proper management.

In January 1976, the Commission issued a Notice of Inquiry seeking public comment on whether it should be involved in programming decisions like format changes. The Commission later issued a Policy Statement in which it concluded that the Communications Act did not compel it to review format changes. Several interest groups challenged the FCC's policy statement and the D.C. Circuit threw out the rules. In *FCC v. WNCN Listeners Guild* (1981), the Supreme Court sided with the FCC, stating that the Commission's position that the market is the best determiner of entertainment did not violate the public interest standard.

FREE ADVERTISING FOR POLITICAL CANDIDATES

Television advertising has become the most expensive part of political campaigns. In 1972, political candidates spent $25 million on television. In the 2004 election cycle, candidates, political parties, and independent groups spent more than $1.6 billion on television ads in the largest 100 television markets. That figure does not include money spent in the 111 smaller markets or on cable. The TNSMI/Campaign Media Analysis Group collected some startling numbers about the 2004 political campaign. In Tampa, Florida, 47,738 political ads were aired leading up the 2004 election. The entire state of Florida saw $236,663,482 worth of ads. One station in the primary lead-off state of New Hampshire, WMUR, sold 16,404 ads. WPVI, in Philadelphia, sold $23,827,987 worth of ads.

In opposition to the waves of advertising, 2004 saw a significant drop in news coverage, particularly of local campaigns. According to the Lear Center Local News Archive, half-hour local news programs in so-called battleground states averaged three minutes of campaign news and six minutes of campaign advertising. Only 29 percent of the stories focused on issues and only 1 percent of the stories examined the claims made in political ads. Most stories focused on the polls and campaign strategy. As Senator John McCain described it, "[i]f a local candidate wants to be on television and can't afford to advertise, his only hope may be to have a freak accident."[14]

Not only is money an issue, but the increasingly negative tone of political ads has also raised concerns. To some activists, the answer to many of the campaign financing woes is mandating that broadcasters give free time to candidates for federal office.

Since 1970, there have been attempts to limit candidate spending. The Political Broadcast Act of 1970 set limits on broadcast spending and was passed by Congress but vetoed by President Nixon. The 1971 Campaign Act, which applied only to the 1972 election cycle, limited federal candidates' media expenditures to no more than ten cents per voter or $50,000, whichever was greater, with a maximum of 60 percent of that money going to broadcast advertising. In 1974, Congress passed the Federal Election Campaign Act amendments that aimed to completely overhaul campaign laws and included mandatory federal campaign spending limits. The FECA amendments never went into effect, however, because the Supreme Court's decision in *Buckley v. Valeo* (1976) determined that political expenditures were essentially speech and thus protected by the First Amendment. Since that case, any attempt to regulate spending has been considered constitutionally suspect.

Various proposals regarding free airtime for candidates have been advanced in the last decade or so. Some involve vouchers given to candidates when they have raised enough small donations from eligible voters in their districts. Others involve stations setting aside time in one- or two-minute increments in the weeks leading up to the elections. Commissioners like Reed Hundt have publicly supported the idea of free time for candidates. The early versions of the Bipartisan Campaign Finance Reform Act of 2002 (also known as McCain-Feingold) included a small amount of free airtime for candidates. Lobbyists for the broadcast industry, however, were so opposed that those sections were removed before the bill came to a vote. Senator McCain and others have continued to lobby for mandatory free time for candidates as part of broadcasting's transition to digital.

HARD LIQUOR ADVERTISING

Beer and wine companies have advertised on television for years, but until 1996, one form of alcohol was missing: so-called hard liquors like whiskey and rum. The Distilled Spirits Council of the United States (DISCUS), which prefers the term "distilled spirits," had imposed a ban on radio advertising by its members in 1936 and extended the ban to television in 1946. The NAB code had also banned hard liquor advertising, while allowing beer and wine.

That all changed in June 1996 when Seagram's broke the self-imposed ban and ran an ad for Crown Royal Whiskey on a Corpus Christi, Texas, television station. In November, DISCUS chose to lift the ban completely, citing the fact that technology and television had advanced to the point that it was easy for their members to place ads at times when the majority of the audience was over twenty-one. In addition, DISCUS research found that in the two years before the ban was lifted, 30 to 50 percent of Americans thought distilled spirits were already advertised on television.

In April 1997, President Bill Clinton called on the FCC to investigate the effects of hard liquor advertising on television. In July of that year, Chairman Reed Hundt wanted the FCC to issue a Notice of Inquiry on the question of regulating hard liquor advertising. Commissioners James Quello and Rachelle Chong voted against it, stating that any advertising regulation was the responsibility of the Federal Trade Commission.

Even after the ban was lifted, the ads were not seen on the broadcast networks. NBC broke ranks in December 2001, when it agreed to run ads for

Smirnoff vodka that focused on designated drivers. The ads were supposed to be followed up with product-focused commercials for Smirnoff and other brands sold by parent company Diageo. NBC cancelled the contract after intense outcry from public interest groups and Congress. DISCUS claims that the real pressure came from beer companies that did not want the competition.

Although the broadcast network's bans still hold, there were more than $100 million worth of ads shown in 2004. They have appeared on more than two dozen cable channels, hundreds of local cable systems, and more than 600 local broadcast stations. CNN became the first news network to accept hard liquor advertising with a March 2005 commercial for Grey Goose vodka. In 2005, NASCAR also lifted its ban on sponsorships of cars by distilled spirits companies, giving further television presence to the hard liquor brands.

Hard liquor advertising is still not seen everywhere, however. A number of states do regulate liquor advertising on television and radio, but those laws are being challenged and overturned. In *44 Liquormart, Inc. v. Rhode Island* (1996), the Supreme Court struck down the state's ban on advertising liquor prices as an unconstitutional restriction of free speech. In *Utah Licensed Beverage Ass'n v. Leavitt* (2001), the U.S. Court of Appeals for the Tenth Circuit enjoined the state of Utah from enforcing a ban on the advertising of hard liquor, also citing free speech concerns.

HOAXES

The FCC's ban on broadcast hoaxes originated with a 1991 stunt by WALE-AM in Providence, Rhode Island. The station's news director announced that an employee had been shot in the head outside the station. Police and other media outlets rushed to the scene. After about ten minutes, the station announced it had been a dramatization. WALE-AM apologized and offered to pay for the police officers' time. The FCC told the station that the announcement was not in the public interest.

The following year, the Commission established a hoax policy. It is now against Commission rules to broadcast *knowingly* false information concerning a crime or a catastrophe if it is foreseeable that the broadcast will cause substantial public harm or the broadcast does, in fact, cause harm. Public harm is defined as immediate and actual damage to property or the health and safety of the general public. Diverting police or other public safety officials away from their duties is also considered a public harm. If a station includes a disclaimer that the program is fiction, it will not be considered an illegal hoax.

LEASED ACCESS CABLE CHANNELS

A cable system has absolute control over what channels come into a subscriber's home. Because of this control, Congress required that large cable systems set aside channel space for sale in the Cable Act of 1984. If a system carried thirty-six to fifty-four channels, it was required to reserve 10 percent of those channels for leased access. If the system carried more than fifty-five channels, it was required to reserve 15 percent for leased access. The belief was that if independent content producers could buy inexpensive airtime, more ideas could come into the marketplace. The FCC was given jurisdiction over the rates that cable systems could charge for these leased access channels. Since these channels are unlikely to be booked twenty-four hours a day, seven days a week, systems are allowed to air regular cable programming until time is requested.

Under the 1984 Cable Act, cable systems were barred from editing or censoring leased access programming in any way. Congress altered this position slightly in the Cable Act of 1992, allowing cable systems to reject sexually explicit leased access programming if it so chose. In the Telecommunications Act of 1996, Congress went even further by requiring that cable systems segregate any sexually explicit programming to one channel. That channel had to be fully scrambled and customers could only get access to the channel if they requested it in writing thirty days in advance.

In *Denver Area Educational Telecommunications Consortium, Inc. v. FCC* (1996), the Supreme Court said that cable systems could reject legally obscene programming, but that it could not reject shows that were merely sexually explicit or featured nudity. The Court also threw out the provisions of the law that required segregation and scrambling of those programs. Finally, the Court said that the requirement that customers request these leased access channels in writing was a violation to the viewers' First Amendment rights.

A case in the U.S. Court of Appeals for the Second Circuit further outlined the First Amendment rights of leased access programming producers. Beginning in 1993, Thomas Loce and Ed Richter produced a program called *Life Without Shame* for the Rochester and Syracuse cable systems owned by Time Warner. The program aired at midnight and featured female nude dancers from area clubs. The program was controversial and community members repeatedly asked Time Warner to stop carrying it.

After the Supreme Court's decision in the *Denver* case, Time Warner adopted a written policy forbidding indecent material on its leased access channels. In 1997, Loce and Richter submitted three episodes of *Life Without Shame* to Time Warner and they were rejected as inappropriate under the new policy. Time Warner also said that it would no longer accept any programming for consideration from Loce and Richter.

Loce and Richter turned to the courts, arguing that Time Warner had trampled on their First Amendment rights by rejecting the programming and by banning them from the cable systems. The Second Circuit upheld Time Warner's policy barring indecent leased access programming. But the court also said that Time Warner's refusal to consider future programming from Loce and Richter was not acceptable. So while cable systems can ban certain sexually explicit programs, they cannot have a blanket refusal for anyone who has submitted an unacceptable program in the past.

LOCALISM

Localism means reflecting the local community's needs and interests. From the beginning of broadcasting, one of the FCC's main concerns was that radio and television stations serve their local market. Localism was first debated as the government considered how to allocate the spectrum for the newly developed technology of radio. There were those who argued that a few clear channel stations with the power to serve the entire country would be the best use of the new technology. But the belief that all local communities should be served locally won out and the Communications Act specifically required the FCC to create a "fair, efficient, and equitable distribution of radio."

Broadcast radio and television stations are licensed to serve local communities. For many years, the Commission favored local ownership and management in deciding between competing applicants for a license. The belief was that a local owner who lived in the local community would be the best judge of that community's needs. The requirement that local stations do ascertainment and keep programming logs was also related to the concept of localism. Ascertainment was seen as a way for the licensees to better know how to serve their local communities (*see* Ascertainment). The requirement to keep programming logs was created so that stations could easily demonstrate how they served the public interest. Both requirements were eliminated in the deregulation of the 1980s.

From the beginning, there have been a few basic rules regarding how a licensee had to serve its local community. Stations had to provide service to the entire local community in which it was licensed. The main studio had to be in or near the community in which it was licensed. The main studio also had to be a toll-free phone call for those within the station's community of license. Finally, the station's public file must be kept at the main studio with the local issues/program list (*see* Public Files).

When the Telecommunications Act of 1996 allowed for further consolidation in both the radio and television industries, many people called for a return to an emphasis on local service. Public interest groups like Free Press have been active in lobbying the FCC and Congress. Much criticism has been levied against large media companies for not adequately serving the needs of their communities of license. The consolidation issue got a lot of attention when a 2002 train accident in Minot, North Dakota, released a toxic cloud at 1:00 A.M. Police tried to reach local radio stations to have them broadcast warnings about the chemical spill and trigger the Emergency Broadcast System [EBS], but no one answered the phones at any of the six stations and the EBS system did not work. All six stations were owned by Clear Channel, the largest radio group in the country, and some say that the reason that no one was at any of the stations was because Clear Channel has done so much cost cutting and uses so much satellite programming.

Localism again became a topic of discussion as part of the FCC's actions on media ownership (*see* Media Ownership). Some at the Commission, including Commissioner Michael Copps, were critical of Chairman Michael Powell's willingness to allow media companies to grow even larger. The Senate Commerce Committee held a hearing that was bipartisan in its criticism of the Commission's attempts to allow a single company to own enough television stations to reach 45 percent of the nation.

In August 2003, Chairman Powell launched a localism initiative. Powell said he would work toward promoting and increasing low power FM stations. He also oversaw the creation of the Localism Task Force, which was charged with studying the issue of localism, organizing public hearings on the topic, advising the Commission on how to promote localism, and advising the Commission on legislative recommendations to Congress to strengthen localism. So far, public hearings on localism have been held in Charlotte, NC (10/22/03), San Antonio, TX (1/28/04), Rapid City, SD (5/26/04), and Monterey, CA (7/21/04).

The final part of the Localism initiative was the issuance of a Notice of Inquiry on July 1, 2004. The Commission presented a long list of questions regarding broadcast licensees' service to their local community. Reponses to the NOI were due in 2005 and respondents were asked to comment on the following questions:

- How can stations best communicate with their communities of license?

- Should the Commission set specific requirements for the nature and amount of community-responsive programming?

- How are broadcasters currently serving their local communities and does the FCC need to take action on this matter?

- Are market forces sufficient motivation for stations to provide community-responsive programming?

- Are there differences between radio and television when considering matters of localism?

- What is the cost of community-responsive programming and can stations afford that cost?

- What types of public service announcements are broadcast on local stations and what times of day do they air?

- Do stations refuse to air public service announcements or require the organization to buy matching commercial time?

- What kinds of political programming are being carried by local stations and should they be required to carry more or different kinds?

- Is there any way the Commission can encourage or require more coverage of local political issues?
- Are stations serving the minority communities in their areas of license?
- Are stations providing adequate warning of impending disasters and are there ways in which stations can improve the disaster warning systems?
- Have stations abdicated control to national networks, rather than making programming decisions based on the needs of the local community?
- Are music-oriented radio stations violating the payola and plugola rules?
- Do music-oriented radio stations serve the needs and tastes of the local community or have practices like voice-tracking (importing out-of-town DJs who simply record announcements to run between songs) and national play lists damaged the local nature of radio?
- Does the FCC's eight-year license term and policy of not allowing competing applications serve the public interest?
- Are new license renewal procedures needed?
- What can the FCC do to further promote low power FM?

LOTTERIES

From the beginning of broadcasting, federal law has restricted information about lotteries from the nation's airwaves. A lottery is defined as a contest or game involving three things: prize, chance, and consideration. For a contest to be considered a lottery, the prize must be of more than token value. Chance means that no real skill is involved. Consideration generally means that money has been exchanged, like in buying a ticket. The Commission tried to ban radio "give away" programs in the 1950s under the lottery restriction. These programs would give prizes to the "right" caller or to audience members who answered a trivia questions correctly. Since there was no consideration involved, the Supreme Court overturned the Commission in *FCC v. American Broadcasting Co.* (1954).

There have been a number of exceptions to the lottery rule added over the years. The first came in the 1970s. Many states had begun lotteries as a way to raise money for education and other funding priorities. As a result, Congress allowed stations to broadcast advertisements and information about state-run lotteries in states where they were legal. But in *United States v. Edge Broadcasting* (1993), the Supreme Court upheld the restriction on lottery advertising in states without a lottery, even if the station's audience is largely in the adjoining state with a lottery.

There are three other exceptions to the lottery rule. The first is that broadcast stations may carry advertising for casinos operated on tribal land. The second exception is the advertisement of lotteries run by a nonprofit or governmental organization, like church bingo games or school fundraising casino nights. Finally, ads may be aired for lotteries conducted as a promotion for a business that is not in the business of lotteries, such as door prizes at furniture stores.

Advertisements for private, for-profit casinos continued to be banned throughout the 1990s. In 1999, however, the Supreme Court ruled that in states where such casinos were legal, broadcast stations could legally carry ads (*Greater New Orleans Broadcasting Association v. United States*).

LOW POWER FM RADIO

Full power FM stations must broadcast at a minimum of 6,000 watts, giving them a reach between eighteen and sixty miles. Most stations are far more powerful broadcasting over a far greater range. Low power FM stations, often called micro radio, generally broadcast at ten or 100-watts, reaching between one and three and a half miles. Although low power FM has been an issue for the last five years, the beginnings of low power broadcasting reach back to the 1940s.

In 1948, the Commission began issuing what were called Class D licenses to educational institutions for stations broadcasting at ten-watts or less. These licenses were a continual source of controversy, and in 1978 the Commission stopped issuing the Class D licenses and encouraged existing stations to up-grade to at least 100-watts if not full power.

The roots of the current low power movement can be seen in two places—"pirate" radio and the Telecommunications Act of 1996. During the 1980s, there was an upsurge in unlicensed micro broadcasters, including Mbanna Kantako's 2-watt station in the John Hay Homes Housing Project in Springfield, Illinois, and Radio Free Berkeley. The FCC did not look kindly on the pirate broadcasters and issued fines whenever an unlicensed broadcaster was caught. The Telecom Act then removed most of the ownership restrictions on radio. As a result, the industry saw enormous consolidation. For example, Clear Channel Communications quickly controlled nearly 1,200 radio stations across the country, representing approximately 9 percent of all stations. That kind of consolidation led many to call for a local radio service that would serve those who were being ignored by giants like Clear Channel.

The current low power FM plan originated with petitions from media activists J. Rodger Skinner, Nickolaus and Judith Leggett, and Donald Schellhardt in 1998. In January 1999, the Commission issued a Notice of Proposed Rulemaking on the matter. A year later, the Commission announced plans for three new classes of radio stations to serve the unmet needs of local communities. The stations would be licensed to noncommercial, educational entities and public safety and transportation organizations. No one with interests in other media, newspapers or broadcast, would be eligible for the new class of stations. The first licenses would be issued at the 100-watt power level. When the first window for construction permits opened in May 2000, 720 applications were filed.

Opposition to the plan was instantaneous and vehement. The NAB was adamantly opposed, claiming that the new stations would interfere with and thus destroy all radio broadcasting. In addition to increasing its Congressional lobbying budget by 800 percent, the NAB asked the U.S. Court of Appeals for the District of Columbia Circuit to prevent the new rules from taking effect. National Public Radio (NPR) was also opposed, claiming that public radio stations would be especially vulnerable to interference. The biggest problems for the Commission's plans, however, came from the Congressional allies of both groups.

FCC engineering studies showed that interference would not be a problem, even in congested city markets. At the behest of the NAB and NPR, Congress required that the Commission make more studies. The Congressional studies reached the same conclusions as the earlier FCC studies—interference was not going to be a problem. The House then passed the Radio Broadcasting Preservation Act, which dictated to the FCC how it was to deal with spectrum allocation issues. The House bill would have made low power FM impossible in most larger markets. The Senate also introduced a version of the Radio Broadcasting Preservation Act, which would have banned low power FM altogether. Eventually, a rider to an appropriations bill mandating certain protections for full power FM stations was passed. The FCC continued to move forward on low power FM during all the industry and Congressional maneuverings.

According the FCC, in March 2005 there were 590 low power stations serving mostly small- and medium-sized markets. Rulemaking on the issue continues through the summer and fall of 2005, as the future shape of the service continues to evolve.

LOW POWER TELEVISION

Low power television (LPTV) was created in 1982 by the FCC. The goal of LPTV is to provide locally oriented television service for small communities. These communities can be in rural areas or be specific communities in urban areas. According to the FCC, LPTV has opened up more opportunities for entry into television and allowed for local self-expression and better use of the broadcast spectrum. LPTV program content faces only minimal FCC regulation, but stations must not broadcast indecent material between 6:00 A.M. and 10:00 P.M.

LPTV stations do not have any particular channels set aside for the service; the FCC merely fits a station where an open channel exists. LPTV stations have "secondary spectrum priority," meaning that they cannot interfere with the signal of any full power television station and they must accept any interference with their own signal from any full power station. LPTV stations are limited in their effective power, although tower placement and height are open. The distance a LPTV signal can travel varies with tower placement and height, transmitter power, and the environment (rural vs. urban, hilly vs. flat).

As of March 31, 2005, there were 2,071 low power television stations licensed in the United States. Unlike low power FM, there are no limits on how many LPTV stations one person or group can own. LPTV stations are operated by a wide variety of groups, from educational institutions like high schools and colleges to civic groups, churches, governments, and even individual citizens. Programming on LPTV is as varied as the owners and includes syndicated programming, movies, and locally produced shows. LPTV often focuses programming or programming blocks on foreign language and ethnic programming to serve minority and immigrant communities.

MEDIA OWNERSHIP

The Telecommunications Act of 1996 rewrote most of the media ownership regulations (see Telecommunications Act of 1996 and Broadcasting; Telecommunications Act of 1996 and Cable). In addition to the immediate changes, Congress ordered the Commission to perform a biennial review of all other media ownership rules to see if the rules continued to be in the public interest or if competition in the marketplace made the rules unnecessary.

After the 1998 Biennial Review, the Commission decided to keep in place the 35 percent cap on national television ownership and the broadcast-cable cross-ownership rule, which banned common ownership of a broadcast station and a cable television system in the same market. Various television networks and cable systems appealed the Commission's decision not to change the rules. In *Fox Television Stations, Inc. v. FCC* (2002), the U.S. Court of Appeals for the District of Columbia Circuit stated that the Commission's decision was not based on any real analysis of competition in the television industry and did not explain why it was necessary to keep the rules. The court ordered the Commission to reconsider whether the two rules were still needed.

On June 2, 2003, the FCC announced that it had completed a review of the media ownership provisions. The review took more than twenty months and compiled a record of more than 520,000 comments. To aid in its analysis, the Commission developed a Diversity Index to measure how many diverse voices a community receives. The Commission also reaffirmed that localism was one of its primary goals. The Commission considered six areas of ownership regulations.

1. *Dual Network Ownership:* The Commission decided to keep the prohibition on any of the Big Four networks merging with each other.

2. *Local Television Multiple Ownership Limit:* The FCC altered these rules. The new rules state:

- Companies may own two television stations in markets with at least five stations. Only one station can be in the top four as measured by ratings.
- Companies may own three television stations in markets with at least eighteen stations. Only one station can be in the top four as measured by ratings.
- Both commercial and noncommercial stations are to be counted when determining ownership levels.
- The Commission established a waiver process for a case-by-case analysis of any situation when two top-rated stations wish to merge in markets with eleven or fewer stations.

3. *National Television Ownership Limits:* The Commission increased the cap on national ownership of television stations to allow companies to own stations that reach 45 percent of the national audience. UHF stations, because of their lower signal strength, will continue to be counted at 50 percent of their market audiences.

4. *Local Radio Ownership Limit:* The FCC kept the local radio ownership limits at the level set by the Telecom Act (*see* Table 5.2 in Telecommunications Act of 1996 and Broadcasting).

5. *Cross-Media Limits:* The FCC drafted a new rule to replace the old broadcast-newspaper and radio-television cross-ownership rules.

- In markets with three or fewer television stations, no cross-ownership is allowed between radio, television, and newspapers.
- In markets with between four and eight television stations, combinations are limited to one of the following:
  - a daily newspaper; one TV station; and up to half of the radio station limit for that market (i.e., if the radio limit in the market is six, the company can only own three) or
  - a daily newspaper; and up to the radio station limit for that market (i.e., no TV stations) or
  - two TV stations (if permissible under local TV ownership rule); up to the radio station limit for that market (i.e., no daily newspapers).
- In markets with more than nine television station, the FCC eliminated all cross-ownership bans.

6. *Radio and Television Transferability Limited to Small Businesses:* Some media companies violate the new ownership limits. These companies will be grandfathered in, allowing them to continue to own above the limit. But companies may not sell any above-the-cap groups as a unit. The FCC made an exception to that prohibition when the sale is being made to what the Commission defines as a small business. This exception was put into place to protect small media companies and aid an effort to increase minority- and female-owned media companies.

The new rules were immediately appealed. In *Prometheus Radio Project v. FCC* (2004), the U.S. Court of Appeals for the Third Circuit said that the Commission had not appropriately justified the changes to the media ownership rules and ordered the Commission to revise the 2003 guidelines. In June 2005, the Supreme Court refused to hear the case. The FCC was supposed to again take up the issue of the media ownership rules at one of its summer 2005 meetings, but the topic was dropped off the agenda without explanation. It is believed that Chairman Kevin Martin will consider each media ownership rule separately, instead of Chairman Powell's attempt at a blanket revisions of all the rules. Commissioners Michael Copps and Jonathan Adelstein have been vocal in their opposition to allowing any further consolidation in the media.

MINORITY OWNERSHIP

Just as there has long been concern about increasing female and minority employment in the media (*see* Equal Employment Opportunities), there has been concern about increasing female and minority ownership of the media. In 1968, the National Advisory Commission on Civil Disorders, or the Kerner Commission, said that the race riots in the summer of 1967 could be blamed, in part, on the failure of the media to cover racial issues and the concerns of the minority communities. This report brought the issue of minority employment and ownership to the forefront at the Commission. Throughout the 1970s, there was debate at the Commission and in the courts over the connection between diversity of ownership and diversity of viewpoints. In 1973, the U.S. Court of Appeals for the District of Columbia Circuit stated in *TV-9, Inc. v. FCC* that increasing minority ownership would lead to an increase in diversity of content. The court went on to point out that in 1971 only ten radio stations and no television stations were minority-owned.

In 1978, the Commission determined that little improvement had been made since the *TV-9* case and that specific remedies were needed. The FCC created two policies to increase ownership among minorities and women: enhanced licensing preferences and the distress sale policy. Enhanced licensing preferences involved how the Commission weighted competing applications for a license. If there were two applicants of equal merit for the same license and one of the applicants was a minority or a women, that application would get enhanced consideration and be weighted more heavily. The distress sale policy said that if a license was set for a revocation hearing, that licensee could sell the station to a minority applicant without the required hearing. These policies were controversial from the very beginning.

In the mid-1980s, the Fowler FCC was deregulating much of broadcasting and sought to removed the two diversity policies. In 1985, after the U.S. Court of Appeals for the District of Columbia Circuit ruled against the use of gender preferences in comparative license hearings in *Steele v. FCC*, the

Commission announced it would abandon all minority-related policies. Even after *Steele* was vacated by the court, the FCC wanted to remove the policies. Congress, however, ordered the Commission to reinstate them in 1988.

In 1989, the U.S. Court of Appeals for the District of Columbia Circuit addressed the FCC's attempts to increase minority ownership. In *Winter Park Communications, Inc. v. FCC* (1989), the court upheld the enhancement policy for minority applicants in a comparative hearing. In *Shurberg Broadcasting of Hartford, Inc. v. FCC* (1989), the court struck down the distress sale policy as unconstitutional, stating that the Commission had never proven any connection between diversity of ownership and diversity of programming. The matter was settled by the Supreme Court in *Metro Broadcasting, Inc. v. FCC* (1990). In *Metro*, the Court ruled that the FCC's policies were constitutional and served to promote the government interest in increasing minority ownership in broadcasting. This decision was later overruled by a nonbroadcasting case, *Adarand Constructors, Inc. v. Peña* (1995).

The U.S. Court of Appeals for the District of Columbia Circuit also reviewed the FCC's policies on increasing gender diversity. In *Lamprecht v. FCC* (1992), the court held that the connection between gender diversity and programming was not as strong as the connection between minority diversity and programming. Thus, the court found that the FCC's policies for increasing gender diversity of media ownership were in violation of the equal protection clause of the Constitution.

The FCC had instituted a third minority-preference policy in 1978 with the introduction of tax certificates as a way to increase minority ownership of broadcast outlets. These tax certificates allowed a licensee to sell a station to a minority-controlled group and defer the capital gains taxes owed as a result of the sale. Cable company sales were added to the tax certificate program in 1982. Tax certificates were used in more than 300 transactions during their seventeen years in existence. The majority, 254, were for the sales of radio stations.

The program gained notoriety and attention from Congress in 1995 when Viacom announced that it was going to sell its cable systems to a minority-controlled group for $2.3 billion. The tax certificate would have allowed Viacom to defer between $280 and $400 million in taxes. The sheer size of the deal led some in Congress to call it corporate welfare and point out that the certificates benefited the nonminority company far more than the minority company. As a result, Congress ended the tax certificate program in 1995.

MUST CARRY AND RETRANSMISSION CONSENT

In the beginning, cable carried only broadcast television stations. In many cases, cable systems were importing distant signals, even when there were local television stations available. Beginning in 1965, the FCC sought to protect local broadcasters by requiring that cable systems carry them, a concept known as must carry. The FCC, along with the broadcast industry, believed that if cable offered larger stations in direct competition with local ones, the local station would likely go out of business. This would mean that anyone without cable would then lose access to television completely. In addition, if a local station was not carried by cable, viewers would have to disconnect the cable and reconnect the rooftop antenna to switch between them. The FCC believed that most people would not do that and thus broadcast stations would go unwatched. When the dawn of satellites came and cable-only networks like HBO were available all across the country, cable systems had even more programming to chose from. The local broadcasters believed these new cable networks made their carriage even less likely.

The must carry rules were designed to protect the broadcast television industry from economic harm, but the cable industry saw them as an infringement of its rights. Cable systems did not like the fact that programming choice was taken away from them. In the early days of cable, it was not unusual for a system to have capacity for fewer than twenty channels. Cable networks did not like must carry because it made it harder for them to find systems that had room to carry them. In *Quincy Cable TV, Inc. v. FCC* (1985), the U.S. Court of Appeals for the District of Columbia Circuit ruled that the must carry regulations were unconstitutional. The FCC scaled back the rules in response to the court's decision, but in 1987, the new rules still failed to pass the court's scrutiny (*Century Communications Corp. v. FCC*). The court never said that must carry was completely disallowed, just that the FCC had never appropriately justified the rules.

With the Cable Act of 1984, Congress officially repealed the must carry provisions. Although cable systems generally continued to carry the local network affiliates, many small, independent, and public stations were dropped. As a result of public outcry over the state of cable, must carry was reinstated with the Cable Act of 1992. As must carry stands, systems with twelve or fewer channels must carry three eligible stations and systems with more than twelve channels must give up to one-third of their channels to local broadcasters.

The 1992 Cable Act added a twist to must carry—retransmission consent. Retransmission consent recognizes that some local signals are valuable to cable systems and if they were not available, some people might choose not to subscribe to cable. If a station chooses retransmission content, it opens a negotiation with the cable system over payment for cable's carriage of the signal. That payment can be in the form of cash, although that has been rare. More common has been the exchange of channel capacity. Several of the broadcast networks are now parts of larger corporations that own cable networks as well. So when Disney, owner of the ABC television network, sought to launch ESPN2, a cable network, it used retransmission consent. If a cable system wanted to carry the local ABC station, it would have to make room for ESPN2.

The choice between must carry and retransmission consent must be made every three years by commercial stations. Public television stations cannot ask for retransmission consent. Negotiations have not always gone smoothly. There have been incidents when broadcast stations have gone dark when negotiations have broken down. These situations rarely last long, however, since the public tends to get angry when stations are not available.

The cable industry continued to fight must carry in courts throughout the 1990s. The case known as *Turner Broadcasting System, Inc. v. FCC* reached the Supreme Court three times, in 1993, 1994, and 1997. Eventually, a divided Court narrowly upheld must carry as an appropriate step by the Commission to protect broadcast channels from extinction.

Although the issue of must carry appeared to be settled, a new twist came about as a result of the Telecommunications Act of 1996. In the act, Congress moved forward on digital television. All broadcasters would get new spectrum space in which to broadcast a new digital signal. What makes digital television different from analog is that the digital signal has the potential to carry multiple program streams at the same time. As the possibilities offered by the new technology became clear, the cable industry questioned the future of must carry. If a single local broadcast station would be able to send, for example, five different channels of programming at the same time, would the cable system have to carry all five channels?

This question is still being debated. In 2005, the FCC affirmed that only the primary signal of a digital television station will come under the requirements of must carry. However, the National Association of Broadcasters is continuing to fight this decision, maintaining that without full carriage, few would be able to receive the multiple program streams. As the transition to digital television approaches, this issue of digital must carry will continue to be debated.

NATIONAL ASSOCIATION OF BROADCASTERS' CODE

In 1929, the National Association of Broadcasters created a voluntary Radio Code of Conduct. A Television Code was added in the 1950s. A 1966 version of the Code states that one of its principal purposes was "[t]o embody a set of professional standards that reflects broadcaster service to the public."[15] As a practical matter, however, a major purpose of the Code was to implement industry self-regulation in an attempt to forestall less flexible FCC regulation. The provisions of the Code were wide ranging and included standards for programming and advertising to which broadcasters could voluntarily subscribe. Whether members of the NAB or not, broadcasters could "join" the Code by agreeing to abide by its provisions. For broadcasters, the incentive to join the Code was the privilege of displaying the NAB Seal of Good Practice, a mark of prestige within the industry. The NAB enforced the Code through their Code Authority, which could suspend members for violations. In 1978, more than 65 percent of all commercial television stations subscribed to the NAB Television Code.

During the 1970s, the Television Code came under attack from advertisers who believed that some of its provisions violated the antitrust laws. Specifically, advertisers argued that several provisions of the Code had the effect of artificially reducing the supply of available advertising time, in essence acting as a restraint of trade under the Sherman Antitrust Act of 1890. In response to these concerns, the U.S. Department of Justice filed suit against the NAB in 1979. In *United States v. NAB*, three specific sections of the code came under attack.

The first section, known as the time standards, limited the amount of commercial material that could be broadcast each hour. This section limited network-affiliated stations to nine and a half minutes of commercials per hour during prime time and sixteen minutes per hour at all other times.

The second group of provisions, the program interruption standards, set maximum limits on the number of commercial interruptions per hour and the number of consecutive announcements per interruption. Network-affiliated stations could only interrupt prime time programs four times per hour with no more than five consecutive announcements per interruption, only four of which could be commercials. Public service announcements did not count.

The third group of challenged code provisions, the multiple product standard, prohibited the advertising of more than one product or service in a single commercial if the commercial was less than sixty seconds in length.

In March 1982, U.S. District Court Judge Harold Greene issued a summary judgment that the multiple product standard violated of the Sherman Antitrust Act. Following the ruling, the NAB immediately suspended all enforcement of the Code. Later that year, the NAB agreed to end the suit by entering into a consent decree that required it to cancel the challenged portions of the code. Individual networks and stations, however, remained free to impose their own advertising limits.

Since 1982, no portion of the Code has ever been reinstated by the NAB. Several of the networks, however, have incorporated some of the NAB standards into their corporate standards and practices policies.

NEWS DISTORTION

In an era of almost constant accusations of news bias, the Commission is very careful not to overstep its regulatory authority over radio and television. By law, the FCC is not allowed to censor broadcasting beyond a few narrow areas like indecency. The Commission is especially careful not to interfere with a licensee's news judgment. There have been situations, however, when the Commission has believed a station has distorted the news in such a way as to violate the public interest standard. Two examples of what is considered inappropriate news distortion occurred in 1969. In one instance, a station in Chicago staged a "pot party" for the cameras. In another case, the CBS documentary *Hunger in America* showed a child described as suffering from malnutrition who actually had another disease.

The FCC's Web site contains the following statement regarding news distortions and its role in regulating them.

> As public trustees, broadcasters may not intentionally distort the news. Broadcasters are responsible for deciding what their stations present to the public. The FCC has stated publicly that "rigging or slanting the news is a most heinous act against the public interest." The FCC does act to protect the public interest where it has received documented evidence of such rigging or slanting. This kind of evidence could include testimony, in writing or otherwise, from "insiders" or persons who have direct personal knowledge of an intentional falsification of the news. Of particular concern would be evidence about orders from station management to falsify the news. In the absence of such documented evidence, the FCC has stressed that it cannot intervene.[16]

OBSCENE, INDECENT, AND PROFANE SPEECH

Federal law has banned the broadcast of material that is obscene, indecent, or profane since radio technology was first developed. Although those terms were considered basically synonymous when they were first added to communications law, they now mean very different things.

Obscenity is rarely an issue for broadcast stations. Although many people use the word obscenity to describe any portrayal of sexual behavior, the legal meaning of obscenity is very narrow. In *Miller v. California* (1973), the Supreme Court created a three-part test to define obscenity:

- An average person, applying contemporary community standards, must find that the material, as a whole, appeals to the prurient interest;

- The material must depict or describe, in a patently offensive way, sexual conduct specifically defined by applicable law; and

- The material, taken as a whole, must lack serious literary, artistic, political, or scientific value.

Obscene speech is not protected by the First Amendment and cannot be broadcast at any time. The Commission has been and continues to be extremely hesitant to get involved in any obscenity cases, leaving that matter to the FBI and others.

That hesitancy has not been an issue with the enforcement of the indecency rules, however. Throughout the history of broadcasting, indecency has been a major regulatory issue. The Commission currently defines indecency as "language or material that, in context, depicts or describes, in terms patently offensive as measured by contemporary community broadcast standards for the broadcast medium, sexual or excretory organs or activities."[17] Indecent broadcast speech is illegal only when there is a reasonable risk that unsupervised children will be in the audience. FCC rules currently state that broadcast stations can air indecent material without fear of a fine after 10:00 P.M. and before 6:00 A.M. This time is known as the safe harbor.

The FCC does not monitor broadcast stations for indecency, but instead relies on complaints from citizens. Anyone wishing to complain to the Commission must include the following information:

- information regarding the specific details of what was said or depicted (saying a program included disgusting sex talk is not enough), submitted as an excerpt, a tape, or a transcript;
- the date and time of the broadcast; and
- the call sign of the station.

If a broadcast is determined to be indecent by the Commission, a Notice of Apparent Liability is issued. The amount of the fine, or forfeiture, is based on a number of factors, including the number of times the indecency policy was violated and the level of explicitness of the broadcast. Congress tried in 2004 and 2005 to raise the minimum fine for indecency to as high as $500,000 per incident. As of yet, the Broadcast Decency Enforcement Act of 2005 has not become law.

The history of the FCC's regulation of indecency is long and complicated. From almost the beginning of broadcasting, the Commission has gotten complaints about sexual material on radio and television. Any kind of enforcement of the indecency policy, however, was infrequent in the early years of broadcasting; warnings, short-term renewals, and fines for other violations of Commission policy were the norm. But in 1970, the Commission began to seek a test case to help it define an indecency policy. After a few small fines were issued and paid without judicial review, the Commission got its test case in a 1973 Pacifica Foundation broadcast of the George Carlin monologue, "Seven Words You Can Never Say on Television" on radio station WBAI-FM.

Although no fine was issued, Pacifica challenged the constitutionality of the FCC's definition of indecency. The U.S. Court of Appeals for the District of Columbia Circuit ruled for Pacifica, saying that the broadcast was protected speech under the First Amendment. The Supreme Court, however, declared in *FCC v. Pacifica* (1978) that the monologue *as broadcast* was not protected by the First Amendment because broadcasting was different from other media. The Court held that the Carlin monologue was fully protected speech when it was performed in nightclubs, on records, and even transcribed in print. But the Court determined that a broadcast of the monologue was different because of the technological realities of broadcasting. Broadcasting, according to the Supreme Court, is uniquely pervasive and intrusive into the home and uniquely accessible to young children. Pervasive means that broadcast signals come into the home uninvited, and no one can choose which signals are available. The Court believed that people should be free of unwanted sexual material in their own homes. And because even very small children can turn on a radio when their parents are not in the room, the Court believed that broadcasting should be free of indecent programming when there was a reasonable risk that unattended children might be in the audience. The Court did declare, however, that indecent material cannot be completely banned from the broadcast media. Adults do have a right to access adult-oriented material through radio and television. The Court's compromise between protecting children and not overprotecting adults was the notion of a safe harbor. Broadcast stations would be free of indecent material from 6:00 A.M. until 10:00 P.M. After 10:00 P.M., stations would be free to air material that could be considered indecent.

After the Supreme Court's decision in *Pacifica*, the FCC stuck to a policy of policing only the so-called seven dirty words and for nearly ten years issued no fines for the broadcast of indecent speech. In 1987, under pressure from Congress and the Religious Right, the Commission "redefined" indecency to include sexual innuendo. This is how the Commission fined shock jocks like Howard Stern who avoided profanity but reveled in sex. Over the years, Stern racked up fines in the millions and eventually he left over-the-air radio for the regulation-free zone of satellite radio.

Fines for indecency came in waves over the next fifteen years. Whenever someone in Congress would decide it was time to "clean up" radio, the Commission would announce some large fines. The smaller fines were usually paid quietly. The larger fines, like a set totaling $1.7 million for Infinity Broadcasting (the home of Howard Stern and other shock jocks), were

Radio "shock jock" Howard Stern has been fined regularly for broadcast indecency by the FCC. (AP/Wide World Photos)

settled. In exchange for a "voluntary" contribution to the U.S. Treasury, a company's record was wiped clean.

Congress also pursued other ways of "cleaning up" radio. Throughout the 1980s and 1990s, members of Congress like Senators Jesse Helms and Robert Byrd attempted to either ban indecency completely or shrink the safe harbor. The parameters of the safe harbor were debated in a series of cases all known as *Action for Children's Television v. FCC* (1988, 1991, 1993, 1995), heard before the U.S. Court of Appeals for the District of Columbia Circuit. After nearly ten years of litigation, the safe harbor remained at 10:00 P.M. until 6:00 A.M.

As is made clear by Table 5.1, the FCC's prosecution of indecency was at a minimal level throughout most of the 1990s. In 2001, the Commission issued a *Policy Statement* on indecency (included in Appendix 2) that was supposed to clarify what would be considered indecent by the Commission. Although the level of fines went up slowly, things remained mostly quiet until the evening of the 2004 Superbowl. During the half time show, singers Janet Jackson and Justin Timberlake performed a song. At the end of the song, Timberlake was supposed to tear away a portion of Jackson's top. Instead, he removed it all and exposed Jackson's breast for about two seconds to the Superbowl audience. CBS called it a wardrobe malfunction and apologized, but nearly a half million complaints poured into the Commission. In the end, the Commission fined CBS stations $500,000 for the broadcast.

After the Superbowl incident, indecency regulations were a major topic of public conversation. Everyone was worrying about the prevalence of sex on television, from White House to Congress to the Commission. An interest group called the Parents Television Council was monitoring all television broadcasts for examples of indecency and flooded the Commission with complaints. Another record fine, $1.18 million, was issued later that year against FOX broadcasting for *Married by America*, a program that aired nearly a year before the Superbowl incident. The reality show contained scenes featuring nude strippers, although the nudity was pixilated.

Two thousand four was a watershed year for indecency fines, with nearly $8 million worth issued. Stations all over the country were in a panic over any programming that might cross the FCC's line. Shows were cancelled and even PBS began heavily editing programming. But both CBS and FOX have refused to pay their large fines. If the Commission wants to collect, it can ask the Justice Department to go to court to force the companies to pay. So far, however, no such action has been taken. In addition, the emphasis on indecency seems to have faded slightly, and no fines were issued in the first eight months of 2005. But the upswing in indecency prosecutions also impacted the way the Commission looked at mere swearing.

Historically, profanity has been connected to the concept of blasphemy. But the Commission redefined profanity in 2004 as language that "denote[s] certain of those personally reviling epithets naturally tending to provoke

TABLE 5.1. Indecency Complaints and Notices of Apparent Liability, 1993–2004

Calendar Year	# of Complaints Received	# of Programs by Service	# of NALs[1]	# of NALs by Service	$ Amount of NALs[2]	Status
2004	1,405,419 (314 programs)	Radio: 145 TV: 140 Cable: 29	12	Radio: 9 TV: 3	$7,928,080[3]	4 paid, 1 agreed to be paid, 6 pending, 1 cancelled
2003	202,032 (375 programs)	Radio: 122 TV: 217 Cable: 36	3	Radio: 3	$440,000	1 paid, 2 agreed to be paid
2002	13,922 (389 programs)	Radio: 185 TV: 166 Cable: 38	7	Radio: 7	$99,400	2 paid, 3 agreed to be paid, 1 pending, 1 cancelled
2001	346 (152 programs)	Radio: 113 TV: 33 Cable: 6	7	Radio: 6 TV: 1	$91,000	5 paid, 2 cancelled
2000	111 (111 programs)	Radio: 85 TV: 25 Cable: 1	7	Radio: 7	$48,000	5 paid, 2 agreed to be paid
1999	N/A	N/A	3	Radio: 3	$49,000	3 paid
1998	N/A	N/A	6	Radio: 6	$40,000	5 paid, 1 not prosecuted by DOJ
1997	N/A	N/A	7	Radio: 6 TV: 1	$35,500	5 paid, 2 cancelled
1996	N/A	N/A	3	Radio: 3	$25,500	1 paid, 2 cancelled
1995	N/A	N/A	1	Radio: 1	$4,000	1 paid
1994	N/A	N/A	7	Radio: 7	$674,500	4 paid, 3 cancelled
1993	N/A	N/A	5	Radio: 5	$665,000	4 paid, 1 cancelled

[1] An NAL may relate to a complaint for a prior year.
[2] These figures represent the amount of the proposed forfeiture (see also note 3). In some instances, the forfeiture was ultimately reduced or rescinded.
[3] In addition to the number of NALs issued for 2004, this figure includes amounts in the 6/9/04 Clear Channel consent decree ($952,500), the 8/12/04 Emmis consent decree ($258,000), and the 11/23/04 Viacom consent decree ($3,059,580) that exceeded the amounts in NALs settled in the consent decrees.
Source: FCC.

violent resentment or denoting language so grossly offensive to members of the public who actually hear it as to amount to a nuisance."[18]

This new definition arose out of events surrounding the live broadcast of the 2003 Golden Globe Awards. After winning the statue for Best Original Song, Bono, the lead singer of U2, said, "This is really, really, f——ing brilliant. Really, really great."[19] The Enforcement Bureau of the Commission initially decided that the broadcast was not indecent since the f-word was not used in a sexual manner. After heavy protest, however, the Commission reversed the decision. The FCC presented the new definition of profanity and said that it would consider whether other swear words are illegally profane on a case-by-case basis. NBC was not fined for the program, and as of August 2005, no other broadcaster has been fined under the new definition of profanity.

PAYOLA AND PLUGOLA

Payola and plugola refer to violations of the FCC's sponsorship identification rules. Plugola is when a station or one of its employees gives an on-air mention, or "plug," to a product or service in which that person or station has an undisclosed financial interest. Payola is generally defined as taking money or gifts in exchange for airplay. According to the web site www.history-of-rock.com, the word payola might be a contraction of "pay" and "Victrola," an early record player.

Throughout much of radio history it was common practice for record companies to give expensive gifts or even cash to disk jockeys in exchange for airplay for their recording artists. Alan Freed, the DJ credited with coining the term rock and roll, saw his career ruined when he admitted to taking $2,500 from record companies. After the payola scandals of the 1950s, Congress made payola a crime.

Section 317 of the Communications Act, known as the Sponsorship Identification rules, requires that if anyone but the licensee pays for all or part of a program carried on the station, that sponsor or donor must be identified at the time the program is aired. Section 508 applies Section 317 to employees, program producers, and program distributors. Programming that is provided for free or at a nominal charge is exempt from the rule. An example of the exemption is when record companies send new CDs to radio stations for free in the hopes of getting airplay. The FCC can also waive the sponsorship rules, such as when a feature film that includes paid product placement airs on television.

Payola and plugola scandals have continued to surface in the broadcast industry. In the 1980s, payola was rumored to have taken the form of gifts of drugs like cocaine in exchange for airplay. In 2005, New York State Attorney General Eliot Spitzer reached a $10 million settlement with Sony's BMG Music Entertainment after a year-long payola investigation. Spitzer said that

BMG bribed radio programmers with expensive trips and electronics and provided prizes for station contests. The company also made payments to radio stations to cover operating expenses and paid for what were called "spin programs," where a song is played as part of a paid advertisement without the audience knowing. After the BMG settlement was announced, Chairman Kevin Martin and Commissioner Jonathan Adelstein called for an additional FCC investigation into the situation.

Concerns about payola in 2005 also took the form of the airing of video news releases (VNR) without proper identification. VNRs are prepackaged programming segments that are designed to look like news footage. In its simplest form, VNRs are background material, like footage of a production line made available to news stations when a new product is released (also known as B-roll). At the other end of the spectrum, VNRs are completely produced segments with actors playing the role of reporters. The VNR controversy came to public attention when it was revealed that various federal agencies were using VNRs to promote Bush Administration policies like the No Child Left Behind Act. The controversy expanded when it became clear that television stations were airing the government VNRs without any editing or explanation. On April 13, 2005, the FCC issued a Public Notice "reminding" licensees of their obligation under the sponsorship identification rules as well as the rules requiring identification of the source of political programming. The Commission used the Public Notice to ask for comments regarding the use of VNRs by broadcast licensees and cable operators. The Commission also requested comments on how the sponsorship rules should apply to the use of VNRs. The Commission stated that it will open a more formal proceeding if the comments it receives warrant further investigation.

POLITICAL BROADCASTING RULES

Section 315 of the Communications Act contains the political broadcasting rules that broadcasters and cable systems must adhere to when they make the decision to give or sell time to candidates for public office. Section 315 requires that when a legally qualified candidate uses a station or cable system, all other legally qualified candidates for the same office must be given the opportunity to use roughly the equivalent amount of time at a similar time of day. In order for Section 315 requirements to apply, however, a series of legal conditions must be met.

First, Section 315 only applies to "legally qualified" candidates. To be considered legally qualified, candidates need not have a formal party affiliation or even a reasonable chance of winning the election. Candidates need only have publicly declared their candidacy, met all legal eligibility requirements (age, residency, etc.), and qualified for a place on the ballot or established themselves as a committed write-in candidate. While legally qualified candidates must be running for the same office, the FCC has determined that

Section 315 applies differently in primary elections. In primaries, Republicans and Democrats are not considered to be running for the "same office" because they are technically not running against one another. Thus, if a station sells time to a Republican candidate during the primary election cycle, it is only obligated under Section 315 to sell time to other Republicans.

Second, in order for Section 315 to kick in, a candidate for a particular office must have "used" a station or cable system, meaning that their picture or voice must identifiably appear in a commercial or program. The appearance could take place within the context of a political advertisement or a regularly scheduled television show with no reference to politics whatsoever. Section 315 does not apply, however, in the case of news events such as news stories, interviews with candidates on regularly scheduled news program, or political debates. Section 315 also does not apply to situations in which a candidate's opponent uses his image or voice in their own political commercial.

Furthermore, candidates must formally request equal opportunity under Section 315: the broadcaster or cable system is under no legal obligation to notify them of their eligibility. Requests for time must be made within seven days of the incident that triggered Section 315 eligibility. Section 315 also requires broadcasters and cable systems to sell time to eligible candidates at the lowest unit rate for forty-five days before a primary election and sixty days before a general election. Lowest unit rate means that stations can only charge candidates the rate charged to their most favored advertisers. Thus, if an advertiser gets a discount when it buys a large number of ads, that discounted per-ad price is the highest price a station can charge a candidate for even one political ad.

Section 315 also specifies that broadcasters and cable systems cannot edit or alter the content of political advertisements or refuse to air an advertisement because they consider it offensive. Even when the content of the ads is extreme, as in the case of the anti-abortion activists in the 1990s, stations are forbidden from altering or channeling the ads (see Anti-Abortion Political Advertising). Because stations cannot alter or censor political ads, the FCC concluded in the 1948 *Port Huron* decision that broadcasts are protected from libel suits resulting from the ads. This position was upheld by the Supreme Court in *Farmers Educational and Cooperative Union of America v. WDAY, Inc.* (1959).

In addition to the provisions of Section 315, broadcasters and cable systems must adhere to an FCC requirement known as the "Zapple Rule," named after the congressional staff member who first raised the issue. The Zapple Rule applies when a candidate's supporters, rather than the candidate herself, uses a station or cable system. In such a situation, the station or cable system must provide equal opportunity to the supporters of opposing candidates.

Finally, it is important to reiterate that Section 315 does not require stations or cable systems to sell time to any candidate for political office; it only requires equal opportunity when time is given or sold to a candidate in the same race. Section 312(a)(7), however, requires broadcast stations to provide candidates for federal office with "reasonable access" to the airwaves. While "reasonable access" is interpreted quite liberally, it is generally understood that broadcasters cannot refuse to sell time to federal candidates. A challenge to this rule came in 1980 when the three major networks refused to sell thirty minutes of time to the Carter-Mondale presidential campaign. The FCC ordered the networks to sell the time under Section 312(a)(7), a position that was later supported by the Supreme Court in CBS, Inc. v. FCC (1981). That doctrine does not, however, apply to advertising involving issues of controversy. Stations are under no obligation to sell time to groups seeking to air opinions on issues of the day. In CBS, Inc. v. Democratic National Committee (1973), the Supreme Court ruled that stations were well within their rights to refuse to sell advertising to groups wishing to advocate a position.

PRIME TIME ACCESS RULE

The FCC has long been concerned about the dominance of the broadcast networks. In 1970, the Commission tried to limit the networks' power by creating the Prime Time Access rule. This rule reduced network prime time from four hours to three in the top fifty markets. In the Eastern Time Zone, that meant that the 7:00 P.M. hour was returned to the affiliates. The Commission's expectation was that the stations would fill this time with innovative local programming. Instead, most stations added game shows and programs like *Entertainment Tonight*.

The Prime Time Access rule did nothing to limit the power of the networks. In fact, by decreasing network programming by an hour, prime time advertising grew more desirable and thus more expensive, which further increased the network's dominance. The FCC repealed the Prime Time Access rule in 1996.

PUBLIC BROADCASTING

Public broadcasting in the United States exists on both radio and television stations. There are more than 780 public radio stations, largely concentrated in the lower end of the FM dial. Public radio stations are owned by a wide variety of organizations, including educational institutions and community groups. Many public radio stations are affiliated with National Public Radio. NPR is a privately supported, not-for-profit membership organization that produces and distributes noncommercial news, talk, and entertainment programming.

Public television's most prominent face comes in the form of the Public Broadcasting Service (PBS). Founded in 1969, PBS is a private, nonprofit company owned and operated by 348 member public television stations. Those stations are licensed to 169 noncommercial, educational licensees, which include eighty-six community organizations, fifty-seven colleges and universities, twenty state authorities, and six local educational or municipal authorities. PBS is a program distributor, rather than a network. The individual station chooses which programs it will air and when. In 2004, PBS's operating revenue was $333 million. That money came from member station assessments (47%); the Corporation for Public Broadcasting and other federal grants (24%); royalties, license fees, satellite services, and investment income (14%); and educational product sales (12%). PBS spends the bulk of its budget on programming and promotion.

While many countries maintained governmental control over broadcasting and thus established public broadcasting services at the beginnings of the technologies, public broadcasting in the United Stations was slower to develop. The Public Broadcasting Act of 1967 began federal aid for noncommercial, educational broadcasting. The act created the Corporation for Public Broadcasting (CPB) as a private, nonprofit corporation that would serve to insulate public radio and television stations from the partisan bickering of Congress and the White House. During the signing ceremony for the act, President Lyndon Johnson spoke of the importance of public broadcasting in general and the CPB in particular:

> While we work every day to produce new goods and to create new wealth, we want most of all to enrich man's spirit. That is the purpose of this act. It will give a wider and, I think, stronger voice to educational radio and television by providing new funds for broadcast facilities. It will launch a major study of television's use in the Nation's classrooms and their potential use throughout the world. Finally—and most important—it builds a new institution: the Corporation for Public Broadcasting. The Corporation will assist stations and producers who aim for the best in broadcasting good music, in broadcasting exciting plays, and in broadcasting reports on the whole fascinating range of human activity. It will try to prove that what educates can also be exciting. It will get part of its support from our Government. But it will be carefully guarded from Government or from party control. It will be free, and it will be independent—and it will belong to all of our people. Television is still a young invention. But we have learned already that it has immense—even revolutionary—power to change, to change our lives.[20]

Despite the lofty goals of the act, public broadcasting has frequently come under attack from politicians seeking to influence the kind of programming that appears on public radio and television stations. Politicians have questioned the concept of state-supported broadcasting and the perceived liberal bias of its programming since the passage of the Act. President Richard Nixon tried to end CPB funding in the 1970s. In the 1980s President Ronald Reagan tried to dramatically cut the budget, as did Speaker of the House Newt Gingrich in the 1990s. One of PBS's most enduring controversies came with a 1980 program called *Death of a Princess*, a dramatized documentary about the execution of a young Saudi Arabian princess for adultery. Protests poured into PBS from the State Department, Congress, the Saudi government, and Mobil Oil, which was one of PBS's biggest sponsors. Some stations refused to air the program and a group of viewers in Alabama and Texas took their local stations to court, hoping to force the airing of the program. In *Muir v. Alabama Educational Television Commission* (1982), the U.S. Court of Appeals for the Fifth Circuit ruled that the individual stations, not the viewers, held the final decision-making power over programming.

A recent example of political impact on PBS came in 2005. Secretary of Education Margaret Spellings criticized the PBS children's show, *Postcards from Buster*. Buster is a cartoon bunny who visits real children around the country. One episode showed Buster visiting a Vermont family headed by a lesbian couple. Spellings wrote to PBS and asked it to remove the Department of Education (DOE) logo from the show (*Buster* is produced with funding from the DOE's Ready to Learn program) and warn individual stations about the program's content. The letter went further and asked that PBS return the DOE money used to produce the program. As a result, PBS chose not to distribute the episode.

The last few years at the CPB have seen much controversy, beginning when President George W. Bush appointed Ken Tomlinson as the head of the CPB in 2003 (he was initially appointed to the board in 2001 by President Bill Clinton). Tomlinson was critical of what he perceived as an extreme liberal bias in PBS programming. In an effort to fight this "bias," he hired two ombudsmen to monitor and critique NPR and PBS news programs. Both services recoiled at these appointments, since each already had an ombudsman. He also replaced the long-time CPB chief executive with a Republican who served as Chairman Michael Powell's media advisor at the FCC. Shortly thereafter, Tomlinson hired a Bush White House communications officer to oversee the ombudsmen as a "special adviser" to CPB's chief executive. Tomlinson again made headlines when he hired someone to evaluate the political bias in *NOW with Bill Moyers* and several other PBS programs and then refused to release the findings of the taxpayer-funded study. This led Moyers, who served in the Johnson Administration and helped draft the Public Broadcasting Act, to say "I always knew Nixon would be back . . . I just didn't know that this time he would ask to be chairman of the Corporation for Public Broadcasting."[21]

Amid the Tomlinson CPB controversies, Congress was debating whether to continue funding the CPB and, by extension, PBS and NPR. Some members perceive both services as being biased against the Bush Administration and the House Appropriations Committee cut the CPB's budget by 25 percent, or $100 million, in June of 2005. Ohio Representative Ralph Regula's original bill would have removed CPB funding completely by 2008, but Democrats on the committee reinstated the future funding. After much public outcry, the full House of Representatives restored the $100 million to the budget.

PUBLIC, EDUCATIONAL, AND GOVERNMENT CABLE ACCESS CHANNELS

Public, educational, and government (PEG) cable access channels are a way for people in local communities to have their voices and ideas heard. PEG channels grew out of early franchise agreements and competition over localities. Cable systems would build studios and provide training to members of the local community as part of the contract with the municipality. The idea was that these channels and studios would be partial payment for the cable system's use of the public rights-of-way.

The FCC began to encourage cable systems to provide PEG channels in 1969. In 1972, the Commission required cable systems to provide both the channels and the equipment for the production of cable access programming. Cable companies protested this new requirement. In *FCC v. Midwest Video* (1979), the Supreme Court struck down the PEG rules, saying that the Commission had exceeded its authority. The Court ruled that while the Commission could require that cable systems produce their own programming, it could not require them to become a common carrier for other people's opinions. In the Cable Act of 1984, Congress gave local franchise authorities the right to require PEG channels.

According to the Alliance for Community Media (ACM), an advocacy group for public access programmers, there are more than 20,000 hours of local PEG programming produced each week by community groups and individual volunteers around the country (more than NBC, CBS, ABC, FOX, and PBS combined). In a year, more than 1 million people get involved in PEG channel production. On their Web site, www.alliancecm.org, ACM lists just a few of the community groups that produce programming for PEG channels, including "the Lions, Kiwanis and Rotary Clubs, the League of Women Voters, NAACP, AARP, the Urban League, public schools, local Chambers of Commerce, religious institutions, colleges and universities, community theaters, labor unions, veterans groups, second language communities, the disabled, politicians, and political organizations." In addition to the local programming, ACM says that PEG channels carry shows from "NASA, the U.S. Department of Education, the Organization of American States, Members of Congress, the National Guard, the U.S. Army, the U.S. Air Force, the Federal Emergency Management Administration (FEMA), the U.S. Department of Housing and Urban Development (HUD), and various arts organizations such as Annenberg/CPB and Classic Arts Showcase."

With thousands of hours of programming, controversy is bound to arise. Cable companies are not allowed to exert control over the content of cable access channels. In exchange, the cable companies are not liable for any material that is aired. The program producers are the only ones with liability. Over the years, PEG channels have seen many controversies, including whether programs containing hate speech should be allowed. The Ku Klux Klan and the White Aryan Resistance have both used PEG channels for programming that features racial and religious hatred. While some localities tried to ban the material, others have counter-programmed with shows from groups like the Anti-Defamation League.

Concerns about sexually explicit PEG programming have been much more prevalent. Taking advantage of the PEG channel's freedom from oversight, many local producers have chosen to present nudity and other sexually explicit programming. In the Cable Act of 1992, Congress allowed cable systems to prohibit sexually explicit programming on PEG channels. This section of the law was overturned by the Supreme Court's decision in *Denver Area Educational Telecommunications Consortium, Inc. v. FCC* (1996). In a later case, *McClellan v. Cablevision of Connecticut* (1998), the U.S. Court of Appeals for the Second Circuit upheld the right of an independent producer to show sexually explicit programming on cable access.

PUBLIC FILES

Beginning in 1973, the FCC required all radio and television stations to maintain a public file. This was done to encourage communication between the station and the public it is obligated to serve. The file must be kept at the station in a location accessible to the public during regular business hours. If the public file is kept on a computer, the station must provide a terminal on which the public can access the material. The file must contain a variety of materials, including the following:

- the station's license, which lists the technical parameters under which the station operates and the expiration date;
- copies of all applications and reports filed with the Commission, including all renewal applications if a temporary renewal has been issued;
- contour maps indicating the station's signal coverage area;
- copies of any Public Notice announcements regarding the license that the station was required to distribute;
- any citizens agreements the station signs with audience members;
- any material relating to complaints being investigated by the Commission;
- ownership reports that detail the ownership structure of the station;
- copies of any contracts that must be filed with the FCC, including any network affiliate agreements or management consulting contracts;

- the station's equal employment opportunity reports;
- a copy of the FCC publication *The Public and Broadcasting*;
- any letters or e-mails received from the public in the last three years;
- a political file that documents the last two years of political activity at the station, including all requests for time by political candidates, any free time given to candidates, and a complete detailed report on when political spots aired and what was charged for those ads;
- an issues/program report written every three months that details which programs aired on the station that addressed community needs (all reports in a license period must be kept in the file);
- the quarterly children's television programming reports, which detail the station's attempts to serve the instructional and educational needs of children sixteen and under (all reports in a license period must be kept in the file);
- reports on the station's compliance with the advertising limits set on children's programming;
- any radio time brokerage agreements, this is, when the station sells a block of time to a broker who supplies the content and sells the advertising;
- a list of donors to noncommercial stations for the last two years; and
- details of any must carry or retransmission consent agreements.

The Commission takes the public file seriously and issues fines when its staff discovers an incomplete file. For example, in 2005, a station in Missouri was fined $10,000 (later reduced to $3,000) for having an incomplete public file.

PUBLIC INTEREST, CONVENIENCE, AND NECESSITY

"Public interest, convenience, and necessity" is the broad standard contained in the Communications Act of 1934 that is supposed to guide the FCC's regulation of the broadcast industry. The authors of the Communications Act took the standard verbatim from the Radio Act of 1927, where it was first used in the context of broadcast regulation. The "public interest" as a standard for regulation, however, actually has a longer history of being applied to common carrier public utilities such as the railroad and trucking industries.

Public utilities were understood to be industries vested with a "public interest," meaning that their goods and services were so essential to the well-being of society that they needed to be made widely available on a nondiscriminatory basis. Broadcasting, while technically not a public utility, was viewed by the mid 1920s as an industry vested with a public interest because it employed the electromagnetic spectrum—a scarce public resource—to deliver its programming content. In exchange for their use of this valuable public resource, broadcasters were expected to engage in nondiscrimination in their programming decisions, providing a wide range of entertaining and informative content that meets the needs of the local service community.

The interpretation of the public interest standard has evolved over time. The Federal Radio Commission was the first body to define the public interest obligations of broadcasters. In 1928, the FRC issued a list of technical and content guidelines for radio. In 1929, the FRC used a conflict between three stations in Chicago to further explain the public interest standard. The suggestions were both technical and content-based. On the technical front, radio stations were obligated by the public interest standard to limit interference and make sure that radio was accessible to the entire country. On the programming front, stations were to provide well-rounded programming and limit the use of phonographic records.

During its tenure, the FRC also revoked station licenses for not serving the public interest. One example was "Doctor" John R. Brinkley. Brinkley had little or no medical training and was most famous for claiming that he could cure impotence with an operation involving goat glands. He owned KFKB in Milford, Kansas, and would prescribe his line of patent medicines to people over the air. He aired a program called the *Medical Question Box*, which featured him reading letters and diagnosing people over the air, as seen in this example:

> Here's one from Tillie. She says she had an operation, had some trouble 10 years ago. I think the operation was unnecessary, and it isn't very good sense to have an ovary removed with the expectation of motherhood resulting therefrom [sic]. My advice to you is to use Women's Tonic No. 50, 67, and 61. This combination will do for you what you desire if any combination will, after three months persistent use.[22]

The FRC revoked his license, claiming Brinkley operated the station solely for financial gain. The U.S. Court of Appeals for the District of Columbia Circuit ruled in *KFKB Broadcasting Ass'n, Inc. v. Federal Radio Commission* (1931) that evaluating the past performance of a licensee in the light of the public interest is not censorship.

After the FCC replaced the FRC, the quest to clearly define what was meant by public interest, convenience, and necessity continued. The Supreme Court upheld the FCC's right to regulate radio in the public interest in a series of cases including *FCC v. Pottsville Broadcasting Co.* (1938) and *FCC v. Sanders Bros. Radio Station* (1940). In 1941, the Commission decided that network domination of radio was not in the public interest and released the *Chain Broadcasting Regulations*. In *National Broadcasting Co., Inc. v. FCC*

(1943), the Supreme Court again supported the FCC's continuing development of the meaning of public interest, convenience, and necessity.

Following the *NBC* case, the Commission hoped to more clearly define what serving the pubic interest meant. In a 1946 report called *Public Service Responsibility of Broadcast Licenses*, more commonly called the *Blue Book*, the Commission tried to give specific guidance to licensees as to their public interest obligations. These guidelines included less advertising and more local live programming. The broadcast industry overwhelming rejected the *Blue Book* and the Commission eventually backed down (*see Blue Book*).

Another attempt was made to clarify the public interest standard in 1960. The En Banc Programming Inquiry created a list of the programming categories that would fit within the Commission's definition of serving the public interest and established a set of criteria by which broadcasters could better ascertain the needs of their local service community (*see Ascertainment*). The list included "opportunity for local self-expression, the development and use of local talent, programs for children, religious programs, educational programs, public affairs programs, editorialization by licensees, political broadcasts, agricultural programs, news programs, weather and market reports, service to minority groups, and entertainment programs."[23] Since the late 1970s, however, the FCC has backed off many of these regulatory requirements, instead preferring to allow the market to determine the public interest in broadcast programming.

The debate over the public interest standard has gotten new attention as the move to digital broadcasting looms. The Commission issued a Notice of Inquiry in December 1999, asking for comments about how television stations could serve the public interest during and after the transition to digital. The Commission asked for comments on the following topics:

1. the application of television stations' public interest obligations to the new flexibility and capabilities of digital television, such as multiple channel transmission;

2. how television stations could best serve their communities in terms of providing their viewers information on their public interest activities, and using digital technology to provide emergency information in new ways;

3. how DTV broadcasters could increase access to television programming by people with disabilities and further the longstanding legislative and regulatory goals of diversity; and

4. whether broadcasters could enhance the quality of political discourse through uses of the airwaves for political issues and debate.[24]

Subsequent to the NOI, the Commission issued two Notices of Proposed Rulemaking that addressed how stations could better disclose their public interest activities and how stations could best serve children in the digital environment.

Debate over the application of the public interest, convenience, and necessity standard to digital broadcasting will continue for years to come as the transition to digital television advances.

QUIZ SHOW SCANDALS

Quiz shows were some of the most popular programs in the 1950s. Early shows offered only small prizes. But on June 7, 1955, CBS debuted *The $64,000 Question*, sponsored by Revlon cosmetics. The series would keep contestants over several weeks and the prizes would escalate in value. Even "losers" would get a "consolation prize" of a new Cadillac. The show was an immediate success and Revlon sales soared. Stores would frequently run out of whatever products were mentioned on the show. When a twenty-eight-year-old Marine captain named Richard S. McCutchen became the first person to win the $64,000 prize, 55 million people, nearly 85 percent of the nation's television sets, were watching. Louis Cowan, the man who packaged *The $64,000 Question*, became a vice president at CBS.

Within months of the debut of *The $64,000 Question*, hordes of imitators followed. Big money shows were king on television. At one point, *The $64,000 Question* and its follow-up show, *the $64,000 Challenge*, were numbers one and two in the ratings. But the question of how to maintain these ratings plagued the shows' producers. They attempted to increase the drama of the programs with devices like isolation booths and armed guards holding the questions. The producers also wanted to keep popular contestants, since people would tune in to see their favorites win and likely tune out when an unlikable contestant won.

The show *21* first appeared on NBC on October 12, 1956, and was sponsored by Geritol. The show moved to the top of the ratings when a young Columbia University English instructor named Charles Van Doren began to win. Van Doren was the son and nephew of

Charles Van Doren was implicated in the quiz show scandals of the 1950s. (AP/Wide World Photos)

Pulitzer Prize winners and was handsome and cultured. He proved to be incredibly popular with audiences. During his fourteen weeks on *21*, he accumulated winnings of $129,000 and was given a $50,000 contract to appear on *The Today Show*.

Rumors that the big money quiz shows were rigged began to surface shortly after the programs got big. In 1957, *Time* magazine ran a story asking if the shows were rigged. The story said that producers did not outright cheat but would ask questions that they knew contestants knew the answers to.

In 1957, Herbert Stempel went to newspapers in New York claiming that *21* was fixed. Stempel was the contestant beaten by Charles Van Doren on December 5, 1956, after three tie matches. Stempel claimed that the producers required him to come across as poorer than he was, wearing bad suits and a cheap watch. He also claimed that they ordered him to take a dive when it became clear that Van Doren was a more popular contestant. The newspapers did not print the story at the time out of fear of a libel suit. It was only after a contestant on the program *Dotto* proved the show was fixed that Stempel's claims got any real attention. When Stempel's claims became public, Van Doren denied he cheated.

In the meantime, New York County District Attorney Frank Hogan began an investigation and impaneled a grand jury to look into the quiz shows. The grand jury sat for nearly a year and interviewed approximately 150 witnesses. In January 1959, Van Doren, along with many other former contestants, told the grand jury that the quiz shows were on the level. The grand jury, however, found some discrepancies in the testimony. But for some unknown reason, the judge sealed the grand jury presentment. Hogan said later that he believed that only about fifty witnesses told the truth.

Suspicious of the judge's actions, Congress became interested in the truthfulness of the quiz shows. Representative Oren Harris held hearings in October and November 1959. Stempel testified on October 6 and described how producers manipulated the show. *21*'s producers testified and did not contradict Stempel. Van Doren testified on November 2, 1959, and talked about his moral struggle with cheating. Van Doren was fired by NBC and allowed to resign from Columbia.

Ten people eventually pled guilty to perjury and a dozen careers were ruined. The networks cancelled all the quiz shows and claimed they were as duped by the quiz show producers as the American public. They used the scandal as an excuse to completely sever sponsor-controlled programming. President Dwight Eisenhower said that the deceptions were a "terrible thing to do to the American public."[25] At the same time, the FCC was embroiled in scandals of its own, resulting in the resignation of Chairman John Doerfer and Commissioner Richard Mack, and was slow to take any action against the rigged programs or the stations that aired them. Eventually Congress made it a violation of the Communications Act to give help to a contestant on a quiz show.

RAISED EYEBROW

A quote that has been attributed to many people, including Supreme Court Justice Thurgood Marshall and Nixon administration official Clay Whitehead, best sums up the concept of regulation by "raised eyebrow": "The value of the sword of Damocles is that it hangs, not falls." Because the FCC issues only temporary licenses, it holds life and death power over broadcasters. Although the Commission has rarely exercised its power by revoking a license, the threat still remains. This makes broadcasters particularly sensitive to the feelings and inclinations of the Commission. That sensitivity allows the Commission to achieve regulatory goals without actual regulations, or regulation by raised eyebrow.

Regulation by raised eyebrow means that if the FCC suggests that it is unhappy with some situation, broadcasters will react as if a regulation has been handed down. These "suggestions" have often come in the form of speeches made by commissioners at the National Association of Broadcasters annual convention. Commissioners, especially chairmen, have been making speeches at the NAB convention since the beginning of the FCC. Some use the speech as a platform to criticize the industry. Chairman Newton Minow's famous "vast wasteland" comment was made at the 1961 convention and is seen as the motivation behind the short-lived decrease in violent television shows.

A classic case of the Commission achieving a regulatory goal without regulation came at the 1973 NAB convention. Topless Radio was a very popular kind of call-in show on which a male host and female callers discussed various sexual matters. The day before the speech, the Commission issued an inquiry asking if such shows were obscene, indecent, or profane. During his speech, Chairman Dean Burch made his feelings clear when he attacked the "prurient trash that is the stock-in-trade of the sex-oriented radio talk show."[26] Burch went on to suggest that broadcasters voluntarily clean up these programs. Although the inquiry as to the legality of these programs had not happened yet, all such shows were cancelled within a few months of Burch's appearance. The Commission raised its eyebrow, and the industry reacted.

The advantage of regulating by raised eyebrow is that hints and speeches are not reviewable by the courts. If the industry does something because it thinks the Commission wants it to, there is no judicial review. And even when the Commission follows with action, the costs of seeking review are high. After Burch's Topless Radio speech, the FCC issued a $2,000 fine to Sonderling Broadcasting for its Topless Radio program, *Femme Forum*. The FCC encouraged Sonderling to seek judicial review of the order because of the First Amendment questions raised by the fine. Sonderling chose to pay the fine, however, knowing that an appeal would cost far more in money and time than $2,000.

Sometimes the eyebrow comes in the form of an announcement from the Commission. In 1971, the FCC issued a Pubic Notice "reminding" broadcasters that they had a duty to exercise responsible judgment with regard to playing songs that promoted or glorified drug use. This notice was released with a list of songs that the Commission believe contained drug-oriented lyrics, including Peter, Paul, and Mary's "Puff the Magic Dragon." In addition to the song list, the FCC included a copy of a statement to Congress made by Chairman Burch in which he said that he would vote to revoke the license of any station playing songs with drug lyrics. "Puff" and other "suspicious" songs were banned from radio from that day forth.

The real threat of the raised eyebrow is that broadcasters may censor themselves out of fear of the Commission's reaction. In the order denying the *en banc* rehearing of *Illinois Citizens Committee for Broadcasting v. FCC* (1974), Chief Judge David Bazelon of the U.S. Court of Appeals for the District of Columbia Circuit, wrote about the raised eyebrow when describing why he would have reheard the case:

> [L]icensees are dependent on the FCC and the government for their economic well-being. The main threat is, of course, that the government can put a licensee out of business but I suppose that the more pervasive threat lies in the sub rosa bureaucratic hassling which the Commission can impose on the licensee, i.e. responding to FCC inquiries, forcing expensive consultation with counsel, immense record-keeping and the various attendant inconveniences.... For better or worse, a licensee confronted with the choice between an economic disadvantage and pleading the government through curtailment of a constitutional right will generally choose curtailment. Thus, licensee political or artistic expression is particularly vulnerable to the "raised eyebrow" of the FCC; faced with the threat of economic injury, the licensee will choose in many cases to avoid controversial speech in order to forestall that injury.[27]

An example of this can be seen in 2004 in the unwillingness of sixty-six ABC affiliates to air the feature film *Saving Private Ryan* for fear of an indecency fine, even though the movie had aired on Veteran's Day in 2001 and 2002 without incident.

The FCC has raised its eyebrow in recent years by creating "voluntary" standards for the industries it regulates. The television ratings system was created "voluntarily" by the industry. (*See* V-Chip and Television Ratings.) It was voluntary in the sense that if the industry had not done it, the FCC said it would. In 2002, Chairman Michael Powell offered a "voluntary" plan to advance digital television, by "encouraging" broadcasters to offer digital programming. So the FCC encourages without requiring, getting the industry to do what it wants without the messy business of regulation.

SATELLITE AND LOCAL INTO LOCAL

The first home satellite dishes appeared in the 1970s and did not bring in local television stations. Because of the size of the large dishes (four to eight feet across) needed by these early satellite services, most did not consider them a reasonable competitor to cable. But as the size of the dish shrank (eighteen to twenty-four inches) to what is commonly seen with Direct Broadcast Satellite (DBS), the potential for DBS to become a wireless competitor with cable became evident. There were many at the Commission and in Congress who supported the idea of competition for cable services without the need to build new cable infrastructure.

Cable's competitive advantage against DBS was its carriage of local broadcast signals. It took both technology and legislative advancements to put DBS on an equal footing. As the technology of DBS advanced to the point that systems could send local channels into the local markets, cable attempted to block DBS from carrying local signals. Senators Patrick Leahy and Orrin Hatch introduced the Satellite Home Viewer Improvement Act (SHVIA) of 1999. SHVIA does not *require* that satellite companies offer local channels; it gives them the *option* to provide what is called local-into-local service. The law also allows DBS to import distant broadcast signals if a subscriber does not live within the broadcast range of any television station. When a DBS provider has chosen to provide local-into-local service, it must carry any local station that asks to be carried. If there are two stations affiliated with the same network in a service area, the DBS company is required to carry only one.

SHVIA had a sunset provision and was set to expire. The Satellite Home Viewer Extension & Reauthorization Act (SHVERA) of 2004 renewed the local-into-local provisions. SHVERA also allowed DBS provider to offer certain "significantly viewed" distant signals.

SPECTRUM SCARCITY

The electromagnetic spectrum over which broadcast signals travel is finite. If a person has enough money, he or she can start a newspaper or magazine any time in any location. Not everyone who wants a radio or television station can start one, however, even if they have the money. It is that "scarcity" that provides the rationale for most broadcast regulation. It is because of spectrum scarcity that broadcast licensees are required to serve the public interest, convenience, and necessity.

The Supreme Court first recognized spectrum scarcity in *National Broadcasting Co., Inc. v. FCC* (1943). In *Red Lion v. FCC* (1969), the Court went further when it placed the First Amendment rights of the listeners over the rights of the broadcasters because the licensees had access to the airwaves that most people did not.

In an era when cable and DBS offer hundreds of channels and the Internet offers almost an infinite supply of web sites, some have raised questions about the scarcity rationale for regulation of the broadcast media. Commission debates over issues like television ownership caps and the proliferation of wireless communication and broadband have all involved issues of spectrum scarcity. When Michael Powell was chairman of the Commission, he was vocal in arguing that scarcity no longer existed, even if the physical limits of the spectrum still did. Powell talked about the diversity of voices available in the media market as the end of spectrum scarcity as a rationale for regulation. Chairman Kevin Martin, while not as dismissive of spectrum scarcity as Chairman Powell, has maintained that the Commission must look at broadcasting and broadcasting regulation differently from the past, without the blind adherence to the scarcity rationale.

TELECOMMUNICATIONS ACT OF 1996 AND BROADCASTING

The Telecommunication Act of 1996 was the first major overhaul of the nation's communications regulatory structure in sixty-two years. Technologies that did not exist when the Communications Act was passed were now household items and the rewrite of the law was long overdue. The Telecom Act was signed into law by President Bill Clinton on February 8, 1996, and affected all aspects of communications policy in the United States.

Broadcasting got a lot of attention in the bill, with particular focus on ownership. Television station ownership caps are based not on the number of stations, but the number of people those stations reach. Before the Act, television station groups could own stations with a maximum reach of 25 percent of the viewing public. The Telecom Act raised that limit to 35 percent. In the years following the Act, the broadcast industry has continued to fight to make that higher (*see* Media Ownership). The Telecom Act also mandated that the one-to-a-market rule that forbade the ownership of radio and television stations in the same market be waived in the top fifty markets.

Radio station ownership caps had always been based on numbers of stations. Before the Telecom Act, radio station groups were limited to twenty AM and twenty FM stations. After the Act, ownership caps on radio were lifted. This allowed companies like Clear Channel to buy huge numbers of stations. By 2000, Clear Channel owned or programmed approximately 1,200 stations, 9 percent of all the radio stations in the United States. Some regulations regarding multiple radio station ownership in a single market did remain in place, however, as shown in Table 5.2. Although the Telecom Act left a number of ownership restrictions in place, it also required the Commission to perform biennial reviews of all remaining ownership rules to see if continuing them serves the public interest (*see* Media Ownership).

Radio and television licenses were extended to eight years by the Telecom Act. The act also made it more difficult for other groups to file competing

TABLE 5.2. Local Radio Ownership Limits under the Telecommunications Act of 1996

Number of Commercial Stations in the Market	Maximum Number of Stations That May Be Held by One Party	Maximum Number of Stations in the Same Service (AM or FM) That May Be Held by One Party
45 or more	8	5
30–44	7	4
15–29	6	4
14 or less	5 or no more than 50%	3

applications when unhappy with the current licensee's performance. Competing applications will now only be accepted if the Commission has already determined that the licensee has not lived up to its public interest obligations.

The Telecom Act also addresses network regulation. The Chain Broadcasting Rules banned companies from owning more than one network in 1941. The Telecom Act permitted the Big Four networks (ABC, CBS, FOX, and NBC) to buy smaller networks or create new ones. This provision led to CBS's relationship with UPN and NBC's relationship with PAX. The Telecom Act also removed the broadcast-cable cross-ownership ban and allowed broadcast networks to own cable television systems. Under the act, stations may also now affiliate with more than one network.

The Telecom Act called for the creation of a ratings system for broadcast and cable programming and mandated that all television sets larger than thirteen inches manufactured after January 1, 2000, include the V-Chip technology (*see* V-Chip and Television Ratings).

The biggest issue for television broadcasters was the assignment of spectrum for digital television. There was much debate during the writing of the Telecom Act over whether stations should pay for their use of the digital spectrum. Powerful senators like Bob Dole and John McCain supported the notion of spectrum fees and claimed they would bring in approximately $70 billion dollars. In the end, however, the television licensees got the new digital channels for the price they had been paying for the old analog ones: nothing. The act also set deadlines for the transition to digital, but those have been altered in the intervening years (*see* Digital and High Definition Television).

TELECOMMUNICATIONS ACT OF 1996 AND CABLE

The cable provisions of the Telecommunications Act of 1996 focused on structural and ownership issues. Cable systems would now face competition from telephone companies or could be owned by them. In addition, cable system could now provide a range of telecommunications services. On other ownership matters the anti trafficking provisions were removed. Previous to the act, a cable system could not be sold less than three years after it was purchased. Now a franchising authority had only 120 days to approve or object to a proposed purchase. The act touched on equipment regulation as well. Local franchising authorities could no longer establish any equipment or technical standards beyond those imposed by the FCC. The act also restructured the way that cable companies record equipment and start-up costs. Finally, the act deregulated rates, mandating that the FCC's rate regulation of the basic cable tier end on March 31, 1999.

UHF

Early television was carried on channels two through thirteen on what was known as the very high frequency band, or VHF. On April 14, 1952, the FCC issued the *Sixth Report and Order* on the development of television, which added channels fourteen through eighty-three to the television allocation. These new channels were on the ultrahigh frequency band, or UHF. With this new allocation, the *Order* called for an additional 2,053 television stations in 1,291 communities. Of these stations, 242 were reserved for noncommercial, educational broadcast stations.

Many people applied for the new channels, but there were problems associated with UHF. One problem was that UHF signals do not travel as far as VHF signals. The FCC tried to compensate for this by allowing UHF stations to broadcast at more than sixteen times the maximum power of VHF. The flaw in that plan, however, was that no one had ever manufactured a UHF transmitter that was that powerful. The second problem with UHF was that few of the more than seventeen million television sets in homes in 1952 could pick up UHF stations. Without viewers, there was little or no advertising revenue. The third problem was that few of the new UHF stations were affiliated with the networks. Most people were primarily interested in watching network programming and thus were not interested in spending the money for a UHF converter. Without the programming, there was no audience and again, without the audience, no advertisers. Most UHF licensees lost money and many let their stations go dark and returned the licenses to the Commission.

By 1956, it was clear that UHF was in deep trouble and the FCC was concerned that it would not survive. In 1961 and 1962, the Commission focused on the transmitter problem and eventually was able to send a UHF signal as far as a VHF one. Although the Commission could do nothing about the network affiliation issue, it did lobby Congress about the receiver issue. In 1962, Congress passed the All-Channel Receiver Act, which required that every television set sold in the United States after April 30, 1964, include UHF. The Commission later imposed rules mandating that sets be designed such that UHF tuning was comparable to VHF tuning. The cable must carry rules also helped strengthen UHF stations, since cable erased any differences between UHF and VHF.

The FCC's attention to UHF paid off by 1975, when UHF stations, as a group, finally made a profit. UHF stations gained even further with the creation of FOX, UPN, and the WB. These start-up networks turned to the previously unaffiliated UHF stations to build their national broadcast services and UHF finally had the network programming that would attract audiences.

UNITED CHURCH OF CHRIST CASE (WBLT)

Despite the fact that the FCC is charged with regulating broadcasting in the *public* interest, convenience, and necessity, members of the actual public were never considered to have a role (or standing) in licensing decisions made by the Commission until 1966. This issue of "standing" was at the heart of the appellate court decision in *Office of Communication of the United Church of Christ v. Federal Communications Commission* (1966).

During the Montgomery Bus Boycott of 1955–1956, Martin Luther King, Jr. met with leaders of northern churches to discuss the issues confronting the Civil Rights movement. One topic of concern was the portrayal of African Americans on southern radio and television stations. One of the people at this meeting was Reverend Everett C. Parker, the director of the Office of Communication of the United Church of Christ (UCC). Following that meeting, Parker went to the South to evaluate the coverage of issues of concern to the African American community, particularly civil rights. Parker found that most stations held the segregationist line.

Parker then went to the NAB with a draft of some suggestions for fair treatment of the African American community. The guidelines asked stations to air diverse programming, to use titles like "Mr." and "Miss" for African Americans, to provide them the opportunity to express their views on the air, and to accord them equal opportunity to buy air time. The president of the NAB, former Florida Governor Le Roy Collins, agreed, but the board of directors of the NAB voted it down unanimously.

The UCC then chose to pursue the matter with the Commission. It decided to challenge the license renewals of two television stations in Jackson, Mississippi: WLBT and WJTV. The population of Jackson at the time was approximately 45 percent African American and the FCC had received a number of complaints over the years about WLBT's programming bias. Parker discovered that WLBT had a habit of blacking out the national news and the *Today* show whenever topics of interest to the African American community were shown. The station would preempt the news with local political programming or even preface network shows with commentary like, "What you are about to see is an example of biased, managed, northern news."[28]

The station manager even publicly bragged that when Thurgood Marshall, then general counsel of the NAACP, appeared on a 1955 broadcast of NBC's *Home*, the station had "cable trouble" and did not air the program.

UCC filed a *Petition to Intervene and to Deny Application for Renewal* when WLBT's license came up for renewal in 1964. Although some at the Commission wanted the UCC's evidence to be considered, the final vote dismissed the UCC's petition because of a lack of standing. WJTV received a full three-year renewal, promising that it would do better. WLBT was given a one-year probationary license, since the station claimed it had done nothing wrong. UCC then appealed the Commission's decision to the U.S. Court of Appeals for the District of Columbia Circuit.

The Court of Appeals held that not only did UCC, in fact, have standing to challenge a license as a representative of the public, but the Commission had erred in renewing WLBT's license. After much legal wrangling, a hearing was held in Jackson in May 1967. The FCC's hearing examiner demonstrated considerable bias toward the station during the hearing, including refusing to allow some UCC witnesses to testify. The hearing examiner recommended that the station be given a full three-year license and the Commission approved the renewal in a five-to-two vote. Commissioners Cox and Johnson filed an angry dissent that was more than seven times longer than the majority opinion.

The UCC then returned to the Court of Appeals. Judge Warren Burger wrote a blistering opinion in which he reversed the renewal and ordered the FCC not only to reconsider its decision but also to invite other applicants to apply for the WLBT license.

UCC stayed active in the fight over the license and eventually helped organize and finance a local, integrated group called Communications Improvement, Inc. to run the station until new owners could be found. WLBT was finally licensed to a group that was 98 percent owned by African Americans in 1983.

UCC's activity on the WLBT license represented a high-water mark for civic involvement at the Commission. It opened the door to many groups to challenge station license renewals because of programming decisions. UCC stayed active in the public interest movement, bringing a number of other suits against the Commission over the years.

V-CHIP AND TELEVISION RATINGS

Concerns about violence on television have existed for as long as television has been in the nation's homes. Since the 1950s, Congress has held hearing after hearing on whether violence should be regulated by the Commission. While no specific laws have ever come out of the hearings, the message about violent television programming gets sent to the broadcast and cable industries (*see* Raised Eyebrow).

With Section 551 of the Telecommunication Act of 1996, Congress sought to give parents greater control over the amounts of sex and violence available to their children through the television set. A new technology, known as the V-Chip, had to be installed in all televisions larger than thirteen

President Clinton holds up a V-Chip at an address in 1996. The term "V-Chip" refers to a technology that allows parents to block out undesirable television programming. (AP/Wide World Photos)

inches manufactured after January 1, 2000. The V-Chip could read any ratings sent with the programs and block them according to parentally set guidelines. Section 551 also encouraged the broadcast and cable industry to "establish voluntary rules for rating programming that contains sexual, violent or other indecent material about which parents should be informed before it is displayed to children," and to voluntarily broadcast signals containing these ratings. The ratings, also known as the TV Parental Guidelines, were developed by the broadcast industry, under the supervision of the FCC. The following ratings and descriptions can be found on the FCC's Parent's Place web site.

TV-Y (All Children—This program is designed to be appropriate for all children.) Whether animated or live-action, the themes and elements in this program are specifically designed for a very young audience, including children from ages 2–6. This program is not expected to frighten younger children.

TV-Y7 (Directed to Older Children—This program is designed for children age 7 and above.) It may be more appropriate for children who have acquired the developmental skills needed to distinguish between make-believe and reality. Themes and elements in this program may include mild fantasy or comedic violence, or may frighten children under the age of 7. Therefore, parents may wish to consider the suitability of this program for their very young children. Note: For those programs where fantasy violence may be more intense or more combative than other programs in this category, such programs will be designated TV-Y7-FV. For programs designed for the entire audience, the general categories are:

TV-G (General Audience—Most parents would find this program suitable for all ages.) Although this rating does not signify a program designed specifically for children, most parents may let younger children watch this program unattended. It contains little or no violence, no strong language and little or no sexual dialogue or situations.

TV-PG (Parental Guidance Suggested—This program contains material that parents may find unsuitable for younger children.) Many parents may want to watch it with their younger children. The theme itself may call for parental guidance and/or the program contains one or more of the following: moderate violence (V), some sexual situations (S), infrequent coarse language (L), or some suggestive dialogue (D).

TV-14 (Parents Strongly Cautioned—This program contains some material that many parents would find unsuitable for children under 14 years of age.) Parents are strongly urged to exercise greater care in monitoring this program and are cautioned against letting children under the age of 14 watch unattended. This program contains one or more of the following: intense violence (V), intense sexual situations (S), strong coarse language (L), or intensely suggestive dialogue (D).

TV-MA (Mature Audience Only—This program is specifically designed to be viewed by adults and therefore may be unsuitable for children under 17.) This program contains one or more of the following: graphic violence (V), explicit sexual activity (S), or crude indecent language (L).[29]

VIDEO DESCRIPTION

Video description is an assistive technology aimed at helping those with impaired vision enjoy television programming. Video description is an audio track that describes settings and actions that are not otherwise conveyed by the dialog. The verbal description is inserted into natural pauses in the audio of a program, allowing people to "hear what they cannot see."[30] The video description is carried over the Secondary Audio Programming (SAP) channel, available on most newer televisions.

The FCC was ordered to make an inquiry regarding video description by Congress in the Telecommunications Act of 1996. The Commission issued the Notice of Proposed Rulemaking on Implementation of Video Description of Video Programming on November 18, 1999, and adopted video description rules on July 21, 2000. The new rules ordered stations in the top twenty-five markets affiliated with ABC, CBS, FOX, and NBC to provide roughly four hours of described prime time or children's programming each week. Cable and DBS systems with more than 50,000 subscribers must provide a similar amount of described programming on any of the top five national non-broadcast networks they carry. Finally, all stations, no matter the market size, must "pass through" any video description it receives from a program producer if it has the technology to do so. The Commission also ruled that emergency programming, like weather warnings or disasters, must be described if that description is vital to understanding the situation. These rules were supposed to take full effect in April of 2002.

The Motion Picture Association of America and other groups asked the FCC to reconsider the video description rules. When the Commission upheld their rules, the groups turned to the courts. The U.S. Court of Appeals for the District of Columbia Circuit overturned the video description rules in November 2002 on two grounds. First, the court held that Congress had only asked the FCC to make an inquiry and not create rules, thus the Commission had gone beyond its statutory authority. Second, the court maintained that the video description rules were an impermissible content regulation on broadcasting.

The Video Description Restoration Act of 2003 was proposed shortly after the D.C. Circuit's decision by the American Foundation for the Blind. The bill was then introduced in Congress by Senator John McCain in June 2003 and would have reinstated the video description rules. The bill was reintroduced in 2004 and in 2005 by Senator McCain and Representative Ed Markey. The 2005 version of the bill currently remains in committee.

NOTES

1. Quoted in Erik Barnouw, *The Golden Web: A History of Broadcasting in the United States from 1933 to 1953* (New York: Oxford University Press, 1968), 232.

2. Quoted in ibid., 231.

3. Quoted in ibid., 233.

4. Quoted in ibid., 234.

5. Richard Campbell, Christopher R. Martin, and Bettina Fabos, *Media and Culture*, 5th ed. (Boston: Bedford/St. Martin's, 2006), 201.

6. Quoted in Barnouw, 172.

7. *Banzhaf v. FCC*, 132 U.S.App.D.C. 14, 405 F.2d 1082 (1968).

8. Federal Communications Commission, "Closed Captioning," www.fcc.gov/cgb/consumerfacts/closedcaption.html (accessed on August 21, 2005).

9. "Television History—The First 75 Years," http://www.tvhistory.tv/timeline 3.htm.

10. Susan L. Brinson, "Reds Need Not Apply: Communism and the FCC, 1940–1960," *Communication Law and Policy* 7 (2002): 107–128.

11. "What Is DTV?" Digital Television, www.dtv.gov/whatisdtv.html (accessed on August 30, 2005).

12. 8 F.C.C. 333 (1941).

13. F. Leslie Smith, John W. Wright, and David Ostroff, *Perspectives on Radio and Television: Telecommunications in the United States* (Mahwah, NJ: Lawrence Erlbaum Associates, 1998), 463.

14. "US Senator John McCain (R-AZ) Holds a News Conference on Broadcasters' Coverage of the 2004 Election Cycle," Congressional Quarterly Transcripts, February 15, 2005.

15. Quoted in Val E. Limburg, "Decline of Broadcast Ethics: US v. NAB," *Journal of Mass Media Ethics* 4 (1989): 218.

16. Federal Communications Commission, "Complaints About Broadcast Journalism," http://ftp.fcc.gov/cgb/consumerfacts/journalism.html (accessed on August 19, 2005).

17. Federal Communications Commission, "Obscene, Profane, and Indecent Broadcasts," www.fcc.gov/cgb/consumerfacts/obscene.html (accessed on August 24, 2005).

18. Ibid.

19. *Complaints against Various Broadcast Licensees Regarding Their Airing of the Golden Globe Awards Program*, F.C.C. 04-43 (released on March 18, 2004).

20. Corporation for Public Broadcasting, "Remarks of President Lyndon B. Johnson upon Signing the Public Broadcasting Act of 1967," www.cpb.org/aboutpb/act/remarks.html (accessed on August 23, 2005).

21. "Bill Moyers Responds to CPB's Tomlinson Charges of Liberal Bias: "We Were Getting It Right, But Not Right Wing," Democracy Now, www.democracynow.org/article.pl?sid=05/05/16/1329245 (accessed on August 28, 2005).

22. *KFKB Broadcasting Ass'n, Inc. v. Federal Radio Commission*, 47 F.2d 670 at 671 (1931).

23. *1960 En Banc Programming Inquiry*, 44 F.C.C. 2303 at 2314.

24. Federal Communications Commission, "FCC Begins Proceeding to Seek Comment on Public Interest Obligations of Television Broadcasters as They Transition to Digital Transmission Technology," http://ftp.fcc.gov/Bureaus/Mass_Media/News_Releases/1999/nrmm9030.html (accessed on August 26, 2005).

25. *Broadcasting*, October 26, 1959, cited in Erik Barnouw, *The Image Empire: A History of Broadcasting in the United States from 1953* (New York: Oxford University Press, 1970), 126.

26. John C. Carlin, "The Rise and Fall of Topless Radio," *Journal of Communications* (Winter 1976), 31.

27. 33 Rad. Reg. 2d (P&F) 117 (1975).

28. Robert B. Horwitz, "Broadcast Reform Revisited: Reverend Everett C. Parker and the 'Standing' Case," *The Communications Review* 2, no. 3 (1997): 311–348.

29. Federal Communications Commission, "The TV Parental Guidelines," www.fcc.gov/parents/parent_guide.html (accessed on August 23, 2005).

30. 47 C.F.R. § 79.3.

★ 6 ★

Biographies of the Commissioners

Federal Communications commissioners are appointed by the president with the advice and consent of the U.S. Senate. When the Commission was established, there were seven commissioners who were appointed to fill staggered seven-year terms. No more than four members of the Commission were allowed to be from the president's political party. The chair of the Commission is designated by the president and is almost always a member of his political party. At first, the commissioners were appointed to oversee particular industries. But by 1937, the commissioners served as a single unit, cooperatively doing all the Commission's business. In the early 1980s, Congress restructured the Commission to only five members with five-year terms.

Sixty-five men and ten women have served as commissioners since 1934. There have been nine minority commissioners, including one Asian American, three Hispanic Americans, and five African Americans. The average age at which the commissioners were appointed was 45.8. Three commissioners were appointed at the youngest age of thirty-two. The oldest was appointed at sixty-four. The average length of service was 69.9 months. If you remove the five longest-serving commissioners (more than eighteen years), that average changes to 54.7 months, less than a full term. There have been thirty-nine Democrats, two Independents, and thirty-four Republicans. In the realm of education, there have been three commissioners with Ph.D.s and four who held master's degrees. Forty-seven of the commissioners had some type of legal education. Fifty-eight had no prior experience at the Commission. Fifty-three of the commissioners were serving in some form of local, state, or federal government position before being appointed, including three members of the House of Representatives and two governors. The majority of those who came from outside the government were lawyers in private practice.

KATHLEEN Q. ABERNATHY (MAY 31, 2001–DECEMBER 9, 2005)

Commissioner Kathleen Abernathy was appointed by President George W. Bush in May 2001. Her experience was mostly in the telecommunications sector, having worked as a legal advisor and a lobbyist for both telephone and wireless companies. Born in Kentucky, Abernathy was educated at Marquette University (B.S., speech pathology) and the Catholic University School of Law. In the early 1990s, Abernathy served as a legal advisor to Commissioners James Quello and Sherrie Marshall. She was president of the Federal Communications Bar Association in 1996–1997.

Abernathy was considered a reliable vote for Chairman Michael Powell while she was at the Commission, and she has avoided public confrontations with the other commissioners. One exception was the clash over the deregulation of media ownership. Commissioner Abernathy wrote that such regulation was "anathema to the First Amendment." In a 2003 Congressional hearing, she was grilled by Democratic lawmakers upset over the FCC's position on the issue.

Abernathy has teamed with the Consumer and Government Affairs Bureau to create the FCC's "Parent's Place," a web site dedicated to helping "parents deal with, decipher, and monitor the communications that their children can access." As part of her Commission duties, Abernathy has also chaired the Federal-State Joint Board on Universal Service. Philosophically, Abernathy has expressed concern that government rules could slow technological development.

Abernathy's term expired in 2004. She remained at the Commission until the end of 2005, awaiting President Bush's announcement of her replacement. When Bush made no move to replace her, she departed the FCC on December 9, 2005.

JONATHAN S. ADELSTEIN (DECEMBER 3, 2002–PRESENT)

Commissioner Jonathan Adelstein was appointed as a Democratic member of the Commission in 2002 to complete Commissioner Gloria Tristani's term and reappointed for a full five-year term in 2004. Before his nomination, Adelstein spent fifteen years as a staff member in the Senate, including seven years as a senior legislative aide to fellow South Dakotan, Senate Majority Leader Tom Daschle. Adelstein was educated at Stanford University, receiving both a bachelors in political science and a master's in history. Adelstein was considered a specialist in telecommunications and technology.

Harkening to his rural roots, Commissioner Adelstein has focused his attention on issues like spectrum management and universal service. Adelstein is best known, however, for his clashes with the Republican majority over the issue of media ownership. His dedication to localism has led him to organize, with fellow Democratic Commissioner Michael Copps, a series of public hearings around the country on the issue of the centralization of the media and the resulting reduction in localism. Adelstein also spoke out in 2005 on the issue of payola and the acceptance of undisclosed promotions in a speech he described as a "major policy statement." The speech, called "Fresh Is Not as Fresh as Frozen: A Response to the Commercialization of American Media," was delivered to the Media Institute.

ANDREW C. BARRETT (SEPTEMBER 8, 1989–MARCH 30, 1996)

Commissioner Andrew Barrett was appointed in 1989 by President George H. W. Bush. He came to the Commission from the Illinois Commerce Commission, where he was known for his advocacy of telecommunications deregulation. Barrett also served as the director of operations of the Illinois Law Commission and the executive director of the Chicago office of the NAACP. Barrett held both a master's in economics from Loyola University and a law degree from DePaul College of Law.

Barrett was considered a swing vote on the Commission and had an acrimonious relationship with Chairman Reed Hundt. He voted frequently in favor of the rights of the broadcast industry, including opposing calls to punish Infinity Broadcasting by not allowing them to buy additional stations as a result of the Howard Stern indecency debacle. He also opposed the rules requiring three hours per week of children's programming. Barrett helped broker a compromise on the network fin-syn rules. In a departure from his normal deregulatory stance, Barrett was vocal on media ownership, particularly concerning the impact of further consolidation on minority broadcasters.

Barrett left the Commission in 1996 to work as a lobbyist and consultant.

ROBERT T. BARTLEY (MARCH 6, 1952–JUNE 30, 1972)

Commissioner Robert T. Bartley was appointed and reappointed by Presidents Truman, Eisenhower, and Johnson. Born in Texas, Bartley studied business at Southern Methodist University and entered government service in 1932. He worked in a variety of positions, including statistician for the House Interstate Commerce Committee. When the FCC was created, he joined the staff as the director of the telegraph division. Commissioner Bartley also had broadcasting experience as the vice president of the Yankee Network in Boston and the National Association of Broadcasters' director of war time activities. Immediately prior to joining the Commission, Bartley served four years as administrative assistant to House Speaker Sam Rayburn, his uncle.

Commissioner Bartley opposed attempts by the FCC to limit the amount of advertising on radio and television. One of the longest serving commissioners, Bartley became critical of the FCC in later years. He believed the agency needed to be abolished or completely restructured because of its inability to deal with rapidly changing technology. Bartley also proposed that the terms of the commissioners be increased to a single fifteen-year term and that they be barred from employment in any industry regulated by the Commission. He thought this would insulate the members of the Commission from industry pressure.

Commissioner Bartley died of heart and lung ailments on January 8, 1988.

THADDEUS H. BROWN (JULY 11, 1934–JUNE 30, 1940)

Commissioner Thad Brown was appointed by President Franklin Roosevelt to the newly created Federal Communications Commission in 1934. He had been a member of the Federal Radio Commission as well as its general counsel. Prior to joining the FRC, Brown was general counsel to the Federal Power Commission. Brown was brought to Washington by his friend Herbert Hoover, whose Ohio campaign he ran in 1928. Brown was the Ohio Secretary of State for four years before moving to Washington. He was educated at Ohio Wesleyan University and the Ohio State University.

Commissioner Brown was renominated by President Roosevelt in 1940, but his hearing was derailed by a scandal involving RCA. After several months of waiting for the Senate, Brown resigned from the Commission and asked the president to withdraw the nomination.

Commissioner Brown died February 25, 1941, at the age of fifty-four.

TYRONE BROWN (NOVEMBER 15, 1977–JANUARY 31, 1981)

Commissioner Tyrone Brown was appointed by President Carter to fill out the term of Commissioner Ben Hooks. Brown graduated from Cornell Law School and then served as a clerk for U.S. Supreme Court Chief Justice Earl Warren. Commissioner Brown's communications experience came in the form of a stint as general counsel for the Post-Newsweek Stations. At the time of his appointment, he was a lawyer in private practice at a tax law firm.

While on the Commission, Brown spoke out on the issues of minority ownership, localism, and the continued need for the public interest standard in broadcasting. As the only African American member at the time, Brown publicly clashed with Commissioner Anne Jones, the only female member, on whether it was the FCC's responsibility to enforce equal opportunity rules on broadcasters. Brown was also known for working closely with Chairman Charles Ferris on the move toward increasing competition and decreasing regulation.

Commissioner Brown resigned from the FCC when Ronald Reagan took office in 1981 to return to private practice.

DEAN BURCH (OCTOBER 31, 1969–MARCH 8, 1974)

Chairman Dean Burch was nominated by President Richard Nixon in 1969. Burch was a conservative Arizona Republican closely associated with Senator Barry Goldwater. He served as an aide to Goldwater in the late 1950s and was the chair of the Republican National Committee in 1964 during Goldwater's presidential run. He was educated at the University of Arizona (L.L.B) and interwove a number of political positions with a private law practice.

While at the Commission, Burch often spoke of the importance of the Fairness Doctrine, diversity of ownership, and the quality of children's television. Burch also perfected the concept of regulation by "raised eyebrow" during a speech to the National Association of Broadcasters in 1973. In that speech, Burch was highly critical of the genre of talk radio programming known as "Topless Radio." Almost immediately after the speech, all programming in that category disappeared.

Chairman Burch left the FCC to become White House political counsel in the waning days of the Nixon administration. He stayed on during the Ford Administration, helping orchestrate Ford's win of the Republican nomination in 1976. In the 1980s Burch stayed active in the Republican party as the chairman of the vice presidential campaign of his close friend George H. W. Bush. Burch was also a top advisor during Bush's successful presidential campaign in 1988.

In 1987, Burch was chosen to be the director general of the scandal-racked communications satellite consortium, Intelsat.

Chairman Burch died of cancer on August 4, 1991.

NORMAN S. CASE (JULY 11, 1934–JUNE 30, 1945)

Commissioner Norman Case was the governor of Rhode Island when brought to the FCC by President Franklin Roosevelt. He and the president were personal friends from the time Roosevelt was governor of New York. Case graduated from Brown University (A.B.) and studied law at Harvard and Boston University. He served as a U.S. Attorney in Rhode Island before becoming lieutenant governor in 1927. He became governor upon the death of Aram J. Pothier in 1928.

While at the Commission, Case chaired a committee studying "superpower" broadcasting. Case dissented in the chain broadcasting decision that forced NBC to sell off the Blue network, believing that the Commission did not have the authority.

Commissioner Case died in Rhode Island in 1967.

RACHELLE B. CHONG (MAY 23, 1994–NOVEMBER 3, 1997)

Commissioner Rachelle Chong was appointed to a Republican seat on the Commission by President Bill Clinton. Chong had a decade of experience practicing telecommunications law in both Washington, D.C., and California. A third-generation Chinese American, she was the first person of Asian descent on the FCC. Chong graduated from the University of California-Berkeley with dual degrees in political science and journalism. A member of Phi Beta Kappa, Chong went on to get her law degree from Hastings College of Law, where she was the editor-in-chief of COMM/ENT, the school's journal of communications and entertainment law.

While at the Commission, Chong was a strong advocate for more competition and less government regulation. Chong viewed herself as a staunch defender of the First Amendment, opposing content regulations on the media. Although an advocate for better programming for children, she opposed the three-hour requirement for children's television, believing a quota would be a threat to the First Amendment. She also opposed Chairman Reed Hundt on the issue of whether to regulate hard liquor advertising.

While some commissioners have gotten attention for not owning a television set when nominated, Chong was an avid media user, regularly surfing the internet and even answering e-mails to the Commission personally. A self-proclaimed "Trekkie," she was known to wear a "Federation" pin while at the Commission.

Chong was expected to be renominated in 1997. Senator John McCain, however, pushed for the appointment of Justice Department attorney Michael Powell in her place. Chong lobbied heavily to keep her job, including marshalling support from National Association of Broadcasters president Eddie Fritts and Cellular Telecommunications Industry Association president Thomas Wheeler. In the end, Senator McCain's wishes prevailed and Michael Powell took her seat on the Commission.

After leaving the FCC, Chong returned to private practice and served on a number of boards, including the Association of Public Television Stations and Corsair Communications. Chong also ran her own mediation firm that specialized in communications, media, and the Internet industries. In addition, she was the president of Carina Jewelry, Inc., a retail store and e-commerce site specializing in Italian jewelry.

MICHAEL J. COPPS (MAY 31, 2001–PRESENT)

Commissioner Michael Copps grew up in Milwaukee, Wisconsin, and was educated at Wofford College (B.A. in history) in South Carolina. After receiving a Ph.D. in American history from the University of North Carolina, he taught at Loyola University of the South for three years. In 1970, Copps moved to Washington to work for Senator Fritz Hollings of South Carolina, eventually becoming his chief of staff. After several lobbying positions, including four years at the American Meat Institute, he joined the Commerce Department, eventually becoming the Assistant Secretary of Commerce for Trade Development. Although he had no background in communications, his academic specialty was the New Deal.

The liberal Democrat was called the "conscience of the FCC"[1] by Commissioner Jonathan Adelstein. He was vocal on the issue of the regulation of indecency, calling for bigger fines and stronger enforcement. He also spoke of the need for regulation of graphic violence in the media.

Copps' biggest issue at the Commission, however, was media consolidation. He publicly clashed with Chairman Michael Powell on a number of occasions. He traveled around the country speaking out about the issue and holding public hearings, often without financial support from the Commission. Copps believed that many of the problems he saw in the media could be related to this issue. He talked at great length about the public interest requirements that broadcasters need to fill now and what they would have to do when the transition to digital was complete. Copps also worried about the disappearance of localism, particularly in news.

On November 9, 2005, Commissioner Copps was renominated by President George W. Bush to an additional five-year term.

KENNETH A. COX (MARCH 25, 1963–AUGUST 31, 1970)

Commissioner Kenneth Cox was appointed in 1963 to fill out the six months remaining in Commissioner T.A.M. Craven's term as well as a seven-year term of his own. At the time of his nomination, Cox had spent three years as the chief of the FCC's Broadcast Bureau. Before that, he was staff counsel for the Senate Commerce Committee and a protégé of Senator Warren G. Magnuson. While working for the Commerce Committee, he wrote reports on issues like FCC jurisdiction over cable and the dominance of the networks over the prime time schedule.

Commissioner Cox was regarded as an aggressive but knowledgeable regulator by many, including Chairman Dean Burch and the broadcasting industry. While considered a champion of the First Amendment, Cox also saw a role for the FCC in some content regulation. Cox supported limiting advertising on radio and television and was concerned about the power of the networks. He argued for the Fairness Doctrine and the Equal Time provision. He opposed the use of Nielsen ratings by TV. In particular, he saw the FCC as playing a role in the racial turmoil of the time, opposing the renewal of WLBT's license in 1968 on the grounds that the station had not served the interest of its African American audience. Cox was considered a strong ally of controversial Commissioner Nicholas Johnson.

After leaving the Commission in 1970, Cox joined upstart phone company MCI as a senior vice president for regulatory matters and maintained a private law practice. He spent time as president of the National Advertising Review Board, the advertising industry's self-regulating organization. He retired from MCI in 1987.

WAYNE C. COY (DECEMBER 29, 1947–FEBRUARY 21, 1952)

Chairman Wayne Coy was a newspaper reporter as a young man, working at *The Franklin Star* soon after graduating from Franklin College. He then bought a weekly newspaper in Delphi, Indiana, and published it until he joined the staff of Governor Paul McNutt in 1933. While working as a regional director of the Works Progress Administration, Coy became friendly with Harry Hopkins and was brought to work in the Roosevelt White House in 1941. He was appointed assistant budget director in 1942. In 1944, Coy became the radio director of *The Washington Post* and vice president and general manager of the WINX broadcasting company.

Coy was appointed to the Commission by President Harry Truman to fill out the unexpired term of Chairman Charles Denny. The primary issue during Coy's chairmanship was the reallocation of frequencies with the introduction of FM, VHF, and UHF television. He was also in charge while the FCC sought a standard for color television.

While supportive of the First Amendment rights of broadcasters, Coy also expressed the belief that the audience has rights. He believed that licensees have an obligation to provide all sides of controversial issues. In 1950, Coy also warned broadcasters that unless they cleaned up some of the "stable humor"[2] that had come to dominate radio Congress might be forced to regulate. He also advocated banning all "gambling information" from the airwaves.

Although nominated for an additional term, Coy resigned in 1952 citing salary as his main reason. In his letter to President Truman, he wrote that with one son in college and another in preparatory school, the $15,000 a year salary was not sufficient to care for his family. He then became a television consultant to Time, Inc.

Soon after returning to his home state of Indiana to become president of WFBM Broadcasting, Chairman Coy died of a heart attack on September 24, 1957.

T.A.M. CRAVEN (AUGUST 25, 1937–JUNE 30, 1944; JULY 2, 1956–MARCH 25, 1963)

Commissioner Tunis Augustus Macdonough Craven is unique in that he served two separate terms on the Commission. Craven, a former Navy engineer and graduate of the U.S. Naval Academy, was the Chief Engineer at the FCC when he was appointed by President Franklin Roosevelt as part of the president's attempt to shake up the Commission. He retired in 1944 after thirty years in government service to become vice president of the Cowles Broadcasting Company. He continued to be publicly critical of the Commission in his role on the National Association of Broadcasters Board. In 1956, President Dwight Eisenhower asked Craven to return to the Commission for another seven-year term.

While Chief Engineer, he often clashed publicly with Commissioner George Henry Payne and members of Congress who oversaw the Commission. After becoming a commissioner, Craven was often at loggerheads with his fellow commissioners, Chairmen Frank McNinch and James Lawrence Fly in particular. Craven often attacked the FCC and the industries it regulated for failing to live up to the public interest standards demanded by the Communications Act and for failing to adequately defend the First Amendment. In fact, Commissioner Craven believed the FCC did not have the authority to regulate programming content at all and would abstain from voting on any license renewal where programming was considered.

He opposed the chain broadcasting decision and the newspaper-radio cross-ownership ban, and in 1942 he described the Commission as "basically unsound."[3]

Craven was considered one of the most technically knowledgeable commissioners to ever sit at the FCC. Because of his engineering background, he was deeply involved in the development of both radio and television.

In 1963, Commissioner Craven reached the mandatory retirement age of seventy and left the Commission. He died on May 31, 1972.

JOHN S. CROSS (MAY 23, 1958–SEPTEMBER 30, 1962)

Commissioner John Cross was nominated by President Dwight Eisenhower to fill out the term of Commissioner Richard Mack. Mack had been forced to resign due to a scandal involving money from an attorney representing a broadcaster with business in front of the Commission. Cross, an electrical engineer by training (Alabama Polytechnic Institute), was a State Department expert on international communications from Arkansas. When asked about his nomination, he told *Broadcasting* magazine that "I may not be awfully smart, but I'm as clean as a hound's tooth."[4]

MARY ANN WEYFORTH DAWSON
(JULY 6, 1981–DECEMBER 3, 1987)

Commissioner Mimi Weyforth Dawson was appointed by Ronald Reagan and came to the FCC from the Senate. Dawson had spent eight years working for Senator Bob Packwood, chair of the Commerce Committee. Before her time in the Senate, she was legislative assistant to two different Missouri congressmen. Commissioner Dawson graduated from Washington University with a degree in government and worked as a social worker in St. Louis before entering government service.

While at the FCC, Dawson was considered a proponent of deregulation and helped to supervise the break up of the Bell system. She rarely dissented from Commission decisions, but she did clash publicly with Chairman Mark Fowler over his plan to eliminate the FCC's cap on individual ownership of broadcast stations.

It was rumored that she was a contender for the chairmanship after Fowler left, but instead she left the Commission to become Deputy Secretary of Transportation in 1987. She resigned from the Department of Transportation in 1989 and entered private practice. She remained active in Republican politics, working on the 1988 and 1992 presidential campaigns.

PATRICIA DIAZ DENNIS (JUNE 25, 1986–SEPTEMBER 29, 1989)

Commissioner Patricia Diaz Dennis was appointed by President Ronald Reagan to fill out the term of Commissioner Henry Rivera. She came to the FCC after three years at the National Labor Relations Board. Dennis had also been an attorney for ABC. She was educated at UCLA and the Loyola University of Los Angeles School of Law.

Commissioner Dennis supported the repeal of the Fairness Doctrine. She was suspicious of the twenty-four-hour ban on indecency but felt that the FCC had to enforce the will of Congress.

In 1989, she asked that President George H. W. Bush not reappoint her and left the Commission to return to private practice. After leaving the Commission, she worked for both SBC and Sprint and in 1992 became Assistant Secretary of State for Human Rights and Humanitarian Affairs. Dennis later served on the boards of the Girl Scouts and the Tomas Rivera Policy Institute and as a member of the Board of Regents of the Texas State University System.

CHARLES R. DENNY (MARCH 30, 1945–OCTOBER 31, 1947)

Charles Denny served as a commissioner, acting chairman (February 26, 1946–December 3, 1946), and then chairman (December 4, 1946–October 31, 1947) during his short time at the Commission. Denny was educated at Amherst College and Harvard Law School. Upon graduation, he entered private practice in Washington, D.C., but moved to the Department of Justice in 1938. He joined the FCC in 1942, first as the assistant general counsel and then as general counsel.

While at the Commission, Denny was involved with the introduction of both FM radio and television. He was chair when the *Blue Book* was released, spelling out the broadcaster's public interest obligations and criticizing excessive commercialization on radio. He was also involved in the development and acceptance of the National Association of Broadcasters' Code.

Denny left the FCC to become the vice president and general counsel at NBC, citing the Commission's $10,000 salary as his main reason.

JOHN C. DOERFER (APRIL 15, 1953–MARCH 10, 1960)

John Doerfer was originally appointed to fulfill the unexpired term of Commissioner Eugene Merrill. Doerfer was nominated for a full seven-year-term in 1954 and became chairman in 1957.

After graduating from the University of Wisconsin and Marquette University law school, Doerfer became the city attorney in his home town of West Allis, Wisconsin. Doerfer then spent four years at the Wisconsin Public Service Commission before joining the FCC in 1953.

The seven years John Doerfer served as both a commissioner and the chairman were marked by scandal. He was considered a close ally of Chairman George McConnaughey and often clashed with Congress and critics of the broadcasting industry. In 1958, Chairman Doerfer and the other commissioners were investigated by Congress for allegedly taking industry money for speaking trips that were being paid for by the FCC and receiving free color televisions for personal use.

During his time at the Commission, the broadcasting industry was rocked by the two major scandals of the 1950s, payola and the quiz shows. Despite congressional and public outcry, Doerfer resisted calls for stronger monitoring. He believed that the quiz shows were fraudulent but not illegal and there was nothing that the FCC could do about it. Many criticized the Commission for failing to act. As a result of the scandals, Doerfer suggested a plan that would have the networks carry cultural programming on a rotating basis as an attempt to clean up the industry's reputation.

Considered by most a reluctant regulator, he rejected calls for the government to monitor program quality. He spoke in favor of repealing the Equal Time provision. Doerfer also oversaw the debates surrounding pay television, UHF, and the appropriate criteria for license renewal.

Always viewed as cozy with the industry, Doerfer was forced to resign by President Eisenhower after it was discovered that he vacationed for six days on a yacht belonging to broadcaster George B. Storer.

After leaving the Commission, he practiced law in Washington, D.C., before moving to Florida and doing legal work for companies affiliated with George Storer.

Chairman Doerfer died on June 9, 1992.

ERVIN S. DUGGAN (FEBRUARY 28, 1990–JANUARY 30, 1994)

Commissioner Ervin Duggan was born and educated in the South (Davidson College, B.A.) but spent his working life in Washington, D.C. Duggan began as a journalist for the *Washington Post* in the early 1960s. He then moved to the Johnson White House as a speech writer and helped draft the Public Broadcasting Act. Duggan went on to work at the Smithsonian, the Department of Health, Education and Welfare, and the State Department. He also spent six years working for Senators Adlai Stevenson and Lloyd Bentsen. Immediately prior to coming to the FCC, Duggan ran his own public relations consulting firm and was a national editor of *Washingtonian Magazine*.

While at the Commission, Duggan opposed lifting the fin-syn restrictions and requiring cable must carry for broadcasters airing only shop-at-home programs. He supported fining a number of television stations for violating the advertising limitations set by the Children's Television Act.

Commissioner Duggan left the FCC to become the president of PBS. He served more than five years in that position, resigning in October of 1999.

CLIFFORD J. DURR (NOVEMBER 1, 1941–JUNE 30, 1948)

Commissioner Clifford Durr was an avid New Dealer whose time in government service was spent at the Reconstruction Finance Corporation and Defense Plant Corporation before he joined the FCC in 1941. He was educated at the University of Alabama and was a Rhodes Scholar, studying Jurisprudence at Oxford.

Commissioner Durr was more concerned about the freedom of radio from the standpoint of the listener, rather than the owner of the broadcast outlets. He spoke out on such issues as the dominance of radio programming by advertisers and the need for broadcasting frequencies for noncommercial educational use. He once opposed the sale of a New England station group to an Ohio tire company on the grounds that absentee ownership might not be in the public interest. He advocated that every radio station be required to spend part of each day broadcasting public service programming. In 1946, he criticized radio set manufacturers for not including the FM band on new sets.

In 1947, he clashed with FBI Director J. Edgar Hoover over the FBI's habit of sending unsolicited reports to the Commission regarding the political leanings of various radio personalities. He was also critical of the House Un-American Activities' Committee's investigations into Hollywood. Upset by the new "loyalty" investigations aimed at routing out Communists in the government, Commissioner Durr refused reappointment to the FCC.

Durr's post-FCC career was one of little financial gain but of historic importance. He was president of the National Lawyers Guild when it recommended in 1950 that the government fund legal aid for low-income people. He and his wife Virginia were deeply involved in the Civil Rights movement. When he returned to Montgomery, Alabama, to practice law in 1954, he was often the only lawyer in the city who would take cases of African Americans claiming their civil rights had been violated. He was the attorney who arranged bail for Rosa Parks after she was arrested for violating the city's bus segregation ordinance, the event that sparked the Montgomery Bus Boycott.

Commissioner Durr died in 1975.

CHARLES D. FERRIS (OCTOBER 17, 1977–APRIL 10, 1981)

Chairman Charles Ferris came to the FCC with no experience in communications but with powerful friends. After graduating from Boston College (undergraduate and law school), Ferris went to Washington to try cases for the Department of Justice. In 1963, he became the chief counsel to the Senate Democrats and Senate Majority Leader Mike Mansfield. In 1977, he switched houses to be general counsel to Speaker Tip O'Neill. During his time in Congress, Ferris was involved in drafting civil rights legislation and was considered one of the most influential staff members on the Hill.

When President Jimmy Carter appointed him to be chair of the Commission, Ferris brought a deregulatory agenda that focused on competition rather than government regulation. One of Ferris's major accomplishments was the Computer II decision that began the process of opening the telephone system to competition. Ferris also brought his deregulatory stance to radio, drastically reducing the paperwork involved in license renewal and removing the requirement for public affairs and news programming. Ferris also created the position of FCC Chief Economist to help the Commission understand the economic impact of its decisions.

During his tenure, the Supreme Court handed down its decision in *FCC v. Pacifica*, the indecency case. Ferris downplayed the ruling, saying that the regulation of indecent speech on radio would be limited to repetitive use of the seven dirty words. Ferris said that it was not the FCC's job to involve itself in "the tangle of taste"[5] but to encourage competition and increase the numbers of media outlets.

Chairman Ferris was intensely disliked by broadcasters but was very popular with the cable industry for his decisions on issues like the carriage of distant broadcast signals. His actions while at the Commission were considered by many to be vital to the development of new communications technologies.

In February 1981, he resigned as Chairman and announced his intention to recuse himself from FCC policymaking until his departure from the Commission on April 10. That date marked the twentieth anniversary of his service to the federal government and the day when he would be eligible for his pension. Chairman Ferris then went into private legal practice.

JAMES LAWRENCE FLY (SEPTEMBER 1, 1939–NOVEMBER 13, 1944)

A native Texan, James Lawrence Fly was educated at the U.S. Naval Academy and Harvard Law School. After a short time in private practice, he became a special assistant attorney general prosecuting monopolies under federal antitrust laws. He joined the Tennessee Valley Authority in 1934, first as solicitor general and then as its general counsel. In 1939, Chairman Fly was appointed by President Franklin Roosevelt to fill out the remainder of Chairman Frank McNinch's term. He was appointed to his own seven-year term in June 1942.

Chairman Fly's time at the Commission was marked by public controversy. He clashed with the military, Congress, and the broadcast industry. He was so unpopular with the industry that in 1941, the National Association of Broadcasters demanded Fly's removal from the Commission. The cause for such hatred: the FCC's chain broadcasting decision. When the Commission determined that NBC's ownership of two radio networks was a detriment to the public interest, invective flew on all sides. Fly was regularly investigated and pilloried by Congress, especially Georgia Representative Eugene Cox. Fly stuck to his guns on the chain broadcasting rules, eventually winning

171

at the Supreme Court and paving the way for the introduction of the ABC network.

Chain broadcasting was not the only matter on which Fly's guidance at the FCC was questioned. He wrangled with David Sarnoff at RCA regarding technical standards for television. Fly blocked the sale of inferior RCA sets, believing that the poor product would hamper the public acceptance of the new technology. Fly was also critical of wiretapping being done by J. Edgar Hoover's FBI.

Fly was appointed by Roosevelt to oversee wartime communications functions in the United States. Members of the Army and Navy also disliked and criticized Fly. At one point they even floated an accusation that the FCC, by allowing Japanese language broadcasts in Hawaii, was responsible for Pearl Harbor.

Fly encouraged broadcasters to cover all sides of controversial issues as required by the public interest standard. One of the last things he worked on at the Commission was the post-war reallocation of the spectrum, ensuring that space was reserved for noncommercial educational broadcasting.

Fly left the Commission in 1944 and spent a year at the Muzak Corporation before returning to private practice. Chairman Fly retired in 1954 and died of cancer on January 6, 1966.

JOSEPH FOGARTY (SEPTEMBER 17, 1976–JUNE 30, 1983)

Commissioner Joseph Fogarty spent ten years as a lawyer for the Senate Commerce Committee before being named by President Gerald Ford to the FCC. While at the Senate, he specialized in the regulation of the telephone industry and later came to be regarded as one of the Commission's leading experts on telecommunications. Fogarty graduated from Holy Cross College and Boston College School of Law.

Fogarty was supportive of deregulation in general but believed that the Commission's Computer II decision happened too quickly. He was also supportive of the advancement of cellular phone technology and he opposed getting rid of the Fairness Doctrine.

Commissioner Fogarty left the FCC to practice telecommunications law in New York City.

FREDERICK W. FORD (AUGUST 29, 1957–DECEMBER 31, 1964)

Commissioner Frederick Ford was appointed by President Dwight Eisenhower after serving several years as assistant to Deputy Attorney General William P. Rogers. Prior to his time at the Justice Department, Ford spent nearly a decade at the FCC, including two years as the chief of the Broadcast Bureau's Hearing Division. Before that, he worked at both the Office of Price Administration and the Federal Security Administration. Ford received both an undergraduate and law degree from West Virginia University.

While Commissioner, Ford had a reputation of not welcoming off-the-record discussions with people from regulated industries. This may have been a factor in his selection to replace the scandal-ridden Chairman John Doerfer. Ford's year as chairman was spent, in part, cleaning up the Commission's image. Ford also had to work to restore confidence in broadcasting following the payola and quiz show scandals.

Upon taking over as chairman, Ford pressed Congress to pass legislation that would aid the Commission in the regulation of deceptive programming. He set up a division within the FCC to monitor program content for information to be used at license renewal time. Although he was concerned about the rise of violence on television, he encouraged self-regulation as a solution. Ford said he viewed spectrum allocation for television as the FCC's number one issue. After concluding that there was no way to increase the number of VHF signals, he advocated that all television sets be manufactured with both VHF and UHF capabilities.

Ford was replaced as chairman by Newton Minow in 1961 but remained on the Commission. He was reappointed by President Lyndon Johnson in 1964 but left at the end of that year to become president of the National Cable Television Association. In 1970, he returned to private practice. He died of cancer on July 26, 1986.

MARK S. FOWLER (MAY 18, 1981–APRIL 17, 1987)

Before attending the University of Florida for both college and law school, Chairman Mark Fowler worked for a decade at radio stations. He then spent eleven years in private legal practice, focusing on broadcast law. Fowler was appointed by President Ronald Reagan, for whom he campaigned in both 1976 and 1980.

While chairman Charles Ferris focused on deregulation to encourage competition, Fowler believed in nonregulation as the answer to all problems brought to the Commission. Chairman Fowler was most famous for referring to television as just a "toaster with pictures."[6]

He viewed any content regulation as censorship, pushing to abolish the Fairness Doctrine and Equal Time provisions. Under his leadership, the Commission ended restrictions on the number of commercials a station could air and eradicated the minimum requirements for news and public affairs programming. He did, however, support the FCC's role in requiring children's programming as part of their license obligations.

Chairman Fowler viewed much of the paperwork required by the Commission as unnecessary. He eliminated the radio program log requirement and cut down on the voluminous license renewal forms.

While Chairman Fowler helped bring direct broadcast satellite (DBS) and lower power television stations to the marketplace, he also damaged the advancement of technology by refusing to set a standard for AM stereo. He

FCC Chairman Mark Fowler (1981–1987) sparked political controversy for his efforts to deregulate the communications industry. (Courtesy of the National Archives. Photograph by Brooks Blunck of Chase Photography.)

maintained that the market should decide what technology was best and refused to choose between four competing models. As a result, AM stereo never moved forward.

Fowler also advocated a number of changes in the ownership regulations. He relaxed rules on regional concentration and wanted to abolish ownership caps in radio completely. He also repealed the antitrafficking regulation requiring that a station be owned for three years before it could be sold. He refused to implement a congressional measure that urged the FCC to give women and minorities preference for low power television licenses.

Fowler believed the FCC should only exist to resolve problems of interference, to keep stations operating at the right power and on the right frequency. The Fowler years were viewed as disastrous by many in the public interest sector, and his relationship with Congress was rocky at best. Fowler's last act at the Commission was to announce a more stringent attitude toward the regulation of indecency, a position that contradicted his belief in nonregulation. He was renominated by President Reagan, but faced an uphill confirmation battle.

Chairman Fowler stepped down in April of 1987 to work in both private practice and the telecommunications industry.

HAROLD W. FURCHTGOTT-ROTH (NOVEMBER 3, 1997–MAY 30, 2001)

Harold Furchtgott was born in Tennessee and educated at MIT (S.B. in economics) and Stanford University (Ph.D. in economics). He added the hyphenated Roth to his name when he married fellow conservative economist Diana Roth. Prior to joining the Commission, he was the chief economist of the House Commerce Committee where he helped draft sections of the Telecommunications Act of 1996. He also spent time as a senior economist for Economists Incorporated and as a research analyst for the Center for Naval Analyses.

The big news when Furchtgott-Roth joined the Commission was that he did not own a television set. Many news reports focused on that issue and when he left the Commission in 2001, his lack of a TV was frequently mentioned.

Commissioner Furchtgott-Roth was called "Dr. Dissent" for his frequent disagreements with the three Democrats and even his fellow Republican, Michael Powell. He was very supportive of deregulation and criticized attempts to regulate new technologies. He also spoke out about government-suggested "voluntary standards," saying that once the government says something, it is no longer voluntary.

Commissioner Furchtgott-Roth declined a second term, saying that as a free market advocate he wanted to return to the private sector. He spent two years as a visiting fellow at the American Enterprise Institute while he completed a book on the implementation of the Telecommunications Act of 1996 and then opened Furchtgott-Roth Economic Enterprises, a consulting firm he runs with his wife.

HAMPSON B. GARY (JULY 11, 1934–JANUARY 1, 1935)

Texan Hampson Gary had a long and interesting career before being named one of the first Federal Communications commissioners. As a young man, he attended the University of Virginia and served in the Texas House of Representatives. He was later on the board of regents for the University of Texas, an attorney in private practice, and a bankruptcy referee. In 1914, he began a career in diplomacy when he was appointed special counsel to the State Department for matters arising out of the war situation in Europe. He also served as assistant solicitor for the State Department. Under President Woodrow Wilson, Gary was counsel general to Egypt and minister to Switzerland.

He left diplomacy in 1921 to practice law in New York and Washington, D.C. In 1934, his friend President Franklin Roosevelt asked him to serve a short appointment at the newly created FCC, heading up the broadcasting division. He resigned from the Commission in January of 1935 to make room for Anning Prall and became the FCC general counsel. Gary was forced to resign in 1938 as part of Chairman Frank McNinch's efforts to clean up the Commission. He went on to serve eight years as the solicitor for the United States Export-Import Bank.

Commissioner Gary died in Florida on April 18, 1952, and was buried at Arlington National Cemetery.

FRIEDA B. HENNOCK (JULY 6, 1948–JUNE 30, 1955)

Appointed by President Harry Truman, Frieda Hennock was the first woman to serve as an FCC Commissioner. In fact, she was the first woman to serve on any independent regulatory commission.

Hennock was born in Poland and immigrated to the United States with her parents at the age of six. In her teens, she decided to become a lawyer and worked at a law firm during the day while attending Brooklyn Law School at night. At age nineteen, she was the youngest woman lawyer in New York when she was admitted to the bar in 1926. She practiced both criminal and civil law in New York before taking a position at the state's Mortgage Commission. She also taught at her alma mater and was active in both local and national Democratic politics.

Commissioner Hennock's time at the FCC was devoted to a crusade for the set-aside of UHF channels for educational use. She publicly accused both politicians and the networks of deliberately strangling educational television in the pursuit of monetary gain. She opposed the concentration of ownership in the media and advocated free airtime for political candidates. Her greatest victory came in 1952 when 242 channels were reserved for noncommercial, educational television.

President Truman nominated Hennock to be a federal district judge in 1951, but the nomination was opposed by members of the New York Bar Association and the Senate Judiciary Committee. Hennock remained at the Commission until the end of her term in 1955. She believed that she was not offered an additional term because she had been so outspoken about the monopolistic tendencies of the television networks.

Hennock entered private practice in Washington, D.C., with her new husband, William Simons, in 1955. She died on June 20, 1960, after surgery for a brain tumor.

E. WILLIAM HENRY (OCTOBER 2, 1962–MAY 1, 1966)

Commissioner E. William Henry was an attorney in Memphis before being appointed by President John F. Kennedy. He was educated at Yale University and Vanderbilt law school. He became chairman in June 1963 after Newton Minow's resignation.

Chairman Henry devoted much of his time at the Commission to issues surrounding advertising. He believed that broadcasting was overcommercialized and advocated codifying the National Association of Broadcasters' code on maximum commercial minutes. This move was opposed by the broadcasting industry and its friends in Congress. He later called for an investigation of the problem of excessive loudness of commercials and criticized the broadcasting industry for running cigarette ads that ignored health controversies.

Commercials were not his only concern while chairman. Henry drew criticism from broadcasters for advocating the need for stations to solicit feedback from the community to determine the public interest. He called for more diversity of ideas on television as well as more public service programming. Chairman Henry supported the decision to give WBLT and WJDX probationary renewals based on their biased presentation of civil rights issues. He also expressed concern over network domination of prime time programming and issued a Notice of Proposed Rulemaking on the topic. Henry also chided broadcasters for being too cautious at times, risking artistic integrity and freedom by overediting programming out of a fear of complaints. Henry was also chairman when the FCC decided cable was within its jurisdiction.

A close personal friend of President Kennedy, Chairman Henry was perceived as losing most of his influence when Lyndon Johnson became president. He resigned in 1966 to work on John J. Hooker Jr.'s campaign for governor of Tennessee.

In the decades after he left the Commission, he practiced law in Washington, D.C., and was active in public television. He served as the director of the National Association of Educational Broadcasters in the late 1960s. He was chairman of WETA, the public television station in Washington, D.C., as well as a director of PBS and chairman of the National Program Policy Committee there.

BENJAMIN L. HOOKS (JULY 5, 1972–JULY 25, 1977)

Commissioner Ben Hooks was a lawyer, a judge, a minister, a businessman, and a TV host before being appointed to the Commission in 1972 by President Richard Nixon. Educated at LeMoyne College and Howard University, Hooks received his law degree from DePaul University in Chicago because no law school in his native Tennessee would admit an African American student. Hooks returned to his hometown of Memphis after law school to work in private practice and as a public defender. In 1965, he became the first African American criminal court judge in Tennessee history. He was active in the Civil Rights movement, as both an attorney and a minister.

Hooks was the first African American commissioner and during his time at the FCC he expressed concern about minority representation in all aspects of the media. He spoke out on the lack of minority ownership of television and radio stations. He also addressed issues of minority employment both in broadcasting and at the FCC. The EEO office at the Commission was started during his time. Hooks was equally concerned with the images of minorities that the media portrayed. He supported the Equal Time provision and the Fairness Doctrine, believing they were often the only paths to airtime open to minorities.

Commissioner Hooks left the FCC in 1977 to become the executive director of the National Association for the Advancement of Colored People, a position he held for fifteen years before his retirement in 1992.

THOMAS J. HOUSER (JANUARY 6, 1971–OCTOBER 5, 1971)

Commissioner Thomas Houser served only nine months, filling out an unexpired term. Houser was a lawyer from Chicago who worked at the law firm where Newton Minow was a partner. Immediately prior to joining the FCC, Houser spent eighteen months as the deputy director of the Peace Corps.

Houser was a specialist in regulatory and administrative law and active in Republican politics, running President Nixon's campaign in Illinois in 1972. In 1976, he was nominated by President Gerald Ford to be the director of the White House Office of Telecommunications Policy.

Although Houser's time at the Commission was short, he drew attention for refusing to vote with the Republican majority to censure CBS for its broadcast of the documentary "The Selling of the Pentagon."

REED E. HUNDT (NOVEMBER 29, 1993–NOVEMBER 3, 1997)

Chairman Reed Hundt once joked that he got his job because he shared a birthday with Alexander Graham Bell. The reality is that he was a prep school classmate and long-time friend of Vice President Al Gore and a Yale University law school classmate of President and Mrs. Clinton. Before joining the Commission, he was an attorney in private practice in Washington, D.C., specializing in antitrust litigation and was a member of Clinton's economic transition team.

Chairman Hundt said that his time at the Commission was guided by two principles: the FCC should make decisions based on the public interest and write fair rules of competition for the communications sector. He believed that the FCC should encourage competition, choice, and business opportunities for all sectors of communications, what he called the five lanes of the information superhighway: broadcasting, cable, satellite, telephony, and wireless communication.

Under Chairman Hundt, the FCC saw much historic action. Hundt initiated the first spectrum auctions in history, raising nearly $20 billion in two years. The Commission established its presence on the internet with the first FCC homepage. In fact, Hundt was the first chairman to have a personal computer on his desk. During his tenure, the Commission wrote the rules to open telephone markets to competition, supported wiring libraries, schools, and rural health facilities to the internet, and guaranteed universal access to all.

Chairman Hundt was especially concerned with children's issues, focusing much attention on bringing computer and internet technology to every school in the nation. He also fought hard to implement the rules requiring all broadcasters to air three hours of educational and instructive programming for children. Hundt focused considerable energy on extending the benefits of the telecommunications revolution to people with disabilities. The FCC's Disabilities Issues Task Force was created during his tenure.

In his last few months at the Commission, Chairman Hundt oversaw the beginnings of the implementation of the Telecommunications Act of 1996.

He left the Commission in November of 1997 to pursue consulting opportunities.

ROSEL H. HYDE (APRIL 17, 1946–OCTOBER 31, 1969)

Commissioner Rosel Hyde joined the Federal Radio Commission in 1928 as an attorney after graduating from George Washington University Law School. He eventually became the general counsel of the FCC before being appointed to the Commission by President Harry Truman. A native of Idaho, Hyde got his undergraduate degree from the Utah Agricultural College in Logan, Utah.

During Hyde's more than twenty-two years as a commissioner, he chaired the FCC three times. In April 1953, he was appointed chair for one year, succeeding Paul Walker. He was named acting chairman in 1966 when E. William Henry resigned. He was then appointed chairman by President Johnson, despite the fact that he was a Republican. This was the first time a president choose a chairman of the Commission who was not from his party.

Including his time as a staff attorney, Rosel Hyde spent nearly forty-one years regulating broadcasting and telephone. He played a pivotal role in the development of most federal communications policies. He was particularly involved with issues of spectrum allocation, having overseen the development of AM and FM radio, black and white and color television, cable television, high-speed data transmissions, and mobile radio. He helped develop the Fairness Doctrine. Although he believed it was not the FCC's job to regulate the content of broadcasting, he did support the ban on tobacco advertising.

He was known as an amiable commissioner, popular with the broadcast industry. He was an advocate of minimal regulation and was recognized for his technical expertise. He presided over many of the ups and downs of AT&T as part of the Commission's Telephone Committee.

Chairman Hyde retired in 1969 and became a partner at a Washington, D.C., law firm. He died in 1992 of complications from a stroke.

EWELL K. JETT (FEBRUARY 15, 1944–DECEMBER 31, 1947)

E. K. Jett spent a lifetime in federal service, joining the Navy as a teenager in 1912. After eighteen years, he moved to the Federal Radio Commission as an engineer, eventually becoming the chief engineer of the FCC before being named a commissioner by President Franklin Roosevelt.

Commissioner Jett was known for his technical expertise, particularly in the area of spectrum allocation. He was chairman for about six weeks between James Lawrence Fly and Paul Porter.

He resigned at the end of 1947 to become vice president of the Baltimore Sun papers and director of its radio interests. He died April 28, 1965, at the age of seventy.

NICHOLAS JOHNSON (JULY 1, 1966–DECEMBER 5, 1973)

Commissioner Nicholas Johnson was born three months after the FCC was formed and would prove to be its most controversial commissioner. Johnson was educated at the University of Texas and clerked for Judge John R. Brown of the 5th Circuit and Supreme Court Justice Hugo Black. He then both taught and practiced law. An unknown, he was named the Administrator of the Maritime Administration by President Lyndon Johnson at age twenty-nine. Two years later he became one the youngest FCC commissioners in history.

Commissioner Johnson's nomination hearing and first few months on the Commission were quiet. But then things changed. The catalyst for his activism was the proposed merger between television network ABC and International Telephone and Telegraph (ITT) in 1966. When the Commission voted to approve the merger, Johnson wrote his first dissent, an eighty-five-page attack on the Commission's actions. When the Commission voted again to approve the merger six months later, he and Commissioner Kenneth Cox co-authored a 131-page dissent. The merger eventually fell apart during a Justice Department investigation and the seeds of the rest of Johnson's time at the Commission were sown.

Johnson's seven-year tenure at the Commission was marked by strong dissents and flamboyant public commentary. He was intensely disliked by the broadcast industry and several of his fellow commissioners, particularly Chairman Dean Burch. An article in *Broadcasting* magazine shortly after his resignation included this description: "To many, he has been a curmudgeon, a burr, a prod to the conscience, a troublemaker, a wrecker, a phony, a publicity seeker. It is not too much to say that, in some quarters, he was hated."[7]

He believed that the broadcasting industry was the single most economically and politically powerful industry in the history of the United States. Following in the footsteps of Newton Minow, he made sweeping criticisms, once referring to the television networks as "child molesters" and "pushers to a junkie nation." In a discussion about paid political advertising, he said "it's kind of like a criminal stealing a woman's wedding band after he's raped her."[8]

Johnson attacked the Commission itself as much as he attacked the broadcasting industry. He was critical of the FCC's practice of renewing stations licenses without examining what the licensees had actually done. He also felt that the FCC's use of probationary renewals was a minor punishment at best, not actually hurting the station despite a clear lack of performance. He also condemned the Commission for going after radio stations for playing songs with drug references but doing nothing about violence on television.

Johnson considered himself an activist for the public, viewing his job as one to stir up debate among all people touched by broadcasting. His most far-reaching impact may have been that he encouraged people to complain to their local broadcasters, the networks, and the Commission when they saw things they did not like. He empowered many to file challenges to license renewals, which they did by the hundreds. He believed that the best defense against poor programming quality was turning the channel or turning off the TV set. He dissented in the Eastern Educational Radio case (a Jerry Garcia interview deemed indecent), saying that there was an absolute right of free expression guaranteed by the First Amendment. He declined to participate in the FCC's "Topless Radio" hearings because he believe that the consumer's opinion, not the Commission's, was most important.

He proposed, with his frequent ally Commissioner Kenneth Cox, that stations be required to dedicate a certain percentage of the broadcast week to public service programming: 5 percent to news, 1 percent to public affairs, and 5 percent to other nonentertainment. He thought that cable would be a check on the power of the telephone companies. His biggest concern about broadcasting, however, was the threat of cross-ownership between communication industries and media consolidation of any kind.

While at the Commission, Johnson published two books, *How to Talk Back to Your TV Set* in 1970 and *Test Pattern for Living* in 1972, and more than 350 articles for publications as varied as *Columbia Journalism Review*, *Playboy*, and *TV Guide*. He was the only FCC commissioner to be featured on the cover of *Rolling Stone*.

Commissioner Johnson did not work within the system, but he did have an impact on the Commission and its decisionmaking. Fear of his blistering dissents is thought to have swayed some of the FCC's decisions, particularly since he made a habit of sending copies of his dissents to the media. In fact, his dissents were often used by the courts to overturn Commission decisions.

President Richard Nixon went to great lengths to remove Johnson from the Commission, even having the FBI follow him on vacation in Europe. Johnson vehemently opposed Nixon's choice for his replacement, broadcaster James Quello.

After leaving the FCC, Commissioner Johnson did public interest work in Washington, D.C. Under President Jimmy Carter, he was an advisor to the White House Conference on Libraries and Information Services, which gave him an early view of what would become the internet. Johnson returned to his home state of Iowa in 1980 to write, teach, and practice law, and to run (unsuccessfully) for Congress. He maintains a mammoth Web site of writing both by and about him at www.nicholasjohnson.org/.

ANNE P. JONES (APRIL 7, 1979–MAY 31, 1983)

Commissioner Anne P. Jones spent ten years at the Securities and Exchange Commission and an additional year as the general counsel at the Federal Home Loan Bank Board before joining the FCC in 1979. Prior to coming to Washington, D.C., she was a lawyer in private practice in her native Massachusetts. She graduated from Boston College with both a B.S. and a law degree. It is believed that her law school classmate, Chairman Charles Ferris, suggested her appointment for the Republican seat on the Commission.

While at the Commission, she favored deregulation unless an explicit reason for a rule could be enunciated. When she arrived at the FCC, she opposed efforts to strengthen equal opportunities for minorities and women, often publicly conflicting with Commissioner Tyrone Brown. She eventually became supportive of these effort toward the end of her time at the Commission. She was also concerned about the state of children's television but did not believe that government regulation was the answer.

Her resignation in 1983 came as a surprise to many and coincided with the reduction of the size of the Commission to five members. She returned to private law practice with two years left on her term.

ROBERT F. JONES (SEPTEMBER 5, 1947–SEPTEMBER 19, 1952)

Commissioner Robert F. Jones was a Republican Congressman from Ohio for more than eight years before being selected by President Harry Truman. His appointment was a surprise since he had been an outspoken critic of both Presidents Roosevelt and Truman.

Jones was born and raised in Ohio, graduating from Ohio Northern University. He practiced law and worked as a prosecuting attorney until his election to Congress in 1938.

During his time at the Commission, he was a controversial figure, often clashing with the broadcasting industry and his fellow commissioners. He was critical of CBS during the testing of color television. He also believed the FCC did not have the authority to regulate give-away programs on radio.

Commissioner Jones quit in September 1952 to enter private practice. In 1954, he became the Chief Counsel of a Senate Commerce Subcommittee investigating radio and television.

Commissioner Jones died in June 1968 at the age of sixty.

WILLIAM E. KENNARD (NOVEMBER 3, 1997–JANUARY 19, 2001)

Chairman William Kennard was a native of Los Angeles and a graduate of Stanford University. After Yale Law School, he worked for the National Association of Broadcasters and a Washington, D.C., law firm specializing in communications law. In the 1980s, he served on the FCC's Advisory Board on Minority Ownership. In December 1993, he became the FCC's general counsel. In 1997, President Bill Clinton named him the first African American Chair of the Commission.

Kennard believed as chairman it was his job to bring competition to the marketplace while still making sure that the benefits of the digital age reached all Americans. The implementation of the Telecommunications Act of 1996 was his main responsibility during his time as general counsel and as chair. He oversaw the development of competitive local phone markets and the explosion in wireless technology and the internet, including broadband. His time at the Commission was marked by the megamergers made possible by the Telecom Act, including AOL-Time Warner, Worldcom-MCI, and CBS-Viacom.

Very concerned about the digital divide, Kennard moved forward with the FCC's e-rate program to bring the internet to schools, libraries, and rural areas. He also worked hard to introduce low power FM, but was largely blocked by Congress and the broadcast industry. His time at the Commission was marked by frequent clashes with Republicans in Congress.

Chairman Kennard also tried to move the Commission itself into the twenty-first century with a five-year strategic plan that focused on making the FCC more efficient. He encouraged the shift to electronic submission of most FCC paperwork. He also oversaw the move to The Portals II, the FCC's new headquarters.

After leaving the Commission in January 2001, Chairman Kennard joined the Aspen Institute, a think tank in Washington, D.C. In May 2001, he joined the Carlyle Group as a managing director in the Global Telecommunications and Media Group.

CHARLES H. KING (JULY 19, 1960–MARCH 2, 1961)

Commissioner Charles King was appointed to fill out the remaining term of disgraced Chairman John Doerfer. King was a graduate of the Detroit College of Law, the Detroit Institute of Technology (A.B.), and the University of Michigan (master's in law). He was a respected attorney and teacher.

At the time of his selection by President Dwight Eisenhower, King had been the dean of the Detroit College of Law for close to sixteen years. Although active in Republican politics, he had no contact with anyone in the broadcasting business. This was key in a time of scandal at the Commission.

Commissioner King returned to academia upon the selection of Newton Minow by newly elected President John F. Kennedy.

H. REX LEE (OCTOBER 28, 1968–DECEMBER 31, 1973)

Commissioner H. Rex Lee began his nearly four decades of government service in 1936 as an economist for the Department of Agriculture after graduating from the University of Idaho. He later worked for the War Relocation Authority and the Bureau of Indian Affairs. In 1961, he was selected to be the Governor of American Samoa. During his six years there, he revolutionized the country with educational television.

Commissioner Lee was a quiet member of the FCC, rarely flamboyant or controversial. When he spoke out in public, it was usually on his pet issue of public television. He also joined Commissioner Nicholas Johnson in his crusade against media concentration, frequently voting against station purchases.

Commissioner Lee chose to leave the Commission eighteen months before the end of his term, saying that it was time to try something else. After retiring from the Commission, he taught at San Diego State University before becoming the founding chairman of the Public Service Satellite Consortium. In retirement, he also helped establish educational television in South America. Commissioner H. Rex Lee died from pneumonia on July 26, 2001, at the age of ninety-one.

ROBERT E. LEE (OCTOBER 6, 1953–JUNE 30, 1981)

Prior to Robert E. Lee's first appointment to the Commission in 1953, he had been a hotel auditor, an FBI agent, an administrative assistant to J. Edgar Hoover, and the director of surveys and investigations for the House Appropriations Committee. He was also a close personal friend of Senator Joe McCarthy. Many thought him completely unqualified to be an FCC commissioner. His confirmation hearing was dominated by questions about his abilities and his relationship with the controversial McCarthy.

Educated at DePaul University, Commissioner Lee served longer than any other commissioner in the history of the FCC. Although he stated in 1954 that he did not believe in government regulation, he stayed at the Commission for almost twenty-eight years during which he was involved in many of the most important decisions made about U.S. communications policy. He was best known for his support of the development of UHF and the expansion of educational television. He played a prominent role in the development of color television as well. He was also an early supporter of what was then called subscription television. He believed that the FCC did have the authority to deal with the quiz show scandals, a position that brought him into conflict with Chairman John Doerfer. He also was a proponent of the regulation of profane and indecent speech.

Commissioner Lee announced his resignation in 1967 at the end of his second term, but was reappointed by President Lyndon Johnson and stayed for two more terms. After his 1981 retirement from the Commission, he consulted for a D.C.-area law firm and promoted the new technology of Direct Satellite Broadcasting.

Commissioner Robert E. Lee died of liver cancer on April 15, 1993.

LEE LOEVINGER (JUNE 11, 1963–JUNE 30, 1968)

Immediately before his appointment to the FCC, Commissioner Lee Loevinger was the chief of the antitrust division of the Justice Department, working with Attorney General Robert F. Kennedy and future Supreme Court justice Byron White. While at the Justice Department, Loevinger argued the landmark antitrust case, *United States v. Philadelphia National Bank*, in front of the Supreme Court. After Loevinger won that case, President John F. Kennedy named him to fill out the remainder of Newton Minow's term at the FCC.

Prior to his time at the Justice Department, Loevinger had been as associate justice on the Minnesota Supreme Court, a trial lawyer for the National Labor

Relations Board, and an attorney in private practice in Kansas City, MO, and Minneapolis. He helped found the American Bar Association's section of science and technology law and *Jurimetrics: The Journal of Law, Science and Technology*. He was educated at the University of Minnesota for both his bachelor's and law degrees.

Commissioner Loevinger's most important legacy at the FCC was the establishment of 911, the nationwide emergency number. AT&T said it was technologically impossible, but Loevinger prevailed.

Commissioner Loevinger was most famous for his commentary on television. He personally viewed it as "the idiot box"[9] and refused to buy a set until his daughter could read the front page of the *New York Times* without making a mistake. But he did not think it was the government's job to interfere and set arbitrary standards. He believed that a better way to influence the quality of television was to work toward more diversity of ownership and control. He considered the regulations that allowed one person to own up to nineteen different radio and television stations too liberal.

Loevinger viewed attempts to regulate the quality of television as elitist. He is famous for remarking, "Television is the golden goose that lays scrambled eggs, and it is futile and probably fatal to beat it for not laying caviar. Anyway, more people like scrambled eggs than caviar."[10] He also said, "It seems to me that television is the literature of the illiterate; the culture of the lowbrow; the wealth of the poor; the privilege of the underprivileged; the exclusive club of the excluded masses." In a nod to the man he replaced, he said that "one man's vast wasteland is another's verdant vineyard."[11]

Commissioner Loevinger took positions on other issues during his time at the FCC, including a suggestion that a station should be required to devote as much time to news as time sold for advertising. He also expressed concern that FCC regulations essentially required stations to air religious programming, something he viewed as a violation of the separation of church and state. He once voted to support an atheist's claim for equal time under the Fairness Doctrine to respond to the broadcast of a church service.

Commissioner Lee Loevinger declined renomination and left the Commission at the end of his term. He practiced antitrust law in Washington, D.C., until his retirement in 1985. He died on April 26, 2004, of complications from heart disease.

RICHARD A. MACK (JULY 7, 1955–MARCH 3, 1958)

Commissioner Richard Mack was appointed by President Dwight Eisenhower for a Democratic seat on the Commission. Prior to his appointment, he was a vice president of the National Association of Railroad and Utility Commissioners. That position came after eight years at the Florida State Railroad and Public Utilities Commission. Mack held a degree in business from the University of Florida.

Commissioner Mack was considered an affable man with a bright political future. But a vote to award a Miami television station to Public Service Television, Inc, a subsidiary of National Airlines, ended his career. He was accused of taking $2,650 from Thurman Whiteside, an attorney representing Public Service Television, Inc. He claimed the money was merely a loan from a childhood friend, but he was forced to resign by the White House.

Several months after he left the Commission, he and Whiteside were indicted on charges of conspiring to defraud the United States. The first trial ended in a mistrial. In 1960, Whiteside was found not guilty. Mack, who was by then a chronic alcoholic with psychiatric problems, had been ruled too ill to stand trial. In May 1961, Whiteside committed suicide in his law office. A few months later, the government dropped the case against Mack.

Commissioner Richard Mack died on November 26, 1963, at the age of fifty-four.

SHERRIE P. MARSHALL (AUGUST 21, 1989–APRIL 30, 1993)

When President George H. W. Bush appointed Sherrie Marshall to the FCC in 1989 she was a lawyer specializing in election and international trade law. In fact, Marshall had spent her entire career in Washington, D.C., working at the White House, the Department of the Treasury, the Federal Elections Commission, and the Senate Committee on Rules and Administration. She even spent time at the FCC as the Director of the Office of Legislative Affairs. Marshall was a graduate of the University of North Carolina (A.B. in English) and the University of North Carolina School of Law.

As word of her nomination leaked out, many believed that Marshall would be named chair. Instead, Alfred Sikes was given the position. Although they were both Republicans, Sikes spent much of his time on the Commission battling Marshall. In addition to her hostility toward Chairman Sikes, she was known for her belief in deregulation and support of the entertainment industry, although she voted to keep the fin-syn rules in place.

Commissioner Sherrie Marshall's term ended in 1992, but she stayed on until April 1993 to allow newly elected President Bill Clinton to appoint her successor. After leaving the Commission, Marshall founded her own consulting firm in Los Angeles and joined an entertainment law firm.

KEVIN J. MARTIN (JULY 3, 2001–PRESENT)

Kevin Martin was a Special Assistant to the President for Economic Policy at the White House and active in the Bush/Cheney 2000 campaign before being appointed to the Commission in 2001. Before working to elect President George W. Bush, he was Commissioner Harold Furchtgott-Roth's legal advisor. He also worked at the Office of the Independent Counsel and spent time in private practice in Washington, D.C. Martin holds a B.S. in Political

Science from the University of North Carolina, a master's in Public Policy from Duke University, and a law degree from Harvard.

Commissioner Martin was often in conflict with Chairman Michael Powell when he first joined the FCC, particularly over Powell's reluctance to regulate indecency. In fact, it was his position on increasing the enforcement of the indecency regulations that brought him the support of many of the Religious Right groups who pushed for his elevation to the chairmanship. Martin was made chairman upon Michael Powell's resignation in March 2005.

Chairman Martin has been a strong advocate of deregulation, particularly on ownership issues. He has endorsed allowing companies to own two or even three stations in a single market and lifting newspaper cross-ownership ban. He has supported broadcast station owners on many issues, including a station's right to preempt programming it finds offensive. Martin has also supported full digital must carry.

Chairman Martin departed from his deregulatory stance on the issue of the active enforcement of the indecency regulation on all media. He advocated a return to the Family Hour and requiring cable companies to provide a family-friendly cable tier.

GEORGE McCONNAUGHEY (OCTOBER 4, 1954–JUNE 30, 1957)

Chairman George McConnaughey was in charge of renegotiating federal defense contracts when he was appointed to the Commission by President Dwight Eisenhower. McConnaughey also served as chairman of the Ohio Public Utilities Commission and president of the National Association of Railroad and Utilities Commissioners. He was educated at Denison University and Western Reserve University Law School in his native Ohio.

McConnaughey believed in as few controls of business as possible. He held that the Commission did not have the authority to regulate programming and supported lengthening license terms to five years. McConnaughey did, however, denounce federal wiretapping as "abominable."[12]

Chairman McConnaughey's time at the FCC was quiet, however there were storms on the horizon regarding the Commission's relationship with the broadcast industry. Some believed that McConnaughey was asked to step down because he was viewed as too friendly with broadcasting executives.

Chairman McConnaughey left the Commission in 1957 to practice law with his son in Ohio. He died of cancer on March 16, 1966, at the age of sixty-nine.

FRANK R. McNINCH (OCTOBER 1, 1937–AUGUST 31, 1939)

After receiving his law degree from the University of North Carolina, Chairman Frank McNinch practiced law in his home state of North Carolina. He also served as a North Carolina state legislator and as the mayor of Charlotte. In 1931, President Herbert Hoover appointed him to a Democratic seat on the Federal Power Commission. In 1933, President Franklin Roosevelt named him chair. In 1937, he was "borrowed" from the Federal Power Commission to put the FCC's "affairs in order."[13]

The Commission had been heavily criticized for being inefficient, unfair, and political, and suffered from much internal dissent. The broadcast division, in particular, was viewed as being a disaster. Roosevelt brought McNinch to the Commission amid calls from Congress for investigations into the agency. McNinch immediately began a massive housekeeping and reorganization, firing people and abolishing divisions. He had a rocky relationship with some inside the Commission, clashing frequently with Commissioner T.A.M. Craven and eventually demanding the resignation of FCC general counsel (and former commissioner) Hampson Gary.

McNinch believed that government censorship of radio was "impracticable and definitely objectionable,"[14] but also warned the industry that it must maintain standards. He was in charge at the Commission during several early controversies, including Orson Wells's production of "War of the Worlds" and NBC's broadcast of a risqué Adam and Eve skit starring Mae West and Charlie McCarthy. Although he declined to take significant action in both cases, he frequently reminded broadcasters that they were required to serve the pubic interest. McNinch also launched the first investigation into chain broadcasting and saw the early germination of the rules that provided for Equal Time and the Fairness Doctrine.

Chairman Frank McNinch resigned in September 1939, citing ill health. He died at the age of seventy-seven on April 20, 1950.

EUGENE H. MERRILL (OCTOBER 6, 1952–APRIL 15, 1953)

Commissioner Eugene Merrill served for only six months at the FCC. He was initially appointed during a Congressional recess and was renominated by President Harry Truman. When Republican Dwight Eisenhower won the election, however, Merrill's name was withdrawn.

Commissioner Merrill held a degree in engineering from the University of Utah and had significant experience in public utility regulation, including time spent as the chief engineer for the Utah Public Utilities Commission and the chief of communication for the Foreign Economic Administration. At the time of his appointment, he was working with the National Production Authority in Washington, D.C.

NEWTON N. MINOW (MARCH 2, 1961–JUNE 1, 1963)

Chairman Newton Minow graduated from Northwestern University with a bachelor's degree in speech and a law degree. He graduated first in his law school class and clerked for Supreme Court Chief Justice Fred Vinson. He then worked as an attorney in private practice and for Governor Adali Stevenson. It was while campaigning for Stevenson that Minow became friends with Robert Kennedy. Minow was active in John F. Kennedy's campaign in 1960, which led to his appointment to the FCC.

Chairman Minow served only two years at the Commission but stirred up enough controversy to last a lifetime. On May 9, 1961, after only a few months in office, he made a speech to the National Association of Broadcasters that forever influenced the debate over the quality of television. Minow told the broadcasters that when:

> television is good, nothing—not theater, not the magazines or newspapers—nothing is better. When television is bad, nothing is worse. I invite you to sit down in front of your television set when your station goes on the air and stay there without a book, magazine, newspaper, profit-and-loss sheet or rating book to distract you—and keep your eyes glued to that set until the station signs off. I can assure you that you will observe *a vast wasteland*.[15]

He went on to focus his speech on the issue of serving the public interest, particularly the interests of children, but it was the "vast wasteland" comment that captured the nation's attention.

Broadcasters were furious and viewed the speech as a move toward government censorship. When Minow was given a special Peabody Award in 1962, *Broadcasting* magazine called for the awards to be abolished. It is also said that television producer Sherwood Schwartz was so upset that he named the shipwrecked S.S. *Minnow* in his comedy *Gilligan's Island* after the chairman.

Many critics argue that Minow's scathing commentary on television lead to little change. He was, however, involved in the passage of some important legislation. Of primary importance was the passage of the All Channel Receiver

Chairman Newton Minow (1961–1963) is pictured testifying before Congress. Minow riled the broadcasting industry when he referred to television as a "vast wasteland." (AP/Wide World Photos)

Act. UHF had been languishing because most television sets did not receive the channels. The act required that all new sets carry both VHF and UHF, thus opening the way for additional television stations. One result of this support of UHF was that it allowed ABC to become a nationwide network, rivaling the power of CBS and NBC. Minow also encouraged the legislation that ushered in the satellite era and he was the only commissioner to vote to encourage Congress to pass legislation giving financial aid to educational television.

Chairman Newton Minow left the FCC in 1963 to work at *Encyclopedia Britannica*. Over the more than forty years since he left the Commission, Minow has held a wide variety of positions, many of which focused on providing quality broadcasting to the American public. He has co-chaired the presidential debates for the League of Women Voters and served on the Commission on Presidential Debates. He also served as the chairman for PBS, the RAND Corporation, and the Carnegie Corporation of New York. In 2004, he called for broadcasters to give free time to local political candidates.

SUSAN NESS (MAY 19, 1994–MAY 30, 2001)

Commissioner Susan Ness was an investment banker and attorney focused on the communication industries when she was appointed to the FCC by President Bill Clinton in 1994. She had been a fundraiser for the Clinton-Gore campaign and had government experience as the assistant counsel to the House Banking Committee. Ness held degrees from Douglass College (B.A.), Boston College Law School (J.D.), and the Wharton School of the University of Pennsylvania (M.B.A.).

Commissioner Ness was considered the FCC's expert on the satellite industry and was active in promoting universal service. She believed that the internet's potential to connect libraries, schools, and rural areas needed to be nurtured. Although she advocated deregulation and greater competition, she supported the effort to establish a government inquiry into the advertising of hard liquor on television. She was also involved in reviewing the AOL-Time Warner merger.

Commissioner Susan Ness was reappointed at the end of President Clinton's term, but later announced that she would step down when President George W. Bush found a Democrat to replace her. She went to work as a consultant and later helped the scandal-rocked Adelphia Communications.

DENNIS R. PATRICK (DECEMBER 2, 1983–AUGUST 7, 1989)

Dennis Patrick was a special assistant to the Assistant Secretary of Commerce for Communications and Information and worked in the personnel office at the Reagan White House before joining the FCC in 1983. He was educated at Occidental College (A.B. in political science) and the University of California at Los Angeles (J.D.). While at UCLA, he clerked for California Supreme Court Justice William Clark. Clark later became Reagan's National Security Advisor and then the Secretary of the Interior. It was Clark who brought Patrick to Washington.

When Chairman Mark Fowler stepped down in 1987, Dennis Patrick was elevated to the chairmanship. He was an ardent free-market supporter who continued the deregulation of the communications industry pursued by Fowler. Chairman Patrick believed that the market was the best regulator. During his time as chair, he eased some of the broadcasting ownership restrictions and supported ending cable must carry. Although he spoke highly of the change in the FCC's indecency policy that was announced the day before he took office, he mostly ignored the complaints pouring into the Commission.

Like his predecessor, Chairman Patrick had a stormy relationship with Congress. It grew particularly bad when the FCC voted to end the Fairness Doctrine. Patrick also provoked controversy among Democrats in Congress over his support of price caps regulation for the telephone industry.

Chairman Patrick resigned from the Commission in 1989 to work as a consultant. He also spent time as the president of AOL Wireless, the chief executive of Time Warner Telecommunications, and the president of National Geographic Ventures.

GEORGE HENRY PAYNE (JULY 11, 1934–JUNE 30, 1943)

Commissioner George Henry Payne spent seventeen years as a city tax commissioner in New York before becoming one of the original seven members of the FCC. Before that, he had been a Republican party activist and a journalist. He studied at City College and the College of Pharmacy and was later a special student at New York Law University.

Payne's time at the Commission was stormy. In 1935, he sponsored a resolution barring any commissioner from doing business in front of the FCC for two years after leaving. That same year, he criticized the broadcast industry for not providing enough programming with educational and cultural value and for being overcommercialized.

Commissioner Payne was renominated in 1936. Not long after, he proposed a tax on broadcasters based on the power of the station and suggested that a license should be renewed based on the quality of the station's programming. He also sued *Broadcasting* magazine for libel for an unflattering commentary.

In 1938, he voted to invite a congressional inquiry into the Commission and told Congress that his colleagues on the FCC were unduly influenced by lobbyists for the broadcasting industry. Georgia Congressman Eugene Cox called for Payne to resign that June, calling him "entirely irresponsible" and a "troublemaker."[16]

Throughout Payne's time at the FCC, he was highly critical of the radio networks, believing them the cause of inferior programming. In 1943, President Roosevelt submitted Payne's name for another term, but it was withdrawn the next day. The move came as a surprise, since Payne, a Republican, had frequently sided with the Democrats and the Roosevelt Administration. After leaving the Commission, he became the vice president of Finch Telecommunications.

Commissioner George Henry Payne died on March 3, 1945, at the age of sixty-eight.

PAUL A. PORTER (DECEMBER 21, 1944–FEBRUARY 25, 1946)

Chairman Paul Porter started working as a journalist at the age of fourteen to help provide for his family after the death of his father. Newspaper work also helped pay his way through the University of Kentucky. After graduation, he practiced law and worked as a radio executive. He was drawn to Washington, D.C., to work for the Roosevelt Administration, spending time at the Agricultural Adjustment Administration, the Defense Advisory Commission, the Office of Price Administration, the War Food Administration, and the Office of Economic Stabilization. He also served as the Washington counsel for CBS. At the time of his appointment, he was the publicity director of the Democratic National Committee.

In his short time at the Commission, he advocated for the development of FM radio and television. The FCC's famous *Blue Book* was released during his tenure.

Porter left the Commission after a little more than a year to head up the Office of Price Administration. In November 1946, he quit the OPA. A month later he headed an economic mission to Greece with the rank of U.S. Ambassador. During the McCarthy Era, Porter and his law firm defended more than 100 government employees against disloyalty charges. In 1971, as a lawyer in private practice, he called for the permanent awarding of licenses to broadcast stations.

Chairman Porter died on November 26, 1975, at the age of seventy-one.

MICHAEL K. POWELL (NOVEMBER 3, 1997–MARCH 17, 2005)

Michael Powell was the chief of staff of the Antitrust Division in the Department of Justice when he was appointed as a Republican member of the Commission by President Bill Clinton. Prior to that position, he had been an attorney in private practice and a policy advisor to Secretary of Defense Richard Cheney. After graduating from the College of William and Mary with a degree in government, Powell joined the Army, following in the footsteps of his father, former secretary of state Colin Powell. Powell was later seriously injured in a training accident and retired from the Army. He then went to Georgetown University for law school.

Commissioner Powell became Chairman Powell shortly after the inauguration of President George W. Bush. Powell was considered a strong advocate of deregulation in all facets of communications policy, believing that regulation hindered the development of technology. Support for technology, particularly digital advancements, was the centerpiece of much of Powell's agenda at the Commission. He advocated for further technological development in many fields, including broadband, voice over internet protocol (VoIP), and digital television. The anti-telemarketing "Do Not Call" list was created during his time at the Commission.

Michael Powell was chairman of the FCC from 2001 to 2005. (Courtesy of the FCC)

The centerpiece of Powell's chairmanship was his loosening of many of the regulations on media ownership. He viewed media scarcity as irrelevant in the internet age. He clashed with Democrats on the Commission and in Congress on the matter and saw the courts overturn his decisions.

He opposed content regulation in theory, but his tenure saw the largest fines for indecency ever issued following the 2004 Super Bowl incident involving Janet Jackson.

Chairman Powell left the Commission in March 2005.

ANNING SMITH PRALL (JANUARY 17, 1935–JULY 23, 1937)

Anning Prall was born on Staten Island (formerly known as Prall Island, after his family), and until he went to Congress, he never lived more than a mile from the house in which he was born. He attended New York University but left to work in a newspaper office. He later served as a clerk in municipal court and spent more than ten years at the Staten Island Savings Bank. He then became involved in local New York City politics and served three years on the New York City Board of Education and two years as a commissioner of taxes and assessment, where he got to know then Governor Franklin Roosevelt. In 1922, he was named to fill the congressional seat of the late Daniel Riordan. He stayed in Congress until January 1935.

Prall was named a commissioner in January 1935 and elevated to chair in March for a one-year term. He was reappointed in 1936 to another term. Shortly after becoming chair, he warned a National Association of Broadcasters meeting that they must bar objectionable programming. During his time at the Commission, he repeatedly encouraged self-regulation to keep within the bounds of what was appropriate. Prall also believed in the need for the Equal Time provision, which required that all qualified federal candidates be given access to the airways. He went so far as to force a radio station in Pittsburgh to carry an address by the Communist candidate for president.

Chairman Prall was strongly supportive of the First Amendment rights of broadcasters. For example, during the Italo-Ethiopian war, he said that radio stations did not have to maintain neutrality, which was the position of the U.S. government. When patriotic groups complained of "subversive" broadcasts, Prall maintained the airwaves belong to all people.

Chairman Anning Prall died of a heart attack at his summer home in Maine on July 23, 1937. As a sign of respect for the departed chairman, all radio stations in the United States and ships at sea broadcast a eulogy and observed a minute of silence on July 27, 1937.

JAMES H. QUELLO (APRIL 30, 1974–NOVEMBER 1997)

Commissioner James Quello frequently said that his six amphibious landings during World War II prepared him for twenty-three years at the FCC. Prior to joining the Commission, he spent twenty-five years as a broadcaster at WJR, Detroit. At the time of his appointment, he was the vice president and general manager. He had also been an executive at Cap Cities Broadcasting. While at WJR, Quello was also involved in civic life in Detroit, serving on the Detroit Housing and Urban Renewal Commission for twenty-one years and as trustee for the Michigan Veterans Trust Fund for twenty-two years.

Quello was a conservative Democrat appointed by President Richard Nixon in 1974. His first confirmation hearing lasted eight days, the longest on record (his last was the shortest, at twelve minutes). His predecessor Nicholas Johnson and many activist groups opposed him because he was so closely associated with the broadcast industry.

Commissioner Quello was a champion for the interests of broadcasters and viewed many regulations as unfairly handicapping the industry in its fight with cable and satellite. He opposed many of Chairman Reed Hundt's pet projects, including the three-hour requirement for children's television, a ban on liquor ads, and free airtime to political candidates. He did believe, however, that it was the FCC's place to regulate indecency and maybe even violence. In 1993, he served eleven months as acting chairman, during which time he voted to repeal the fin-syn rules.

After leaving the Commission, he founded the James H. and Mary B. Quello Center for Telecommunications Management and Law at his alma mater, Michigan State University, and served as a consultant on government affairs to a Washington, D.C., law firm.

CHARLOTTE THOMPSON REID (OCTOBER 8, 1971–JULY 1, 1976)

Commissioner Charlotte Thompson Reid came to the FCC from Congress, having spent ten years representing Illinois. Born in 1913, she attended Illinois College and was a featured vocalist (under the name Annette King) on *Don McNeill's Breakfast Club* at the age of twenty-three. She retired from entertaining to be a wife and a mother. She reentered public life when her husband, who was running for Congress, died. She took his place on the ballot and was reelected four times. Reid was considered very conservative, described by the *Chicago Daily News* as "slightly to the right of Marie Antoinette."[17] She voted against most of Lyndon Johnson's Great Society measures and for the Vietnam War.

Reid was considered a fairly disinterested commissioner, missing more than 15 percent of the votes while at the FCC. She believed in media self-regulation and disliked television. She opposed a Commission inquiry into broadcast obscenity.

After remarrying in 1976, Commissioner Reid resigned.

HENRY M. RIVERA (AUGUST 10, 1981–SEPTEMBER 15, 1985)

Commissioner Henry Rivera held both a B.A. in economics and a law degree from the University of New Mexico. He was a lawyer in private practice and had no experience in communications when appointed by President Ronald Reagan.

Commissioner Rivera was a frequent dissenter during the highly deregulatory tenure of Chairman Mark Fowler. He was supportive of the deregulation of the telephone industry but often opposed Fowler on broadcasting issues. He was especially concerned about advertising and children's television. He also opposed increasing media ownership caps and allowing newspaper cross-ownership. Commissioner Rivera, the first Hispanic on the FCC, was vocal about the need for more minorities in broadcasting and often clashed with Fowler over the issue.

After leaving the Commission in frustration, Rivera returned to private practice, focusing on communications law. He later served as the chairman of the Minority Media and Telecommunications Council, a lobbying group.

GLEN O. ROBINSON (JULY 10, 1974–AUGUST 30, 1976)

Commissioner Glen Robinson was educated at Harvard University and Stanford University Law School. He practiced law in Washington, D.C., for six years and taught at the University of Minnesota Law School for seven years before being appointed to the Commission in 1974.

Commissioner Robinson was an early advocate of deregulation and believed the Fairness Doctrine should be repealed.

After leaving the Commission in 1976, he joined the faculty of the law school at the University of Virginia and has taught there for more than thirty years.

STEPHEN A. SHARP (OCTOBER 4, 1982–JUNE 30, 1983)

Commissioner Stephen Sharp had considerable FCC experience when he was nominated by President Ronald Reagan. At the time of his nomination, he was the FCC's general counsel. He had also served as a legal assistant to Commissioner Margita White and as a staff attorney. Sharp also spent time as an attorney in private practice. He graduated from Washington and Lee University (B.A.) and the University of Virginia School of Law. He worked on the Reagan campaign and was considered a deregulatory ally of Chairman Mark Fowler.

Sharp's nomination was strongly supported by Mark Fowler and Moral Majority leader Jerry Falwell but opposed by Senate Democrats and Republican Senator Ted Stevens, who backed another candidate.

Although Commissioner Sharp was originally nominated to a seven-year term, he served only nine months. His place on the Commission was eliminated when Congress reduced the FCC to five members. He then returned to private practice.

ALFRED C. SIKES (AUGUST 8, 1989–JANUARY 19, 1993)

Chairman Alfred Sikes came to the Commission from the Commerce Department, where he spent three years as the assistant secretary of commerce for the Telecommunications and Information Administration. Prior to that, he was the president of his own broadcast management and media consulting company and owned and operated a radio station group. Sikes spent considerable time in Missouri government and politics, including the Department of Consumer Affairs, Regulation, and Licensing. Sikes had also been a practicing attorney, graduating from Westminster College (B.A.) and the University of Missouri Law School.

Although a proponent of deregulation, Chairman Sikes believed that the FCC should step in when the market was not competitive, such as in the case of monopolistic cable rates. Sikes was committed to advancing technology and keeping the regulators out of the way. One of the first things he did at the Commission was to replace the old dial telephones with push button ones.

During his tenure, the FCC cleared the way for telephone companies to provide video programming and relaxed limits on radio station ownership and network and cable cross-ownership. Sikes's biggest defeat came with the close vote on the repeal of the fin-syn regulations.

Chairman Sikes had a much better relationship with Congress than Mark Fowler or Dennis Patrick did and some say he achieved much more in the way of deregulation as a result. His confirmation hearing was dominated by senators clamoring for more active enforcement of the indecency regulations. As a result, Sikes's FCC became more aggressive on the indecency front, handing out record fines. Sikes was particularly concerned with the "shock jock" trend and frequently fined people like Infinity Broadcasting's Howard Stern. Stern, in turn, regularly attacked Sikes on the air, including wishing that Sikes's prostate cancer would spread.

After leaving the FCC, Chairman Sikes joined the Hearst Group as the president of its interactive media division.

GEORGE E. STERLING (JANUARY 2, 1948–SEPTEMBER 30, 1954)

Commissioner George Sterling started in the burgeoning radio field in the beginning and at the bottom, building the first amateur station in Maine in 1908. After the passage of the Radio Act of 1912, he received one of the first radio licenses issued. His first job with the FCC came in 1935 as an inspector in the Third Radio District. Three years later, he became the assistant chief of the field division of the FCC's Engineering Department. After a variety of other positions at the Commission, he was named Chief Engineer in May 1947. Sterling attended Johns Hopkins University and Baltimore City College.

During his time on the Commission, Sterling was viewed as an expert in amateur radio and the other commissioners often deferred to him. He also brought his perspective of being at the center of the birth of radio to the Commission's wrangling over the birth of television.

By 1954, Commissioner Sterling was suffering from ill health and resigned in September upon the advice of his physician.

IRVIN STEWART (JULY 11, 1934–JUNE 30, 1937)

Commissioner Irvin Stewart was highly educated and deeply involved in the early development of radio. He earned a bachelors, a masters in government and public administration, a law degree from the University of Texas, and a Ph.D. in constitutional law from Columbia University. He interspersed government service, such as being the assistant solicitor at the State Department, with academic pursuits like teaching constitutional law at the University of Texas for two years and spending a year as the chair of the government department at American University.

Commissioner Stewart was deeply involved in many of the early radio conferences. His first foray into the radio world was when he was appointed to supervise radio matters insofar as they impacted treaties. He helped draft the Communications Act of 1934 while on loan from the State Department to Representative Sam Rayburn. Commissioner Stewart believed that the domination of broadcasting by the chains was hurting program quality.

When Commissioner Stewart's term ended in 1937, he asked that he not be reappointed. He then became the head of the Committee of Scientific Aids to Learning, appointed by the National Research Council. In 1940, he was named the executive secretary of the National Defense Research Committee (later the Office of Scientific Research and Development), which oversaw the development of the atomic bomb. Stewart was president of West Virginia University from 1946 to 1958 and then he taught constitutional law there until his retirement in 1967. In the 1960s, he also acted as the director of telecommunications management in the Office of Emergency Planning. Commissioner Stewart died on December 24, 1990, after a series of strokes.

EUGENE O. SYKES (JULY 11, 1934–APRIL 5, 1939)

Eugene Sykes was charged with bringing order out of the chaos that was the early radio industry. Sykes attended St. John's College and the U.S. Naval Academy, eventually graduating from the University of Mississippi. After several years as an attorney in private practice, he was named a judge on the Supreme Court of Mississippi in 1916. After eight years, he returned to private practice. In 1927, he was named a federal radio commissioner by President Calvin Coolidge. He was the acting chairman of the FRC at the time of the creation of the FCC. He was very supportive of the passage of the Communications Act of 1934.

The most important issue faced by the FCC under Chairman Sykes was spectrum allocation. Sykes was also concerned that rural America be served adequately by radio. At a National Association of Broadcasters convention in 1936 Commissioner Sykes warned broadcasters to remember that children were listening to their programs and they should act accordingly.

Chairman Sykes stepped down from the chairmanship on March 8, 1935, but remained on the Commission until 1939. He then returned to private practice in Washington, D.C. He died of a heart attack in June 1945.

FREDERICK I. THOMPSON (APRIL 13, 1939–JUNE 30, 1941)

Commissioner Frederick Thompson was appointed in 1939 to complete the unfinished term of Commissioner Eugene Sykes. He had spent his career in the newspaper business and was a newspaper publisher for thirty-five years. He also spent ten years as a director for the Associated Press. He was active in Democratic politics through the 1910s and 1920s. He was on the U.S. Shipping Board for five years and was appointed by President Franklin Roosevelt to serve on the Advisory Board on Public Works in 1935.

Commissioner Thompson died on February 20, 1952, in Mobile, Alabama.

GLORIA TRISTANI (NOVEMBER 3, 1997–SEPTEMBER 7, 2001)

Commissioner Gloria Tristani had a family history of public service. Her grandfather was U.S. Senator Dennis Chavez, who represented New Mexico from 1931 until 1962. Her father, Jorge Tristani, served as the administrator of the Puerto Rico Industrial Development Company. She was born and raised in San Juan, Puerto Rico, and Spanish was her first language. She graduated from Barnard College and the University of New Mexico School of Law. In 1994, Tristani was the first woman elected to the New Mexico State Corporation Commission and was the chair in 1996. While at the SCC, she helped implement the Telecommunications Act of 1996 at the state level.

Commissioner Tristani was committed to bringing the benefits of the telecommunications revolution to all Americans. She was very concerned with the promulgation of the FCC's universal service policies. She also demonstrated great concern for the impact of the media on children, serving as the chair of the FCC's V-Chip Task Force and pushing for greater enforcement of the indecency regulations. Tristani opposed media consolidation and voted against allowing Viacom to own both the CBS and UPN television networks. Tristani also supported the EEO rules, increasing minority ownership of the media, and low power FM.

Commissioner Tristani left the FCC in 2001 to run as the Democratic candidate for the U.S. Senate from New Mexico. She lost to the Republican incumbent, Senator Pete Domenici. She went on to serve as the managing director of the Office of Communications of the United Church of Christ.

JAMES J. WADSWORTH (MAY 5, 1965–OCTOBER 31, 1969)

Commissioner James Wadsworth spent his life in public service after graduating from Yale University. The son of a U.S. senator and a grandson of President Abraham Lincoln's private secretary and secretary of state, he was a New York State Assemblyman for ten years and then became a special assistant with the Economic Cooperation Administration. He also served two years at the War Assets Board and two years at the Air Transportation Association. Wadsworth then went to the United Nations. Appointed in 1953, he was deputy chief of the delegation for seven years and then rose to the head of the mission when Henry Cabot Lodge left to run for vice president.

A Republican appointed by President Lyndon Johnson, he was later described as an "unpredictable maverick"[18] on the Commission by *The New York Times*. He believed that the less regulation, the better. He cast a key vote to revoke a television station's license for the first time. He dissented from the FCC ban on cigarette advertising, believing that the Commission did not have the authority to ban the ads.

Commissioner Wadsworth resigned from the FCC to join the negotiations that resulted in the chartering of Intelsat—the international satellite consortium. After retiring from public life in 1970, he managed his family's dairy farm until his death in March 1984.

ROY C. WAKEFIELD (MARCH 22, 1941–JUNE 30, 1947)

Commissioner Roy Wakefield was on the California Railroad Commission when he was appointed by President Franklin Roosevelt in 1941. He held a B.A. and a law degree from Stanford University. He practiced law and was active in Republican politics in his home state of California.

In 1947, Commissioner Wakefield said that radio in America was not living up to its responsibilities or potential, but he did not believe the FCC could guarantee that stations do so.

Commissioner Wakefield was renominated in May 1947. In June, his nomination was withdrawn and Congressman Robert Jones was put forward instead. No explanation was given for the switch. He then went to Switzerland to represent the State Department on the International Provisional Radio Frequency Board. Fifteen months later, he returned to the United States, suffering from acute insomnia and ill health. On September 29, 1949, he was found dead in his apartment, an apparent suicide.

PAUL A. WALKER (JULY 11, 1934–JUNE 30, 1953)

Commissioner Paul Walker was an expert on telephone and telegraph rates who spent his career overseeing public utilities. Beginning in 1915, he was an attorney for the Oklahoma Corporation Commission, the state public service control board. Four years later, he became a special referee for the Oklahoma Supreme Court. In 1921, he returned to the Oklahoma Corporation Commission and was elected a commissioner in 1930. He was chairman at the time of his appointment to the newly formed FCC. Walker held degrees from the University of Chicago and the University of Oklahoma law school. He had also spent time as a lawyer and a high school principal.

Walker served on the FCC from 1934 until 1953, one of the longest tenures at the Commission. He served as acting chairman for a few months in 1947 and was the chair from February 28, 1952, until April 17, 1953. Commissioner Walker was heavily involved in the regulation of AT&T from the very beginning, overseeing many of the investigations into the telephone industry and the rates it could charge.

During his time at the Commission, Walker was involved in most of the major issues of the time and was especially proud of his role in encouraging educational television. He once proposed that the FCC be given the power to license the broadcast networks as a way to protect the individual stations.

After his retirement from the Commission, Walker practiced law in Washington, D.C., for a few years. He then retired to Oklahoma in 1957, living near the University of Oklahoma campus where he and his wife met. Commissioner Walker died of pneumonia on November 3, 1965, at the age of eighty-four.

ABBOTT WASHBURN (JULY 10, 1974–OCTOBER 1, 1982)

Commissioner Abbott Washburn had a long career in public relations, government service, and Republican politics, serving Presidents Eisenhower, Nixon, and Reagan in a variety of capacities. After graduating from Harvard University, Washburn worked in public relations at General Mills for fifteen years. He brought those PR skills to government service as the executive vice chairman of Crusade for Freedom, which raised money for Radio Free Europe. He then spent seven years as the deputy director of the U.S. Information Agency. After leaving the USIA, he ran his own PR firm in Washington, D.C., for six years and then joined Citizens for Nixon as its PR director. Immediately before his appointment to the Commission, Washburn spent three years as chairman (with the rank of ambassador) of the U.S. delegation to the Intelsat Conference on Definitive Arrangements International Telecommunications Satellite Organization.

While at the FCC, Commissioner Washburn advocated setting aside bandwidth for cellular telephone development and encouraged more educational programming on television. Washburn also co-authored the FCC opinion in the *Pacifica* case, helping to determine what constituted indecent speech on radio.

After leaving the FCC, Washburn returned to diplomacy and chaired the International Telecommunication Union Radio Conference on Direct-to-Home Satellite Broadcasting Western Hemisphere. He remained involved in Republican politics and government for many years, advising the Reagan Administration and the State Department.

Commissioner Washburn died at the age of eighty-eight on December 11, 2003.

EDWARD M. WEBSTER (APRIL 10, 1947–JUNE 30, 1956)

Commissioner E. M. Webster was a retired commodore in the U.S. Coast Guard who first joined the FCC as an assistant chief engineer in 1934. He was then recalled to active military duty during World War II. Following the war, Webster became the director of the division of telecommunications of the National Federation of American Shipping. President Harry Truman appointed him to the Commission in 1947.

Considering his background, it is not surprising that Commissioner Webster was an expert on the use of radio frequencies on the high seas, particularly as it related to safety concerns. He represented the Commission and the U.S. government at a number of conferences on issues relating to shipping before and during his time at the FCC. He was also deeply involved with the development of television.

Commissioner Webster died in July 1976 at the age of eighty-seven.

ROBERT WELLS (NOVEMBER 6, 1969–NOVEMBER 1, 1971)

Before being appointed by President Richard Nixon, Commissioner Robert Wells was the President of KIUL in Garden City, Kansas, and general manager of the Harris Radio Group, a chain of nine stations in Kansas, Iowa, Illinois, and Colorado. He was also a member of the National Association of Broadcasters' radio code review board. At the time of his appointment to the Commission, he was already on the record against allowing competitive challenges to license renewals.

Commissioner Wells brought experience to the Commission that very few had—what it was actually like to run a small radio station. His appointment and his service were applauded by the broadcasting industry, who felt that the appointment of an experienced broadcaster was long overdue.

Commissioner Wells was originally appointed to fill out the term of Commissioner James Wadsworth. In January 1971, he was given his own seven-year term. In October of that year, Wells announced his resignation from the Commission, citing a desire to return to his home state of Kansas.

MARGITA E. WHITE (SEPTEMBER 23, 1976–FEBRUARY 28, 1979)

Commissioner Margita White was born in Sweden and immigrated to California with her parents when she was a child. She graduated from the University of the Redlands with a degree in government and went on to earn a master's in political science from Rutgers University. She first went to Washington, D.C., in 1958 as an intern and spent the bulk of her career in politics and government. Throughout the 1960s, she worked for a variety of politicians, including Richard Nixon's 1960 presidential campaign and Barry Goldwater's 1964 presidential campaign.

White began working for the Nixon administration in 1969 in the White House Office of Communications. In 1973, she became the assistant director for pubic information at the U.S. Information Agency. In 1975, she returned to the White House to become an assistant press secretary to President Gerald Ford and then the director of the White House Office of Communications. She was appointed to the FCC in the fall of 1976. White was originally nominated for a full seven-year term, but her nomination ran into some trouble when senators perceived a potential conflict of interest in that her husband's law firm handled communications cases. Instead of the seven-year term, she was instead confirmed to finish out two years on an unexpired term.

White left the Commission at the end of her term and became a director of Radio Free Europe. She then spent four years as a consultant and the coordinator of the Television Operators Caucus before being named the president of the Association for Maximum Service Television in 1988. White retired from the MSTV in 2001. On November 20, 2002, Commissioner White died of lung cancer.

RICHARD E. WILEY (JANUARY 5, 1972–OCTOBER 13, 1977)

Richard Wiley had earned an undergraduate and law degree from Northwestern University when he joined the U.S. Army Judge Advocate General's Office at the Pentagon. While in Washington, D.C., he earned an LL.M. degree from Georgetown University. He then returned to Illinois to enter private practice. He also taught law at the John Marshall Law School in Chicago.

It was through his work on Nixon's 1968 presidential campaign that Wiley first came to the FCC. After interviewing with Chairman Dean Burch, he was hired to be the Commission's general counsel in 1970. In 1972, he was appointed a commissioner. When Burch left the FCC to counsel the president during Watergate, Wiley was elevated to chairman.

Wiley's time as chairman was marked by increased efficiency and consensus-building at the Commission, both at the staff level and with his fellow commissioners. It was routine to see 7-to-0 votes under Chairman Wiley. It was also during Wiley's tenure that the FCC and the three broadcast networks agreed to create the Family Viewing Hour. He supported increasing competition and lightening the regulatory load on the broadcast industry.

After leaving the Commission in 1977, Chairman Wiley returned to private legal practice and stayed active in Republican politics. In 1983, he co-founded Wiley, Rein, and Fielding, considered one of the most important communications law firms in the

Chairman Richard Wiley was known as a consensus-builder among his fellow commissioners. (Courtesy of the National Archives)

country. Wiley himself has been recognized as one of the most powerful lawyers in Washington, D.C., and is often referred to as the "sixth commissioner." He played an important role in the development of HDTV, serving for nine years as the chairman of the FCC's Advisory Committee on Advanced Television Service.

WILLIAM H. WILLS (JULY 23, 1945–MARCH 6, 1946)

Commissioner William Wills was a two-term governor of Vermont when he was appointed to the FCC by President Harry Truman. He had been a successful businessman in his home town of Bennington, where he founded Wills Insurance and later helped establish the Bennington Co-operative Savings and Loan Association. He also served in the Vermont House of Representatives, the Vermont State Senate, and as the state's lieutenant governor.

Commissioner Wills died of a heart attack on March 6, 1946, after serving only seven months at the FCC.

NOTES

1. Catherine Yang, "The FCC's Loner Is No Longer So Lonely," *Business Week*, March 24, 2003, 78.

2. *New York Times*, "Coy Warns Radio on Crime and Smut," March 15, 1950, 54.

3. *New York Times*, "Communications Act Criticized by Craven," July 3, 1942, 20.

4. Ken Ditto and Gerald Flannery, "John S. Cross," in *Commissioners of the FCC, 1927–1994*, ed. Gerald V. Flannery (Lanham, MD: University Press of America, 1995), 120–121.

5. *New York Times*, "Cleaning Up After Dirty Words," July 31, 1978, A14.

6. *The Economist*, "The FCC: Compete or Die," January 31, 1987, 34.

7. Leonard Zeidenberg, "Seven Years and Five Months: A Look Back at the Tenure of Nick Johnson," *Broadcasting*, December 10, 1973, 20.

8. Zeidenberg, "Seven Years," 20.

9. Trudi Hahn, "Jurist, Regulator, Trustbuster Dies," *Star Tribune*, May 1, 2004, 1B.

10. Adam Bernstein, "Lawyer Lee Loevinger, 91, Dies," *Washington Post*, May 5, 2004, B06.

11. *New York Times*, "FCC's Loevinger Wary of US Role," August 27, 1963, 63.

12. *New York Times*, "Wire-Tapping Denounced," February 24, 1955, 17.

13. *New York Times*, "President Begins Shake-Up of FCC," August 18, 1937, 34.

14. *New York Times*, "Bars Radio Censorship," November 13, 1938, 42.

15. *Chicago Tribune*, "'Vast Wasteland' Speech Holds True After All These Years," April 24, 2004, 17; italics added.

16. *New York Times*, "Plans Radio Rules on Political Talks," June 24, 1938, 6.

17. Carol A. Weisenberger, "Women of the FCC: Activists or Tokens?" *Business and Economic History* 21 (1992): 194.

18. Joseph B. Treaster, "James J. Wadsworth Dies at 78: Headed US Delegation to UN," *New York Times*, March 15, 1984, B12.

─────── ☆ **7** ☆ ───────

Annotated Supreme Court Decisions, 1930–2004

The Federal Communications Commission regulates complicated and diverse industries with complicated and diverse rules. It is not surprising, then, that the Commission often finds itself in court. According to the Office of the General Counsel, the FCC has been involved in well over 1,700 appellate and Supreme Court cases. The cases in which the Supreme Court issued a decision have been annotated below. A list of all appellate cases involving the Commission is included in Appendix 1. Although there have been appellate cases of enormous significance, there were far too many non-Supreme Court cases to annotate here. Instead, cases with significance to the Commission and the regulated industries have been dealt with in other chapters, particularly Chapter 5.

Arkansas Educ. Television Comm'n v. Forbes, 523 U.S. 666, 140 L.Ed.2d 875, 118 S.Ct. 1633 (1998)

Candidate debates have long been considered "bona fide news events" according to the FCC and thus exempt from the Equal Time requirements of Section 315 of the Communications Act. The debate in question in this case was on a public television station, thus triggering questions regarding the power of the state to suppress political speech. The Supreme Court concluded that even public stations could exclude minor candidates from a debate without triggering the Equal Time requirements as long as the exclusion was not based on the candidate's views.

Ashbacker Radio Corp. v. FCC, 326 U.S. 327, 90 L.Ed.2d 108, 66 S.Ct. 148 (1945)

One of the FCC's biggest challenges in the early days of broadcasting was spectrum allocation and licensing. The Supreme Court concluded that when mutually exclusive applications for a broadcast station are filed, the FCC must hold a hearing to determine which applicant will receive the license.

AT&T Corp. v. Iowa Util. Bd., 525 U.S. 366, 142 L.Ed.2d 835, 119 S.Ct. 721 (1999)

The Telecommunications Act of 1996 was a far-reaching rewrite of the federal laws governing the communications industries in this country. Telephone regulation, in particular, changed dramatically. Local telephone service had always been a regulated monopoly. The new law required that local phone service be opened to competition and that the local phone companies be required to share their infrastructure with competitors. The FCC wrote a number of rules to move the phone industry into competition. Local phone companies sued, claiming the FCC did not have the authority to write the rules as it had. The Supreme Court sided with the Commission.

Capital Cities Cable v. Crisp, 467 U.S. 691, 81 L.Ed.2d 580, 104 S.Ct. 2694 (1984)

The state of Oklahoma passed a law that banned alcoholic beverage advertising coming in on out-of-state channels carried on cable systems. This was in conflict with FCC must carry rules, which mandated that signals be carried without editing. The Supreme Court held that federal law trumped state law and the FCC, not the local or state authorities, had the power to regulate the content of cable.

CBS, Inc. v. Democratic National Comm., 412 U.S. 94, 36 L.Ed.2d 772, 93 S.Ct. 2080 (1973)

Two groups, the Democratic National Committee and Business Executives Move for Vietnam Peace, sought to buy time on radio and television stations to run ads that advocated a position on issues of public controversy. Many stations had policies of refusing such ads. The DNC and the BEM argued that this violated the Fairness Doctrine and the First Amendment. The Supreme Court held that stations were within their rights to promulgate a ban on advertising of controversial issues.

CBS, Inc. v. FCC, 316 U.S. 407, 86 L.Ed. 1563, 62 S.Ct. 1194 (1942)

In 1941, the FCC issued the Chain Broadcasting Regulations to regulate the affiliate agreements stations had with the networks. CBS was particularly concerned because the contracts it had with its seven owned-and-operated stations and 115 affiliates violated the new orders, and thus the stations' licenses were subject to revocation. The Supreme Court affirmed that the new rules were subject to judicial review. The Supreme Court later ruled more specifically on the Chain Broadcasting Regulations in *National Broadcasting Co., Inc. v. United States*, 319 U.S. 190 (1943).

CBS, Inc. v. FCC, 453 U.S. 367, 69 L.Ed.2d 706, 101 S.Ct. 2813 (1981)

In 1979, the Carter-Mondale campaign asked the major television networks to sell it thirty minutes of airtime. The networks refused, despite the fact that Section 312(a)(7) of the Communications Act required broadcasters to provide reasonable access to all qualified federal candidates. The FCC ruled that the networks' refusal violated Section 312(a)(7) and the Supreme Court upheld the Commission's ruling.

City of Los Angeles v. Preferred Communications, Inc., 476 U.S. 488, 90 L.Ed.2d 480, 106 S.Ct. 2034 (1986)

Preferred Communications wanted to offer cable service to a part of Los Angeles that already had a cable company with an exclusive franchise. Preferred challenged the city's right to award exclusive franchises on the basis of the First Amendment, since the utility poles could support more than one company's wires. The court of appeals sided with Preferred, saying that cable deserved the same First Amendment protection as newspapers. The Supreme Court refused to go that far, but did agree that exclusive franchises raised First Amendment issues. The case was then sent back to a trial court for a factual analysis of whether Los Angeles utility poles could support additional wires. A judge later ruled that the poles could support additional cables and thus opened some of the cable markets to competition.

City of New York v. FCC, 486 U.S. 57, 100 L.Ed.2d 48, 108 S.Ct. 1637 (1988)

New York City argued that the technical standards set for cable by the FCC were too low. The city maintained that it should be allowed to set higher standards. The Supreme Court ruled that the FCC's national standards could not be overruled by local governments.

Community Television of Southern Calif. v. Gottfried, 459 U.S. 498, 74 L.Ed.2d 705, 103 S.Ct. 1885 (1983)

Section 504 of the Rehabilitation Act of 1973 provides that no otherwise qualified handicapped individual shall, solely by reason of his handicap, be excluded from participation in, be denied the benefits of, or be subjected to discrimination under any program or activity receiving federal financial assistance. Sue Gottfried asked the FCC to deny the license renewals of eight Los Angeles television stations that were not providing sufficient closed captioning of their programming. The FCC concluded that the seven commercial stations did not receive federal funding and thus were not subject to Section 504. The public station in question, however, did receive federal funds and could be subject to the requirements of Section 504. The Supreme Court concluded that Section 504 did not mean that the FCC should base license renewals of public television stations on different criteria from those applied to commercial stations.

Denver Area Educ. Telecommunications Consortium, Inc. v. FCC, 518 U.S. 727, 135 L.Ed.2d 888, 116 S.Ct. 2374 (1996)

Three provisions of the Cable Act of 1992 dealt with the broadcast of sexually explicit material over public and leased access channels. The Supreme Court upheld Section 10(a), guaranteeing a cable company's right to refuse to carry explicit programming on leased access channels. The Court deemed two other sections, 10(b) and 10(c), unconstitutional. Section 10(b) stated that any cable company that chose to accept sexually explicit material on leased access channels had to segregate that programming to a single channel and block that channel for all subscribers unless they requested the channel in writing thirty days in advance. The Court said that this was an undue burden on viewers' First Amendment freedoms. Section 10(c) required that cable operators censor sexually explicit programming on all pubic, educational, and governmental channels. The Court said public access channels had traditionally been a public forum and thus could not be subject to censorship.

Farmers Educational and Cooperative Union of America v. WDAY, Inc., 360 U.S. 525, 3 L.Ed.2d 1407, 79 S.Ct. 1302 (1959)

Section 315 of the Communications Act bars broadcasters from censoring or controlling the content of political ads and other candidate messages. In 1959, a candidate for the U.S. Senate from North Dakota went on radio station WDAY and accused a local nonprofit of being a Communist organization. The nonprofit sued the candidate and the station for slander. A federal district judge removed the station from the suit on the basis of the no-censorship provision and the Supreme Court upheld the ruling.

FCC v. Allentown Broadcasting Corp., 349 U.S. 358, 99 L.Ed. 1147, 75 S.Ct. 855 (1955)

The Communications Act requires that broadcast stations be fairly, efficiently, and equitably distributed throughout the United States. The Supreme Court determined that when different communities were competing to use the same broadcast frequency, the FCC should base the license decision on which community has the greatest need for the station, not on the qualifications of the particular applicants.

FCC v. American Broadcasting Co., 347 U.S. 284, 98 L.Ed.2d 699, 74 S.Ct. 793 (1954)

The federal criminal code prohibits broadcast stations from airing information about lotteries. As a result, the FCC banned "give-away" programs that gave prizes to audience members selected by chance or who answered questions correctly but who were not required to contribute any money or other valuable consideration. The Supreme Court held that this position went beyond the power of the Commission and was thus invalid.

FCC v. Beach Communications, Inc., 508 U.S. 307, 124 L.Ed.2d 211, 113 S.Ct. 2096 (1993)

Satellite master antenna television systems (SMATV) are essentially private cable systems that serve apartments, condominiums, and other private multi-unit buildings. SMATV is largely unregulated, with one exception. The Supreme Court upheld an FCC ruling that if any SMATV wires crossed a public right-of-way, such as a public street, the SMATV system became a cable system subject to all the rules and regulations that apply to franchised cable companies.

FCC v. Columbia Broadcasting System of Calif., Inc., 311 U.S. 132, 85 L.Ed. 87, 61 S.Ct. 152 (1940)

The FCC denied an application to transfer a license from Associated Broadcasters to the Columbia Broadcasting System of California. The companies then appealed the decision to the U.S. Court of Appeals for the District of Columbia Circuit. The Commission argued that the appeals court did not have jurisdiction in the case. The Supreme Court sided with the Commission, stating the lower court did not have jurisdiction over this type of FCC decision.

FCC v. Florida Power Corp., 480 U.S. 245, 94 L.Ed.2d 282, 107 S.Ct. 1107 (1987)

The Pole Attachments Act gave the FCC the authority to regulate the rates charged by utility companies to cable companies seeking to hang the cable wires on utility poles. When the FCC reduced the rates that Florida Power was charging the cable companies in the state, Florida Power claimed it was a case of unlawful "takings" under the Fifth Amendment. The Supreme Court held that the FCC's ability to set rates did not violate the Fifth Amendment.

FCC v. ITT World Communications, Inc., 466 U.S. 463, 80 L.Ed.2d 480, 104 S.Ct. 1936 (1984)

The federal Sunshine Act prohibits members of government agencies from meeting in private. The Supreme Court concluded that when FCC commissioners represent the United States at international communication conferences, the open meeting laws do not apply.

FCC v. League of Women Voters, 468 U.S. 364, 82 L.Ed.2d 278, 104 S.Ct. 3106 (1984)

In Section 399 of the Communications Act, Congress banned editorializing by public broadcasters. The belief was that since public stations receive government funding, they would feel compelled to support government positions in order not to endanger that funding. The Supreme Court struck down the ban, citing the First Amendment and stating that there were other ways to protect public stations from undue government influence over editorial policies.

FCC v. Midwest Video Corp., 440 U.S. 689, 59 L.Ed.2d 692, 99 S.Ct. 1435 (1979)

Midwest Video was a cable system that challenged the FCC's access channel requirements. The Commission had mandated that cable systems provide channels and equipment to the public, educational institutions, and local government. The Supreme Court held that the FCC did not have the authority to promulgate these cable regulations and that the Commission had to ask Congress to grant it the ability to do so.

FCC v. National Broadcasting Co., Inc., 319 U.S. 239, 87 L.Ed. 1374, 63 S.Ct. 1035 (1943)

NBC operated KOA in Denver, Colorado, a "clear channel" station that could be heard throughout much of the country and that was given exclusive nighttime access to the frequency. WHDH was a daytime-only station in Boston that operated on the same frequency. In 1938, WHDH requested an upgrade in power and permission to broadcast at night. Because of possible interference issues, the FCC set a hearing. As part of the WHDH consideration, the FCC intended to reconsider the clear channel rule. NBC wanted to participate in the WHDH hearing, but was turned down by the Commission. The FCC then granted WHDH's request to broadcast at night. The Supreme Court held that NBC should have been allowed to participate in the hearing.

FCC v. National Citizens Comm. for Broadcasting, 436 U.S. 775, 56 L.Ed.2d 697, 98 S.Ct. 2096 (1978)

From the beginning of broadcasting, the FCC was concerned about the impact on diversity when newspapers owned broadcast stations in the same market. In 1975, the Commission made this ownership structure illegal but grandfathered in most existing cross-ownership situations. In sixteen cases, the Commission ordered divestiture. The Supreme Court upheld the Commission's rules requiring some to divest and allowing others to continue.

FCC v. NextWave Personal Communications, Inc., 537 U.S. 293, 154 L.Ed.2d 863, 123 S.Ct. 832 (2003)

NextWave won an auction for spectrum space for high-speed wireless services. The company later filed for Chapter 11 bankruptcy and the FCC revoked the licenses. Section 525 of the Bankruptcy Code prohibits the FCC from revoking licenses for failure to make payments, but the Communications Act as amended required the FCC to take back the licenses when NextWave failed to make a payment. The Supreme Court determined that the FCC could not revoke a license for nonpayment.

FCC v. Pacifica Foundation, 438 U.S. 726, 57 L.Ed.2d 1073, 98 S.Ct. 3026 (1978)

In 1973, Pacifica radio station WBAI broadcast a George Carlin monologue called "Seven Words You Can Never Say on Television." One complaint was sent to the Commission and a letter was placed in WBAI's file. The Commission used this order to define a new indecency policy. Pacifica challenged the constitutionality of the new policy. The Supreme Court held that over-the-air broadcasting was different from other media because broadcasting was uniquely accessible to young children (even those too young to read) and pervasive and intrusive into the home. The Court wrote that because of these differences, sexually explicit content could be regulated at times of the day when there was a reasonable risk that children were in the audience.

FCC v. Pottsville Broadcasting Co., 309 U.S. 134, 84 L.Ed. 656, 60 S.Ct. 437 (1940)

In May 1936, the Pottsville Broadcasting Company applied for a construction permit to build a station in Pottsville, Pennsylvania. The FCC did not award the permit, stating the company was financially disqualified and did not represent the local interests of the Pottsville community. Pottsville appealed and the U.S. Court of Appeals for the District of Columbia Circuit held that the FCC had made a mistake in its determination of the company's financial status and ordered the FCC to reconsider. In the meantime, two other applicants applied for the same frequency. The FCC scheduled a comparative hearing to consider all three license requests together. The Court of Appeals then stated the FCC had to consider the Pottsville application separately since when the proceeding started, it was the only applicant. The Supreme Court overturned the lower court, stating that the FCC had the authority to set the parameters of a license hearing however it believed would best determine the public interest, convenience, and necessity.

FCC v. RCA Communications, Inc., 346 U.S. 86, 97 L.Ed. 1470, 73 S.Ct. 998 (1953)

The Mackay Radio and Telegraph Co. wanted to open telegraph lines to European countries already being served by RCA. The FCC approved the new lines, saying that competition would serve the public interest. RCA appealed and the Supreme Court held that the idea of competition alone was not enough to warrant granting the license. The Court stated that the FCC must be able to point to a specific benefit from competition before approving a new license.

FCC v. Sanders Bros. Radio Station, 309 U.S. 470, 84 L.Ed. 869, 60 S.Ct. 693 (1940)

In January 1936, the *Telegraph Herald* newspaper applied for a construction permit to build a radio station in Dubuque, Iowa. A few months later, Sanders

Bros. applied to move their East Dubuque, Illinois, station across the Mississippi River to Dubuque. Sanders later claimed that there was not enough revenue or talent to support two stations in the area and asked the FCC to reject the *Telegraph Herald*'s application. The FCC eventually granted both construction permits and Sanders Bros. appealed. The Supreme Court held that a broadcast station may get involved in the license process for another station when it believes that it will suffer financially if the license is granted. This claim of financial harm, however, only allows the station to be involved in the process. Once the station is granted entry to the hearing, any request to deny the license must then be based on the public interest standard.

FCC *v. Schreiber*, 381 U.S. 279, 14 L.Ed.2d 383, 85 S.Ct. 1459 (1965)

In 1959 Congress asked the FCC to investigate the roles played by the networks, advertisers, agencies, talent, film producers, and distributors in the television industry. In October 1960, a hearing was held in Los Angeles to examine the practices of television companies, talent agencies and representatives, program "packagers," sales representatives, and others. One witness called to testify was Schreiber, a vice president of Music Corporation of America, Inc., one of the largest packagers and producers of network television programs. He was told to bring a list of the programs that MCA produced and packaged. Schreiber brought the list of produced programming but refused to reveal the packaged programs without a guarantee of privacy. He claimed that revealing the list would disclose trade secrets and confidential data. The Supreme Court held that Schreiber was required to submit the documents because the FCC has the authority to establish the parameters of a hearing.

FCC *v. WJR, The Goodwill Station, Inc.*, 337 U.S. 265, 93 L.Ed. 1353, 69 S.Ct. 1097 (1949)

The FCC granted a construction permit to Coastal Plains Broadcasting Company for a station in Tarboro, North Carolina. WJR was a powerful station based in Detroit, Michigan, that had been broadcasting exclusively on the frequency awarded to Coastal Plains. WJR asked the FCC to reconsider. Without holding a hearing, the FCC decided in favor of Coastal Plains. WJR claimed that the lack of a hearing violated its due process rights. The Supreme Court held that the FCC was under no obligation to hold hearings on license matters.

FCC *v. WNCN Listeners Guild*, 450 U.S. 582, 67 L.Ed.2d 521, 101 S.Ct. 1266 (1981)

During the 1970s, a number of classical music stations around the country changed formats. Listener groups petitioned the FCC to get involved, since the stations were the only outlet for classical music in these particular markets. The FCC maintained that content decisions like the types of music played on a station were purely the choice of the licensee, based on whatever market factors it choose to consider. In 1974, the U.S. Court of Appeals for the District of Columbia Circuit ordered the FCC to hold a hearing whenever a unique format was being changed and a substantial number of people objected (*Citizens Committee to Save WEFM v. FCC*, 506 F.2d 246). The FCC refused and the Supreme Court ruled that the Commission was correct to stay out of format disputes and that entertainment programming was within the broadcaster's discretion.

213

FCC v. WOKO, Inc., 329 U.S. 223, 91 L.Ed. 204, 67 S.Ct. 213 (1946)

For twelve years, the manager of WOKO concealed from the FCC that a network vice president secretly owned 24 percent of the station's stock. The Commission discovered the lie and did not renew the station's license. The station appealed, claiming that the Commission had not harshly punished other stations for lying in the past. The Supreme Court upheld the FCC's decision to deny the renewal, saying that past actions did not preclude the Commission from more stringently enforcing its rules.

Fly v. Heitmeyer, 309 U.S. 146, 60 S.Ct. 443, 84 L.Ed. 664 (1940)

The FCC denied a construction permit to Heitmeyer for a radio station in Wyoming. He appealed, and the appellate court determined that the FCC had made an error in evaluating Heitmeyer's financial viability. In the meantime, several other applicants had applied for the same frequency. When the FCC scheduled a new hearing, they reopened the record and gathered new evidence. Heitmeyer claimed that the FCC should have made the decision based on the existing record only. The Supreme Court said that the FCC had the right to decide how best to evaluate which applicant would serve the public interest, and if the Commission believed more evidence was necessary, it had the right to gather such material.

FRC v. General Electric Co., 281 U.S. 464, 74 L.Ed. 969, 50 S.Ct. 389 (1930)

General Electric was operating a radio station at Schenectady, New York, when the Radio Act of 1927 was passed. A new license was granted, but the hours during which the station could operate were greatly reduced. GE appealed and the U.S. Court of Appeals for the District of Columbia Circuit held that the license should be issued for the same terms as the previous license. The FRC appealed to the Supreme Court. The Court held that since the matter was administrative, not constitutional, it had no jurisdiction and dismissed the case.

FRC v. Nelson Bros. Bond & Mortgage Co., 289 U.S. 266, 77 L.Ed. 1166, 563 S.Ct. 627 (1933)

WJKS was the only station that operated in Gary, Indiana, and offered many programs of local interest. WIBO (owned by Nelson Bros. Bond & Mortgage Co.) and WPPC (owned by the North Shore Church) shared the same frequency and broadcast out of Chicago, Illinois. These signals were interfering with WJKS and as a result, the FRC gave WIBO and WPPC temporary licenses until it could determine what to do about WJKS. The stations appealed and the D.C. Circuit Court said the FRC had overstepped its bounds by deleting the two stations. The Supreme Court sided with the FRC, stating that the Commission had the authority to delete stations if it served the public interest.

Greater New Orleans Broadcasting Ass'n v. United States, 527 U.S. 173, 144 L.Ed.2d 161, 119 S.Ct. 1923 (1999)

Federal law prohibited broadcast stations from carrying advertising for privately owned, for-profit casinos, even if such casinos were legal in the state where the station was licensed. The Supreme Court determined that such restrictions violated the free speech provisions of the First Amendment.

Head v. New Mexico Board of Examiners in Optometry, 374 U.S. 424, 10 L.Ed.2d 983, 83 S.Ct. 1759 (1963)

The state of New Mexico prohibited the advertising of prices and terms of sale of eyeglasses. A Texas optometrist wanted to advertise on a radio station in Hobbs, New Mexico, whose broadcast reached his service area in Texas. The Supreme Court held that New Mexico's authority to regulate professional advertising practices did not conflict with the Communications Act.

Louisiana Public Serv. Comm'n v. FCC, 476 U.S. 355, 90 L.Ed.2d 369, 106 S.Ct. 1890 (1986)

In the early 1980s, the FCC issued rules concerning rates for depreciating telephone facilities and equipment. According to the Communications Act, the Commission has jurisdiction over all interstate and foreign communications, but the states regulate intrastate communication. The Supreme Court concluded that the FCC could not issue rules that contradicted state laws regarding intrastate communication.

MCI Telecommunications Corp. v. American Tel. & Tel. Co., 512 U.S. 218, 129 L.Ed.2d 182, 114 S.Ct. 2223 (1994)

Federal law requires that all long distance telephone companies file a document called a tariff to initiate changes in rates, services, or other corporate policies. The FCC decided to make the filing of tariffs optional for nondominant telephone companies. This meant that while AT&T had to file tariffs, all other long distance companies did not. The Commission claimed that it had the authority to "modify" the requirements laid out by the Communications Act. The Supreme Court held that the decision to make tariffs optional was a change well beyond the definition of "modify" and was therefore beyond the Commission's authority.

Metro Broadcasting, Inc. v. FCC, 497 U.S. 547, 111 L.Ed.2d 445, 110 S.Ct. 2997 (1990), overruled, *Adarand Constructors, Inc. v. Peña*, 515 U.S. 200, 132 L.Ed.2d 158, 115 S.Ct. 2097 (1995)

The FCC and Congress have established policies to encourage minority (defined as "those of Black, Hispanic Surnamed, American Eskimo, Aleut, American Indian, and Asiatic American extraction") ownership of broadcast stations. When deciding between competing applicants for the same broadcast license, the FCC weights the ownership and participation of minorities. In addition, when a licensee's qualifications to own a station are called into question, that licensee may transfer its license to a minority company without the required hearing. Two groups challenged these policies, claiming they violated the equal protection component of the Fifth Amendment. The Supreme Court held that the policies were constitutional and served to promote the government interest in increasing minority ownership in broadcasting. This holding was later overturned by a nonbroadcasting case, *Adarand Constructors, Inc. v. Peña* (1995).

National Broadcasting Co., Inc. v. United States, 319 U.S. 190, 87 L.Ed. 1344, 63 S.Ct. 997 (1943)

By the late 1930s, the FCC was growing increasingly concerned about the dominance of the networks over radio programming. In 1941, the Commission issued the Chain Broadcasting Regulations, which attempted to regulate the power of the networks through their affiliate agreements. The rules also banned any company from owning more than one network, thus requiring NBC to sell off one of its networks. NBC took the Commission to court, claiming it had gone well beyond its role as a "traffic cop" of the airwaves. The Supreme Court upheld the FCC's rules, stating that the powers of the Commission extended beyond the engineering and technical aspects of broadcasting. The Court also affirmed that the FCC had the right to regulate the content of broadcasting in the public interest, convenience, and necessity, as set forth by the Communications Act of 1934. This right stemmed from the scarce nature of radio frequencies. As a result, NBC was required to sell off the Blue network and ABC was born.

National Cable & Telecommunications Ass'n, Inc. v. Gulf Power Co., 534 U.S. 327, 151 L.Ed.2d 794, 122 S.Ct. 782 (2002)

The Pole Attachments Act allowed the FCC to set the rates that utility companies could charge for "any attachment by a cable television system or provider of telecommunications service." A number of utility companies challenged the FCC, saying that the law did not apply to wireless companies or to cable companies who also used the wires to provide high-speed internet. The Supreme Court sided with the FCC, saying that the act should be interpreted to cover these new services.

National Cable Television Ass'n, Inc. v. United States, 415 U.S. 336, 94 S.Ct. 1146, 39 L.Ed.2d 370 (1974)

The Independent Offices Appropriation Act was passed by Congress in 1952 and allowed government agencies, like the FCC, to set up a fee schedule for the services it provided to regulated industries. When the Commission imposed a thirty-cent-per-subcriber fee on cable systems, the National Cable Television Association challenged the Commission's methodology for determining the fee. The Supreme Court agreed with the NCTA and ordered the FCC to find another way to decide the appropriate fee structure.

Nixon v. Missouri Municipal League, 541 U.S. 125, 124 S.Ct. 1555, 158 L.Ed.2d 291 (2004)

Section 253 of the Telecommunications Act of 1996 authorized the FCC to preempt state and local laws and regulations "that prohibit or have the effect of prohibiting the ability of any entity" to provide telecommunications services. Missouri passed a law that barred local governments in Missouri from providing telecommunications services and facilities. The question before the Court was whether local governments in Missouri were considered "entities" under Section 253. The Supreme Court concluded that the local governments were not "entities" under Section 253 and FCC was therefore not required to preempt the Missouri statute.

Radio Corp. of America v. United States, 341 U.S. 412, 95 L.Ed. 1062, 71 S.Ct. 806 (1951)

Throughout the 1940s, the FCC sought to create technical standards for color television. In 1950, the Commission choose the CBS standard, which was not compatible with existing sets. RCA, which was developing another type of color television that was compatible, said that the FCC had been arbitrary and capricious in its selection of the CBS standard and that the Commission should have waited until better technologies were developed. The Supreme Court held that the Commission had appropriately decided to go forward with color television to give the public the opportunity to receive color television if it wished.

Radio Station WOW, Inc. v. Johnson, 326 U.S. 120, 89 L.Ed. 2092, 65 S.Ct. 1475 (1945)

Woodmen of the World Life Insurance Society owned radio station WOW, but leased it to Radio Station WOW, Inc., a Nebraska corporation formed to operate the station. Both groups later applied to the Commission to transfer the license to Radio Station WOW, Inc. The application was approved. In the meantime, a member of the Society brought a fraud suit against Radio Station WOW, Inc. and demanded the license be returned. What followed was a conflict between the Nebraska Supreme Court and the FCC over the disposition of the license. The U.S. Supreme Court concluded that a state court could not override the Commission on matters of broadcast licensing.

Red Lion Broadcasting Co. v. FCC, 395 U.S. 367, 23 L.Ed.2d 371, 89 S.Ct. 1794 (1969)

In 1964, a radio evangelist named Billy James Hargis attacked a man named Fred Cook who had authored a book that criticized Republican presidential candidate Barry Goldwater. Among other things, Hargis said that Cook had been fired from a newspaper job for making false charges against a city official and that he had worked for a magazine affiliated with Communism. Cook demanded time on the station to reply to the charges, but Red Lion Broadcasting (the station owner) told Cook he should buy advertising time. Cook went to the FCC and the Commission ordered Red Lion to give him free time under the Personal Attack Rule, part of the FCC's Fairness Doctrine. Red Lion claimed this would be a violation of its First Amendment rights. The Supreme Court ruled for the Commission, saying that radio frequencies were a scarce resource and thus the First Amendment rights of the listeners were paramount over the First Amendment rights of the broadcasters.

Regents of the Univ. System of Ga. v. Carroll, 338 U.S. 586, 94 L.Ed. 363, 70 S.Ct. 370 (1950)

The Georgia School of Technology received radio station WGST in 1923 as a gift and operated it until 1930. The school then contracted with the Southern Broadcasting Company to operate the station, in exchange for a percentage of the profits. In 1940, the FCC initiated a hearing regarding whether the contractual arrangement violated the Communications Act requirement that a licensee maintain control over its station. After concluding the arrangement was not acceptable, the FCC ruled that the license would only be renewed if the contract was severed. After some legal wrangling with stock purchases that did not remove Southern from the picture, the FCC again maintained that the school had abdicated responsibility for the station. The school then agreed to assume full control of the station. In doing so, the school did not fulfill some of the contractual obligations it had with Southern. When Southern sued, the school claimed that any decision by the state court would improperly interfere with the FCC's power to regulate broadcasting. The Supreme Court held that since the FCC had no authority over contractual relationships, the Georgia court's decision did not interfere with the FCC's regulatory authority.

Rochester Telephone Corp. v. United States, 307 U.S. 125, 83 L.Ed.2d 1147 (1939)

Rochester operated a telephone system in and around the city of Rochester, New York. Rochester engaged in interstate communications solely through physical connections with the facilities of the New York Telephone Company. In 1935, the FCC ordered Rochester to abide by the mandates of the Communications Act by filing a number of documents including a schedule of charges and copies of contracts with other telephone carriers. Rochester maintained that since it operated solely in the state of New York, it was outside the jurisdiction of the FCC. An FCC hearing found that Rochester was controlled by the New York Telephone Company and thus was subject to the Commission's rules. Rochester appealed and the New York courts supported the FCC's decision. The Commission then asked the Supreme Court to consider whether the decision was, in fact, reviewable by the courts. The Supreme Court held that FCC orders were indeed open to judicial review for errors of law, but not on matters of fact. Matters of fact were the responsibility of the Commission.

Sable Communications of Calif., Inc. v. FCC, 492 U.S. 115, 109 S.Ct. 2829, 106 L.Ed.2d 93 (1989)

In the 1980s, some members of Congress grew concerned with the proliferation of sexually oriented prerecorded telephone messages, known as "dial-a-porn." As a result, the Communications Act was amended in 1988 to completely ban both indecent and obscene communications by telephone. Sable Communications, a Los Angeles-based dial-a-porn provider, challenged the constitutionality of the law. The Supreme Court refused to overturn the obscenity provisions. But a unanimous Court declared that the indecency provisions violated adults' First Amendment right to access sexually explicit material. The Court concluded that dial-a-porn was different from broadcasting in that it was not intrusive, since individuals had to initiate the call. In addition, dial-a-porn was not accessible, since technology existed to easily block minors from accessing the material.

Scripps-Howard Radio v. FCC, 316 U.S. 4, 86 L.Ed. 1229, 62 S.Ct. 875 (1942)

In 1939, the FCC issued a construction permit to WCOL, Columbus, Ohio, for a change in its frequency and power. Scripps-Howard Radio owned WCPO in Cincinnati, Ohio, and it believed that the new, more-powerful station would interfere with its signal. Scripps-Howard asked the Commission to reconsider and schedule a hearing on the matter. The Commission turned down the request. Scripps-Howard then appealed, claiming the FCC could not grant the permit without a hearing. During the appeals process, Scripps-Howard wanted the court to block the issuance of the construction permit until the case was resolved. The Supreme Court concluded that the appellate courts did have the right to order a stay although the Court made no comment as to the appropriateness of the stay in question.

Turner Broadcasting System, Inc. v. FCC, 507 U.S. 1301, 123 L.Ed.2d 642, 113 S.Ct. 1806 (1993); *Turner Broadcasting System, Inc. v. FCC*, 512 U.S. 622, 129 L.Ed.2d 497, 114 S.Ct. 2445 (1994); and *Turner Broadcasting System, Inc. v. FCC*, 520 U.S. 180, 137 L.Ed.2d 369, 117 S.Ct. 1174 (1997)

The Cable Television Consumer Protection and Competition Act of 1992 required cable systems to carry local broadcast stations, a concept known as must carry. In 1993, cable companies asked the Supreme Court to issue an injunction against the enforcement of the must carry requirement. The Court refused. In 1994, the cable companies asked the Supreme Court to strike down the must carry provisions on the basis of the First Amendment. In a complicated and fractured decision, the Court upheld must carry as a suitable solution to the government concern over maintaining over-the-air broadcasting. This time, the case hinged on the standard of review that should be used to evaluate content regulations on cable. Once the Court settled on a standard, the case was sent back to the lower court for review. The cable companies again returned to the Supreme Court in 1997 after additional fact-finding and again the Supreme Court upheld the regulations as acceptable under the First Amendment.

United States v. Edge Broadcasting, 509 U.S. 418, 125 L.Ed.2d 345, 113 S.Ct. 2696 (1993)

Federal law prohibits stations from broadcasting advertising for a lottery, except when the lottery is operated by the state. Edge Broadcasting ran a station that was licensed in North Carolina, a state without a lottery. Ninety percent of the station's audience, however, lived in Virginia and Edge wanted to run advertisements for the Virginia state lottery. The Supreme Court ruled against Edge, stating that the prohibition of lottery advertising in states without a lottery was constitutional.

United States v. Midwest Video Corp., 406 U.S. 649, 32 L.Ed.2d 390, 92 S.Ct. 1860 (1972)

An FCC rule stated that a cable system with more than 3,500 subscribers must carry locally produced, cable-only programming and provide the production facilities to create such programming if it wanted to carry the local broadcast channels. Although the Supreme Court was split on the rationale, it held that the FCC was within its authority to enact such rules over cable systems.

United States v. New Jersey State Lottery Comm'n, 420 U.S. 371, 43 L.Ed.2d 260, 95 S.Ct. 941 (1975)

In the 1970s, federal law banned the broadcast of any information about a lottery, including those lotteries run by the state. A New Jersey radio station wanted to broadcast the winning numbers in the New Jersey state lottery, but the FCC refused. While the case was working its way through the appeals process, Congress modified the law to allow the broadcast of information regarding state-run lotteries. The Supreme Court sent the case back to the lower court to determine whether the Congressional action made the case moot.

United States v. Playboy Entertainment Group, Inc., 529 U.S. 803, 146 L.Ed.2d 865, 120 S.Ct. 1878 (2000)

The Telecommunications Act of 1996 required that cable companies either fully scramble indecent programming or carry the channels only during the safe harbor (10:00 P.M. to 6:00 A.M.), the time of day when children were less likely to be in the audience. Since fully scrambling channels was enormously expensive and difficult, most cable companies chose to only carry the channels during the safe harbor hours. Playboy challenged the law on the basis of the First Amendment and the Supreme Court agreed. The Court held that since there were less restrictive ways of keeping indecent cable programming away from children, the Telecom Act was too restrictive.

United States v. Southwestern Cable Co., 392 U.S. 157, 20 L.Ed.2d 1001, 88 S.Ct. 1994 (1968)

Cable television got its start in the 1940s, simply importing distant broadcast signals to rural and mountainous areas. In the 1960s, the FCC promulgated its first rules regarding cable, claiming cable was within its jurisdiction because the service was ancillary to broadcasting. Many in the burgeoning cable industry disagreed and asked the Court to determine if the FCC had regulatory jurisdiction over cable. The Supreme Court concluded that the FCC did indeed have the authority to regulate the cable industry.

United States v. Storer Broadcasting Co., 351 U.S. 192, 100 L.Ed. 1081, 76 S.Ct. 763 (1956)

In 1953, the FCC issued rules that limited the number of stations one entity could own to seven AM, five FM, and five television stations in an effort to prevent overconcentration in the media. Storer Broadcasting had reached the limit under the rules and wished to acquire additional stations. The Supreme Court concluded that the FCC had the authority to create ownership caps for broadcast stations.

Verizon Communications Inc. v. FCC, 535 U.S. 467, 152 L.Ed.2d 701, 122 S.Ct. 1646 (2002)

The Telecommunications Act of 1996 required that local telephone companies open their systems to competitors through a lease arrangement. This was done to encourage competition in the local telephone market. The FCC created rules that determined how state utility boards set the rates for those leases and required the phone companies to unbundle services upon the lessee's request. The phone companies challenged these rules, saying they went beyond the Commission's authority. The Supreme Court held the rules were within the mandate of the Commission.

Verizon Communications Inc. v. Law Offices of Curtis V. Trinko, LLP, 540 U.S. 398, 157 L.Ed.2d 823, 124 S.Ct. 872 (2004)

One of the main goals of the Telecommunications Act of 1996 was to open telephone markets to competition. As part of a long and complicated attempt to enter the New York market, an antitrust suit was brought against Verizon by a law firm that used another telephone carrier. The Supreme Court held that Verizon's slowness in implementing the requirements of the Telecommunications Act did not represent a violation of the Sherman Antitrust Act.

★ 8 ★
Chronology of Key Events

1934

Congress passes the Communications Act of 1934, creating the FCC. The Commission is made up of seven commissioners appointed to staggered seven-year terms.

1935

Edwin Howard Armstrong makes the first public demonstration of FM broadcasting.

1936

Chairman Anning Prall forces a Pittsburgh radio station to carry the speech of the presidential candidate from the Communist Party under the Equal Time provisions of the Fairness Doctrine.

1938

The FCC announces that it will investigate chain broadcasting.

1939

The FCC completes the telephone investigation mandated by the Communications Act of 1934.

The FCC issues the Mayflower Doctrine, ruling that broadcast stations cannot editorialize.

1940

The FCC authorizes commercial broadcasting on FM and decides that television will use FM technology for its audio soundtrack.

1941

The FCC issues the *Report on Chain Broadcasting*, which regulates the kinds of contracts individual stations can make with networks. The report also requires that NBC sell one of its radio networks, leading to the creation of ABC.

1946

The FCC issues the *Blue Book*, detailing the public interest obligations of broadcast licensees.

1948

Commissioner Clifford Durr refuses reappointment to the Commission because of his opposition to the anti-Communist loyalty oaths being required by the Truman administration.

Frieda Hennock becomes the first woman to serve as an FCC commissioner.

Harold Tuttle, inventor of the Hush-A-Phone, petitions the FCC to overturn AT&T's foreign attachments policy. The FCC denies this request in both 1951 and 1955.

1949

The FCC creates the Common Carrier Bureau to regulate the telephone and telegraph industries.

The FCC overturns the Mayflower Doctrine, saying that the right of the public to be informed is more important than the right of a station to air only the licensee's opinion.

1950

The FCC announces that the CBS mechanical system will be the technical standard for color television.

1952

Congress mandates the use of integrated bureaus to organize FCC staff.

The FCC adds UHF channels fourteen through eighty-three to the television allocation.

1953

The FCC approves the RCA electronic system as the national standard for color television.

1956

The Hush-a-Phone controversy is resolved after a court appeal by Harold Tuttle. The FCC requires AT&T to amend its foreign attachment rules.

The FCC rules that cable is outside of its statutory authority.

1959

The FCC completes the Above 890 inquiry. As a result, the Commission allows the licensing of private-line microwave systems.

1960

The FCC issues the *1960 Programming Policy Statement*, which introduces formal ascertainment for broadcast stations.

Chairman John Doerfer is forced to resign following a scandal involving a yachting vacation with a broadcast station owner.

1961

The FCC authorizes FM stereo broadcasting.

Chairman Newton Minow makes his "vast wasteland" speech at the National Association of Broadcasters Convention.

1962

The FCC decides that it can deny a microwave license for cable if economic harm would be caused to a local broadcast station.

Congress passes the All-Channel Receiver Act, which requires that every television set sold after April 1964 include the ability to receive UHF.

1964

The FCC rules that public interest groups like the United Church of Christ do not have standing to challenge a license renewal.

1965

The FCC issues its first cable rules, declaring it an ancillary service to broadcasting.

1966

A lawyer named John F. Banzhaf III asks WCBS TV in New York to provide free airtime to antismoking activists under the Fairness Doctrine. The Commission later supports Banzhaf's request.

The U.S. Court of Appeals for the District of Columbia Circuit rules that public interest groups do have standing to challenge license renewals in front of the FCC.

1967

The FCC formalizes the Personal Attack rule, stating that any person whose honesty, character, or integrity are attacked in a broadcast has the right to reply on air.

Congress passes the Public Broadcasting Act of 1967, beginning federal aid for noncommercial broadcasting and creating the Corporation for Public Broadcasting.

1968

The U.S. Supreme Court upholds the FCC's position that cable is within its jurisdiction.

The Carterfone controversy is resolved. The FCC requires AT&T to abandon its policy against foreign attachments.

The FCC issues *Ascertainment of Community Needs by Broadcast Applicants*, a report that further details formal ascertainment.

1969

The U.S. Supreme Court upholds the Fairness Doctrine based on the scarcity of broadcast frequencies.

The FCC approves MCI's application for construction of a commercial microwave communications system.

The FCC begins to encourage cable systems to provide cable access channels to public, educational, and governmental institutions.

1970

The FCC issues the Telephone/Cable Cross-ownership ban.

The FCC creates the Financial Interest and Syndication rules as a way to limit the power of the networks and increase program diversity.

The FCC issues the Prime Time Access rule, reducing network prime time from four hours to three in the top fifty markets.

1971

The Congressional ban on the broadcast of cigarette advertising takes effect.

The FCC issues the Specialized Common Carrier Decision, which institutes a general policy for the licensing of commercial microwave communications systems.

The FCC completes the first Computer Inquiry, specifying the role of telephone companies in the provision of data communication services.

The FCC issues the *Primer on Ascertainment of Community Problems by Broadcast Applicants*, requiring extensive public surveys as part of the formal ascertainment process.

1972

The FCC promulgates the Cable Exclusivity and Non-Duplication rules, which are aimed at protecting local station programming from cable.

The FCC requires that cable systems be franchised by local franchising authorities.

The FCC requires cable systems to provide equipment and cable access channels to public, educational, and governmental institutions.

Benjamin Hooks becomes the first African American to serve as an FCC commissioner.

1973

The FCC requires all radio and television stations to maintain a public file.

FCC Chairman Dean Burch criticizes "topless radio" programming at a National Association of Broadcasters convention and all such programming disappears within weeks.

1974

Congress asks the Commission to take action on what is perceived as excessive sex, crime, and violence on television, leading to the establishment of the Family Viewing Hour.

1975

The FCC revises the ascertainment primer to reduce the burden on broadcast licensees.

The FCC issues the Cable Anti-Siphoning rule, aimed at protecting broadcasters from losing programming to the new cable networks.

The FCC defines a formal indecency policy.

1976

Congress completely revises U.S. copyright law, declaring that cable systems owe no copyright fees to local television stations for the carriage of their signals.

1977

The U.S. Court of Appeals for the District of Columbia Circuit strikes down the Anti-Siphoning rule.

The Execunet controversy is resolved, effectively allowing for full competition in public long distances telephone services.

The FCC begins investigating the possibility of AM stereo broadcasting.

1980

The FCC completes the second Computer Inquiry, revising its policy regarding telephone company provision of data communication services and deregulating terminal equipment.

1981

The FCC removes formal ascertainment requirements for radio stations.

Henry Rivera becomes the first Hispanic FCC commissioner.

1982

AT&T and the U.S. Department of Justice enter into a consent decree mandating the breakup of the Bell System.

The FCC creates low power television to provide local programming for small communities.

The National Association of Broadcasters suspends all enforcement of the radio and television codes.

1983

Congress reduces the FCC to five members, serving staggered five-year terms.

1984

The consent decree mandating the breakup of the Bell System takes effect.

The FCC mandates the use of access charges to compensate local telephone companies for the delivery of long distance telephone services following the breakup of the Bell System.

Congress passes the Cable Act of 1984, granting the FCC the authority to regulate all cable communications and deregulated cable rates and remove must carry provisions.

The FCC removes formal ascertainment requirements for television stations.

1985

The FCC, led by Mark Fowler, announces that scarcity is no longer an issue and questions the need for the Fairness Doctrine.

1986

The FCC completes the third Computer Inquiry, further revising its policy regarding telephone company provision of data communication services.

The U.S. Supreme Court concludes that exclusive franchising of cable systems is appropriate only when there are technical reasons why an area cannot support multiple cable systems.

1987

The FCC removes the Fairness Doctrine.

The FCC appoints the Advisory Committee on Advanced Television Service to recommend a technical standard for HDTV.

1989

The FCC approves the use of price caps for the regulation of interstate telephone services.

1990

Congress passes the Children's Television Act of 1990, requiring that broadcasters serve the educational and informational needs of children.

1992

Congress passes the Cable Act of 1992, re-regulating cable rates, re-instituting must carry, and introducing retransmission consent.

The FCC establishes the initial framework for the provision of video dial tone services by telephone companies.

The FCC issues a policy banning hoaxes on broadcast stations.

1993

The FCC votes to repeal the Financial Interest and Syndication rules.

Congress authorizes the licensing of land mobile radio services through spectrum auctions.

Congress directs the FCC to designate a single technical standard for AM stereo.

The Congressional requirement that all television sets include closed captioning technology takes effect.

1994

The FCC announces that nothing in the Communications Act bars a television station from channeling explicit political advertising (anti-abortion imagery) to a time when children are unlikely to be in the viewing audience.

Rachelle Chong becomes the first person of Asian descent to serve as an FCC commissioner.

1996

Congress passes the Telecommunications Act of 1996, instituting deregulation throughout the communications industries.

The U.S. Court of Appeals for the District of Columbia Circuit rules that channeling of anti-abortion political advertising violates the Communications Act.

The FCC approves a technical standard for digital television.

The FCC issues a report requiring that television stations provide at least three hours of children's programming per week.

The FCC repeals the Prime Time Access rule.

1997

William Kennard becomes the first African American FCC chairman.

1999

The FCC's regulation of cable rates ends.

2000

The FCC announces plans for low power FM.

2003

The FCC adopts the Broadcast Flag rule to aid in the prevention of the piracy of digital television programming.

2004

The House Commerce Committee orders the FCC to investigate the impact of a la carte cable programming on rates.

2005

The U.S. Court of Appeals for the District of Columbia Circuit overturns the Broadcast Flag rule.

APPENDIX 1
Case List, 1928–2004

A/B Financial, Inc. v. FCC, 316 U.S.App.D.C. 191, 76 F.3d 1244 (1996)

Abacoa Radio Corp. v. FCC, 123 U.S.App.D.C. 218, 358 F.2d 849 (1966)

ABC, Inc. v. FCC, 682 F.2d 25 (2nd Cir. 1982)

Accuracy in Media, Inc. v. FCC, 172 U.S.App.D.C. 188, 521 F.2d 288 (1975), cert. denied, 425 U.S. 934 (1976)

Achernar Broadcasting Co. v. FCC, 314 U.S.App.D.C. 109, 62 F.3d 1441 (1995)

ACS of Anchorage, Inc. v. FCC, 351 U.S.App.D.C. 317, 290 F.3d 403 (2002)

Action for Children's Television v. FCC, 183 U.S.App.D.C. 437, 564 F.2d 458 (1977)

Action for Children's Television v. FCC, 546 F.Supp. 872 (D.D.C. 1982)

Action for Children's Television v. FCC, 244 U.S.App.D.C. 190, 756 F.2d 899 (1985)

Action for Children's Television v. FCC, 261 U.S.App.D.C. 253, 821 F.2d 741 (1987)

Action for Children's Television v. FCC, 271 U.S.App.D.C. 365, 852 F.2d 1332 (1988)

Action for Children's Television v. FCC, 285 U.S.App.D.C. 58, 906 F.2d 752 (1990)

Action for Children's Television v. FCC, 290 U.S.App.D.C. 4, 932 F.2d 1504 (1991), cert. denied, 503 U.S. 914 (1992)

Action for Children's Television v. FCC, 999 F.2d 19 (1st Cir. 1993)

Action for Children's Television v. FCC, 304 U.S.App.D.C. 126, 11 F.3d 170 (1993), vacated, 304 U.S.App.D.C. 367, 15 F.3d 186 (1994)

Action for Children's Television v. FCC, 313 U.S.App.D.C. 94, 58 F.3d 654 (1995), cert. denied, 516 U.S. 1043 (1996)

Action for Children's Television v. FCC, 313 U.S.App.D.C. 261, 59 F.3d 1249 (1995), cert. denied, 516 U.S. 1072 (1996)

Action for Children's Television v. FCC, 827 F.Supp. 4 (D.D.C. 1993), aff'd, 313 U.S.App.D.C. 261, 59 F.3d 1249 (1995), cert. denied, 516 U.S. 1072 (1996)

Ad Hoc Telecommunications Users Comm. v. FCC, 220 U.S.App.D.C. 241, 680 F.2d 790 (1982)

Adams Communications Corp. v. FCC, 333 U.S.App.D.C. 45, 159 F.3d 635 (1998)

Adams Telcom, Inc. v. FCC, 302 U.S.App.D.C. 265, 997 F.2d 955 (1993)

Adams Telcom, Inc. v. FCC, 309 U.S.App.D.C. 1, 38 F.3d 576 (1994)

Adelphi Broadcasting Corp. v. FCC, 267 U.S.App.D.C. 273, 838 F.2d 571 (1988)

Adelphia Communications Corp. v. FCC, 319 U.S.App.D.C. 187, 88 F.3d 1250 (1996)

Advanced Communications Corp. v. FCC, 318 U.S.App.D.C. 78, 84 F.3d 1452 (1996), cert. denied, 519 U.S. 1071 (1997)

Advanced Communications Corp. v. FCC, 363 U.S.App.D.C. 117, 376 F.3d 1153 (2004)

Advanced Electronics, Inc. v. FCC, 218 U.S.App.D.C. 159, 673 F.2d 550 (1982)

Aeronautical Radio, Inc. v. FCC, 206 U.S.App.D.C. 253, 642 F.2d 1221 (1980), cert. denied, 451 U.S. 920, 976 (1981)

Aeronautical Radio, Inc. v. FCC, 289 U.S.App.D.C. 16, 928 F.2d 428 (1991)

Aeronautical Radio, Inc. v. FCC, 299 U.S.App.D.C. 250, 983 F.2d 275 (1993)

Aeronautical Radio, Inc. v. United States, 335 F.2d 304 (7th Cir. 1964), cert. denied, 379 U.S. 966 (1965)

Affiliated Communications Corp. v. FCC, 246 U.S.App.D.C. 43, 762 F.2d 137 (1985)

AirTouch Paging v. FCC, 234 F.3d 815 (2nd Cir. 2000)

Alabama Power Company v. FCC, 249 U.S.App.D.C. 99, 773 F.2d 362 (1985)

Alabama Power Company v. FCC, 311 F.3d 1357 (11th Cir. 2002), cert. denied, 124 S.Ct. 50 (2003)

Alarm Industry Communications Comm. v. FCC, 327 U.S.App.D.C. 412, 131 F.3d 1066 (1997)

Alascom, Inc. v. FCC, 234 U.S.App.D.C. 113, 727 F.2d 1212 (1984)

Alaskans For Better Media v. FCC, 236 U.S.App.D.C. 351, 735 F.2d 617 (1984)

Albertson v. FCC, 87 U.S.App.D.C. 39, 182 F.2d 397 (1950)

Albertson v. FCC, 100 U.S.App.D.C. 103, 243 F.2d 209 (1957)

ALC Communications Corp. v. FCC, 288 U.S.App.D.C. 256, 925 F.2d 487 (1991)

Alden Communications Corp. v. FCC, 286 U.S.App.D.C. 348, 917 F.2d 62 (1990)

Alee Cellular Communications v. FCC, 2000 WL 521487 (D.C. Cir. 2000)

Alegria I, Inc. v. FCC, 284 U.S.App.D.C. 366, 905 F.2d 471 (1990)

Alegria, Inc. v. FCC, 292 U.S.App.D.C. 120, 947 F.2d 986 (1991)

Alenco Communications, Inc. v. FCC, 201 F.3d 608 (5th Cir. 2000)

Alianza Federal de Mercedes v. FCC, 176 U.S.App.D.C. 253, 539 F.2d 732 (1976)

All America Cables and Radio, Inc. v. FCC, 237 U.S.App.D.C. 143, 736 F.2d 752 (1984)

Allegany County Broadcasting Co. v. FCC, 121 U.S.App.D.C. 166, 348 F.2d 778 (1965)

Allen B. Dumont Laboratories, Inc. v. Carroll, 184 F.2d 153 (3rd Cir. 1950), cert. denied, 340 U.S. 929 (1951)

Allen B. Dumont Laboratories, Inc. v. Carroll, 86 F.Supp. 813 (E.D. Pa. 1949), aff'd, 184 F.2d 153 (3rd Cir. 1950), cert. denied, 340 U.S. 929 (1951)

Allentown Broadcasting Corp. v. FCC, 94 U.S.App.D.C. 353, 222 F.2d 781 (1954), cert. denied, 349 U.S. 358 (1955)

Allentown Broadcasting Corp. v. FCC, 98 U.S.App.D.C. 57, 232 F.2d 57 (1955), cert. denied, 350 U.S. 1015 (1956)

Alliance for Community Media v. FCC, 304 U.S.App.D.C. 37, 10 F.3d 812 (1993), vacated, 304 U.S.App.D.C. 367, 15 F.3d 186 (1994)

Alliance for Community Media v. FCC, 312 U.S.App.D.C. 141, 56 F.3d 105 (1995) (en banc), aff'd in part and rev'd in part, *Denver Area Educ. Tele. Consortium, Inc. v. FCC*, 518 U.S. 727 (1996)

Allied Broadcasting, Inc. v. FCC, 140 U.S.App.D.C. 264, 435 F.2d 68 (1970)

Allnet Communication Services, Inc. v. FCC, 800 F.Supp. 984 (D.D.C. 1992)

ALLTEL Corp. v. FCC, 267 U.S.App.D.C. 253, 838 F.2d 551 (1988)

American Broadcasting Co., Inc. v. FCC, 85 U.S.App.D.C. 343, 179 F.2d 437 (1949)

American Broadcasting Co., Inc. v. FCC, 89 U.S.App.D.C. 298, 191 F.2d 492 (1951)

American Broadcasting Co., Inc. v. United States, 110 F.Supp. 374 (S.D.N.Y. 1953), aff'd, 347 U.S. 284 (1954)

American Broadcasting Cos., Inc. v. FCC, 207 U.S.App.D.C. 68, 643 F.2d 818 (1980)

American Broadcasting Cos., Inc. v. FCC, 213 U.S.App.D.C. 369, 663 F.2d 133 (1980)

American Broadcasting Cos., Inc. v. FCC, 662 F.2d 155 (2nd Cir. 1981)

American Broadcasting Cos., Inc. v. FCC, 682 F.2d 25 (2nd Cir. 1982)

American Broadcasting-Paramount Theatres, Inc. v. FCC, 108 U.S.App.D.C. 83, 280 F.2d 631 (1960)

American Broadcasting-Paramount Theatres, Inc. v. FCC, 113 U.S.App.D.C. 1, 303 F.2d 766 (1962)

American Broadcasting-Paramount Theatres, Inc. v. FCC, 120 U.S.App.D.C. 264, 345 F.2d 954 (1965), cert. denied, 383 U.S. 906 (1966)

American Civil Liberties Union v. FCC, 158 U.S.App.D.C. 344, 486 F.2d 411 (1973)

American Civil Liberties Union v. FCC, 523 F.2d 1344 (9th Cir. 1975)

American Civil Liberties Union v. FCC, 774 F.2d 24 (1st Cir. 1985)

American Civil Liberties Union v. FCC, 262 U.S.App.D.C. 244, 823 F.2d 1554 (1987), cert. denied, 485 U.S. 959 (1988)

American Communications Ass'n v. United States, 298 F.2d 648 (2nd Cir. 1962)

American Family Association Ass'n v. FCC and United States, 361 U.S.App.D.C. 231, 365 F.3d 1156 (2004)

American Family Life Assurance Co. v. FCC, 327 U.S.App.D.C. 133, 129 F.3d 625 (1997)

American Federation of Musicians v. FCC, 123 U.S.App.D.C. 74, 356 F.2d 827 (1966)

American Legal Foundation v. FCC, 257 U.S.App.D.C. 189, 808 F.2d 84 (1987)

American Message Centers, Inc. v. FCC, 311 U.S.App.D.C. 64, 50 F.3d 35 (1995)

American Public Communications Council v. FCC, 342 U.S.App.D.C. 51, 215 F.3d 51 (2000)

American Radio Ass'n v. FCC, 690 F.2d 334 (2nd Cir. 1982), cert. denied, 460 U.S. 1051 (1983)

American Radio Relay League, Inc. v. FCC, 199 U.S.App.D.C. 293, 617 F.2d 875 (1980)

American Radio Relay League, Inc. v. FCC, 287 U.S.App.D.C. 38, 918 F.2d 978 (1990)

American Scholastic TV Programming Found. v. FCC, 310 U.S.App.D.C. 256, 46 F.3d 1173 (1995)

American Security Council v. FCC, 236 U.S.App.D.C. 135, 733 F.2d 966 (1984)

American Security Council Educ. Foundation v. FCC, 197 U.S.App.D.C. 124, 607 F.2d 438 (1979), cert. denied, 444 U.S. 1013 (1980)

American Tel. & Tel. Co. v. FCC, 449 F.2d 439 (2nd Cir. 1971)

American Tel. & Tel. Co. v. FCC, 487 F.2d 865 (2nd Cir. 1973)

American Tel. & Tel. Co. v. FCC, 503 F.2d 612 (2nd Cir. 1974)

American Tel. & Tel. Co. v. FCC, 519 F.2d 322 (2nd Cir. 1975)

American Tel. & Tel. Co. v. FCC, 176 U.S.App.D.C. 288, 539 F.2d 767 (1976)

American Tel. & Tel. Co. v. FCC, 179 U.S.App.D.C. 328, 551 F.2d 1287 (1977)

American Tel. & Tel. Co. v. FCC, 572 F.2d 17 (2nd Cir.), cert. denied, 439 U.S. 875 (1978)

American Tel. & Tel. Co. v. FCC, 195 U.S.App.D.C. 223, 602 F.2d 401 (1979)

American Tel. & Tel. Co. v. FCC, 266 U.S.App.D.C. 47, 832 F.2d 1285 (1987)

American Tel. & Tel. Co. v. FCC, 267 U.S.App.D.C. 38, 836 F.2d 1386 (1988)

American Tel. & Tel. Co. v. FCC, 298 U.S.App.D.C. 1, 974 F.2d 1351 (1992)

American Tel. & Tel. Co. v. FCC, 298 U.S.App.D.C. 230, 978 F.2d 727 (1992), cert. denied, 509 U.S. 913 (1993)

American Tel. & Tel. Co. v. FCC, 1993 WL 260778, No. 92-1628 (D.C. Cir. June 4, 1993), aff'd, *MCI Telecommunications Corp. v. American Tel. & Tel. Co.*, 512 U.S. 218 (1994)

American Tel. & Tel. Co. v. United States, 14 F.Supp. 121 (S.D.N.Y. 1936)

American Trucking Ass'ns, Inc. v. FCC, 126 U.S.App.D.C. 236, 377 F.2d 21 (1966), cert. denied, 386 U.S. 943 (1967)

Ameritel, Inc. v. FCC, 323 U.S.App.D.C. 289, 107 F.3d 922 (1996)

Amigos Broadcasting, Inc. v. FCC, 225 U.S.App.D.C. 46, 696 F.2d 128 (1982)

Amor Family Broadcasting Group v. FCC, 287 U.S.App.D.C. 20, 918 F.2d 960 (1990)

AMSC Subsidiary Corp. v. FCC, 342 U.S.App.D.C. 311, 216 F.3d 1154 (2000)

Anderson v. FCC, 403 F.2d 61 (2nd Cir. 1968)

Anniston Broadcasting Co. v. FCC, 668 F.2d 829 (5th Cir. 1982)

Ansley v. FRC, 60 U.S.App.D.C. 19, 46 F.2d 600 (1930)

Anti-Defamation Ass'n of Emigres from Post-1917 Russia v. FCC, 261 U.S.App.D.C. 333, 821 F.2d 821 (1987)

Anti-Defamation League v. FCC, 131 U.S.App.D.C. 146, 403 F.2d 169 (1968), cert. denied, 394 U.S. 930 (1969)

Apple Valley Broadcasting, Inc. v. FCC, 168 U.S.App.D.C. 77, 512 F.2d 991 (1975)

Appledore Communications, Inc. v. FCC, 301 U.S.App.D.C. 251, 993 F.2d 913 (1993)

Arkansas AFL-CIO v. FCC, 980 F.2d 1190 (8th Cir. 1992), vacated, 980 F.2d 1197 (8th Cir. 1993)

Arkansas AFL-CIO v. FCC, 11 F.3d 1430 (8th Cir. 1993) (en banc)

Arkansas Educ. Television Comm'n v. Forbes, 523 U.S. 666, 140 L.Ed.2d 875, 118 S.Ct. 1633 (1998)

Arthur Fulmer, Inc. v. FCC, 186 U.S.App.D.C. 328, 569 F.2d 159 (1977)

Artlite Broadcasting Co. v. FCC, 252 U.S.App.D.C. 18, 786 F.2d 431 (1986)

Ashbacker Radio Corp. v. FCC, 326 U.S. 327, 90 L.Ed.2d 108, 66 S.Ct. 148 (1945)

Associated Broadcasters, Inc. v. FCC, 71 U.S.App.D.C. 206, 108 F.2d 737 (1939), rev'd, 311 U.S. 132 (1940)

Associated Press v. FCC, 145 U.S.App.D.C. 172, 448 F.2d 1095 (1971)

Associated Press v. FCC, 146 U.S.App.D.C. 361, 452 F.2d 1290 (1971)

Association of Communications Enterprises v. FCC, 344 U.S.App.D.C. 290, 235 F.3d 662 (2001)

Association of Communications Enterprises v. FCC, 346 U.S.App.D.C. 325, 253 F.3d 29 (2001)

Association of Maximum Service Telecasters v. FCC, 253 U.S.App.D.C. 36, 791 F.2d 207 (1986)

Association of Maximum Service Telecasters v. FCC, 272 U.S.App.D.C. 42, 853 F.2d 973 (1988)

Association of Public Safety Communications Officials International, Inc. v. FCC, 316 U.S.App.D.C. 134, 76 F.3d 395 (1996)

Astroline Communications Co. v. FCC, 273 U.S.App.D.C. 118, 857 F.2d 1556 (1988)

AT&T Corp. v. City of Portland, 216 F.3d 871 (9th Cir. 2000)

AT&T Corp. v. FCC, 318 U.S.App.D.C. 168, 86 F.3d 242 (1996)

AT&T Corp. v. FCC, 324 U.S.App.D.C. 272, 113 F.3d 225 (1997)

AT&T Corp. v. FCC, 343 U.S.App.D.C. 23, 220 F.3d 607 (2000)

AT&T Corp. v. FCC, 344 U.S.App.D.C. 362, 236 F.3d 729 (2001)

AT&T Corp. v. FCC, 292 F.3d 808 (2002)

AT&T Corp. v. FCC, 354 U.S.App.D.C. 325, 317 F.3d 227 (2003)

AT&T Corp. v. FCC, 355 U.S.App.D.C. 322, 323 F.3d 1081 (2003)

AT&T Corp. v. FCC and United States, No. 03-1017 (2004)

AT&T Corp. v. FCC and United States, No. 03-1035 (2004)

AT&T Corp. v. Iowa Util. Bd., 525 U.S. 366, 142 L.Ed.2d 835, 119 S.Ct. 721 (1999)

AT&T Information Systems, Inc. v. FCC, 272 U.S.App.D.C. 225, 854 F.2d 1442 (1988)

AT&T Wireless Services, Inc., et al. v. FCC, 348 U.S.App.D.C. 135, 270 F.3d 959 (2001)

AT&T Wireless Services, Inc., et al. v. FCC, 361 U.S.App.D.C. 170, 365 F.3d 1095 (2004)

Atlantic Tele-Network, Inc. v. FCC, 313 U.S.App.D.C. 396, 59 F.3d 1384 (1995)

Atlas Broadcasting Co. v. FCC, 111 U.S.App.D.C. 196, 295 F.2d 183 (1961)

Bachow Communications, Inc. v. FCC, 345 U.S.App.D.C. 45, 237 F.3d 683 (2001)

Baker v. FCC, 266 U.S.App.D.C. 155, 834 F.2d 181 (1987)

Bakersfield Broadcasting Co. v. United States, 105 U.S.App.D.C. 293, 266 F.2d 697 (1959)

Baltimore Mobile Telephone Co. v. FCC, 197 U.S.App.D.C. 179, 607 F.2d 493 (1979)

Bamford v. FCC, 175 U.S.App.D.C. 250, 535 F.2d 78, cert. denied, 429 U.S. 895 (1976)

Banzhaf v. FCC, 132 U.S.App.D.C. 14, 405 F.2d 1082 (1968), cert. denied, 396 U.S. 842 (1969)

Bartholdi Cable Co., Inc. v. FCC, 324 U.S.App.D.C. 420, 114 F.3d 274 (1997)

Basic Media, Ltd. v. FCC, 182 U.S.App.D.C. 209, 559 F.2d 830 (1977)

Baxter v. FCC, 249 U.S.App.D.C. 210, 774 F.2d 510 (1985)

Bay State Beacon v. FCC, 84 U.S.App.D.C. 216, 171 F.2d 826 (1948)

Beach Communications, Inc. v. FCC, 294 U.S.App.D.C. 377, 959 F.2d 975 (1992)

Beach Communications, Inc. v. FCC, 296 U.S.App.D.C. 141, 965 F.2d 1103 (1992), rev'd, 508 U.S. 307, 124 L.Ed.2d 34, 113 S.Ct. 2096 (1993)

Beach Communications, Inc. v. FCC, 304 U.S.App.D.C. 36, 10 F.3d 811 (1993)

Beachview Broadcasting Corp. v. FCC, 104 U.S.App.D.C. 377, 262 F.2d 688, reh. denied, 106 U.S.App.D.C. 341, 273 F.2d 76 (1958), cert. denied, 359 U.S. 936 (1959)

Beaufort County Broadcasting Co. v. FCC, 252 U.S.App.D.C. 89, 787 F.2d 645 (1986)

Beaumont Branch of the NAACP v. FCC, 272 U.S.App.D.C. 92, 854 F.2d 501 (1988)

Beaumont Broadcasting Corp. v. FCC, 91 U.S.App.D.C. 111, 202 F.2d 306 (1952)

Bechtel v. FCC, 294 U.S.App.D.C. 124, 957 F.2d 873 (1992), cert. denied, 506 U.S. 816 (1992)

Bechtel v. FCC, 304 U.S.App.D.C. 100, 10 F.3d 875 (1993)

Becker v. FCC, 320 U.S.App.D.C. 387, 95 F.3d 75 (1996)

Beebe v. FRC, 61 U.S.App.D.C. 273, 61 F.2d 914 (1932)

Beehive Tel. Co. v. FCC, 336 U.S.App.D.C. 331, 179 F.3d 941 (1999)

Beehive Tel. Co. v. FCC, 336 U.S.App.D.C. 379, 180 F.3d 314 (1999)

Beehive Tel. Co. v. FCC, 343 U.S.App.D.C. 50, 221 F.3d 195 (2000)

Bell Atlantic Telephone Cos. v. FCC, 306 U.S.App.D.C. 333, 24 F.3d 1441 (1994)

Bell Atlantic Telephone Cos. v. FCC, 316 U.S.App.D.C. 395, 79 F.3d 1195 (1996)

Bell Atlantic Telephone Cos. v. FCC, 327 U.S.App.D.C. 390, 131 F.3d 1044 (1997)

Bell Atlantic Telephone Cos v. FCC, 340 U.S.App.D.C. 328, 206 F.3d 1 (2000)

Bell County Broadcasting Co. v. FCC, 292 U.S.App.D.C. 388, 950 F.2d 797 (1991)

Bell Telephone Co. of Pa. v. FCC, 503 F.2d 1250 (3rd Cir. 1974), cert. denied, 422 U.S. 1026 (1975)

Bell Telephone Co. of Pa. v. FCC, 245 U.S.App.D.C. 386, 761 F.2d 789 (1985)

BellSouth Corp. v. FCC, 286 U.S.App.D.C. 378, 917 F.2d 600 (1990)

BellSouth Corp. v. FCC, 305 U.S.App.D.C. 134, 17 F.3d 1487 (1994)

BellSouth Corp. v. FCC, 960 F.3d 849 (6th Cir. 1996)

BellSouth Corp. v. FCC, 333 U.S.App.D.C. 253, 162 F.3d 678 (1998)

BellSouth Corp. v. FCC, 330 U.S.App.D.C. 109, 144 F.3d 58 (1998), cert. denied, 526 U.S. 1086 (1999)

BellSouth Corp. v. FCC, 333 U.S.App.D.C. 308, 162 F.3d 1215 (1999)

Belluso v. Turner Communications Corp., 633 F.2d 393 (5th Cir. 1980)

Beloit Broadcasters, Inc. v. FCC, 125 U.S.App.D.C. 29, 365 F.2d 962 (1966)

Bendix Aviation Corp. v. FCC, 106 U.S.App.D.C. 304, 272 F.2d 533 (1959), cert. denied, 361 U.S. 965 (1960)

Benkelman Telephone Co. v. FCC, 343 U.S.App.D.C. 17, 220 F.3d 601 (2000)

Berg v. FCC, 217 U.S.App.D.C. 358, 672 F.2d 892 (1981)

Berlin Communications, Inc. v. FCC, 200 U.S.App.D.C. 5, 626 F.2d 869 (1979)

Bernstein-Rein Advertising, Inc. v. FCC, 265 U.S.App.D.C. 304, 830 F.2d 1188 (1987)

Berwick v. FCC, 109 U.S.App.D.C. 241, 286 F.2d 97 (1960)

Bethel Broadcasting Inc. v. FCC, 255 U.S.App.D.C. 397, 801 F.2d 1436 (1986)

Bethesda-Chevy Chase Broadcasters, Inc. v. FCC, 128 U.S.App.D.C. 185, 385 F.2d 967 (1967)

Big Valley Cablevision, Inc. v. FCC, 174 U.S.App.D.C. 111, 529 F.2d 353 (1976)

Bilingual Bicultural Coalition v. FCC, 160 U.S.App.D.C. 390, 492 F.2d 656 (1974)

Bilingual Bicultural Coalition v. FCC, 193 U.S.App.D.C. 236, 595 F.2d 621 (1978)

Biltmore Forest Broadcasting FM, Inc. v. FCC, 355 U.S.App.D.C. 170, 321 F.3d 155, cert. denied, 124 S.Ct. 463 (2003)

Black v. FCC, 252 U.S.App.D.C. 136, 788 F.2d 38 (1986)

Black Broadcasting Coalition of Richmond v. FCC, 181 U.S.App.D.C. 182, 556 F.2d 59 (1977)

Black Citizens for a Fair Media v. FCC, 231 U.S.App.D.C. 163, 719 F.2d 407 (1983), cert. denied, 467 U.S. 1255 (1984)

Black Hills Video Corp. v. FCC, 399 F.2d 65 (8th Cir. 1968)

Black River Valley Broadcasts v. McNinch, 69 U.S.App.D.C. 311, 101 F.2d 235 (1938), cert. denied, 307 U.S. 623 (1939)

Blanco Pi v. FCC, 219 U.S.App.D.C. 114, 675 F.2d 1339 (1982)

Blumenthal v. FCC, 115 U.S.App.D.C. 305, 318 F.2d 276, cert. denied, 373 U.S. 951 (1963)

Boedker v. FCC, 295 U.S.App.D.C. 209, 961 F.2d 963 (1992)

Booth American Co. v. FCC, 126 U.S.App.D.C. 97, 374 F.2d 311 (1967)

Borrow v. FCC, 109 U.S.App.D.C. 244, 285 F.2d 666, cert. denied, 364 U.S. 892 (1960)

Boston Broadcasting Co. v. FRC, 62 U.S.App.D.C. 299, 67 F.2d 505 (1933)

Boston Community Media Comm. v. FCC, 166 U.S.App.D.C. 183, 509 F.2d 516 (1975)

Bradwin Corp. v. FCC, 186 U.S.App.D.C. 328, 569 F.2d 159 (1977)

Brahy v. FRC, 61 U.S.App.D.C. 204, 59 F.2d 879 (1932)

Branch v. FCC, 262 U.S.App.D.C. 310, 824 F.2d 37 (1987), cert. denied, 485 U.S. 959 (1988)

Brand X Internet Services v. FCC, 345 F.3d 1120 (9th Cir. 2003)

Brandywine-Main Line Radio, Inc. v. FCC, 153 U.S.App.D.C. 305, 473 F.2d 16 (1972), cert. denied, 412 U.S. 922 (1973)

Branton v. FCC, 301 U.S.App.D.C. 244, 993 F.2d 906 (1993), cert. denied, 511 U.S. 1052 (1994)

Brigham v. FCC, 276 F.2d 828 (5th Cir. 1960)

Broadcast Enterprises, Inc. v. FCC, 129 U.S.App.D.C. 68, 390 F.2d 483 (1968)

Broadcast Good Music! Comm. v. FCC, 177 U.S.App.D.C. 269, 543 F.2d 416 (1976)

Broadcasting Service Organization, Inc. v. FCC, 84 U.S.App.D.C. 152, 171 F.2d 1007 (1948), rev'd, 337 U.S. 901 (1949)

Brookhaven Cable TV, Inc. v. FCC, 428 F.Supp. 1216 (S.D.N.Y. 1977), aff'd, 573 F.2d 765 (2nd Cir. 1978), cert. denied, 441 U.S. 904 (1979)

Brookhaven Cable TV, Inc. v. FCC, 573 F.2d 765 (2nd Cir. 1978), cert. denied, 441 U.S. 904 (1979)

Brown v. FCC, 199 U.S.App.D.C. 9, 615 F.2d 1368 (1980)

Brown v. FCC, 281 U.S.App.D.C. 201, 888 F.2d 898 (1989)

Brown Telecasters, Inc. v. FCC, 110 U.S.App.D.C. 127, 289 F.2d 868, cert. denied, 368 U.S. 916 (1961)

Buckeye Cablevision, Inc. v. FCC, 128 U.S.App.D.C. 262, 387 F.2d 220 (1967)

Buckeye Cablevision, Inc. v. United States, 438 F.2d 948 (6th Cir. 1971)

Buckley v. United States, 110 U.S.App.D.C. 81, 289 F.2d 458 (1961)

Buckley-Jaeger Broadcasting Corp. v. FCC, 130 U.S.App.D.C. 90, 397 F.2d 651 (1968)

Bucks County Cable TV, Inc. v. United States, 299 F.Supp. 1325 (E.D. Pa. 1969), rev'd, 427 F.2d 438 (3rd Cir.), cert. denied, 400 U.S. 831 (1970)

Bucks County Cable TV, Inc. v. United States, 427 F.2d 438 (3rd Cir.), cert. denied, 400 U.S. 831 (1970)

Buffalo Broadcasting Co., Inc. v. FCC, 188 U.S.App.D.C. 199, 578 F.2d 441 (1978)

Building Owners & Mgrs Ass'n, Intl. v. FCC, 349 U.S.App.D.C. 12, 254 F.3d 89 (2001)

Bunkfeldt Broadcasting Corp. v. FCC, 226 U.S.App.D.C. 210, 701 F.2d 221 (1983)

Bursam Communications Corp. v. FCC, 292 U.S.App.D.C. 37, 946 F.2d 127 (1991)

Business Executives Move for Vietnam Peace v. FCC, 146 U.S.App.D.C. 181, 450 F.2d 642 (1971), rev'd, *CBS v. DNC*, 412 U.S. 94 (1973)

Busse Broadcasting Corp. v. FCC, 318 U.S.App.D.C. 447, 87 F.3d 1456 (1996)

Bywater Neighborhood Ass'n v. Tricarico, 879 F.2d 165 (5th Cir. 1989), cert. denied, 494 U.S. 1004 (1990)

Cable & Wireless PLC v. FCC, 334 U.S.App.D.C. 261, 166 F.3d 1224 (1999)

Cable TV Co. v. FCC, 154 U.S.App.D.C. 307, 475 F.2d 418 (1973)

Cable TV of Santa Barbara, Inc. v. FCC, 428 F.2d 672 (9th Cir. 1970)

California v. FCC, 185 U.S.App.D.C. 217, 567 F.2d 84 (1977), cert. denied, 434 U.S. 1010 (1978)

California v. FCC, 255 U.S.App.D.C. 84, 798 F.2d 1515 (1986)

California v. FCC, 39 F.3d 919 (9th Cir. 1994)

California Ass'n of the Physically Handicapped, Inc. v. FCC, 721 F.2d 667 (9th Cir. 1983), cert. denied, 469 U.S. 832 (1984)

California Ass'n of the Physically Handicapped, Inc. v. FCC, 250 U.S.App.D.C. 202, 778 F.2d 823 (1985)

California Ass'n of the Physically Handicapped, Inc. v. FCC, 268 U.S.App.D.C. 208, 840 F.2d 88, rehearing en banc denied, 270 U.S.App.D.C. 272, 848 F.2d 1304 (1988)

California Ass'n of the Physically Handicapped, Inc. v. FCC, 833 F.2d 1333 (9th Cir. 1987)

California Ass'n of the Physically Handicapped, Inc. v. FCC, 905 F.2d 1540 (9th Cir. 1990), cert. denied, 499 U.S. 975 (1991)

California Citizens Band Ass'n v. United States, 375 F.2d 43 (9th Cir.), cert. denied, 389 U.S. 844 (1967)

California Interstate Telephone Co. v. FCC, 117 U.S.App.D.C. 255, 328 F.2d 556 (1964)

California Paralyzed Veterans Ass'n v. FCC, 496 F.Supp. 125 (C.D. Cal. 1980), aff'd, *California Ass'n of the Physically Handicapped, Inc. v. FCC*, 721 F.2d 667 (9th Cir. 1983), cert. denied, 469 U.S. 832 (1984)

California Public Broadcasting Forum v. FCC, 243 U.S.App.D.C. 213, 752 F.2d 670 (1985)

California Public Broadcasting Forum v. FCC, 292 U.S.App.D.C. 89, 947 F.2d 505 (1991)

Calumet Broadcasting Corp. v. FCC, 82 U.S.App.D.C. 59, 160 F.2d 285 (1947)

Camden Radio v. FCC, 94 U.S.App.D.C. 312, 220 F.2d 191 (1954)

Campos v. FCC, 487 F.Supp. 865 (D. Ill. 1980), appeal dismissed, 650 F.2d 890 (7th Cir. 1981)

Campos v. FCC, 650 F.2d 890 (7th Cir. 1981)

Capital Broadcasting Co. v. Mitchell, 333 F.Supp. 582 (D.D.C. 1971), aff'd, *Capital Broadcasting Co. v. Kleindienst*, 405 U.S. 1000 (1972)

Capital Cities/ABC, Inc. v. FCC, 29 F.3d 309 (7th Cir. 1994)

Capital Cities Cable v. Crisp, 467 U.S. 691, 81 L.Ed.2d 580, 104 S.Ct. 2694 (1984)

Capital Cities Communications, Inc. v. FCC, 180 U.S.App.D.C. 276, 554 F.2d 1135 (1976)

Capital City Television, Inc. v. FCC, 106 U.S.App.D.C. 35, 269 F.2d 226 (1959)

Capital Communications, Inc. v. FCC, 229 U.S.App.D.C. 141, 711 F.2d 419 (1983)

Capital Network System, Inc. v. FCC, 294 U.S.App.D.C. 162, 957 F.2d 911 (1992)

Capital Network System, Inc. v. FCC, 296 U.S.App.D.C. 181, 966 F.2d 701 (1992)

Capital Network System, Inc. v. FCC, 303 U.S.App.D.C. 242, 3 F.3d 1526 (1993)

Capital Network System, Inc. v. FCC, 307 U.S.App.D.C. 334, 28 F.3d 201 (1994)

Capital Telephone Co. v. FCC, 162 U.S.App.D.C. 192, 498 F.2d 734 (1974)

Capital Telephone Co. v. FCC, 777 F.2d. 868 (2nd Cir. 1985)

Capital Transit Co. v. United States, 97 F.Supp. 614 (D.D.C. 1951)

Capitol Broadcasting Co. v. FCC, 103 U.S.App.D.C. 252, 257 F.2d 630 (1958)

Capitol Broadcasting Co. v. FCC, 116 U.S.App.D.C. 370, 324 F.2d 402 (1963)

Capitol Radiotelephone Co., Inc. v. FCC, 324 U.S.App.D.C. 203, 111 F.3d 962 (1997)

Caples Co. v. United States, 100 U.S.App.D.C. 126, 243 F.2d 232 (1957)

Carlin Communications, Inc. v. FCC, 749 F.2d 113 (2nd Cir. 1984)

Carlin Communications, Inc. v. FCC, 787 F.2d 846 (2nd Cir. 1986)

Carlin Communications, Inc. v. FCC, 837 F.2d 546 (2nd Cir.), cert. denied, 488 U.S. 924 (1988)

Carlson v. FCC, 84 U.S.App.D.C. 415, 172 F.2d 766, cert. denied, 337 U.S. 930 (1949)

Carpenter v. FCC, 176 U.S.App.D.C. 240, 539 F.2d 242 (1976)

Carpenter v. FCC, 177 U.S.App.D.C. 269, 543 F.2d 416 (1976)

Carpenter v. FCC, 774 F.2d 1161 (6th Cir. 1985)

Carrell v. FRC, 59 U.S.App.D.C. 131, 36 F.2d 117 (1929)

Carroll Broadcasting Co. v. FCC, 103 U.S.App.D.C. 346, 258 F.2d 440 (1958)

Carter Mountain Transmission Corp. v. FCC, 116 U.S.App.D.C. 93, 321 F.2d 359, cert. denied, 375 U.S. 951 (1963)

Cascade Broadcasting Group v. FCC, 262 U.S.App.D.C. 110, 822 F.2d 1172 (1987)

Cassell v. FCC, 332 U.S.App.D.C. 156, 154 F.3d 478 (1998)

Catoctin Broadcasting Corp. v. FCC, 287 U.S.App.D.C. 245, 920 F.2d 1039 (1990)

CBS, Inc. v. FCC, 202 U.S.App.D.C. 369, 629 F.2d 1 (1980), aff'd, 453 U.S. 367 (1981)

CBS, Inc. v. FCC, 453 U.S. 367, 69 L.Ed.2d 706, 101 S.Ct. 2813 (1981)

CBS Television Network Affiliates Ass'n v. FCC, 181 U.S.App.D.C. 48, 555 F.2d 985 (1977)

Cedar Rapids Television Co. v. FCC, 128 U.S.App.D.C. 270, 387 F.2d 228 (1967)

CEETRUTH v. FCC, 225 U.S.App.D.C. 51, 696 F.2d 133 (1982)

Celcom Communications Corp. v. FCC, 252 U.S.App.D.C. 235, 789 F.2d 67 (1986)

Celcom Communications Corp. v. FCC, 268 U.S.App.D.C. 145, 839 F.2d 824 (1988)

Celcom Communications Corp. of Ga. v. FCC, 252 U.S.App.D.C. 53, 787 F.2d 609 (1986)

Cellco Partnership d/b/a Verizon Wireless v. FCC and United States, 360 U.S.App.D.C. 73, 357 F.3d 88 (2004)

Cellnet Communications, Inc. v. FCC, 296 U.S.App.D.C. 144, 965 F.2d 1106 (1992)

Cellnet Communications, Inc. v. FCC, 149 F.3d 429 (6th Cir. 1998)

Cellular Mobile Systems of Illinois, Inc. v. FCC, 251 U.S.App.D.C. 132, 782 F.2d 214 (1986)

Cellular Mobile Systems of Pa., Inc. v. FCC, 251 U.S.App.D.C. 100, 782 F.2d 182 (1985)

Cellular Mobile Systems of Pa., Inc. v. FCC, 253 U.S.App.D.C. 171, 792 F.2d 239 (1986)

Cellular Phone Taskforce v. FCC, 205 F.3d 82 (2nd Cir. 2000)

Cellular Telecommunications & Internet Ass'n v. FCC, 356 U.S.App.D.C. 238, 330 F.3d 502 (2003)

Cellular Telecommunications Industry Ass'n v. FCC, 335 U.S.App.D.C. 32, 168 F.3d 1332 (1999)

Cellwave Telephone Services, L.P. v. FCC, 308 U.S.App.D.C. 166, 30 F.3d 1533 (1994)

Celtronix Telemetry, Inc v. FCC, 348 U.S.App.D.C. 183, 272 F.3d 585 (2001)

Central Broadcasting Co. v. FCC, 126 U.S.App.D.C. 257, 377 F.2d 142 (1966)

Central California Communications v. FCC, 179 U.S.App.D.C. 126, 549 F.2d 829 (1977)

Central Florida Enterprises, Inc. v. FCC, 194 U.S.App.D.C. 118, 598 F.2d 37 (1978), cert. dismissed, 441 U.S. 957 (1979)

Central Florida Enterprises, Inc. v. FCC, 221 U.S.App.D.C. 162, 683 F.2d 503 (1982), cert. denied, 460 U.S. 1084 (1983)

Central Television, Inc. v. FCC, 266 U.S.App.D.C. 160, 834 F.2d 186 (1987)

Century Communications Corp. v. FCC, 266 U.S.App.D.C. 228, 835 F.2d 292 (1987), clarified, 267 U.S.App.D.C. 94, 837 F.2d 517 (1988), cert. denied, 486 U.S. 1032 (1988)

Century Federal, Inc. v. FCC, 270 U.S.App.D.C. 20, 846 F.2d 1479 (1988)

C.F. Communications Corp. v. FCC, 327 U.S.App.D.C. 1, 128 F.3d 735 (1997)

Chaconas v. FCC, 159 U.S.App.D.C. 54, 486 F.2d 1314 (1973)

Chadmoore Communications, Inc. v. FCC, 324 U.S.App.D.C. 282, 113 F.3d 235 (1997)

Chambersburg Broadcasting Co. v. FCC, 125 U.S.App.D.C. 346, 372 F.2d 919 (1966), cert. denied, 386 U.S. 1004 (1967)

Channel 9 Syracuse, Inc. v. FCC, 128 U.S.App.D.C. 187, 385 F.2d 969 (1967)

Channel 16 of Rhode Island, Inc. v. FCC, 97 U.S.App.D.C. 179, 229 F.2d 520 (1956)

Channel 16 of Rhode Island, Inc. v. FCC, 142 U.S.App.D.C. 238, 440 F.2d 266 (1971)

Channel 32 Hispanic Broadcasters, Inc. v. FCC, 22 Fed.Appx. 12, 2001 WL 1699415 (D.C. Cir. 2001)

Channel 51 of San Diego, Inc. v. FCC, 316 U.S.App.D.C. 387, 79 F.3d 1187 (1996)

Channel One Systems, Inc. v. FCC, 270 U.S.App.D.C. 273, 848 F.2d 1305 (1988)

Charles P. B. Pinson, Inc. v. FCC, 116 U.S.App.D.C. 106, 321 F.2d 372 (1963)

Chase Communications, Inc. v. FCC, 304 U.S.App.D.C. 298, 13 F.2d 421 (1993)

Chesapeake & Potomac Tel. Co. of Va. v. United States, 42 F.3d 181 (4th Cir. 1994), vacated, 516 U.S. 415 (1996)

Chesapeake & Potomac Tel. Co. of Va. v. United States, 830 F.Supp. 909 (E.D. Va. 1993), aff'd, 42 F.3d 181 (4th Cir. 1994), vacated, 516 U.S. 415 (1996)

Chicago Board of Trade v. United States, 96 U.S.App.D.C. 56, 223 F.2d 348 (1955)

Chicago Federation of Labor v. FRC, 59 U.S.App.D.C. 333, 41 F.2d 422 (1930)

Chickasaw Telephone Co. v. FCC, 306 U.S.App.D.C. 356, 24 F.3d 1464 (1994)

Chisholm v. FCC, 176 U.S.App.D.C. 1, 538 F.2d 349, cert. denied, 429 U.S. 890 (1976)

CHM Broadcasting Ltd. Partnership v. FCC, 306 U.S.App.D.C. 345, 24 F.3d 1453 (1994)

Christian Children's Network, Inc. v. FCC, 277 U.S.App.D.C. 61, 872 F.2d 496 (1989)

Christian Voice of Central Ohio v. FCC, 217 U.S.App.D.C. 359, 672 F.2d 893 (1981)

Chronicle Publishing Co. v. FCC, 125 U.S.App.D.C. 53, 366 F.2d 632 (1966)

Churchill Tabernacle v. FCC, 81 U.S.App.D.C. 411, 160 F.2d 244 (1947)

Cincinnati Bell Tel. Co. v. FCC, 69 F.3d 752 (6th Cir. 1995)

Citizens Comm. v. FCC, 141 U.S.App.D.C. 109, 436 F.2d 263 (1970)

Citizens Comm. to Keep Progressive Rock v. FCC, 156 U.S.App.D.C. 16, 478 F.2d 926 (1973)

Citizens Comm. to Save WEFM v. FCC, 165 U.S.App.D.C. 185, 506 F.2d 246 (1973)

Citizens Communications Center v. FCC, 145 U.S.App.D.C. 32, 447 F.2d 1201 (1971), clarified, 149 U.S.App.D.C. 419, 463 F.2d 822 (1972)

Citizens for Jazz on WRVR v. FCC, 249 U.S.App.D.C. 342, 775 F.2d 392 (1985)

Citizens TV Protest Comm. v. FCC, 121 U.S.App.D.C. 50, 348 F.2d 56 (1965)

City Cabs, Inc. v. FCC, 107 U.S.App.D.C. 136, 275 F.2d 165 (1960)

City of Abilene v. FCC, 334 U.S.App.D.C. 49, 164 F.3d 49 (1999)

City of Angels Broadcasting, Inc. v. FCC, 240 U.S.App.D.C. 280, 745 F.2d 656 (1984)

City of Brookings Municipal Telephone Co. v. FCC, 262 U.S.App.D.C. 91, 822 F.2d 1153 (1987)

City of Chicago v. FCC, 199 F.3d 424 (7th Cir. 1999)

City of Dallas, Tx. v. FCC, 118 F.3d 393 (5th Cir. 1997)

City of Dallas, Tx. v. FCC, 165 F.3d 341 (5th Cir. 1999)

City of Jacksonville v. FCC, 89 U.S.App.D.C. 411, 195 F.2d 198 (1951)

City of Los Angeles v. Preferred Communications, Inc., 476 U.S. 488, 90 L.Ed.2d 480, 106 S.Ct. 2034 (1986)

City of New York Municipal Broadcasting System v. FCC, 96 U.S.App.D.C. 172, 223 F.2d 637 (1955)

City of New York Municipal Broadcasting System v. FCC, 240 U.S.App.D.C. 203, 744 F.2d 827 (1984), cert. denied, 470 U.S. 1084 (1985)

City of New York v. FRC, 59 U.S.App.D.C. 129, 36 F.2d 115 (1929)

City of New York v. FRC, 62 U.S.App.D.C. 81, 64 F.2d 719 (1933)

City of New York v. FCC, 259 U.S.App.D.C. 191, 814 F.2d 720 (1987), aff'd, 486 U.S. 57 (1988)

City of New York v. FCC, 486 U.S. 57, 100 L.Ed.2d 48, 108 S.Ct. 1637 (1988)

City of Peoria v. General Electric Cablevision Corp., 690 F.2d 116 (7th Cir. 1982)

City of Portland, Ore. v. AT&T Corp., 45 Fed.Supp.2d 1146 (W.D. Or. 1999), rev'd, 216 F.3d 871 (9th Cir. 2000)

City of Rochester v. Bond, 195 U.S.App.D.C. 345, 603 F.2d 927 (1979)

City of Trenton v. FCC, 441 F.2d 1329 (3rd Cir. 1971)

Civic Communications Corp. v. FCC, 149 U.S.App.D.C. 205, 462 F.2d 309 (1972)

Civic Telecasting Corp. v. FCC, 173 U.S.App.D.C. 236, 523 F.2d 1185 (1975), cert. denied, 426 U.S. 949 (1976)

C.J. Community Services, Inc. v. FCC, 100 U.S.App.D.C. 379, 246 F.2d 660 (1957)

Clarksburg Publishing Co. v. FCC, 96 U.S.App.D.C. 211, 225 F.2d 511 (1955)

Clay Broadcasting Corp. v. United States, 464 F.2d 1313 (5th Cir. 1972), rev'd, NCTA, Inc. v. United States, 415 U.S. 336 (1974)

Clear Channel Broadcasting Service v. United States, 109 U.S.App.D.C. 88, 284 F.2d 222 (1960)

Cleveland Television Corp. v. FCC, 235 U.S.App.D.C. 360, 732 F.2d 962 (1984)

Coalition for a Healthy California v. FCC, 87 F.3d 383 (9th Cir. 1996)

Coalition for Noncommercial Media v. FCC, 346 U.S.App.D.C. 11, 249 F.3d 1005 (2001)

Coalition for the Preservation of Hispanic Broadcasting v. FCC, 282 U.S.App.D.C. 200, 893 F.2d 1349 (1990), vacated in part and aff'd in part, 289 U.S.App.D.C. 228, 931 F.2d 73 (en banc), cert. denied, 502 U.S. 907 (1991)

Coast Television Broadcasting Corp. v. FCC, 187 U.S.App.D.C. 425, 574 F.2d 636 (1978)

Coastal Bend Television Co. v. FCC, 97 U.S.App.D.C. 339, 231 F.2d 498 (1956)

Coastal Bend Television Co. v. FCC, 98 U.S.App.D.C. 251, 234 F.2d 686 (1956)

Colby-Bates-Bowdoin Educ. Telecasting Corp. v. FCC, 534 F.2d 11 (1st Cir. 1976)

Colby-Bates-Bowdoin Educ. Telecasting Corp. v. FCC, 574 F.2d 639 (1st Cir. 1978)

Colonial Broadcasters Inc. v. FCC, 70 U.S.App.D.C. 258, 105 F.2d 781 (1939)

Colonial Television v. FCC, 95 U.S.App.D.C. 7, 217 F.2d 21 (1954)

Colorado Radio Corp. v. FCC, 73 U.S.App.D.C. 225, 118 F.2d 24 (1941)

Colorado Television, Inc. v. FCC, 255 U.S.App.D.C. 397, 801 F.2d 1436 (1986)

Columbia Broadcasting System v. FCC, 316 U.S. 407, 86 L.Ed. 1563, 62 S.Ct. 1194 (1942)

Columbia Broadcasting System, Inc. v. Democratic National Comm., 412 U.S. 94, 36 L.Ed.2d 772, 93 S.Ct. 2080 (1973)

Columbia Broadcasting System, Inc. v. FCC, 147 U.S.App.D.C. 175, 454 F.2d 1018 (1971)

Columbia Broadcasting System of California v. FCC, 93 U.S.App.D.C. 399, 211 F.2d 644, cert. denied, 348 U.S. 876 (1954)

Columbia Communications Corp. v. FCC, 265 U.S.App.D.C. 421, 832 F.2d 189 (1987)

Columbia Empire Telecasters, Inc. v. FCC, 97 U.S.App.D.C. 112, 228 F.2d 459 (1955)

Columbia Television Broadcasters, Inc. v. FCC, 229 U.S.App.D.C. 141, 711 F.2d 419 (1983)

Columbus Broadcasting Coalition v. FCC, 164 U.S.App.D.C. 213, 505 F.2d 320 (1974)

Commercial Realty St. Pete, Inc. v. FCC, 325 U.S.App.D.C. 320, 116 F.3d 941, cert. denied, 522 U.S. 983 (1997)

Committee for Community Access v. FCC, 237 U.S.App.D.C. 292, 737 F.2d 74 (1984)

Committee for Effective Cellular Rules v. FCC, 311 U.S.App.D.C. 345, 53 F.3d 1309 (1995)

Committee for Open Media v. FCC, 174 U.S.App.D.C. 333, 533 F.2d 1 (1976)

Committee for Open Media v. FCC, 177 U.S.App.D.C. 376, 543 F.2d 861 (1976)

Committee for Scientific Investigation of Claims of Paranormal v. FCC, 198 U.S.App.D.C. 91, 612 F.2d 586 (1980)

Committee to Save WEAM v. FCC, 257 U.S.App.D.C. 218. 808 F.2d 113 (1986)

Commodity News Services, Inc. v. FCC, 183 U.S.App.D.C. 128, 561 F.2d 1021 (1977)

Communications and Control, Inc. v. FCC, 362 U.S.App.D.C. 504, 374 F.3d 1329 (2004)

Communications Investment Corp. v. FCC, 206 U.S.App.D.C. 1, 641 F.2d 954 (1981)

Communications Satellite Corp. v. FCC, 198 U.S.App.D.C. 60, 611 F.2d 883 (1977)

Communications Satellite Corp. v. FCC, 266 U.S.App.D.C. 459, 836 F.2d 623 (1988)

Communications Systems, Inc. v. FCC, 193 U.S.App.D.C. 412, 595 F.2d 797 (1978)

Communications Vending Corp. of Arizona v. FCC and United States, 361 U.S.App.D.C. 139, 365 F.3d 1064 (2004)

Communi-Centre Broadcasting, Inc. v. FCC, 272 U.S.App.D.C. 389, 856 F.2d 1551 (1988), cert. denied, 489 U.S. 1083 (1989)

Community Broadcasting Co. v. FCC, 107 U.S.App.D.C. 95, 274 F.2d 753 (1960)

Community Broadcasting Corp. v. FCC, 124 U.S.App.D.C. 230, 363 F.2d 717 (1966)

Community Broadcasting of Boston, Inc. v. FCC, 178 U.S.App.D.C. 256, 546 F.2d 1022 (1976)

Community Broadcasting Service, Inc. v. FCC, 126 U.S.App.D.C. 258, 377 F.2d 143 (1967)

Community Coalition for Better Broadcasting v. FCC, 218 U.S.App.D.C. 160, 673 F.2d 551 (1982)

Community Coalition for Media Change v. FCC, 207 U.S.App.D.C. 278, 646 F.2d 613 (1980)

Community First Corp. v. FCC, 131 U.S.App.D.C. 172, 403 F.2d 578 (1968)

Community Service, Inc. v. United States, 418 F.2d 709 (6th Cir. 1969)

Community-Service Broadcasting of Mid-America, Inc. v. FCC, 192 U.S.App.D.C. 448, 593 F.2d 1102 (1978)

Community Telecasters of Cleveland, Inc. v. FCC, 187 U.S.App.D.C. 425, 574 F.2d 636 (1978)

Community Telecasting Co. v. FCC, 103 U.S.App.D.C. 139, 255 F.2d 891 (1958)

Community Telecasting Corp. v. FCC, 115 U.S.App.D.C. 181, 317 F.2d 592 (1963)

Community Television, Inc. v. United States, 404 F.2d 771 (10th Cir. 1969)

Community Television, Inc. v. FCC, 342 U.S.App.D.C. 290, 216 F.3d 1133 (2000)

Community Television of Southern Calif. v. Gottfried, 459 U.S. 498, 74 L.Ed.2d 705, 103 S.Ct. 1885 (1983)

Competitive Telecommunications Ass'n v. FCC, 302 U.S.App.D.C. 423, 998 F.2d 1058 (1993)

Competitive Telecommunications Ass'n v. FCC, 318 U.S.App.D.C. 288, 87 F.3d 522 (1996)

Competitive Telecommunications Ass'n v. FCC, 117 F.3d 1068 (8th Cir. 1997)

Competitive Telecommunications Ass'n v. FCC, 309 F.3d 8 (D.C. Cir. 2002)

Computer and Communications Industry Ass'n v. FCC, 224 U.S.App.D.C. 83, 693 F.2d 198 (1982), cert. denied, 461 U.S. 938 (1983)

COMSAT Corp. v. FCC, 316 U.S.App.D.C. 240, 77 F.3d 1419 (1996)

COMSAT Corp. v. FCC, 324 U.S.App.D.C. 369, 114 F.3d 223 (1997)

COMSAT Corp. v. FCC, 250 F.3d 931 (5th Cir. 2001)

COMSAT Corp. v. FCC, 350 U.S.App.D.C. 191, 283 F.3d 344 (2002)

Comtronics, Inc. v. Puerto Rico Telephone Co., 409 F.Supp. 800 (D.P.R. 1975), aff'd, 553 F.2d 701 (1st Cir. 1977)

Comtronics, Inc. v. Puerto Rico Telephone Co., 553 F.2d 701 (1st Cir. 1977)

Concerned Citizens of Roanoke v. FCC, 252 U.S.App.D.C. 403, 790 F.2d 604 (1986)

Conley Electronics Corp. v. FCC, 394 F.2d 620 (10th Cir.), cert. denied, 393 U.S. 858 (1968)

Connecticut Comm. Against Pay TV v. FCC, 112 U.S.App.D.C. 248, 301 F.2d 835, cert. denied, 371 U.S. 816 (1962)

Connecticut Dept. of Public Util. Control v. FCC, 78 F.3d 842 (2nd Cir. 1996)

Connecticut Office of Consumer Council v. FCC, 915 F.2d 75 (2nd Cir. 1990), cert. denied, 499 U.S. 920 (1991)

Consolidated Nine, Inc. v. FCC, 131 U.S.App.D.C. 179, 403 F.2d 585 (1968)

Consumer Electronics Ass'n v. FCC, 358 U.S.App.D.C. 180, 347 F.3d 291 (2003)

Consumer Federation of America v. FCC, 358 U.S.App.D.C. 271, 348 F.3d 1009 (2003)

Contemporary Media, Inc. v. FCC, 341 U.S.App.D.C. 427, 214 F.3d 187 (2000)

Continental Broadcasting, Inc. v. FCC, 142 U.S.App.D.C. 70, 439 F.2d 580, cert. denied, 403 U.S. 905 (1971)

Continental Cellular v. FCC, 287 U.S.App.D.C. 377, 923 F.2d 200 (1990)

Cook, Inc. v. United States, 394 F.2d 84 (7th Cir. 1968)

Copley Press, Inc. v. FCC, 144 U.S.App.D.C. 109, 444 F.2d 984 (1971)

Coral Television Corp. v. FCC, 217 U.S.App.D.C. 359, 672 F.2d 893 (1981)

Cornell University v. United States, 427 F.2d 680 (2nd Cir. 1970)

Corporate Telecom Services, Inc. v. FCC, 312 U.S.App.D.C. 107, 55 F.3d 672 (1995)

Cosmopolitan Broadcasting Corp. v. FCC, 189 U.S.App.D.C. 139, 581 F.2d 917 (1978)

Costa de Oro Television, Inc. v. FCC, 294 F.3d 123 (2002)

Council for Employment and Economic Energy Use v. FCC, 575 F.2d 311 (1st Cir.), cert. denied, 439 U.S. 911 (1978)

Courier Post Publishing Co. v. FCC, 70 U.S.App.D.C. 90, 104 F.2d 213 (1939)

Courier-Journal Co. v. FRC, 60 U.S.App.D.C. 33, 46 F.2d 614 (1931)

Crisler v. FCC, 287 U.S.App.D.C. 73, 919 F.2d 182 (1990)

Crockett Telephone Co. v. FCC, 295 U.S.App.D.C. 397, 963 F.2d 1564 (1992)

Cronan v. FCC, 109 U.S.App.D.C. 208, 285 F.2d 288 (1960), cert. denied, 366 U.S. 904 (1961)

Crosley Corp. v. FCC, 70 U.S.App.D.C. 312, 106 F.2d 833, cert. denied, 308 U.S. 605 (1939)

Crosthwait v. FCC, 189 U.S.App.D.C. 392, 584 F.2d 550 (1978)

Crowder v. FCC, 130 U.S.App.D.C. 198, 399 F.2d 569, cert. denied, 393 U.S. 962 (1968)

Cumberland Broadcasting Corp. v. FCC, 208 U.S.App.D.C. 212, 647 F.2d 1341 (1980)

Dacre v. FCC, 122 U.S.App.D.C. 171, 352 F.2d 647 (1965)

Da-Gon Broadcasting Co. v. FCC, 287 U.S.App.D.C. 377, 923 F.2d 200 (1991)

Daly v. United States, 286 F.2d 146 (7th Cir.), cert. denied, 368 U.S. 949 (1961)

Damsky v. FCC, 339 U.S.App.D.C. 314, 199 F.3d 527 (2000)

Daniels Cablevision, Inc. v. United States, 835 F.Supp. 1 (D.D.C. 1993), aff'd in part and rev'd in part, *Time Warner Entertainment Co., L.P. v. FCC*, 320 U.S.App.D.C. 294, 93 F.3d 957 (1996)

David Ortiz Radio Corp. v. FCC, 291 U.S.App.D.C. 336, 941 F.2d 1253 (1991)

David Ortiz Radio Corp. v. FCC, 316 U.S.App.D.C. 367, 79 F.3d 169 (1996)

Davidson v. FRC, 61 U.S.App.D.C. 249, 61 F.2d 401 (1932)

de Perez v. FCC, 238 U.S.App.D.C. 158, 738 F.2d 1304 (1984)

Deep South Broadcasting Co. v. FCC, 107 U.S.App.D.C. 384, 278 F.2d 264 (1960)

Deep South Broadcasting Co. v. FCC, 120 U.S.App.D.C. 365, 347 F.2d 459 (1965)

Deitz v. FCC, 268 U.S.App.D.C. 306, 841 F.2d 428 (1988)

Delaware, L. & W. R. Co. v. FCC, 272 F.2d 706 (2nd Cir. 1959)

Delta Communications Corp. v. FCC, 777 F.2d 226 (5th Cir. 1985)

Delta Radio, Inc. v. FCC, 363 U.S.App.D.C. 312, 387 F.3d 897 (2004)

Democrat Printing Co. v. FCC, 91 U.S.App.D.C. 72, 202 F.2d 298 (1952)

Democratic National Comm. v. FCC, 148 U.S.App.D.C. 383, 460 F.2d 891, cert. denied, 409 U.S. 843 (1972)

Democratic National Comm. v. FCC, 148 U.S.App.D.C. 405, 460 F.2d 913 (1972)

Democratic National Comm. v. FCC, 156 U.S.App.D.C. 368, 481 F.2d 543 (1973)

Democratic National Comm. v. FCC, 230 U.S.App.D.C. 414, 717 F.2d 1471 (1983)

Denver Area Educ. Telecommunications Consortium, Inc. v. FCC, 518 U.S. 727, 135 L.Ed.2d 888, 116 S.Ct. 2374 (1996)

Destination Ventures, Ltd. v. FCC, 844 F.Supp. 632 (D. Or. 1994), aff'd, 46 F.3d 54 (1995)

Diamond International Corp. v. FCC, 201 U.S.App.D.C. 30, 627 F.2d 489 (1980)

Dickinson Broadcasting Corp. v. FCC, 193 U.S.App.D.C. 217, 593 F.2d 1371 (1979)

Didriksen v. FCC, 103 U.S.App.D.C. 17, 254 F.2d 354 (1958)

Direct Marketing Ass'n, Inc. v. FCC, 249 U.S.App.D.C. 48, 772 F.2d 966 (1985)

DIRECTV, Inc. v. FCC, 324 U.S.App.D.C. 72, 110 F.3d 816 (1997)

Dobronski v. FCC, 17 F.3d 275 (9th Cir. 1994)

Don Lee Broadcasting System v. FCC, 64 U.S.App.D.C. 228, 76 F.2d 439 (1935)

Ettlinger Broadcasting Corp. v. FCC, 233 U.S.App.D.C. 166, 725 F.2d 125 (1983)

Evangelical Lutheran Synod v. FCC, 70 U.S.App.D.C. 270, 105 F.2d 793 (1939)

Evans v. FCC, 72 U.S.App.D.C. 159, 113 F.2d 166 (1940)

Faber v. FCC, 295 U.S.App.D.C. 284, 962 F.2d 1076 (1992)

Fairness In Media v. FCC, 271 U.S.App.D.C. 273, 851 F.2d 1500, cert. denied, 488 U.S. 893 (1988)

Faith Center, Inc. v. FCC, 220 U.S.App.D.C. 84, 679 F.2d 261 (1982), cert. denied, 459 U.S. 1203 (1983)

Faith Center, Inc. v. FCC, 246 U.S.App.D.C. 43, 762 F.2d 137 (1985)

Fancher v. FCC, 226 U.S.App.D.C. 210, 701 F.2d 221 (1983)

Farmers Educational and Cooperative Union of America v. WDAY, Inc., 360 U.S. 525, 3 L.Ed.2d 1407, 79 S.Ct. 1302 (1959)

Farmers Tel. Co., Inc. v. FCC, 184 F.3d 1241 (10th Cir. 1999)

Faulkner Radio, Inc. v. FCC, 181 U.S.App.D.C. 243, 557 F.2d 866 (1977)

FCC v. Allentown Broadcasting Corp., 349 U.S. 358, 99 L.Ed. 1147, 75 S.Ct. 855 (1955)

FCC v. American Broadcasting Co., 347 U.S. 284, 98 L.Ed.2d 699, 74 S.Ct. 793 (1954)

FCC v. Beach Communications, Inc., 508 U.S. 307, 124 L.Ed.2d 211, 113 S.Ct. 2096 (1993)

FCC v. Broadcasting Service Organization, 337 U.S. 901, 69 S.Ct. 1047, 93 L.Ed. 1715 (1949)

FCC v. Cohn, 154 F.Supp. 899 (S.D.N.Y. 1957)

FCC v. Columbia Broadcasting System of Calif., Inc., 311 U.S. 132, 85 L.Ed. 87, 61 S.Ct. 152 (1940)

FCC v. Florida Power Corp., 480 U.S. 245, 94 L.Ed.2d 282, 107 S.Ct. 1107 (1987)

FCC v. ITT World Communications, Inc., 466 U.S. 463, 80 L.Ed.2d 480, 104 S.Ct. 1936 (1984)

FCC v. League of Women Voters, 468 U.S. 364, 82 L.Ed.2d 278, 104 S.Ct. 3106 (1984)

FCC v. Midwest Video Corp., 440 U.S. 689, 59 L.Ed.2d 692, 99 S.Ct. 1435 (1979)

FCC v. National Broadcasting Co., Inc., 319 U.S. 239, 87 L.Ed. 1374, 63 S.Ct. 1035 (1943)

FCC v. National Citizens Comm. for Broadcasting, 436 U.S. 775, 56 L.Ed.2d 697, 98 S.Ct. 2096 (1978)

FCC v. NextWave Personal Communications, Inc., 200 F.3d 43 (2d Cir.), cert. denied, 531 U.S. 924 (2000)

FCC v. NextWave Personal Communications, Inc., 537 U.S. 293, 154 L.Ed.2d 863, 123 S.Ct. 832 (2003)

FCC v. Pacifica Foundation, 438 U.S. 726, 57 L.Ed.2d 1073, 98 S.Ct. 3026 (1978)

FCC v. Pottsville Broadcasting Co., 309 U.S. 134, 84 L.Ed. 656, 60 S.Ct. 437 (1940)

FCC v. RCA Communications, Inc., 346 U.S. 86, 97 L.Ed. 1470, 73 S.Ct. 998 (1953)

FCC v. Sanders Bros. Radio Station, 309 U.S. 470, 84 L.Ed. 869, 60 S.Ct. 693 (1940)

FCC v. Schreiber, 201 F.Supp. 421 (S.D. Cal. 1962), modified, 329 F.2d 517 (9th Cir. 1964), modified, 381 U.S. 279 (1965)

FCC v. Schreiber, 381 U.S. 279, 14 L.Ed.2d 383, 85 S.Ct. 1459 (1965)

FCC v. Stahlman, 40 F.Supp. 338 (D.D.C. 1941), aff'd, 75 U.S.App.D.C. 176, 126 F.2d 124 (1941)

FCC v. WJR, The Goodwill Station, Inc., 337 U.S. 265, 93 L.Ed. 1353, 69 S.Ct. 1097 (1949)

FCC v. WNCN Listeners Guild, 450 U.S. 582, 67 L.Ed.2d 521, 101 S.Ct. 1266 (1981)

FCC v. WOKO, Inc., 329 U.S. 223, 91 L.Ed. 204, 67 S.Ct. 213 (1946)

Federal Broadcasting System, Inc. v. FCC, 96 U.S.App.D.C. 260, 225 F.2d 560, cert. denied, 350 U.S. 923 (1955)

Federal Broadcasting System, Inc. v. FCC, 97 U.S.App.D.C. 293, 231 F.2d 246 (1956)

Federal Broadcasting System, Inc. v. FCC, 99 U.S.App.D.C. 320, 239 F.2d 941 (1956)

Federal Broadcasting System, Inc. v. FCC, 105 U.S.App.D.C. 324, 266 F.2d 922, cert. denied, 361 U.S. 822 (1959)

Federal Broadcasting System, Inc. v. FCC, 106 U.S.App.D.C. 162, 270 F.2d 914 (1959), cert. denied, 362 U.S. 935 (1960)

Fidelity Television, Inc. v. FCC, 163 U.S.App.D.C. 441, 502 F.2d 443 (1974)

Fidelity Television, Inc. v. FCC, 169 U.S.App.D.C. 225, 515 F.2d 684, cert. denied, 423 U.S. 926 (1975)

Fidelity Voices, Inc. v. FCC, 155 U.S.App.D.C. 363, 477 F.2d 1248 (1973)

Fiesta Productions, Inc. v. FCC, 260 U.S.App.D.C. 358, 819 F.2d 318 (1987)

Fischer v. FCC, 135 U.S.App.D.C. 134, 417 F.2d 551 (1969)

560 Broadcast Corp. v. FCC, 135 U.S.App.D.C. 330, 418 F.2d 1166 (1969)

Flagstaff Broadcasting Foundation v. FCC, 298 U.S.App.D.C. 356, 979 F.2d 1566 (1992)

Fleming v. FCC, 96 U.S.App.D.C. 223, 225 F.2d 523 (1955)

Florida Broadcasting Co. v. FCC, 71 U.S.App.D.C. 231, 109 F.2d 668 (1939)

Florida Cellular Mobil Communications Corp. v. FCC, 307 U.S.App.D.C. 324, 28 F.3d 191 (1994), cert. denied, 514 U.S. 1016 (1995)

Florida Gulfcoast Broadcasters, Inc. v. FCC, 122 U.S.App.D.C. 250, 352 F.2d 726 (1965)

Florida Inst. of Tech. v. FCC, 293 U.S.App.D.C. 193, 952 F.2d 549 (1992)

Florida Power Corp. v. FCC, 772 F.2d 1537 (11th Cir. 1985), rev'd, 480 U.S. 245 (1987)

Florida Public Telecommunications Ass'n, Inc. v. FCC, 312 U.S.App.D.C. 24, 54 F.3d 857 (1995)

Florida State Conf. of Branches of the NAACP v. FCC, 306 U.S.App.D.C. 265, 24 F.3d 271 (1994)

Florida State Conf. of Branches of the NAACP v. FCC, 309 U.S.App.D.C. 218, 40 F.3d 474 (1994)

Flory v. FCC, 528 F.2d 124 (7th Cir. 1975)

Floyd v. FCC, 338 U.S.App.D.C. 393, 194 F.3d 173 (1999), cert. denied, 120 S.Ct. 799 (2000)

Fly v. Heitmeyer, 309 U.S. 146, 60 S.Ct. 443, 84 L.Ed. 664 (1940)

Folden, et al. v. United States, 56 Fed.Cl. 43 (Fed.Cl. 2003)

Folkways Broadcasting Co. v. FCC, 126 U.S.App.D.C. 123, 375 F.2d 299 (1967)

Folkways Broadcasting Co. v. FCC, 126 U.S.App.D.C. 393, 379 F.2d 447 (1967)

Forbes v. Arkansas Educ. Tel. Comm'n, 22 F.3d 1423 (8th Cir. 1994) (en banc), cert. denied, 513 U.S. 995 (1994)

Forbes v. Arkansas Educ. Tel. Comm'n, 93 F.3d 497 (8th Cir. 1996), rev'd, 523 U.S. 666 (1998)

Forbes v. Arkansas Educ. Tel. Comm'n, 145 F.3d 1017 (8th Cir. 1998)

Fort Collins Telecasters v. FCC, 268 U.S.App.D.C. 306, 841 F.2d 428 (1988)

Fort Harrison Telecasting Corp. v. FCC, 111 U.S.App.D.C. 368, 297 F.2d 779 (1961)

Fort Harrison Telecasting Corp. v. FCC, 116 U.S.App.D.C. 347, 324 F.2d 379 (1963), cert. denied, 376 U.S. 915 (1964)

Fort Mill Telephone Co. v. FCC, 719 F.2d 89 (4th Cir. 1983)

Fort Mojave Indian Tribe v. FCC, 299 U.S.App.D.C. 273, 983 F.2d 298 (1992)

Fox Television Stations, Inc. v. FCC, 280 F.3d 1027, rehearing granted in part, 294 F.3d 123 (D.C. Cir. 2002)

FRC v. General Electric Co., 281 U.S. 464, 74 L.Ed. 969, 50 S.Ct. 389 (1930)

FRC v. Nelson Bros. Bond & Mortgage Co., 289 U.S. 266, 77 L.Ed. 1166, 563 S.Ct. 627 (1933)

Free Air Corp. v. FCC, 327 U.S.App.D.C. 218, 130 F.3d 447 (1997)

Free Speech v. Reno & FCC, 200 F.3d 63 (2nd Cir. 1999)

Freeman v. Burlington Broadcasters, Inc., 204 F.3d 311 (2nd Cir. 2000)

Freeman Engineering Associates, Inc. v. FCC, 322 U.S.App.D.C. 263, 103 F.3d 169 (1997)

Fresno Mobile Radio, Inc. v. FCC, 334 U.S.App.D.C. 178, 165 F.3d 965 (1999)

Friedman v. FCC, 105 U.S.App.D.C. 47, 263 F.2d 493 (1959)

Friends of the Earth v. FCC, 146 U.S.App.D.C. 88, 449 F.2d 1164 (1971)

Frontier Broadcasting Co. v. FCC, 111 U.S.App.D.C. 321, 296 F.2d 443 (1961)

Frontier Broadcasting Co. v. FCC, 134 U.S.App.D.C. 31, 412 F.2d 162 (1969)

Frontier Broadcasting Co. v. United States, 105 U.S.App.D.C. 161, 265 F.2d 353 (1959)

FTC Communications, Inc. v. FCC, 750 F.2d 226 (2nd Cir. 1984)

Fulani v. FCC, 49 F.3d 904 (2nd Cir. 1995)

Functional Music, Inc. v. FCC, 107 U.S.App.D.C. 34, 274 F.2d 543 (1958), cert. denied, 361 U.S. 813 (1959)

Gloria Borland Hawaii PCS, Inc. v. FCC, 340 U.S.App.D.C. 182, 203 F.3d 52 (2000)

Gonzalez v. FCC, 299 U.S.App.D.C. 417, 984 F.2d 1255 (1993)

Goodman v. FCC, 294 U.S.App.D.C. 162, 957 F.2d 911 (1992)

Goodman v. FCC, 337 U.S.App.D.C. 188, 182 F.2d 987 (1999)

Goodwill Stations, Inc. v. FCC, 117 U.S.App.D.C. 64, 325 F.2d 637 (1963)

Gordon County Broadcasting Co. v. FCC, 144 U.S.App.D.C. 334, 446 F.2d 1335 (1971)

Goss v. FRC, 62 U.S.App.D.C. 301, 67 F.2d 507 (1933)

Gottfried v. FCC, 210 U.S.App.D.C. 184, 655 F.2d 297 (1981), cert. denied, 454 U.S. 1144 (1982), and rev'd in part, *Community Television of Southern Calif. v. Gottfried,* 459 U.S. 498 (1983)

Gottfried v. FCC, 229 U.S.App.D.C. 142, 711 F.2d 420 (1983)

Graceba Total Communications, Inc. v. FCC, 325 U.S.App.D.C. 135, 115 F.3d 1038 (1997)

Graceba Total Communications, Inc. v. FCC & USA, 349 U.S.App.D.C. 238, 254 F.3d 315 (2000)

Granik v. FCC, 98 U.S.App.D.C. 247, 234 F.2d 682 (1956)

Granik v. FCC, 102 U.S.App.D.C. 258, 252 F.2d 822 (1958)

Graphnet, Inc. v. FCC, 316 U.S.App.D.C. 367, 79 F.3d 169 (1996)

Great Eastern Communications Co. v. FCC, 180 U.S.App.D.C. 342, 554 F.2d 1202 (1977)

Great Falls Community TV Cable Co. v. FCC, 416 F.2d 238 (9th Cir. 1969)

Great Lakes Broadcasting Co. v. FRC, 59 U.S.App.D.C. 195, 37 F.2d 993, cert. dismissed, 281 U.S. 706 (1930)

Great Lakes Broadcasting Co. v. FCC, 110 U.S.App.D.C. 88, 289 F.2d 754 (1960)

Great Western Broadcasting Ass'n v. FCC, 68 U.S.App.D.C. 119, 94 F.2d 244 (1937)

Great Western Cellular Partners v. FCC, 315 U.S.App.D.C. 280, 72 F.3d 919 (1995)

Greater Boston Television Corp. v. FCC, 118 U.S.App.D.C. 162, 334 F.2d 552 (1964)

Greater Boston Television Corp. v. FCC, 143 U.S.App.D.C. 383, 444 F.2d 841 (1970), cert. denied, 403 U.S. 923 (1971)

Greater Boston Television Corp. v. FCC, 149 U.S.App.D.C. 322, 463 F.2d 268 (1971), cert. denied, 406 U.S. 950 (1972)

Greater Kampeska Radio Corp. v. FCC, 71 U.S.App.D.C. 117, 108 F.2d 5 (1939)

Greater Los Angeles Council on Deafness, Inc. v. Community Television of Southern Calif., 719 F.2d 1017 (9th Cir. 1983), cert. denied, 467 U.S. 1252 (1984)

Greater Los Angeles Council on Deafness, Inc. v. Community Television of Southern Calif., 813 F.2d 217 (9th Cir. 1987)

Greater Mansfield Broadcasting Co. v. FCC, 256 U.S.App.D.C. 149, 803 F.2d 1227 (1986)

Greater New Orleans Broadcasting Ass'n, Inc. v. United States, 866 F.Supp. 975 (E.D. La. 1994), aff'd, 69 F.3d 1296 (5th Cir. 1995), vacated & remanded, 419 U.S. 801 (1996)

Greater New Orleans Broadcasting Ass'n v. United States, 149 F.3d 334 (5th Cir. 1998), rev'd, 527 U.S. 173 (1999)

Greater New Orleans Broadcasting Ass'n v. United States, 527 U.S. 173, 144 L.Ed.2d 161, 119 S.Ct. 1923 (1999)

Green v. FCC, 144 U.S.App.D.C. 363, 447 F.2d 323 (1971)

Green Country Mobilephone, Inc. v. FCC, 246 U.S.App.D.C. 366, 765 F.2d 235 (1985)

Greene v. FCC, 252 U.S.App.D.C. 18, 786 F.2d 431 (1986)

Greensboro Television Co. v. FCC, 164 U.S.App.D.C. 15, 502 F.2d 475 (1974)

Greenville Television Co. v. FCC, 95 U.S.App.D.C. 314, 221 F.2d 870 (1955)

Greenwich Broadcasting Corp. v. FCC, 111 U.S.App.D.C. 129, 294 F.2d 913 (1961)

Gregory v. FCC, 223 F.3d 912 (Fed. Cir. 2000)

Greylock Broadcasting Co. v. United States, 97 U.S.App.D.C. 414, 231 F.2d 748 (1956)

Grid Radio v. FCC, 349 U.S.App.D.C. 365, 278 F.3d 1314 (2002)

Gross v. FCC, 480 F.2d 1288 (2nd Cir. 1973)

GTE California, Inc. v. FCC, 39 F.3d 940 (9th Cir. 1994)

GTE Service Corp. v. FCC, 474 F.2d 724 (2nd Cir. 1973)

GTE Service Corp. v. FCC, 246 U.S.App.D.C. 45, 762 F.2d 1024 (1985)

GTE Service Corp. v. FCC, 251 U.S.App.D.C. 181, 782 F.2d 263 (1986)

GTE Service Corp. v. FCC, 308 U.S.App.D.C. 313, 36 F.3d 127 (1994)

GTE Service Corp. v. FCC, 340 U.S.App.D.C. 308, 205 F.3d 416 (2000)

GTE Service Corp. v. FCC, 343 U.S.App.D.C. 125, 224 F.3d 768 (2000)

GTE Sprint Communications Corp. v. FCC, 236 U.S.App.D.C. 135, 733 F.2d 966 (1984)

Guinan v. FCC, 111 U.S.App.D.C. 371, 297 F.2d 782 (1961)

Gulf Coast Communications, Inc. v. FCC, 230 U.S.App.D.C. 70, 713 F.2d 864 (1983)

Gulf Power Co. v. FCC, 187 F.3d 1324 (11th Cir. 1999)

Gulf Power Co. v. FCC, 208 F.3d 1263 (11th Cir. 2000), cert. denied, 531 U.S. 1125 (2001)

Gulf Power Co. v. FCC, 307 F.3d 1317 (11th Cir. 2002)

GWI PCS, Inc. v. United States, 230 F.3d 788 (5th Cir. 2000)

H & B Communications Corp. v. FCC, 137 U.S.App.D.C. 70, 420 F.2d 638 (1969)

Hale v. FCC, 138 U.S.App.D.C. 125, 425 F.2d 556 (1970)

Hale v. FCC, 250 U.S.App.D.C. 268, 778 F.2d 889 (1985)

Haley v. FCC, 266 U.S.App.D.C. 489, 836 F.2d 653 (1988)

Hall v. FCC, 99 U.S.App.D.C. 86, 237 F.2d 567 (1956)

Hall v. FCC, 103 U.S.App.D.C. 248, 257 F.2d 626 (1958)

Halpern v. FCC, 118 U.S.App.D.C. 28, 331 F.2d 774, cert. denied, 379 U.S. 827 (1964)

Hansen v. FCC, 134 U.S.App.D.C. 100, 413 F.2d 374 (1969)

Harbenito Broadcasting Co. v. FCC, 94 U.S.App.D.C. 329, 218 F.2d 28 (1954)

Harrell v. FCC, 105 U.S.App.D.C. 352, 267 F.2d 629 (1959)

Hartford Communications Comm. v. FCC, 151 U.S.App.D.C. 354, 467 F.2d 408 (1972)

Harvey Radio Laboratories, Inc. v. United States, 110 U.S.App.D.C. 81, 289 F.2d 458 (1961)

Havens & Martin v. FRC, 59 U.S.App.D.C. 393, 45 F.2d 295 (1930)

Hawaiian Telephone Co. v. FCC, 162 U.S.App.D.C. 229, 498 F.2d 771 (1974)

Hawaiian Telephone Co. v. FCC, 191 U.S.App.D.C. 124, 589 F.2d 647 (1978)

HBZ Communications, Inc. v. FCC, 263 U.S.App.D.C. 379, 825 F.2d 516 (1987)

Head v. New Mexico Board of Examiners in Optometry, 374 U.S. 424, 10 L.Ed.2d 983, 83 S.Ct. 1759 (1963)

Head-of-the-Lakes Broadcasting Co. v. FCC, 66 U.S.App.D.C. 19, 84 F.2d 396 (1936)

Healey v. FCC, 148 U.S.App.D.C. 409, 460 F.2d 917 (1972)

Health and Medicine Policy Research Group v. FCC, 257 U.S.App.D.C. 123, 807 F.2d 1038 (1986)

Hearst Radio v. FCC, 73 F.Supp. 308 (D.D.C. 1947), aff'd, 83 U.S.App.D.C. 63, 167 F.2d 225 (1948)

Hearst Radio v. FCC, 83 U.S.App.D.C. 63, 167 F.2d 225 (1948)

Hecksher v. FCC, 102 U.S.App.D.C. 350, 253 F.2d 872 (1958)

Heitmeyer v. FCC, 68 U.S.App.D.C. 180, 95 F.2d 91 (1937)

Helena TV, Inc. v. FCC, 269 F.2d 30 (9th Cir. 1959)

Helena TV, Inc. v. FCC, 107 U.S.App.D.C. 289, 277 F.2d 88 (1960)

Henry v. FCC, 112 U.S.App.D.C. 257, 302 F.2d 191, cert. denied, 371 U.S. 821 (1962)

Hernstadt v. FCC, 219 U.S.App.D.C. 305, 677 F.2d 893 (1980)

Hernstadt v. FCC, 287 U.S.App.D.C. 73, 919 F.2d 182 (1990)

High Point Television Co. v. FCC, 118 U.S.App.D.C. 192, 334 F.2d 582 (1964)

High Plains Wireless, L.P. v. FCC, 349 U.S.App.D.C. 17, 276 F.3d 599 (2002)

High Sierra Broadcasting, Inc. v. FCC, 251 U.S.App.D.C. 327, 784 F.2d 1131 (1986)

Hilding v. FCC, 835 F.2d 1435 (9th Cir. 1987)

Hispanic Information & Telecommunications Network, Inc. v. FCC, 275 U.S.App.D.C. 190, 865 F.2d 1289 (1989)

Hi-Tech Furnace Systems v. FCC, 343 U.S.App.D.C. 138, 224 F.3d 781 (2000)

Hoffart v. FCC, 252 U.S.App.D.C. 119, 787 F.2d 675 (1986)

Home Box Office, Inc. v. FCC, 185 U.S.App.D.C. 142, 567 F.2d 9, cert. denied, 434 U.S. 829 (1977)

Home Box Office, Inc. v. FCC, 190 U.S.App.D.C. 351, 587 F.2d 1248 (1978)

Home TV, Inc. v. FCC, 252 U.S.App.D.C. 18, 786 F.2d 431 (1986)

Hoover v. Intercity Radio Co., 52 U.S.App.D.C. 339, 286 F. 1003 (1923)

Hope Valley FM Ltd. Partnership v. FCC, 304 U.S.App.D.C. 298, 13 F.2d 421 (1993)

Hotel Astor v. United States, 325 U.S. 837, 89 L.Ed. 1964, 65 S.Ct. 1401 (1945)

Houston Consolidated Television Co. v. FCC, 99 U.S.App.D.C. 378, 240 F.2d 409 (1956)

Houston Post Co. v. United States, 79 F.Supp. 199 (S.D. Tex. 1948)

Hubbard Broadcasting, Inc. v. FCC, 128 U.S.App.D.C. 197, 385 F.2d 979 (1967)

Hubbard Broadcasting, Inc. v. FCC, 184 U.S.App.D.C. 115, 564 F.2d 600 (1977)

Hubbard Broadcasting, Inc. v. FCC, 214 U.S.App.D.C. 43, 663 F.2d 220 (1980)

Hubbard Broadcasting, Inc. v. FCC, 684 F.2d 594 (8th Cir. 1982), cert. denied, 459 U.S. 1202 (1983)

Huddy v. FCC, 344 U.S.App.D.C. 353, 236 F.3d 720 (2001)

Hudson Valley Broadcasting Corp. v. FCC, 116 U.S.App.D.C. 1, 320 F.2d 723 (1963)

Huntington Broadcasting Co. v. FCC, 89 U.S.App.D.C. 222, 192 F.2d 33 (1951)

Hush-A-Phone Corp. v. United States, 99 U.S.App.D.C. 190, 238 F.2d 266 (1956)

Iacopi v. FCC, 451 F.2d 1142 (9th Cir. 1971)

IBM Corp. v. FCC, 570 F.2d 452 (2nd Cir. 1978)

ICBC Corp. v. FCC, 230 U.S.App.D.C. 275, 716 F.2d 926 (1983)

ICORE, Inc. v. FCC, 300 U.S.App.D.C. 16, 985 F.2d 1075 (1993)

Idaho Microwave, Inc. v. FCC, 122 U.S.App.D.C. 253, 352 F.2d 729 (1965)

Illinois Bell Tel. Co. v. FCC, 740 F.2d 465 (7th Cir. 1984)

Illinois Bell Tel. Co. v. FCC, 280 U.S.App.D.C. 32, 883 F.2d 104 (1989)

Illinois Bell Tel. Co. v. FCC, 286 U.S.App.D.C. 34, 911 F.2d 776 (1990)

Illinois Bell Tel. Co. v. FCC, 296 U.S.App.D.C. 197, 966 F.2d 1478 (1992)

Illinois Bell Tel. Co. v. FCC, 300 U.S.App.D.C. 296, 988 F.2d 1254 (1993)

Illinois Citizens Comm. for Broadcasting v. FCC, 467 F.2d 1397 (7th Cir. 1972)

Illinois Citizens Comm. for Broadcasting v. FCC, 169 U.S.App.D.C. 166, 515 F.2d 397 (1974)

Illinois Public Telecommunications Ass'n v. FCC, 326 U.S.App.D.C. 1, 117 F.3d 555. clarified, 326 U.S.App.D.C. 315, 123 F.3d 693 (1997), cert. denied, 523 U.S. 1046 (1998)

Ilowite v. United States, 390 F.2d 589 (3rd Cir.), vacated, 393 U.S. 15 (1968)

Immaculate Conception Church v. FCC, 116 U.S.App.D.C. 73, 320 F.2d 795, cert. denied, 375 U.S. 904 (1963)

Independent Broadcasting Co. v. FCC, 89 U.S.App.D.C. 396, 193 F.2d 900 (1951), cert. denied, 344 U.S. 837 (1952)

Indiana Broadcasting Corp. v. FCC, 132 U.S.App.D.C. 218, 407 F.2d 681 (1968)

Industrial Broadcasting Co. v. FCC, 141 U.S.App.D.C. 247, 437 F.2d 680 (1970)

Information Providers' Coalition v. FCC, 928 F.2d 866 (9th Cir. 1991)

Innovative Women's Media Ass'n v. FCC, 305 U.S.App.D.C. 76, 16 F.3d 1287 (1994)

Intercity Radio Telephone Co. v. FRC, 60 U.S.App.D.C. 21, 46 F.2d 602 (1931)

Intercontinental Ministries, Inc. v. FCC, 181 U.S.App.D.C. 410, 559 F.2d 187 (1977)

International Broadcast Corp. v. FCC, 99 U.S.App.D.C. 51, 237 F.2d 205, cert. denied, 352 U.S. 895 (1956)

International Communications Ass'n v. FCC, 274 U.S.App.D.C. 134, 862 F.2d 361 (1988)

International Telecard Ass'n v. FCC, 334 U.S.App.D.C. 259, 166 F.3d 387, cert. denied, 526 U.S. 1146 (1999)

Interstate Broadcasting Co. v. FCC, 105 U.S.App.D.C. 224, 265 F.2d 598 (1959)

Interstate Broadcasting Co. v. FCC, 108 U.S.App.D.C. 78, 280 F.2d 626 (1960)

Interstate Broadcasting Co. v. FCC, 109 U.S.App.D.C. 190, 285 F.2d 270 (1960)

Interstate Broadcasting Co. v. FCC, 116 U.S.App.D.C. 327, 323 F.2d 797 (1963)

Interstate Broadcasting Co. v. United States, 109 U.S.App.D.C. 255, 286 F.2d 539 (1960)

Interstate Broadcasting Co. v. United States, 109 U.S.App.D.C. 260, 286 F.2d 544 (1960)

Interstate Broadcasting System, Inc. v. FCC, 267 U.S.App.D.C. 60, 836 F.2d 1408 (1988)

Iowa v. FCC, 342 U.S.App.D.C. 389, 218 F.3d 156 (2000)

Iowa Acorn Broadcasting Corp. v. FCC, 328 U.S.App.D.C. 135, 132 F.3d 1481 (1997), cert. denied, 523 U.S. 1076 (1998)

Iowa Utilities Bd. v. FCC, 120 F.3d 753 (8th Cir. 1997)

Iowa Utilities Bd. v. FCC, 135 F.3d 535 (8th Cir. 1998), vacated and remanded, mem., 525 U.S. 1133 (1999)

Iowa Utilities Bd v. FCC, 219 F.3d 744 (8th Cir. 2000)

Iowa Utilities Bd v. FCC, 302 F.3d 957 (8th Cir. 2002)

Iowans for WOI TV, Inc., 311 U.S.App.D.C. 144, 50 F.3d 1096 (1995)

ITT World Communications, Inc. v. FCC, 555 F.2d 1125 (2nd Cir. 1977)

ITT World Communications, Inc. v. FCC, 595 F.2d 897 (2nd Cir. 1979)

ITT World Communications, Inc. v. FCC, 621 F.2d 1201 (2nd Cir. 1980)

ITT World Communications, Inc. v. FCC, 635 F.2d 32 (2nd Cir. 1980)

ITT World Communications, Inc. v. FCC, 635 F.2d 45 (2nd Cir. 1980)

ITT World Communications, Inc. v. FCC, 226 U.S.App.D.C. 67, 699 F.2d 1219 (1983), rev'd, 466 U.S. 463 (1984)

ITT World Communications, Inc. v. FCC, 233 U.S.App.D.C. 205, 725 F.2d 732 (1984)

Ivy Broadcasting Co. v. American Tel. & Tel. Co., 391 F.2d 486 (2nd Cir. 1968)

Jackson Broadcasting & Television Corp. v. FCC, 108 U.S.App.D.C. 128, 280 F.2d 676 (1960)

Jacksonville Broadcasting Corp. v. FCC, 121 U.S.App.D.C. 69, 348 F.2d 75, cert. denied, 382 U.S. 893 (1965)

Jacksonville Journal Co. v. FCC, 101 U.S.App.D.C. 12, 246 F.2d 699 (1957)

Jahnke v. FCC, 219 U.S.App.D.C. 115, 675 F.2d 1340 (1982)

JAJ Cellular v. FCC, 312 U.S.App.D.C. 1, 54 F.3d 834 (1995)

In re: James M. Tennant, 360 U.S.App.D.C. 171, 359 F.3d 523 (2004)

James River Broadcasting Corp. v. FCC, 130 U.S.App.D.C. 210, 399 F.2d 581 (1968)

James S. Rivers, Inc. v. FCC, 122 U.S.App.D.C. 29, 351 F.2d 194 (1965)

Jaramillo v. FCC, 333 U.S.App.D.C. 250, 162 F.3d 675 (1998)

Jefferson Amusement Co. v. FCC, 96 U.S.App.D.C. 375, 226 F.2d 277 (1955)

Jefferson Radio Co. v. FCC, 119 U.S.App.D.C. 256, 340 F.2d 781 (1964)

Jefferson Standard Broadcasting Co. v. FCC, 297 F.Supp. 784 (W.D.N.C. 1969)

Jefferson Standard Broadcasting Co. v. FCC, 305 F.Supp. 744 (W.D.N.C. 1969)

Jelks v. FCC, 330 U.S.App.D.C. 365, 146 F.3d 878 (1998), cert. denied, 525 U.S. 1147 (1999)

JEM Broadcasting, Inc. v. FCC, 306 U.S.App.D.C. 11, 22 F.3d 320 (1994)

Jersey Shore Broadcasting Corp. v. FCC, 308 U.S.App.D.C. 404, 37 F.3d 1531 (1994)

Johnson v. FCC, 264 U.S.App.D.C. 372, 829 F.2d 157 (1987)

Johnston v. FCC, 246 U.S.App.D.C. 44, 762 F.2d 138 (1985)

Johnston Broadcasting Co. v. FCC, 85 U.S.App.D.C. 40, 175 F.2d 351 (1949)

Johnston Broadcasting Co. v. FCC, 88 U.S.App.D.C. 90, 187 F.2d 202 (1950)

Joint Council on Educational Broadcasting v. FCC, 113 U.S.App.D.C. 86, 305 F.2d 755 (1962)

Joseph v. FCC, 131 U.S.App.D.C. 207, 404 F.2d 207 (1968)

Journal Co. v. FRC, 60 U.S.App.D.C. 92, 48 F.2d 461 (1931)

Joyner Communications v. FCC, 292 U.S.App.D.C. 85, 946 F.2d 1565 (1991)

Jupiter Associates, Inc. v. FCC, 136 U.S.App.D.C. 266, 420 F.2d 108 (1969)

KA5E54 Television Partnership v. FCC, 318 U.S.App.D.C. 78, 84 F.3d 1452 (1996)

Kahn v. FCC, 311 U.S.App.D.C. 277, 52 F.3d 1122 (1995)

KAKE-TV and Radio, Inc. v. FCC, 537 F.2d 1121 (10th Cir. 1976), cert. denied, 429 U.S. 1072 (1977)

Kansas City TV 62 Ltd. Partnership v. FCC, 301 U.S.App.D.C. 405, 995 F.2d 305 (1993)

Kansas State Network v. FCC, 232 U.S.App.D.C. 10, 720 F.2d 185 (1983)

Kay v. FCC, 143 U.S.App.D.C. 223, 443 F.2d 638 (1970)

Kay v. FCC, 867 F.Supp. 11 (D.D.C. 1994)

Kay v. FCC, Nos. 02-1175, 04-1045 (2004)

KCMC, Inc. v. FCC, 600 F.2d 546 (5th Cir. 1979)

KCST-TV, Inc. v. FCC, 226 U.S.App.D.C. 33, 699 F.2d 1185 (1983)

Keller & Heckman v. FCC, 299 U.S.App.D.C. 417, 984 F.2d 1255 (1993)

Keller Communications, Inc. v. FCC, 327 U.S.App.D.C. 280, 130 F.3d 1073 (1997), cert. denied, 524 U.S. 954 (1998)

Kennedy for President Comm. v. FCC, 204 U.S.App.D.C. 145, 636 F.2d 417 (1980)

Kennedy for President Comm. v. FCC, 204 U.S.App.D.C. 160, 636 F.2d 432 (1980)

Kenter v. FCC, 259 U.S.App.D.C. 390, 816 F.2d 8 (1987)

Kentucky Broadcasting Corp. v. FCC, 84 U.S.App.D.C. 383, 174 F.2d 38 (1949)

KERM, Inc v. FCC and United States, 359 U.S.App.D.C. 200, 353 F.3d 57 (2004)

Kessler v. FCC, 117 U.S.App.D.C. 130, 326 F.2d 673 (1963)

Keystone Cable-Vision Corp. v. FCC, 464 F.Supp. 740 (W.D. Pa. 1979)

KFKB Broadcasting Ass'n, Inc. v. FRC, 60 U.S.App.D.C. 79, 47 F.2d 670 (1931)

KFAB Broadcasting Co. v. FCC, 85 U.S.App.D.C. 160, 177 F.2d 40 (1949)

KGMO Radio-Television, Inc. v. FCC, 119 U.S.App.D.C. 1, 336 F.2d 920 (1964)

Kidd v. FCC, 112 U.S.App.D.C. 288, 302 F.2d 873 (1962)

King Broadcasting Co. v. FCC, 273 U.S.App.D.C. 380, 860 F.2d 465 (1988)

King's Garden, Inc. v. FCC, 162 U.S.App.D.C. 100, 498 F.2d 51 (1974)

KIRO, Inc. v. FCC, 141 U.S.App.D.C. 300, 438 F.2d 141 (1970)

KIRO, Inc. v. FCC, 178 U.S.App.D.C. 126, 545 F.2d 204 (1976)

KIRO, Inc. v. FCC, 203 U.S.App.D.C. 318, 631 F.2d 900 (1980)

KIST Corp. v. FCC, 255 U.S.App.D.C. 397, 801 F.2d 1436 (1986)

Kitchen v. FCC, 150 U.S.App.D.C. 292, 464 F.2d 801 (1972)

Klein v. FCC, 98 U.S.App.D.C. 73, 232 F.2d 73 (1956)

Knollwood Ltd. v. FCC, 318 U.S.App.D.C. 78, 84 F.3d 1452 (1996)

Koplar Communications of Calif., Inc. v. FCC, 243 U.S.App.D.C. 17, 750 F.2d 1093 (1984)

KSIG Broadcasting Co. v. FCC, 144 U.S.App.D.C. 228, 445 F.2d 704 (1971)

Kuczo v. Western Conn. Broadcasting Co., 424 F.Supp. 1325 (D. Conn. 1976), rev'd, 566 F.2d 384 (2nd Cir. 1977)

Kuczo v. Western Conn. Broadcasting Co., 566 F.2d 384 (2nd Cir. 1977)

KVUE, Inc. v. Moore, 709 F.2d 922 (5th Cir. 1983), aff'd, mem., 465 U.S. 1092 (1984)

KWK Radio, Inc. v. FCC, 119 U.S.App.D.C. 144, 337 F.2d 540 (1964), cert. denied, 380 U.S. 910 (1965)

KXIV, Inc. v. FCC, 227 U.S.App.D.C. 165, 704 F.2d 1294 (1983)

La Rose v. FCC, 161 U.S.App.D.C. 226, 494 F.2d 1145 (1974)

La Star Cellular Telephone Co. v. FCC, 283 U.S.App.D.C. 248, 899 F.2d 1233 (1990)

La Voz Radio de la Communidad v. FCC, 223 F.3d 313 (6th Cir. 2000)

Lafayette Radio Electronics Corp. v. United States, 345 F.2d 278 (2nd Cir. 1965)

Lake v. United States, 338 F.2d 787 (10th Cir. 1964)

Lake Carriers Ass'n v. United States, 414 F.2d 567 (6th Cir. 1969)

Lake Huron Broadcasting Corp. v. FCC, 106 U.S.App.D.C. 286, 272 F.2d 515 (1958)

Lakeshore Broadcasting, Inc. v. FCC, 339 U.S.App.D.C. 255, 199 F.3d 468 (1999)

Lakewood Broadcasting Service, Inc. v. FCC, 156 U.S.App.D.C. 9, 478 F.2d 919 (1973)

Lamb v. Hyde, 96 U.S.App.D.C. 181, 223 F.2d 646 (1955)

Lamprecht v. FCC, 294 U.S.App.D.C. 164, 958 F.2d 382 (1992)

Larus & Brother Co. v. FCC, 447 F.2d 876 (4th Cir. 1971)

Las Cruces TV Cable v. FCC, 207 U.S.App.D.C. 116, 645 F.2d 1041 (1981)

Las Misiones de Bejar Television Co. v. FCC, 249 U.S.App.D.C. 61, 772 F.2d 979 (1985)

Las Vegas Valley Broadcasting Co. v. FCC, 191 U.S.App.D.C. 71, 589 F.2d 594 (1978), cert. denied, 441 U.S. 931 (1979)

Law Offices of Seymour M. Chase, P.C. v. FCC, 269 U.S.App.D.C. 24, 843 F.2d 517 (1988)

L. B. Wilson, Inc. v. FCC, 83 U.S.App.D.C. 176, 170 F.2d 793 (1948)

L. B. Wilson, Inc. v. FCC, 130 U.S.App.D.C. 156, 397 F.2d 717 (1968)

LBC, Inc. v. FCC, 275 U.S.App.D.C. 230, 865 F.2d 1329 (1988)

League of Women Voters Educ. Fund v. FCC, 235 U.S.App.D.C. 293, 731 F.2d 995 (1984)

League of Women Voters of Calif. v. FCC, 489 F.Supp. 517 (C.D. Cal. 1980)

League of Women Voters of Calif. v. FCC, 547 F.Supp. 379 (C.D. Cal. 1982), aff'd, 468 U.S. 364 (1984)

League of Women Voters of Calif. v. FCC, 751 F.2d 986 (9th Cir. 1985)

League of Women Voters of Calif. v. FCC, 568 F.Supp. 295 (C.D. Cal. 1983), aff'd, 798 F.2d 1255 (9th Cir. 1986)

League of Women Voters of Calif. v. FCC, 798 F.2d 1255 (9th Cir. 1986)

Lebanon Valley Radio, Inc. v. FCC, 164 U.S.App.D.C. 105, 503 F.2d 196 (1974)

Lechman v. FCC, 323 U.S.App.D.C. 290, 107 F.3d 923 (1997)

Lee v. FCC, 126 U.S.App.D.C. 45, 374 F.2d 259 (1967)

Lefebvre v. FCC, 288 U.S.App.D.C. 342, 926 F.2d 1215 (1991)

Leflore Broadcasting Co., Inc. v. FCC, 204 U.S.App.D.C. 182, 636 F.2d 454 (1980)

Leland Broadcasting Group, Inc. v. FCC, 304 U.S.App.D.C. 35, 10 F.3d 13 (1993)

Leland Broadcasting Group, Inc. v. FCC, 316 U.S.App.D.C. 367, 79 F.3d 169 (1996)

LEOSat Corp. v. FCC, 311 U.S.App.D.C. 277, 52 F.3d 1122 (1990)

Levin v. FCC, 251 U.S.App.D.C. 327, 784 F.2d 1131 (1986)

Levinson v. FCC, 298 U.S.App.D.C. 98, 976 F.2d 46 (1992)

Levinson v. FCC, 1995 WL 224851 (D.C. Cir.), cert. denied, 516 U.S. 1011 (1995)

Lillard v. United States, 249 F.2d 315 (8th Cir. 1957)

Lincoln Tel. & Tel. Co. v. FCC, 212 U.S.App.D.C. 208, 659 F.2d 1092 (1981)

Listeners' Guild, Inc. v. FCC, 259 U.S.App.D.C. 103, 813 F.2d 465 (1987)

Little Rock Television Co. v. FCC, 646 F.2d 1271 (8th Cir. 1981)

Llerandi v. FCC, 274 U.S.App.D.C. 173, 863 F.2d 79 (1988)

Logansport Broadcasting Corp. v. United States, 93 U.S.App.D.C. 342, 210 F.2d 24 (1954)

Long Island Multimedia, Inc. v. FCC, 340 U.S.App.D.C. 182, 203 F.3d 52 (1999)

Long Island Music Broadcasting Corp. v. Patrick, 1989 WL 31656 (S.D.N.Y. 1989)

Longshore v. United States, 77 F.3d 440 (Fed. Cir. 1996)

Lorain Journal Co. v. FCC, 122 U.S.App.D.C. 127, 351 F.2d 824 (1965), cert. denied, 383 U.S. 967 (1966)

Los Angeles SMSA Ltd. Partnership v. FCC, 315 U.S.App.D.C. 146, 70 F.3d 1358 (1995)

Los Angeles Women's Coalition for Better Broadcasting v. FCC, 190 U.S.App.D.C. 108, 584 F.2d 1089 (1978)

Los Angeles Women's Coalition for Better Broadcasting v. FCC, 218 U.S.App.D.C. 161, 673 F.2d 552 (1982)

Louisiana Public Serv. Comm'n v. FCC, 476 U.S. 355, 90 L.Ed.2d 369, 106 S.Ct. 1890 (1986)

Louisiana Television Broadcasting Corp. v. FCC, 121 U.S.App.D.C. 24, 347 F.2d 808 (1965)

Loveday v. FCC, 228 U.S.App.D.C. 38, 707 F.2d 1443, cert. denied, 464 U.S. 1008 (1983)

Loyola Univ. v. FCC, 216 U.S.App.D.C. 403, 670 F.2d 1222 (1982)

Lutheran Church—Missouri Synod v. FCC, 329 U.S.App.D.C. 381, 141 F.3d 344, reh. denied, 332 U.S.App.D.C. 172, 154 F.3d 494 (1998)

Lutter v. Fowler, 257 U.S.App.D.C. 242, 808 F.2d 137 (1986)

Lynch v. United States, 114 U.S.App.D.C. 59, 310 F.2d 864 (1962)

M & M Communications, Inc. v. FCC, 271 U.S.App.D.C. 274, 851 F.2d 1501 (1988)

MacKay Radio & Telegraph Co. v. FCC, 68 U.S.App.D.C. 336, 97 F.2d 64 (1938)

Mackey v. United States, 103 U.S.App.D.C. 146, 255 F.2d 898 (1958)

Magnolia Petroleum Co. v. FCC, 64 U.S.App.D.C. 189, 76 F.2d 439 (1935)

Maier v. FCC, 735 F.2d 220 (7th Cir. 1984)

Mainstream Marketing Services, Inc. v. FCC, No. 03-9571 (2003), U.S. App. LEXIS 20067

Mainstream Marketing Services, Inc. v. FTC, 358 F.3d 1228 (2004)

Malkan FM Associates v. FCC, 290 U.S.App.D.C. 194, 935 F.2d 1313 (1991)

Malrite TV of New York, Inc. v. FCC, 652 F.2d 1140 (2nd Cir. 1981), cert. denied, 454 U.S. 1143 (1982)

Mansfield Journal Co. v. FCC, 84 U.S.App.D.C. 341, 173 F.2d 646 (1949)

Mansfield Journal Co. v. FCC, 86 U.S.App.D.C. 102, 180 F.2d 28 (1950)

Maricopa Media, Inc. v. FCC, 293 U.S.App.D.C. 57, 951 F.2d 1324 (1991)

Marin TV Services Partners, Ltd. v. FCC, 290 U.S.App.D.C. 247, 936 F.2d 1304 (1991)

Marin TV Services Partners, Ltd. v. FCC, 301 U.S.App.D.C. 222, 993 F.2d 261 (1993)

Marine Telephone Operators Ass'n v. FCC, 230 U.S.App.D.C. 423, 717 F.2d 1480 (1983)

Mark v. FCC, 468 F.2d 266 (1st Cir. 1972)

Marlin Broadcasting of Central Fla., Inc. v. FCC, 293 U.S.App.D.C. 151, 952 F.2d 507 (1992)

Marquette University v. FRC, 60 U.S.App.D.C. 44, 47 F.2d 406 (1931)

Marsh v. FCC, 140 U.S.App.D.C. 384, 436 F.2d 132 (1970)

Marsh Media, Ltd. v. FCC, 798 F.2d 772 (5th Cir. 1986), cert. denied, 479 U.S. 1085 (1987)

Marshall County Broadcasting Co., Inc. v. FCC, 187 U.S.App.D.C. 240, 571 F.2d 674 (1978)

Martell v. FCC, 184 U.S.App.D.C. 212, 565 F.2d 788 (1977)

Martin-Trigona v. FCC, 139 U.S.App.D.C. 249, 432 F.2d 682 (1970)

Martin-Trigona v. FCC, 229 U.S.App.D.C. 389, 712 F.2d 1421 (1983)

Martin-Trigona v. FCC, 240 U.S.App.D.C. 45, 743 F.2d 45 (1984)

Martin-Trigona v. FCC, 253 U.S.App.D.C. 77, 791 F.2d 979 (1986)

Mass Communicators, Inc. v. FCC, 105 U.S.App.D.C. 277, 266 F.2d 681, cert. denied, 361 U.S. 828 (1959)

Massachusetts Bay Telecasters, Inc. v. FCC, 104 U.S.App.D.C. 226, 261 F.2d 55 (1958), cert. denied, 366 U.S. 918 (1961)

Massachusetts Bay Telecasters, Inc. v. FCC, 111 U.S.App.D.C. 144, 295 F.2d 131 (1961)

Massachusetts Broadcasting Corp. v. FCC, 71 U.S.App.D.C. 138, 107 F.2d 1007 (1939)

Matias v. FCC, 309 U.S.App.D.C. 34, 38 F.3d 609 (1994), cert. denied, 514 U.S. 1004 (1995)

Maxcell Telecom Plus, Inc. v. FCC, 259 U.S.App.D.C. 350, 815 F.2d 1551 (1987)

May v. FCC, 894 F.2d 407 (6th Cir. 1990)

Mazo Radio Co. v. FCC, 305 U.S.App.D.C. 193, 18 F.3d 953 (1994)

McCarthy v. FCC, 129 U.S.App.D.C. 56, 390 F.2d 471 (1968)

McClatchey Broadcasting Co. v. FCC, 99 U.S.App.D.C. 195, 239 F.2d 15, rehearing denied, 99 U.S.App.D.C. 199, 239 F.2d 19 (1956), cert. denied, 353 U.S. 918, 952 (1957)

McClendon v. Jackson Television, Inc., 603 F.2d 1174 (5th Cir. 1979)

McCrary v. FCC, 620 F.2d 298 (5th Cir. 1980)

McElroy Electronics Corp. v. FCC, 301 U.S.App.D.C. 81, 990 F.2d 1351 (1993)

McElroy Electronics Corp. v. FCC, 318 U.S.App.D.C. 174, 86 F.3d 248 (1996)

McGraw-Hill Broadcasting v. FCC, 217 U.S.App.D.C. 361, 672 F.2d 895 (1981)

MCI Cellular Telephone Co. v. FCC, 238 U.S.App.D.C. 176, 738 F.2d 1322 (1984)

MCI Telecommunications Corp. v. American Tel. & Tel. Co., 512 U.S. 218, 129 L.Ed.2d 182, 114 S.Ct. 2223 (1994)

MCI Telecommunications Corp. v. FCC, 182 U.S.App.D.C. 367, 561 F.2d 365 (1977), cert. denied, 434 U.S. 1040 (1978)

MCI Telecommunications Corp. v. FCC, 188 U.S.App.D.C. 327, 580 F.2d 590, cert. denied, 439 U.S. 980 (1978)

MCI Telecommunications Corp. v. FCC, 200 U.S.App.D.C. 269, 627 F.2d 322 (1980)

MCI Telecommunications Corp. v. FCC, 214 U.S.App.D.C. 482, 665 F.2d 1300 (1981)

MCI Telecommunications Corp. v. FCC, 218 U.S.App.D.C. 389, 675 F.2d 408 (1982)

MCI Telecommunications Corp. v. FCC, 229 U.S.App.D.C. 203, 712 F.2d 517 (1983)

MCI Telecommunications Corp. v. FCC, 242 U.S.App.D.C. 287, 750 F.2d 135 (1984)

MCI Telecommunications Corp. v. FCC, 247 U.S.App.D.C. 32, 765 F.2d 1186 (1985)

MCI Telecommunications Corp. v. FCC, 255 U.S.App.D.C. 120, 799 F.2d 773 (1986)

MCI Telecommunications Corp. v. FCC, 261 U.S.App.D.C. 348, 822 F.2d 80 (1987)

MCI Telecommunications Corp. v. FCC, 269 U.S.App.D.C. 1, 842 F.2d 1296 (1988)

MCI Telecommunications Corp. v. FCC, 286 U.S.App.D.C. 316, 917 F.2d 30 (1990)

MCI Telecommunications Corp. v. FCC, 304 U.S.App.D.C. 67, 10 F.3d 842 (1993)

MCI Telecommunications Corp. v. FCC, 313 U.S.App.D.C. 51, 57 F.3d 1136 (1995)

MCI Telecommunications Corp. v. FCC, 313 U.S.App.D.C. 419, 59 F.3d 1407 (1995), cert. denied, 517 U.S. 1240 (1996)

MCI Telecommunications Corp. v. FCC, 330 U.S.App.D.C. 92, 143 F.3d 606 (1998)

MCI Telecommunications Corp. v. FCC, 341 U.S.App.D.C. 132, 209 F.3d 760 (2000)

MCI WorldCom Network Services, et al. v. FCC & USA, 348 U.S.App.D.C. 259, 274 F.3d 542 (2001)

McIntire v. Wm. Penn Broadcasting Co., 151 F.2d 597 (3rd Cir. 1945), cert. denied, 327 U.S. 779 (1946)

McKean v. FCC, 111 U.S.App.D.C. 148, 295 F.2d 135 (1961)

McKenney v. FCC, 116 U.S.App.D.C. 412, 324 F.2d 444 (1963)

McNinch v. Heitmeyer, 70 U.S.App.D.C. 162, 105 F.2d 41 (1939), rev'd, 309 U.S. 146 (1940)

MD/DC/DE Broadcasters Ass'ns v. FCC, 344 U.S.App.D.C. 322, 236 F.3d 13, reh. denied, 347 U.S.App.D.C. 19, 253 F.3d 732 (2001)

Meadville Master Antenna, Inc. v. FCC, 443 F.2d 282 (3rd Cir. 1971)

Meadville Master Antenna, Inc. v. FCC, 535 F.2d 2114 (3rd Cir. 1976)

Mebane Home Telephone Co. v. FCC, 175 U.S.App.D.C. 362, 535 F.2d 1324 (1976)

Media Access Project v. FCC, 280 U.S.App.D.C. 119, 883 F.2d 1063 (1989)

Media One Group v. County of Henrico, Va., 257 F.3d 356 (4th Cir. 2001)

Melcher v. FCC, 328 U.S.App.D.C. 319, 134 F.3d 1143 (1998)

Melody Music, Inc. v. FCC, 120 U.S.App.D.C. 241, 345 F.2d 730 (1965)

Meredith Broadcasting Co. v. FCC, 124 U.S.App.D.C. 379, 365 F.2d 912 (1966)

Meredith Corp. v. FCC, 258 U.S.App.D.C. 22, 809 F.2d 863 (1987)

Merkeley v. FCC, 249 U.S.App.D.C. 399, 776 F.2d 365 (1985)

Mesa Microwave, Inc. v. FCC, 105 U.S.App.D.C. 1, 262 F.2d 723 (1958)

Mester v. United States, 70 F.Supp. 118 (E.D.N.Y.), aff'd, 332 U.S. 749 (1947)

Metro Broadcasting, Inc. v. FCC, 497 U.S. 547, 111 L.Ed.2d 445, 110 S.Ct. 2997 (1990), overruled, Adarand Constructors, Inc. v. Peña, 515 U.S. 200, 132 L.Ed.2d 158, 115 S.Ct. 2097 (1995)

Metro Cellular Telecommunications, Inc. v. FCC, 259 U.S.App.D.C. 110, 813 F.2d 472 (1987)

Metro Mobile CTS, Inc. v. FCC, 252 U.S.App.D.C. 240, 789 F.2d 72 (1986)

Metro-Act of Rochester, Inc. v. FCC, 216 U.S.App.D.C. 44, 670 F.2d 202 (1981)

Metropolitan Council of NAACP Branches v. FCC, 310 U.S.App.D.C. 237, 46 F.3d 1154 (1995)

Metropolitan Television Co. v. FCC, 110 U.S.App.D.C. 133, 289 F.2d 874 (1961)

Metropolitan Television Co. v. United States, 95 U.S.App.D.C. 326, 221 F.2d 879 (1955)

MG-TV Broadcasting Co. v. FCC, 133 U.S.App.D.C. 54, 408 F.2d 1257 (1968)

Miami MDS Co. v. FCC, 304 U.S.App.D.C. 360, 14 F.3d 658 (1994)

Michelman v. FCC, 486 F.2d 1394 (2nd Cir. 1972)

Michigan Channel 38, Inc. v. FCC, 257 U.S.App.D.C. 242, 808 F.2d 137 (1986)

Microwave Acquisition Corp. v. FCC, 330 U.S.App.D.C. 340, 145 F.3d 1410 (1998)

Microwave Communications, Inc. v. FCC, 169 U.S.App.D.C. 154, 515 F.2d 385 (1974)

Mid-America Cellular Systems, Inc. v. FCC, 251 U.S.App.D.C. 327, 784 F.2d 1131 (1986)

Mid-Florida Radio Corp. v. FCC, 101 U.S.App.D.C. 342, 248 F.2d 755 (1957)

Mid-Ohio Communications, Inc. v. FCC, 292 U.S.App.D.C. 85, 946 F.2d 1565, cert. denied, 502 U.S. 956 (1991)

Mid-Ohio Radio, Ltd. v. FCC, 301 U.S.App.D.C. 107, 990 F.2d 1377 (1993)

Midwest Television, Inc. v. FCC, 124 U.S.App.D.C. 281, 364 F.2d 674 (1966)

Midwest Television, Inc. v. FCC, 138 U.S.App.D.C. 228, 426 F.2d 1222 (1970)

Midwest Video Corp. v. FCC, 571 F.2d 1025 (8th Cir. 1978), aff'd, 440 U.S. 689 (1979)

Midwest Video Corp. v. United States, 362 F.2d 259 (8th Cir. 1966)

Midwest Video Corp. v. United States, 441 F.2d 1322 (8th Cir. 1971), rev'd, *United States v. Midwest Video Corp.*, 406 U.S. 649 (1972)

Millar v. FCC, 228 U.S.App.D.C. 125, 707 F.2d 1530 (1983)

Miller v. FCC, 229 U.S.App.D.C. 142, 711 F.2d 420 (1983)

Miller v. FCC, 66 F.3d 1140 (11th Cir. 1995), cert. denied, 517 U.S. 1155 (1996)

Mills v. FCC, 301 U.S.App.D.C. 251, 993 F.2d 913 (1993)

Miner v. FCC, 213 U.S.App.D.C. 388, 663 F.2d 152 (1980)

Miners Broadcasting Service, Inc. v. FCC, 121 U.S.App.D.C. 222, 349 F.2d 199 (1965)

Mission Broadcasting Corp. v. FCC, 324 U.S.App.D.C. 301, 113 F.3d 254 (1997)

Missouri Broadcasting Corp. v. FCC, 68 U.S.App.D.C. 154, 94 F.2d 623 (1937), cert. denied, 303 U.S. 655 (1938)

Missouri Municipal League, et al. v. FCC, 299 F.3d 949 (8th Cir. 2002)

Mobile Broadcast Service, Inc. v. FCC, 175 U.S.App.D.C. 362, 535 F.2d 1324 (1976)

Mobile Communications Corp. of America v. FCC, 316 U.S.App.D.C. 220, 77 F.3d 1399, cert. denied, 519 U.S. 823 (1996)

MobileTel, Inc. v. FCC, 323 U.S.App.D.C. 255, 107 F.3d 888, cert. denied, 522 U.S. 948 (1997)

Mobilfone of Northeastern Pa., Inc. v. FCC, 221 U.S.App.D.C. 14, 682 F.2d 269 (1982)

Mobilfone of Northeastern Pa., Inc. v. FCC, 246 U.S.App.D.C. 44, 762 F.2d 138 (1985)

Mobilfone Service, Inc. v. FCC, 196 U.S.App.D.C. 56, 605 F.2d 572 (1979)

Mobilfone Service, Inc. v. FCC, 212 U.S.App.D.C. 206, 659 F.2d 252 (1981)

Monongahela Power Co. v. FCC, 211 U.S.App.D.C. 24, 655 F.2d 1254 (1981)

In re Monroe Communications Corp., 268 U.S.App.D.C. 235, 840 F.2d 942 (1988)

Monroe Communications, Inc. v. FCC, 283 U.S.App.D.C. 367, 900 F.2d 351 (1990)

Montgomery County Radio, Inc. v. FCC, 217 U.S.App.D.C. 362, 672 F.2d 896 (1981)

Montierth v. FCC, 333 U.S.App.D.C. 46, 159 F.3d 636 (1998)

Morriseau v. Mt. Mansfield Television, Inc., 380 F.Supp. 512 (D. Vt. 1974)

Moser v. FCC, 811 F.Supp. 541 (D. Or. 1992)

Moser v. FCC, 826 F.Supp. 360 (D. Or. 1993), rev'd, 46 F.3d 970 (9th Cir. 1995), cert. denied, 515 U.S. 1161 (1995)

Motion Picture Association of America, Inc., et al. v. FCC, 353 U.S.App.D.C. 405, 309 F.3d 796 (D.C. Cir. 2002)

Mt. Mansfield Television, Inc. v. FCC, 442 F.2d 470 (2nd Cir. 1971)

Mount Wilson FM Broadcasters, Inc. v. FCC, 280 U.S.App.D.C. 252, 884 F.2d 1462 (1989)

Mountain Communication, Inc. v. FCC and United States, 359 U.S.App.D.C. 349, 355 F.3d 644 (2004)

Mountain Solutions, Ltd., Inc. v. FCC, 339 U.S.App.D.C. 42, 197 F.3d 512 (1999)

Mountain States Tel. & Tel. Co. v. FCC, 291 U.S.App.D.C. 193, 939 F.2d 1021 (1991)

Mountain States Tel. & Tel. Co. v. FCC, 291 U.S.App.D.C. 207, 939 F.2d 1035 (1991)

Mountain States Tel. & Tel. Co. v. FCC, 951 F.2d 1259 (10th Cir. 1991)

Moving Phones Partnership L.P. v. FCC, 302 U.S.App.D.C. 416, 998 F.2d 1051 (1993), cert. denied, 511 U.S. 1004 (1994)

Multi-State Communications, Inc. v. FCC, 192 U.S.App.D.C. 1, 590 F.2d 1117 (1978), cert. denied, 440 U.S. 959 (1979)

Multi-State Communications, Inc. v. FCC, 234 U.S.App.D.C. 285, 728 F.2d 1519 (1984), cert. denied, 469 U.S. 1017 (1984)

Multi-State Communications, Inc. v. United States, 648 F.Supp. 1203 (S.D.N.Y. 1986)

Murphy v. United States, 252 F.2d 389 (7th Cir. 1958)

Music Broadcasting Co. v. FCC, 95 U.S.App.D.C. 12, 217 F.2d 339 (1954)

NAACP v. FCC, 221 U.S.App.D.C. 44, 682 F.2d 993 (1982)

NAACP v. FCC, 227 U.S.App.D.C. 165, 704 F.2d 1294 (1983)

NAACP v. FCC, 309 U.S.App.D.C. 218, 40 F.3d 474 (1994)

Nader v. FCC, 172 U.S.App.D.C. 1, 520 F.2d 182 (1975)

Natick Broadcast Associates, Inc. v. FCC, 128 U.S.App.D.C. 203, 385 F.2d 985 (1967)

National Anti-Vivisection Society v. FCC, 234 F.Supp. 696 (N.D. Ill. 1964)

National Ass'n for Better Broadcasting v. FCC, 192 U.S.App.D.C. 203, 591 F.2d 812 (1978)

National Ass'n for Better Broadcasting v. FCC, 265 U.S.App.D.C. 122, 830 F.2d 270 (1987)

National Ass'n for Better Broadcasting v. FCC, 270 U.S.App.D.C. 334, 849 F.2d 665 (1988)

National Ass'n for Better Broadcasting v. FCC, 284 U.S.App.D.C. 183, 902 F.2d 1009 (1990)

National Ass'n of Broadcast Employees & Technicians v. FCC, 120 U.S.App.D.C. 358, 346 F.2d 839 (1965)

National Ass'n of Broadcasters v. FCC, 180 U.S.App.D.C. 259, 554 F.2d 1118 (1976)

National Ass'n of Broadcasters v. FCC, 198 U.S.App.D.C. 58, 610 F.2d 1000 (1979)

National Ass'n of Broadcasters v. FCC, 239 U.S.App.D.C. 87, 740 F.2d 1190 (1984)

National Ass'n of Indpt. Television Producers & Distributors v. FCC, 502 F.2d 249 (2nd Cir. 1974)

National Ass'n of Indpt. Television Producers & Distributors v. FCC, 170 U.S.App.D.C. 167, 516 F.2d 760 (1975)

National Ass'n of Indpt. Television Producers & Distributors v. FCC, 516 F.2d 526 (2nd Cir. 1975)

National Ass'n of Motor Bus Owners v. FCC, 460 F.2d 561 (2nd Cir. 1972)

National Ass'n of Regulatory Utility Commissioners v. FCC, 173 U.S.App.D.C. 413, 525 F.2d 630, cert. denied, 425 U.S. 992 (1976)

National Ass'n of Regulatory Utility Commissioners v. FCC, 174 U.S.App.D.C. 374, 533 F.2d 601 (1976)

National Ass'n of Regulatory Utility Commissioners v. FCC, 233 U.S.App.D.C. 166, 725 F.2d 125 (1984)

National Ass'n of Regulatory Utility Commissioners v. FCC, 241 U.S.App.D.C. 175, 746 F.2d 1492 (1984)

National Ass'n of Regulatory Utility Commissioners v. FCC, 237 U.S.App.D.C. 390, 737 F.2d 1095 (1984), cert. denied, 469 U.S. 1227 (1985)

National Ass'n of Regulatory Utility Commissioners v. FCC, 279 U.S.App.D.C. 99, 880 F.2d 422 (1989)

National Ass'n of State Utility Consumer Advocates v. FCC and United States, 362 U.S.App.D.C. 87, 372 F.3d 454 (2004)

National Ass'n of Theatre Owners, Inc. v. FCC, 136 U.S.App.D.C. 352, 420 F.2d 194 (1969), cert. denied, 397 U.S. 922 (1970)

National Ass'n of Theatre Owners, Inc. v. FCC, 155 U.S.App.D.C. 281, 477 F.2d 450 (1973)

National Automotive Long Lines, Inc. v. FCC, 193 U.S.App.D.C. 217, 593 F.2d 1371 (1979)

National Black Media Coalition v. FCC, 191 U.S.App.D.C. 55, 589 F.2d 578 (1978)

National Black Media Coalition v. FCC, 226 U.S.App.D.C. 211, 701 F.2d 222 (1983)

National Black Media Coalition v. FCC, 227 U.S.App.D.C. 320, 706 F.2d 1224 (1983)

National Black Media Coalition v. FCC, 232 U.S.App.D.C. 40, 720 F.2d 215 (1983)

National Black Media Coalition v. FCC, 245 U.S.App.D.C. 273, 760 F.2d 1297 (1985)

National Black Media Coalition v. FCC, 246 U.S.App.D.C. 44, 762 F.2d 138 (1985)

National Black Media Coalition v. FCC, 249 U.S.App.D.C. 292, 775 F.2d 342 (1985)

National Black Media Coalition v. FCC, 252 U.S.App.D.C. 273, 789 F.2d 955 (1986)

National Black Media Coalition v. FCC, 791 F.2d 1016 (2nd Cir. 1986)

National Black Media Coalition v. FCC, 822 F.2d 277 (2nd Cir. 1987)

National Broadcasting Co., Inc. v. FCC, 76 U.S.App.D.C. 238, 132 F.2d 545 (1942), aff'd, 319 U.S. 239 (1943)

National Broadcasting Co., Inc. v. FCC, 124 U.S.App.D.C. 116, 362 F.2d 946 (1966)

National Broadcasting Co., Inc. v. FCC, 170 U.S.App.D.C. 173, 516 F.2d 1101 (1974), judgment vacated & remanded, 170 U.S.App.D.C. 252, 516 F.2d 1180 (1975), cert. denied, 424 U.S. 910 (1976)

National Broadcasting Co., Inc. v. United States, 319 U.S. 190, 87 L.Ed. 1344, 63 S.Ct. 997 (1943)

National Cable & Telecommunications Ass'n, Inc. v. Gulf Power Co., 534 U.S. 327, 151 L.Ed.2d 794, 122 S.Ct. 782 (2002)

National Cable Television Ass'n, Inc. v. FCC, 156 U.S.App.D.C. 91, 479 F.2d 183 (1973)

National Cable Television Ass'n, Inc. v. FCC, 180 U.S.App.D.C. 235, 554 F.2d 1094 (1976)

National Cable Television Ass'n, Inc. v. FCC, 241 U.S.App.D.C. 389, 747 F.2d 1503 (1984)

National Cable Television Ass'n, Inc. v. FCC, 286 U.S.App.D.C. 229, 914 F.2d 285 (1990)

National Cable Television Ass'n, Inc. v. FCC, 308 U.S.App.D.C. 221, 33 F.3d 66 (1994)

National Cable Television Ass'n, Inc. v. United States, 415 U.S. 336, 94 S.Ct. 1146, 39 L.Ed.2d 370 (1974)

National Cellular Resellers Ass'n v. FCC, 295 U.S.App.D.C. 209, 961 F.2d 963 (1992)

National Citizens Comm. for Broadcasting v. FCC, 181 U.S.App.D.C. 1, 555 F.2d 938 (1977), aff'd in part and rev'd in part, 436 U.S. 775 (1978)

National Citizens Comm. for Broadcasting v. FCC, 181 U.S.App.D.C. 30, 555 F.2d 967 (1977), aff'd in part and rev'd in part, 436 U.S. 775 (1978)

National Citizens Comm. for Broadcasting v. FCC, 181 U.S.App.D.C. 410, 559 F.2d 187 (1977)

National Citizens Comm. for Broadcasting v. FCC, 186 U.S.App.D.C. 102, 567 F.2d 1095 (1977), cert. denied, 436 U.S. 926 (1978)

National Comm. for Responsive Philanthropy v. FCC, 209 U.S.App.D.C. 196, 652 F.2d 189 (1981)

National Exchange Carrier Ass'n v. FCC, 346 U.S.App.D.C. 297, 253 F.3d 1 (2001)

National Latino Media Coalition v. FCC, 259 U.S.App.D.C. 481, 816 F.2d 785 (1987)

National Mobile Radio Ass'n v. FCC, 241 U.S.App.D.C. 174, 746 F.2d 907 (1984)

National Organization for Women v. FCC, 181 U.S.App.D.C. 65, 555 F.2d 1002 (1977)

National Public Radio, Inc. v. FCC, 349 U.S.App.D.C. 149, 254 F.3d 226 (2001)

National Rural Telecom Ass'n v. FCC, 300 U.S.App.D.C. 226, 988 F.2d 174 (1993)

National Welfare Rights Organization v. FCC, 191 U.S.App.D.C. 213, 589 F.2d 1115 (1978)

Neckritz v. FCC, 446 F.2d 501 (9th Cir. 1971)

Neckritz v. FCC, 163 U.S.App.D.C. 409, 502 F.2d 411 (1974)

Neighborhood TV Co., Inc. v. FCC, 239 U.S.App.D.C. 292, 742 F.2d 629 (1984)

Nelson Broadcasters v. FCC, 287 U.S.App.D.C. 378, 923 F.2d 201 (1990)

Nelson Bros. Bond & Mtg. Co. v. FRC, 61 U.S.App.D.C. 315, 62 F.2d 854 (1932)

Network Project v. FCC, 167 U.S.App.D.C. 220, 511 F.2d 786 (1975)

New East Communications, Inc. v. FCC, 323 U.S.App.D.C. 290, 107 F.3d 923 (1997)

New England Public Communications Council v. FCC, 357 U.S.App.D.C. 231, 334 F.3d 69 (2003)

New England Tel. and Tel. Co. v. FCC, 264 U.S.App.D.C. 85, 826 F.2d 1101 (1987), cert. denied, 490 U.S. 1039(1989)

New Jersey Coalition for Fair Broadcasting v. FCC, 188 U.S.App.D.C. 354, 580 F.2d 617 (1978)

New Jersey Coalition for Fair Broadcasting v. FCC, 574 F.2d 1119 (3rd Cir. 1978)

New Jersey State Lottery Comm'n v. United States, 491 F.2d 219 (3rd Cir. 1974), vacated & remanded, 420 U.S. 371 (1975)

New Jersey State Lottery Comm'n v. United States, 519 F.2d 1398 (3rd Cir. 1975)

New Jersey Television Corp. v. FCC, 393 F.3d 219 (2004)

New Life Evangelistic Center, Inc. v. FCC, 282 U.S.App.D.C. 404, 895 F.2d 809 (1990)

New Orleans Channel 20, Inc. v. FCC, 265 U.S.App.D.C. 213, 830 F.2d 361 (1987)

New Radio Corp. v. FCC, 256 U.S.App.D.C. 211, 804 F.2d 756 (1986)

New South Broadcasting Corp. v. FCC, 279 U.S.App.D.C. 21, 879 F.2d 867 (1989)

New South Media Corp. v. FCC, 207 U.S.App.D.C. 85, 644 F.2d 37 (1981)

New South Media Corp. v. FCC, 222 U.S.App.D.C. 258, 685 F.2d 708 (1982)

New World Radio, Inc. v. FCC, 352 U.S.App.D.C. 366, 294 F.3d 164 (2002)

New York State Broadcasters Ass'n v. United States, 414 F.2d 990 (2nd Cir. 1969), cert. denied, 396 U.S. 1061 (1970)

New York State Comm'n on Cable Television v. FCC, 571 F.2d 95 (2nd Cir.), cert. denied, 439 U.S. 820 (1978)

New York State Comm'n on Cable Television v. FCC, 669 F.2d 58 (2nd Cir. 1982)

New York State Comm'n on Cable Television v. FCC, 242 U.S.App.D.C. 126, 749 F.2d 804 (1984)

New York State Dept. of Law v. FCC, 299 U.S.App.D.C. 371, 984 F.2d 1209 (1993)

New York Telephone Co. v. FCC, 631 F.2d 1059 (2nd Cir. 1980)

Newark Radio Broadcasting Ass'n v. FCC, 246 U.S.App.D.C. 160, 763 F.2d 450 (1985)

News America Publishing, Inc. v. FCC, 269 U.S.App.D.C. 182, 844 F.2d 800 (1988)

Newton v. FCC, 287 U.S.App.D.C. 378, 923 F.2d 201 (1990)

NextWave Personal Communications, Inc. v. FCC, 349 U.S.App.D.C. 53, 254 F.3d 130 (2001), aff'd, 537 U.S. 293 (2003)

Nixon v. Missouri Municipal League, 541 U.S. 125, 124 S.Ct. 1555, 158 L.Ed.2d 291 (2004)

Noe v. FCC, 104 U.S.App.D.C. 221, 260 F.2d 739 (1958), cert. denied, 359 U.S. 924 (1959)

North American Telecommunications Ass'n v. FCC, 751 F.2d 207 (7th Cir. 1984)

Offshore Telephone Co. v. FCC, 258 U.S.App.D.C. 334, 811 F.2d 676 (1987)

Offshore Telephone Co. v. FCC, 277 U.S.App.D.C. 195, 873 F.2d 408 (1989)

Offshore Telephone Co. v. FCC, 295 U.S.App.D.C. 98, 959 F.2d 1102 (1992)

O'Hair v. United States, 281 F.Supp. 815 (D.D.C. 1968)

Ohio Bell Tel. Co. v. FCC, 949 F.2d 864 (6th Cir. 1991)

Omnipoint Corp. v. FCC, 316 U.S.App.D.C. 259, 78 F.3d 620 (1996)

Omnipoint Corp. v. FCC, 341 U.S.App.D.C. 363, 213 F.3d 720 (2000)

O'Neill Broadcasting Co. v. United States, 100 U.S.App.D.C. 38, 241 F.2d 443 (1956)

Orange Park Florida TV, Inc. v. FCC, 258 U.S.App.D.C. 322, 811 F.2d 664 (1987)

Orion Communications Ltd. v. FCC, 327 U.S.App.D.C. 326, 131 F.3d 176 (1997), cert. denied, 525 U.S. 820 (1998)

Orion Communications Ltd. v. FCC, 341 U.S.App.D.C. 404, 213 F.3d 761 (2000)

Orloff v. FCC and USA, 359 U.S.App.D.C. 132, 352 F.3d 415 (2003), cert. denied, 124 S.Ct. 2907 (2004)

Owens v. FCC, 227 U.S.App.D.C. 165, 704 F.2d 1294 (1983)

Owensboro-on-the-Air, Inc. v. United States, 104 U.S.App.D.C. 391, 262 F.2d 702 (1958), cert. denied, 360 U.S. 911 (1959)

Oyster v. FCC, 249 U.S.App.D.C. 399, 776 F.2d 365 (1985)

P & R Temmer v. FCC, 240 U.S.App.D.C. 74, 743 F.2d 918 (1984)

Pacific & Southern Co. v. FCC, 132 U.S.App.D.C. 101, 405 F.2d 1371 (1968)

Pacific Bell v. FCC, 317 U.S.App.D.C. 191, 81 F.3d 1147 (1996)

Pacific Development Radio Co. v. FRC, 60 U.S.App.D.C. 378, 55 F.2d 540 (1931)

Pacific FM, Inc. v. FCC, 123 U.S.App.D.C. 352, 359 F.2d 1018 (1966)

Pacifica Foundation v. FCC, 181 U.S.App.D.C. 132, 556 F.2d 9 (1977), rev'd, 438 U.S. 726 (1978)

Pacifica Foundation v. FCC, 191 U.S.App.D.C. 210, 589 F.2d 733 (1978)

Paducah Newspapers, Inc. v. FCC, 134 U.S.App.D.C. 287, 414 F.2d 1183

Page Enterprises, Inc. v. FCC, 292 U.S.App.D.C. 86, 946 F.2d 1566 (1991)

Paging Associates, Inc. v. FCC, 310 U.S.App.D.C. 61, 43 F.3d 712 (1994)

PanAmSat Corp. v. FCC, 339 U.S.App.D.C. 143, 198 F.3d 890 (1999)

PanAmSat Corp. v. FCC, 361 U.S.App.D.C. 444, 370 F.3d 1168 (2004)

Pappas v. FCC, 257 U.S.App.D.C. 104, 807 F.2d 1019 (1986)

Pappas Television, Inc. v. FCC, 185 U.S.App.D.C. 133, 566 F.2d 798 (1977)

Paragon Cable Television, Inc. v. FCC, 262 U.S.App.D.C. 21, 822 F.2d 152 (1987)

Parcel 49 Ltd. Partnership v. United States, 31 F.3d 1147 (Fed. Cir. 1994)

Parr v. FCC, 120 U.S.App.D.C. 154, 344 F.2d 539 (1965)

Parsons v. FCC, 320 U.S.App.D.C. 323, 93 F.3d 986 (1996)

Pasadena Broadcasting Co. v. FCC, 181 U.S.App.D.C. 109, 555 F.2d 1046 (1977)

Pass Word, Inc. v. FCC, 218 U.S.App.D.C. 181, 673 F.2d 1363, cert. denied, 459 U.S. 840 (1982)

Pauley v. FCC, 86 U.S.App.D.C. 294 181 F.2d 292 (1950)

Paulsen v. FCC, 491 F.2d 887 (9th Cir. 1974)

Pegasus Broadcasting of San Juan, Inc. v. FCC, 284 U.S.App.D.C. 78, 901 F.2d 1130 (1990)

Peninsula Communications, Inc. v. FCC, 55 Fed.Appx. 1 (D.C. Cir. 2003)

Pennsylvania State Univ. v. FCC, 113 U.S.App.D.C. 80, 304 F.2d 956 (1962)

People of the State of California v. FCC, 905 F.2d 1217 (9th Cir. 1990)

People of the State of California v. FCC, 4 F.3d 1505 (9th Cir. 1993)

People of the State of California v. FCC, 39 F.3d 919 (9th Cir. 1994), cert. denied, 514 U.S. 1050 (1995)

People of the State of California v. FCC, 75 F.3d 1350 (9th Cir.), cert. denied, 517 U.S. 1216 (1996)

People of the State of California v. FCC, 124 F.3d 934 (8th Cir. 1997)

People of the State of New York v. FCC, 267 F.3d 91 (2nd Cir. 2001)

Peoples Broadcasting Co. v. United States, 93 U.S.App.D.C. 78, 209 F.2d 286 (1953)

Petroleum Communications, Inc. v. FCC, 306 U.S.App.D.C. 82, 22 F.3d 1164 (1994)

Philadelphia Community Cable Coalition v. FCC, 531 F.2d 1240 (3rd Cir. 1976)

Philadelphia Television Broadcasting Co. v. FCC, 123 U.S.App.D.C. 298, 359 F.2d 282 (1966)

Philco Corp. v. FCC, 103 U.S.App.D.C. 278, 257 F.2d 656 (1958), cert. denied, 358 U.S. 946 (1959)

Philco Corp. v. FCC, 110 U.S.App.D.C. 387, 293 F.2d 864 (1961)

Piedmont Electronics & Fixture Corp. v. FCC, 104 U.S.App.D.C. 77, 259 F.2d 807 (1958)

Pike Family Broadcasting, Inc. v. FCC, 310 U.S.App.D.C. 142, 44 F.3d 1031 (1994)

Pikes Peak Broadcasting Co. v. FCC, 137 U.S.App.D.C. 234, 422 F.2d 671 (1969)

Pikes Peak Broadcasting Co. v. FCC, 187 U.S.App.D.C. 240, 571 F.2d 674 (1978)

Pinellas Broadcasting Co. v. FCC, 97 U.S.App.D.C. 236, 230 F.2d 204, cert. denied, 350 U.S. 1007 (1956)

Pittsburgh Radio Supply House v. FCC, 69 U.S.App.D.C. 22, 98 F.2d 303 (1938)

Plains Radio Broadcasting Co. v. FCC, 85 U.S.App.D.C. 48, 175 F.2d 359 (1949)

Plains Television Corp. v. FCC, 108 U.S.App.D.C. 20, 278 F.2d 854 (1960)

Plains Television Corp. v. FCC, 142 U.S.App.D.C. 248, 440 F.2d 276 (1971)

Plantation Broadcasting Corp. v. FCC, 259 U.S.App.D.C. 49, 812 F.2d 1443 (1987)

Playboy Entertainment Group, Inc. v. United States, 945 F.Supp. 772 (D. De. 1996), aff'd, mem., 520 U.S. 1141 (1997)

Playboy Entertainment Group, Inc. v. United States, 30 F.Supp.2d 702 (D. De. 1998), aff'd, mem., 520 U.S. 1141 (2000)

Pleasant Broadcasting Co. v. FCC, 164 U.S.App.D.C. 202, 504 F.2d 271 (1974)

Pleasant Broadcasting Co. v. FCC, 184 U.S.App.D.C. 11, 564 F.2d 496 (1977)

PLMRS Narrowband Corp. v. FCC, 337 U.S.App.D.C. 196, 182 F.3d 395 (1999)

Pocket Phone Broadcast Service, Inc. v. FCC, 176 U.S.App.D.C. 99, 538 F.2d 447 (1976)

Polar Broadcasting, Inc. v. FCC, 306 U.S.App.D.C. 102, 22 F.3d 1184 (1994)

Polish American Congress v. FCC, 520 F.2d 1248 (7th Cir. 1975), cert. denied, 424 U.S. 927 (1976)

Polite Society, Inc. v. FCC, 541 F.2d 283 (7th Cir. 1976)

Pontchartrain Broadcasting Co., Inc. v. FCC, 304 U.S.App.D.C. 364, 15 F.3d 183 (1994)

Poole Broadcasting Co. v. FCC, 143 U.S.App.D.C. 103, 442 F.2d 825 (1971)

Port Angeles Telecable, Inc. v. FCC, 416 F.2d 243 (9th Cir. 1969)

Post v. FCC, 245 U.S.App.D.C. 234, 759 F.2d 960 (1985)

Pote v. FRC, 62 U.S.App.D.C. 303, 67 F.2d 509, cert. denied, 290 U.S. 680 (1933)

Pottsville Broadcasting Co. v. FCC, 69 U.S.App.D.C. 7, 98 F.2d 288 (1938)

Pottsville Broadcasting Co. v. FCC, 70 U.S.App.D.C. 157, 105 F.2d 36 (1939), rev'd, 309 U.S. 134 (1940)

Prater & Durham v. FCC, 299 U.S.App.D.C. 273, 983 F.2d 298 (1992)

Prayze FM v. FCC, 214 F.3d 245 (2d Cir. 2000)

Presque Isle TV Co. v. United States, 387 F.2d 502 (1st Cir. 1967)

Press Broadcasting Co., Inc. v. FCC, 287 U.S.App.D.C. 378, 923 F.2d 201 (1990)

Press Broadcasting Co., Inc. v. FCC, 313 U.S.App.D.C. 377, 59 F.3d 1365 (1995)

Press Communications LLC v. FCC, 338 U.S.App.D.C. 384, 194 F.3d 174 (1999)

Press Wireless, Inc. v. FCC, 105 U.S.App.D.C. 86, 264 F.2d 372 (1959)

Pressley v. FCC, 141 U.S.App.D.C. 283, 437 F.2d 716 (1970)

Price Broadcasters, Inc. v. FCC, 111 U.S.App.D.C. 179, 295 F.2d 166 (1961)

Progressive Cellular III B-3 v. FCC, 300 U.S.App.D.C. 83, 986 F.2d 546, cert. denied, 510 U.S. 860 (1993)

Prometheus Radio Project v. FCC, 373 F.3d 372 (2004)

PSWF Corp. v. FCC, 323 U.S.App.D.C. 300, 108 F.3d 354 (1997)

Public Interest Research Group v. FCC, 522 F.2d 1060 (1st Cir. 1975), cert. denied, 424 U.S. 965 (1976)

Public Media Center v. FCC, 190 U.S.App.D.C. 425, 587 F.2d 1322 (1978)

Public Serv. Comm'n of Md. v. FCC, 285 U.S.App.D.C. 329, 909 F.2d 1510 (1990)

Public Serv. Comm'n of the District of Columbia v. FCC, 283 U.S.App.D.C. 146, 897 F.2d 1168 (1990)

Public Serv. Comm'n of the District of Columbia v. FCC, 285 U.S.App.D.C. 19, 906 F.2d 713 (1990)

Public Serv. Co. of Col. v. FCC, 356 U.S.App.D.C. 137, 328 F.3d 675 (2003)

Public Service Television, Inc. v. FCC, 115 U.S.App.D.C. 200, 317 F.2d 900 (1962)

Public Utility Comm'n of Calif. v. United States, 356 F.2d 236 (9th Cir.), cert. denied, 385 U.S. 816 (1966)

Public Utility Comm'n of Texas v. FCC, 281 U.S.App.D.C. 25, 886 F.2d 1325 (1989)

Puerto Rico Broadcasting, Inc. v. FCC, 212 U.S.App.D.C. 206, 659 F.2d 252 (1981)

Puerto Rico Telephone Authority v. FCC, 211 U.S.App.D.C. 311, 656 F.2d 900 (1981)

Puerto Rico Telephone Co. v. FCC, 553 F.2d 694 (1977)

Pulitzer Publishing Co. v. FCC, 68 U.S.App.D.C. 124, 94 F.2d 249 (1937)

Pyle v. FCC, 292 U.S.App.D.C. 388, 950 F.2d 797 (1992)

Qualcomm, Inc. v. FCC, 337 U.S.App.D.C. 78, 181 F.3d 1370 (1999)

Quality Telecasting Corp. v. FCC, 160 U.S.App.D.C. 149, 489 F.2d 1273 (1974)

Queen City Cellular Communications v. FCC, 273 U.S.App.D.C. 265, 859 F.2d 241 (1988)

QWEST Communications, Inc. v. FCC, 343 U.S.App.D.C. 324, 229 F.3d 1172 (2000)

QWEST Corp. v. FCC, 240 F.3d 886 (10th Cir. 2001)

QWEST Corp. v. FCC, 258 F.3d 1191 (10th Cir. 2001)

QWEST Corp. v. FCC, 346 U.S.App.D.C. 271, 252 F.3d 462 (2001)

Quincy Cable TV, Inc. v. FCC, 235 U.S.App.D.C. 119, 730 F.2d 1549 (1984)

Quincy Cable TV, Inc. v. FCC, 248 U.S.App.D.C. 1, 768 F.2d 1434 (1985), cert. denied, 476 U.S. 1169 (1986)

Quinnipiac College v. FCC, 310 U.S.App.D.C. 386, 48 F.3d 562 (1995)

Radio Athens, Inc. v. FCC, 130 U.S.App.D.C. 333, 401 F.2d 398 (1968)

Radio Atlanta v. FCC, 99 U.S.App.D.C. 347, 240 F.2d 33 (1956)

Radio Cincinnati v. FCC, 85 U.S.App.D.C. 292, 177 F.2d 92 (1949)

Radio Corp. of America v. United States, 95 F.Supp 660 (N.D. Ill. 1950), aff'd, 341 U.S. 412 (1951)

Radio Corp. of America v. United States, 341 U.S. 412, 95 L.Ed. 1062, 71 S.Ct. 806 (1951)

Radio Gaithersburg v. FCC, 217 U.S.App.D.C. 362, 672 F.2d 896 (1981)

Radio Investment Co. v. FRC, 61 U.S.App.D.C. 296, 62 F.2d 381 (1932)

Radio Relay Corp. v. FCC, 409 F.2d 322 (2nd Cir. 1969)

Radio Representatives, Inc. v. FCC, 288 U.S.App.D.C. 342, 926 F.2d 1215 (1991)

Radio Service Corp. v. FCC, 64 U.S.App.D.C. 228, 76 F.2d 998 (1935)

Radio Station KFH Co. v. FCC, 101 U.S.App.D.C. 164, 247 F.2d 570 (1957)

Radio Station WOW, Inc. v. FCC, 87 U.S.App.D.C. 226, 184 F.2d 257 (1950)

Radio Station WOW, Inc. v. Johnson, 326 U.S. 120, 89 L.Ed. 2092, 65 S.Ct. 1475 (1945)

Radio Television S.A. de C.V. v. FCC, 327 U.S.App.D.C. 285, 130 F.3d 1078 (1997)

Radio-Electronics Officers Union v. FCC, 282 U.S.App.D.C. 404, 895 F.2d 809 (1990)

Radio-Television News Directors Ass'n v. United States, 400 F.2d 1002 (7th Cir. 1968), rev'd, *Red Lion Broadcasting Co. v. FCC*, 395 U.S. 367 (1969)

Radio-Television News Directors Ass'n v. FCC, 258 U.S.App.D.C. 19, 809 F.2d 860, vacated, 265 U.S.App.D.C. 389, 831 F.2d 1148 (1987)

Radio-Television News Directors Ass'n v. FCC, 337 U.S.App.D.C. 292, 184 F.3d 872 (1999)

Radio-Television News Directors Ass'n v. FCC, 343 U.S.App.D.C. 305, 229 F.3d 269 (2000)

Radiofone, Inc. v. FCC, 245 U.S.App.D.C. 210, 759 F.2d 936 (1985)

Rainbow Broadcasting Co. v. FCC, 292 U.S.App.D.C. 230, 949 F.2d 405 (1991)

Rainbow Broadcasting, Inc. v. FCC, 1995 WL 224866 (D.C. Cir. 1995)

Rainbow/PUSH Coalition v. FCC, 356 U.S.App.D.C. 275, 330 F.3d 539 (2003)

Ralph C. Wilson Industries, Inc. v. FCC, 232 U.S.App.D.C. 263, 721 F.2d 1424 (1983)

RAM Broadcasting of Texas, Inc. v. FCC, 166 U.S.App.D.C. 197, 509 F.2d 530 (1974)

Rancocas Valley Broadcasting Co., Inc. v. FCC, 236 U.S.App.D.C. 351, 735 F.2d 617 (1984)

Ranger v. FCC, 111 U.S.App.D.C. 44, 294 F.2d 240 (1961)

Ranger Cellular v. FCC, 357 U.S.App.D.C. 134, 333 F.3d 255 (2003)

Ranger Cellular v. FCC, 358 U.S.App.D.C. 306, 348 F.3d 1044 (2003)

RCA American Communications, Inc. v. FCC, 235 U.S.App.D.C. 294, 731 F.2d 996 (1984)

RCA Communications v. FCC, 91 U.S.App.D.C. 289, 201 F.2d 694 (1952), rev'd, 346 U.S. 86 (1953)

RCA Communications v. FCC, 99 U.S.App.D.C. 163, 238 F.2d 241 (1956), cert. denied, 352 U.S. 1004 (1957)

RCA Global Communications, Inc. v. FCC, 559 F.2d 881 (2nd Cir. 1977)

RCA Global Communications, Inc. v. FCC, 563 F.2d 1 (2nd Cir. 1977)

RCA Global Communications, Inc. v. FCC, 574 F.2d 727 (2nd Cir. 1978)

RCA Global Communications, Inc. v. FCC, 524 F.Supp. 579 (D. De. 1981)

RCA Global Communications, Inc. v. FCC, 230 U.S.App.D.C. 372, 717 F.2d 1429 (1983)

RCA Global Communications, Inc. v. FCC, 244 U.S.App.D.C. 402, 758 F.2d 722 (1985)

Reading Broadcasting Co. v. FRC, 60 U.S.App.D.C. 89, 48 F.2d 458 (1931)

Red Lion Broadcasting Co. v. FCC, 127 U.S.App.D.C. 129, 381 F.2d 908 (1967), aff'd, 395 U.S. 367 (1969)

Red Lion Broadcasting Co. v. FCC, 395 U.S. 367, 23 L.Ed.2d 371, 89 S.Ct. 1794 (1969)

Red River Broadcasting Co. v. FCC, 69 U.S.App.D.C. 1, 98 F.2d 282, cert. denied, 305 U.S. 625 (1938)

Red River Broadcasting Co. v. FCC, 105 U.S.App.D.C. 376, 267 F.2d 653 (1959)

Red River Valley Broadcasting Corp. v. FCC, 106 U.S.App.D.C. 333, 272 F.2d 562 (1959)

Red Rock Broadcasting, Inc. v. FCC, 320 U.S.App.D.C. 364, 94 F.3d 698 (1996)

Reeder v. FCC, 275 U.S.App.D.C. 199, 865 F.2d 1298 (1989)

Regents of the Univ. System of Ga. v. Carroll, 338 U.S. 586, 94 L.Ed. 363, 70 S.Ct. 370 (1950)

Reiser v. FCC, 217 U.S.App.D.C. 362, 672 F.2d 896 (1981)

Reno Minority Broadcasting Corp. v. FCC, 292 U.S.App.D.C. 86, 946 F.2d 1566 (1991)

Reservation Telephone Cooperative v. FCC, 264 U.S.App.D.C. 113, 826 F.2d 1129 (1987)

Resort Broadcasting Co., Inc. v. FCC, 167 U.S.App.D.C. 210, 511 F.2d 448 (1975)

Reston v. FCC, 492 F.Supp. 697 (D.D.C. 1980)

Retail Store Employees Union v. FCC, 141 U.S.App.D.C. 94, 436 F.2d 248 (1970)

Reuters Limited v. FCC, 251 U.S.App.D.C. 93, 781 F.2d 946 (1986)

Rhode Island Television Corp. v. FCC, 116 U.S.App.D.C. 40, 320 F.2d 762 (1963)

Rice v. FCC, 60 Fed.Appx. 332 (D.C. Cir. 2003)

Richard F. Lewis, Jr., Inc. v. FCC, 110 U.S.App.D.C. 269, 292 F.2d 762 (1961)

Richardson v. FCC, 983 F.2d 1073 (7th Cir. 1992)

Richardson v. Wiley, 186 U.S.App.D.C. 309, 569 F.2d 140 (1977)

Richman Bros. Records, Inc. v. FCC, 326 U.S.App.D.C. 330, 124 F.3d 1302 (1997)

Richmond Development Co. v. FRC, 59 U.S.App.D.C. 113, 35 F.2d 883 (1929)

Ricks v. FCC, 188 U.S.App.D.C. 201, 578 F.2d 443 (1978)

Ridge Radio Corp. v. FCC, 110 U.S.App.D.C. 277, 292 F.2d 770 (1961)

Riker v. FRC, 60 U.S.App.D.C. 373, 55 F.2d 535 (1931)

Rio Grande Family Radio Fellowship, Inc. v. FCC, 132 U.S.App.D.C. 128, 406 F.2d 664 (1968)

Rippe v. FCC, 528 F.2d 771 (6th Cir. 1976)

RKO General, Inc. v. FCC, 216 U.S.App.D.C. 57, 670 F.2d 215 (1981), cert. denied, 456 U.S. 927 and 457 U.S. 1119 (1982)

Robinson v. FCC, 118 U.S.App.D.C. 144, 334 F.2d 534, cert. denied, 379 U.S. 843 (1964)

Rochester Telephone Corp. v. United States, 23 F.Supp. 634 (W.D.N.Y. 1938), aff'd, 307 U.S. 125 (1939)

Rochester Telephone Corp. v. United States, 307 U.S. 125, 83 L.Ed.2d 1147 (1939)

Rockler v. FCC, 268 U.S.App.D.C. 145, 839 F.2d 824 (1988)

Rocky Mountain Radar, Inc. v. FCC, 158 F.3d 1118 (10th Cir. 1998), cert. denied, 525 U.S. 1147 (1999)

Rogers Radio Communications Services, Inc. v. FCC, 193 U.S.App.D.C. 71, 593 F.2d 1225 (1978)

Rogers Radio Communications Services, Inc. v. FCC, 243 U.S.App.D.C. 32, 751 F.2d 408 (1985)

Rounsaville of Louisville, Inc. v. FCC, 114 U.S.App.D.C. 275, 314 F.2d 280 (1963)

Royce International Broadcasting Co. v. FCC, 246 U.S.App.D.C. 44, 762 F.2d 138, cert. denied, 474 U.S. 995 (1985)

Royce International Broadcasting Co. v. FCC, 261 U.S.App.D.C. 153, 820 F.2d 1332 (1987)

RT Communications, Inc. v. FCC, 201 F.3d 1264 (10th Cir. 2000)

Ruggiero v. FCC, 349 U.S.App.D.C. 374, 278 F.3d 1323 (2002)

Ruggiero v. FCC, 354 U.S.App.D.C. 337, 317 F.3d 239, cert. denied, 124 S.Ct. 62 (2003)

Rural Telephone Coalition v. FCC, 267 U.S.App.D.C. 357, 838 F.2d 1307 (1988)

Russian River Vintage Broadcasting v. FCC, 303 U.S.App.D.C. 326, 5 F.3d 1518 (1993)

Rust Broadcasting Co. v. FCC, 126 U.S.App.D.C. 426, 379 F.2d 480 (1967)

Sable Communications, Inc. v. FCC, 827 F.2d 640 (9th Cir. 1987)

Sable Communications of Calif., Inc. v. FCC, 692 F.Supp. 1208 (C.D. Cal. 1988), aff'd, 492 U.S. 115 (1989)

Sable Communications of Calif., Inc. v. FCC, 492 U.S. 115, 109 S.Ct. 2829, 106 L.Ed.2d 93 (1989)

Saco River Cellular, Inc. v. FCC, 328 U.S.App.D.C. 162, 133 F.3d 25, cert. denied, 525 U.S. 813 (1998)

Sacramento Broadcasters v. FCC, 98 U.S.App.D.C. 394, 236 F.2d 689 (1956)

Sacramento RSA Ltd. Partnership v. FCC, 312 U.S.App.D.C. 461, 56 F.3d 1531 (1995)

Saginaw Broadcasting Co. v. FCC, 68 U.S.App.D.C. 282, 96 F.2d 554, cert. denied, 305 U.S. 613 (1938)

Saginaw Mobile Telephone System v. FCC, 283 U.S.App.D.C. 284, 900 F.2d 268 (1990)

St. Joseph Tel. & Tel. Co. v. FCC, 164 U.S.App.D.C. 369, 505 F.2d 476 (1974)

St. Louis Amusement Co. v. FCC, 104 U.S.App.D.C. 45, 259 F.2d 202, cert. denied, 358 U.S. 894 (1958)

Saltzman v. Stromberg-Carlson Telephone Mfg. Co., 60 U.S.App.D.C. 31, 46 F.2d 612 (1931)

Salzer v. FCC, 250 U.S.App.D.C. 248, 778 F.2d 869 (1985)

Sanders Bros. Radio Station v. FCC, 70 U.S.App.D.C. 297, 106 F.2d 321 (1939), rev'd, 309 U.S. 470 (1940)

Sangamon Valley Television Corp. v. United States, 103 U.S.App.D.C. 113, 255 F.2d 191, vacated, 358 U.S. 49 (1958)

Sangamon Valley Television Corp. v. United States, 106 U.S.App.D.C. 30, 269 F.2d 221 (1959)

Sangamon Valley Television Corp. v. United States, 111 U.S.App.D.C. 113, 294 F.2d 742 (1961)

Sangre de Christo Communications, Inc. v. FCC, 329 U.S.App.D.C. 260, 139 F.3d 953 (1998)

Sarasota-Charlotte Broadcasting Corp. v. FCC, 298 U.S.App.D.C. 135, 976 F.2d 1439 (1992)

Satellite Broadcasting & Communications Ass'n v. FCC, 275 F.3d 337 (4th Cir. 2001)

Satellite Broadcasting Co., Inc. v. FCC, 246 U.S.App.D.C. 44, 762 F.2d 138 (1985)

Satellite Broadcasting Co., Inc. v. FCC, 262 U.S.App.D.C. 274, 824 F.2d 1 (1987)

Satellite Cellular Systems v. FCC, 287 U.S.App.D.C. 378, 923 F.2d 201 (1990)

Savannah College of Art and Design and Diocese Savannah v. FCC, 115 Fed.App. 444 (2004)

Sayger v. FCC, 114 U.S.App.D.C. 112, 312 F.2d 352 (1962)

SBC Communications, Inc. v. FCC, 312 U.S.App.D.C. 414, 56 F.3d 1484 (1995)

SBC Communications, Inc. v. FCC, 329 U.S.App.D.C. 133, 138 F.3d 410 (1998)

SBC Communications, Inc. v. FCC and United States, 981 F.Supp. 996 (N.D. Tx. 1997), rev'd, 154 F.3d 226 (5th Cir. 1998), cert. denied, 525 U.S. 1113 (1999)

SBC Communications, Inc. v. FCC and United States, 362 U.S.App.D.C. 131, 373 F.3d 140 (2004)

Schoenbohm v. FCC, 340 U.S.App.D.C. 205, 204 F.3d 243 (2000)

School District #1 v. FCC, 198 U.S.App.D.C. 58, 610 F.2d 1000 (1979)

Schultz v. FCC, 288 U.S.App.D.C. 403, 927 F.2d 1258, cert. denied, 502 U.S. 974 (1991)

Schurz Communications, Inc. v. FCC, 982 F.2d 1043 (7th Cir. 1992)

Scranton Broadcasters, Inc. v FCC, 218 U.S.App.D.C. 161, 673 F.2d 552 (1981)

Scripps-Howard Radio v. FCC, 316 U.S. 4, 86 L.Ed. 1229, 62 S.Ct. 875 (1942)

Scripps-Howard Radio v. FCC, 89 U.S.App.D.C. 13, 189 F.2d 677, cert. denied, 342 U.S. 830 (1951)

Sea Island Broadcasting Corp. v. FCC, 200 U.S.App.D.C. 187, 627 F.2d 240 (1980), cert. denied, 449 U.S. 834 (1980)

Serafyn v. FCC, 331 U.S.App.D.C. 340, 149 F.3d 1213 (1998)

Service Electric Cable TV, Inc. v. FCC, 153 U.S.App.D.C. 393, 473 F.2d 104 (1972)

Service Electric Cable TV, Inc. v. FCC, 468 F.2d 674 (3rd Cir. 1972)

Services Unlimited, Inc. v. FCC, 477 F.2d 593 (4th Cir. 1973)

Shenandoah Valley Academy v. FCC, 324 U.S.App.D.C. 204, 111 F.3d 963 (1997)

Shorter v. Adler, 103 U.S.App.D.C. 311, 258 F.2d 163 (1958)

Showtime Entertainment v. FCC, 235 U.S.App.D.C. 294, 731 F.2d 996 (1984)

Showtime Networks, Inc. v. FCC, 289 U.S.App.D.C. 348, 932 F.2d 1 (1991)

Shurberg Broadcasting of Hartford, Inc. v. FCC, 278 U.S.App.D.C. 24, 876 F.2d 902, rehearing denied, 278 U.S.App.D.C. 80, 876 F.2d 958 (1989), rev'd, *Metro Broadcasting, Inc. v. FCC*, 497 U.S. 547 (1990)

Shurberg Broadcasting of Hartford, Inc. v. FCC, 617 F.Supp. 825 (D.D.C. 1985)

Simmons v. FCC, 79 U.S.App.D.C. 264, 145 F.2d 578 (1944), abandoned, *Orange Park Florida TV, Inc. v. FCC*, 258 U.S.App.D.C. 322, 811 F.2d 664 (1987)

Simmons v. FCC, 83 U.S.App.D.C. 262, 169 F.2d 670, cert. denied, 335 U.S. 846 (1948)

Sinclair Broadcast Group, Inc. v. FCC, 350 U.S.App.D.C. 261, 294 F.3d 148 (2002)

Singleton v. FCC, 293 U.S.App.D.C. 250, 952 F.2d 1444 (1992)

Sioux Valley Rural Television, Inc. v. FCC, 358 U.S.App.D.C. 344, 349 F.3d 667 (2003)

Skidelsky v. FCC, 303 U.S.App.D.C. 418, 8 F.3d 71 (1993)

Sky Way Broadcasting Corp. v. FCC, 85 U.S.App.D.C. 425, 176 F.2d 951 (1949)

SL Communications, Inc. v. FCC, 335 U.S.App.D.C. 54, 168 F.3d 1354 (1999)

Small Business in Telecommunications v. FCC, 346 U.S.App.D.C. 200, 251 F.3d 1015 (2001)

Smith v. FCC, 101 U.S.App.D.C. 109, 247 F.2d 100 (1957)

Smith v. FCC, 491 F.2d 751 (3rd Cir. 1974)

Smith v. FCC, 168 U.S.App.D.C. 78, 512 F.2d 992 (1975)

Snyder v. FCC and United States, No. 04-1022, 2004 U.S.APP LEXIS 9755 (2004)

Sotomayer v. FCC, 232 U.S.App.D.C. 247, 721 F.2d 1408 (1983)

South Florida Television Corp. v. FCC, 121 U.S.App.D.C. 293, 349 F.2d 971 (1965), cert. denied, 382 U.S. 987 (1966)

South Missouri Broadcasting Co. v. FCC, 304 U.S.App.D.C. 429, 15 F.3d 1160 (1993)

South Star Communications, Inc. v. FCC, 292 U.S.App.D.C. 37, 946 F.2d 127 (1991)

South Star Communications, Inc. v. FCC, 292 U.S.App.D.C. 275, 949 F.2d 450 (1991)

Southeast Arkansas Broadcasters, Inc. v. FCC, 185 U.S.App.D.C. 133, 566 F.2d 798 (1977)

Southeast Florida Broadcasting v. FCC, 292 U.S.App.D.C. 89, 947 F.2d 505 (1991)

Southern Bell Tel. & Tel. Co. v. FCC, 251 U.S.App.D.C. 33, 781 F.2d 209 (1986)

Southern Company v. FCC, 293 F.3d 1338 (11th Cir. 2002)

Southern Company Services, Inc. v. FCC, 354 U.S.App.D.C. 124, 313 F.3d 574 (2002)

Southern Indiana Broadcasting, Ltd. v. FCC, 290 U.S.App.D.C. 221, 935 F.2d 1340 (1991)

Southern Pacific Communications Co. v. FCC, 220 U.S.App.D.C. 397, 682 F.2d 232 (1982)

Southland Industries v. FCC, 69 U.S.App.D.C. 82, 99 F.2d 117 (1938)

Southland Television Co. v. FCC, 105 U.S.App.D.C. 282, 266 F.2d 686 (1959)

Southside Virginia Telecasting Corp. v. FCC, 97 U.S.App.D.C. 130, 228 F.2d 644 (1955), cert. denied, 350 U.S. 1001 (1956)

Southwest Broadcasting Co. v. FCC, 181 U.S.App.D.C. 411, 559 F.2d 188 (1977)

Southwest Pa. Cable TV, Inc. v. FCC, 169 U.S.App.D.C. 102, 514 F.2d 1343 (1975)

Southwestern Bell Corp. v. FCC, 283 U.S.App.D.C. 80, 896 F.2d 1378 (1990)

Southwestern Bell Corp. v. FCC, 310 U.S.App.D.C. 90, 43 F.3d 1515 (1995)

Southwestern Bell Tel. Co. v. FCC, 304 U.S.App.D.C. 117, 10 F.3d 892 (1993), cert. denied, 512 U.S. 1204 (1994)

Southwestern Bell Tel. Co. v. FCC, 305 U.S.App.D.C. 272, 19 F.3d 1475 (1994)

Southwestern Bell Tel. Co. v. FCC, 307 U.S.App.D.C. 298, 28 F.3d 165 (1994)

Southwestern Bell Tel. Co. v. FCC, 321 U.S.App.D.C. 390, 100 F.3d 1004 (1996)

Southwestern Bell Tel. Co. v. FCC, 325 U.S.App.D.C. 249, 116 F.3d 593 (1997)

Southwestern Bell Tel. Co. v. FCC, 138 F.3d 746 (8th Cir. 1998)

Southwestern Bell Tel. Co. v. FCC, 153 F.3d 597 (8th Cir. 1998)

Southwestern Bell Tel. Co. v. FCC, 153 F.3d 523 (8th Cir. 1998), vacated and remanded, 525 U.S. 1113 (1999)

Southwestern Bell Tel. Co. v. FCC, 335 U.S.App.D.C. 44, 168 F.3d 1344 (1999)

Southwestern Bell Tel. Co. v. FCC, 336 U.S.App.D.C. 372, 180 F.3d 307 (1999)

Southwestern Bell Tel. Co. v. FCC, 225 F.3d 942 (8th Cir. 2000)

Southwestern Cable Co. v. United States, 378 F.2d 118 (9th Cir. 1967), rev'd, 392 U.S. 157 (1968)

Southwestern Operating Co. v. FCC, 122 U.S.App.D.C. 137, 351 F.2d 834 (1965)

Southwestern Publishing Co. v. FCC, 100 U.S.App.D.C. 251, 243 F.2d 829 (1957)

Spain v. FCC, 178 U.S.App.D.C. 77, 543 F.2d 1390 (1976)

Spanish International Broadcasting Co. v. FCC, 128 U.S.App.D.C. 93, 385 F.2d 615 (1967)

Spanish International Network, Inc. v. FCC, 219 U.S.App.D.C. 115, 675 F.2d 1340 (1982)

Spartan Radiocasting Co. v. FCC, 619 F.2d 314 (4th Cir. 1980)

Spectron Broadcasting Corp. v. FCC, 273 U.S.App.D.C. 179, 858 F.2d 774 (1988)

Spectrum Telecommunications Corp. v. FCC, 252 U.S.App.D.C. 19, 786 F.2d 432 (1986)

Spentonbush Fuel Transport Service, Inc. v. FCC, 315 F.2d 188 (2nd Cir. 1963)

Springfield Television Broadcasting Corp. v. FCC, 104 U.S.App.D.C. 13, 259 F.2d 170 (1958)

Springfield Television Broadcasting Corp. v. FCC, 117 U.S.App.D.C. 214, 328 F.2d 186 (1964)

Springfield Television Broadcasting Corp. v. FCC, 168 U.S.App.D.C. 78, 512 F.2d 992 (1975)

Springfield Television Corp. v. FCC, 609 F.2d 1014 (1st Cir. 1979)

Springfield Television of Utah, Inc. v. FCC, 710 F.2d 620 (10th Cir. 1983)

Sprint Communications Co. v. FCC, 316 U.S.App.D.C. 168, 76 F.3d 1221 (1996)

Sprint Communications Company L.P. v. FCC, 348 U.S.App.D.C. 266, 274 F.3d 549 (2001)

Sprint Corp. v. FCC, 354 U.S.App.D.C. 288, 315 F.3d 369 (2003)

Sprint Corp. v. FCC, 356 U.S.App.D.C. 367, 331 F.3d 952 (2003)

Sproul v. FRC, 60 U.S.App.D.C. 333, 54 F.2d 444 (1931)

Stahlman v. FCC, 75 U.S.App.D.C. 176, 126 F.2d 124 (1942)

Star Television, Inc. v. FCC, 135 U.S.App.D.C. 71, 415 F.2d 1086, cert. denied, 396 U.S. 888 (1969)

Starpower Communications, Inc. v. FCC, 357 U.S.App.D.C. 328, 334 F.2d 1150 (2003)

State Corporation Comm'n of Kansas v. FCC, 787 F.2d 1421 (10th Cir. 1986)

State of Oregon v. FCC, 322 U.S.App.D.C. 185, 102 F.3d 583 (1996)

Steele v. FCC, 248 U.S.App.D.C. 279, 770 F.2d 1192 (1985), vacated & reh. en banc granted, Order of Oct. 31, 1985, remanded, Order of Oct. 9, 1986, mandate recalled, Order of June 9, 1988, remanded, Order of Aug. 15, 1988

Stereo Broadcasters, Inc. v. FCC, 209 U.S.App.D.C. 229, 652 F.2d 1026 (1981)

Stewart v. FCC, 164 U.S.App.D.C. 369, 505 F.2d 476 (1974)

Stone v. FCC, 151 U.S.App.D.C. 145, 466 F.2d 316 (1972)

Storer Broadcasting Co. v. United States, 95 U.S.App.D.C. 97, 220 F.2d 204 (1955), rev'd, 351 U.S. 192 (1956)

Storer Broadcasting Co. v. United States, 99 U.S.App.D.C. 369, 240 F.2d 55 (1956)

Storer Communications, Inc. v. FCC, 246 U.S.App.D.C. 146, 763 F.2d 436 (1985)

Straus Communications, Inc. v. FCC, 174 U.S.App.D.C. 149, 530 F.2d 1001 (1976)

Strawbridge & Clothier v. FRC, 61 U.S.App.D.C. 68, 57 F.2d 434 (1932)

Stuart v. FCC, 70 U.S.App.D.C. 265, 105 F.2d 788 (1939)

Sudbrink Broadcasting, Inc. v. FCC, 166 U.S.App.D.C. 85, 509 F.2d 418 (1974)

Sun Communications, Inc. v. FCC, 293 U.S.App.D.C. 303, 971 F.2d 766 (1992), cert. denied, 507 U.S. 921 (1993)

Sunbeam Television Corp. v. FCC, 100 U.S.App.D.C. 82, 243 F.2d 26 (1957)

SunCom Mobile & Data, Inc. v. FCC, 318 U.S.App.D.C. 377, 87 F.3d 1386 (1996)

Sunshine State Broadcasting Co. v. FCC, 114 U.S.App.D.C. 271, 314 F.2d 276 (1963)

Swan Creek Communications, Inc. v. FCC, 309 U.S.App.D.C. 125, 39 F.3d 1217 (1994)

Sykes v. Jenny Wren Co., 64 U.S.App.D.C. 379, 78 F.2d 729 (1935)

Symons Broadcasting Co. v. FRC, 62 U.S.App.D.C. 46, 64 F.2d 381 (1933)

Syracuse Coalition v. FCC, 193 U.S.App.D.C. 16, 593 F.2d 1170 (1978)

Syracuse Peace Council v. FCC, 276 U.S.App.D.C. 38, 867 F.2d 654 (1989), cert. denied, 493 U.S. 1019 (1990)

Tallahassee Branch of the NAACP v. FCC, 276 U.S.App.D.C. 290, 870 F.2d 704 (1989)

Tampa Times Co. v. FCC, 97 U.S.App.D.C. 256, 230 F.2d 224 (1956)

Technical Aeroservice, Inc. v. FCC, 193 U.S.App.D.C. 218, 593 F.2d 1372 (1979)

Technical Radio Laboratory v. FRC, 59 U.S.App.D.C. 125, 36 F.2d 111 (1929)

Telanserphone, Inc. v. FCC, 97 U.S.App.D.C. 398, 231 F.2d 732 (1956)

Tel-Central of Jefferson City v. FCC, 287 U.S.App.D.C. 245, 920 F.2d 1039 (1990)

Telecommunications Research and Action Center v. FCC, 242 U.S.App.D.C. 222, 750 F.2d 70 (1984)

Telecommunications Research and Action Center v. FCC, 255 U.S.App.D.C. 156, 800 F.2d 1181 (1986)

Telecommunications Research and Action Center v. FCC, 255 U.S.App.D.C. 287, 801 F.2d 501, rehearing en banc denied, 257 U.S.App.D.C. 23, 806 F.2d 1115 (1986), cert. denied, 482 U.S. 919 (1987)

Telecommunications Research and Action Center v. FCC, 267 U.S.App.D.C. 1, 836 F.2d 1349 (1988)

Telecommunications Research and Action Center v. FCC, 286 U.S.App.D.C. 363, 917 F.2d 585 (1990)

Telecommunications Research and Action Center v. FCC, 307 U.S.App.D.C. 44, 26 F.3d 185 (1994)

Telecommunications Resellers Ass'n v. FCC, 329 U.S.App.D.C. 409, 141 F.3d 1193 (1998)

Teledesic LLC v. FCC, 348 U.S.App.D.C. 296, 275 F.3d 75 (2001)

Telegraph Herald Co. v. FRC, 62 U.S.App.D.C. 240, 66 F.2d 220 (1933)

Tele-Media Corp. v. FCC, 225 U.S.App.D.C. 160, 697 F.2d 402 (1983)

Telemundo, Inc. v. FCC, 255 U.S.App.D.C. 437, 802 F.2d 513 (1986)

Telephone and Data Systems, Inc. v. FCC, 305 U.S.App.D.C. 195, 19 F.3d 42 (1994).

Telephone and Data Systems, Inc. v. FCC, 305 U.S.App.D.C. 216, 19 F.3d 655 (1994).

Telephone Users Ass'n v. FCC, 126 U.S.App.D.C. 178, 375 F.2d 923 (1967)

Teleprompter Cable Communications Corp. v. FCC, 184 U.S.App.D.C. 161, 565 F.2d 736 (1977)

Teleprompter Cable Systems, Inc. v. FCC, 178 U.S.App.D.C. 66, 543 F.2d 1379 (1976)

Teleprompter Corp. v. FCC, 159 U.S.App.D.C. 55, 486 F.2d 1315 (1973)

Telerama, Inc. v. United States, 419 F.2d 1047 (6th Cir. 1969)

TeleSTAR, Inc. v. FCC, 281 U.S.App.D.C. 119, 888 F.2d 132 (1989)

TeleSTAR, Inc. v. FCC, 281 U.S.App.D.C. 24, 886 F.2d 442 (1989), cert. denied, 498 U.S. 812 (1990)

TeleSTAR, Inc. v. FCC, 283 U.S.App.D.C. 283, 899 F.2d 1268 (1990)

TeleSTAR, Inc. v. FCC, 284 U.S.App.D.C. 79, 901 F.2d 1131 (1990)

Television Corp of Mich., Inc. v. FCC, 111 U.S.App.D.C. 101, 294 F.2d 730 (1961)

Telocator Network of America, Inc. v. FCC, 214 U.S.App.D.C. 238, 665 F.2d 394 (1981)

Telocator Network of America, Inc. v. FCC, 223 U.S.App.D.C. 336, 691 F.2d 525 (1982)

Telocator Network of America, Inc. v. FCC, 245 U.S.App.D.C. 360, 761 F.2d 763 (1985)

Tennessee Television, Inc. v. FCC, 104 U.S.App.D.C. 316, 262 F.2d 28 (1958)

Texas Coalition of Cities for Utility Issues v. FCC, 324 F.3d 802 (5th Cir. 2003)

Texas Office of Public Utility Counsel v. FCC, 183 F.3d 393 (5th Cir. 1999)

Texas Office of Public Utility Counsel, et al. v. FCC, 265 F.3d 313 (5th Cir. 2001)

Texas Power and Light Co. v. FCC, 784 F.2d 1265 (5th Cir. 1986)

Texas Two-Way, Inc. v. FCC, 246 U.S.App.D.C. 44, 762 F.2d 138 (1985)

Texas Utilities Elec. Co. v. FCC, 302 U.S.App.D.C. 235, 997 F.2d 925 (1993)

Thomas Radio Co. v. FCC, 230 U.S.App.D.C. 270, 716 F.2d 921 (1983)

TI Broadcasting, Inc. v. FCC, 126 U.S.App.D.C. 54, 374 F.2d 268 (1966)

Time Warner Entertainment Co., L.P. v. FCC, 810 F.Supp. 1302 (D.D.C. 1992)

Time Warner Entertainment Co., L.P. v. FCC, 312 U.S.App.D.C. 187, 56 F.3d 151 (1995), cert. denied, 516 U.S. 1112 (1996)

Time Warner Entertainment Co., L.P. v. FCC, 320 U.S.App.D.C. 294, 93 F.3d 957 (1996), reh. denied, 323 U.S.App.D.C. 109, 105 F.3d 723 (1997)

Time Warner Entertainment Co., L.P. v. FCC, 330 U.S.App.D.C. 126, 144 F.3d 75 (1998)

Time Warner Entertainment Co., L.P., v. FCC, 341 U.S.App.D.C. 255, 211 F.3d 1313 (2000)

Time Warner Entertainment Co., L.P. v. FCC, 345 U.S.App.D.C. 186, 240 F.3d 1126 (2001)

Titusville Cable TV, Inc. v. United States, 404 F.2d 1187 (3rd Cir. 1968)

Tomah-Mauston Broadcasting Co. v. FCC, 113 U.S.App.D.C. 204, 306 F.2d 811 (1962)

Total Telecable, Inc. v. FCC, 411 F.2d 639 (9th Cir. 1969)

Town of Deerfield v. FCC, 992 F.2d 420 (2nd Cir. 1993)

Transcontinent Television Corp. v. FCC, 113 U.S.App.D.C. 384, 308 F.2d 339 (1962)

Transportation Intelligence, Inc. v. FCC, 357 U.S.App.D.C. 386, 336 F.3d 1058 (2003)

Treasure Valley CATV Comm. v. FCC, 562 F.2d 1182 (9th Cir. 1977)

Triangle Publications, Inc. v. FCC, 110 U.S.App.D.C. 214, 291 F.2d 342 (1961)

Tribune Co. v. FCC, 328 U.S.App.D.C. 198, 133 F.3d 61 (1998)

Trinity Broadcasting of Florida, Inc. v. FCC, 341 U.S.App.D.C. 191, 211 F.3d 618 (2000)

Trinity Methodist Church, South v. FRC, 61 U.S.App.D.C. 311, 62 F.2d 850 (1932)

Tri-State Broadcasting Co. v. FCC, 68 U.S.App.D.C. 292, 96 F.2d 564 (1938)

Tri-State Broadcasting Co. v. FCC, 71 U.S.App.D.C. 157, 107 F.2d 956 (1939)

TRT Telecommunications Corp. v. FCC, 273 U.S.App.D.C. 97, 857 F.2d 1535 (1988)

TRT Telecommunications Corp. v. FCC, 277 U.S.App.D.C. 375, 876 F.2d 134 (1989)

Tucson FM Broadcasting Corp. v. FCC, 292 U.S.App.D.C. 89, 947 F.2d 505 (1991)

Tucson Radio, Inc. v. FCC, 147 U.S.App.D.C. 48, 452 F.2d 1380 (1971)

Turner v. FCC, 169 U.S.App.D.C. 113, 514 F.2d 1354 (1975)

Turner Broadcasting System, Inc. v. FCC, 810 F.Supp. 1308 (D.D.C. 1992)

Turner Broadcasting System, Inc. v. FCC, 507 U.S. 1301, 123 L.Ed.2d 642, 113 S.Ct. 1806 (1993)

Turner Broadcasting System, Inc. v. FCC, 819 F.Supp. 32 (D.D.C. 1993), vacated, 512 U.S. 622 (1994)

Turner Broadcasting System, Inc. v. FCC, 512 U.S. 622, 129 L.Ed.2d 497, 114 S.Ct. 2445 (1994)

Turner Broadcasting System, Inc. v. FCC, 520 U.S. 180, 137 L.Ed.2d 369, 117 S.Ct. 1174 (1997)

Turner Broadcasting System, Inc. v. FCC, 910 F.Supp. 734 (D.D.C. 1995), aff'd, 520 U.S. 180 (1997)

Turro v. FCC, 273 U.S.App.D.C. 351, 859 F.2d 1498 (1988)

TV 9, Inc. v. FCC, 161 U.S.App.D.C. 349, 495 F.2d 929 (1973), cert. denied, 419 U.S. 986 (1974)

21st Century Telesis v. FCC, 355 U.S.App.D.C. 1, 318 F.3d 192 (2003)

United American Telecasters, Inc. v. FCC, 255 U.S.App.D.C. 397, 801 F.2d 1436 (1986), cert. denied, 481 U.S. 1050 (1987)

United Broadcasting, Co., Inc. v. FCC, 184 U.S.App.D.C. 124, 565 F.2d 699 (1977)

United Detroit Theatres Corp. v. FCC, 85 U.S.App.D.C. 239, 178 F.2d 700 (1949)

United States v. American Tel. & Tel. Co., 57 F.Supp. 451 (S.D.N.Y. 1944), aff'd, 325 U.S. 837 (1945)

United States v. Any and All Radio Station Transmission Equip., 169 F.3d 548 (8th Cir. 1999)

United States v. Any and All Radio Station Transmission Equip., 204 F.3d 658 (6th Cir. 2000)

United States v. Any and All Radio Station Transmission Equip., 207 F.3d 458 (8th Cir. 2000)

United States v. Dunifer, 997 F.Supp. 1235 (N.D.Cal. 1998), aff'd, 219 F.3d 1004 (9th Cir. 2000)

United States v. Dunifer, 219 F.3d 1004 (9th Cir. 2000)

United States v. Edge Broadcasting, 509 U.S. 418, 125 L.Ed.2d 345, 113 S.Ct. 2696 (1993)

United States v. FCC, 209 U.S.App.D.C. 79, 652 F.2d 72 (1980)

United States v. FCC, 227 U.S.App.D.C. 413, 707 F.2d 610 (1983)

United States v. High Country Broadcasting, Inc., 3 F.3d 1244 (9th Cir. 1993)

United States v. Midwest Video Corp., 406 U.S. 649, 32 L.Ed.2d 390, 92 S.Ct. 1860 (1972)

United States v. Neset, 235 F.3d 415 (8th Cir. 2000)

United States v. New Jersey State Lottery Comm'n, 420 U.S. 371, 43 L.Ed.2d 260, 95 S.Ct. 941 (1975)

United States v. Peninsula Communications, Inc., 287 F.3d 832, (9th Cir. 2002)

United States v. Playboy Entertainment Group, Inc., 529 U.S. 803, 146 L.Ed.2d 865, 120 S.Ct. 1878 (2000)

United States v. Reveille, 21 F.3d 1118 (9th Cir. 1994)

United States v. Southwestern Cable Co., 392 U.S. 157, 20 L.Ed.2d 1001, 88 S.Ct. 1994 (1968)

United States v. Storer Broadcasting Co., 351 U.S. 192, 100 L.Ed. 1081, 76 S.Ct. 763 (1956)

United States Cellular Corp. v. FCC, 349 U.S.App.D.C. 1, 254 F.3d 78 (2001)

United States Satellite Broadcasting Co., Inc. v. FCC, 239 U.S.App.D.C. 74, 740 F.2d 1177 (1984)

United States Tel. Ass'n v. FCC, 338 U.S.App.D.C. 1, 188 F.3d 521 (1999)

United States Tel. Ass'n v. FCC, 343 U.S.App.D.C. 278, 227 F.3d 450 (2000)

United States Telecom Association v. FCC, 351 U.S.App.D.C. 329, 290 F.3d 415 (2002)

United States Telecom Association v. FCC, 353 U.S.App.D.C. 59, 295 F.3d 1326 (2002)

United States Telecom Association v. FCC, 2004 U.S. App. LEXIS 20967 (2004)

United Telegraph Workers, AFL-CIO v. FCC, 141 U.S.App.D.C. 190, 436 F.2d 920 (1970)

United Telephone Co. v. FCC, 182 U.S.App.D.C. 99, 559 F.2d 720 (1977)

United Telephone Co. of Pa. v. FCC, 375 F.Supp. 992 (M.D. Pa. 1974)

United Telephone Workers v. FCC, 141 U.S.App.D.C. 190, 436 F.2d 920 (1970)

United Television Co., Inc. v. FCC, 168 U.S.App.D.C. 383, 514 F.2d 279 (1975)

United Video, Inc. v. FCC, 281 U.S.App.D.C. 368, 890 F.2d 1173 (1989)

Unity School of Christianity v. FRC, 62 U.S.App.D.C. 52, 64 F.2d 550 (1933)

Unity School of Christianity v. FRC, 63 U.S.App.D.C. 84, 69 F.2d 570 (1934)

Universal Service Wireless v. FRC, 59 U.S.App.D.C. 319, 41 F.2d 113 (1930)

Up North Broadcasting Co. v. FCC, 259 U.S.App.D.C. 245, 814 F.2d 774 (1987)

U.S. Airwaves, Inc. v. FCC, 344 U.S.App.D.C. 10, 232 F.3d 227 (2000)

U.S. West, Inc. v. FCC, 250 U.S.App.D.C. 150, 778 F.2d 23 (1985)

U. S. West, Inc. v. FCC, 336 U.S.App.D.C. 224, 177 F.3d 1057 (1999), cert. denied, 120 S.Ct. 1240 (2000)

U. S. West, Inc. v. FCC, 182 F.3d 1224 (10th Cir. 1999)

U. S. Telephone Communications, Inc. v. FCC, 233 U.S.App.D.C. 167, 725 F.2d 126 (1984)

U. S. Telephone Ass'n v. FCC, 307 U.S.App.D.C. 365, 28 F.3d 1232 (1994)

U. S. Telephone Ass'n v. FCC, 309 U.S.App.D.C. 34, 38 F.3d 609 (1994)

Valley Broadcasting Co. v. FCC, 99 U.S.App.D.C. 156, 237 F.2d 784 (1956)

Valley Broadcasting Co. v. United States, 820 F.Supp. 519 (D. Nev. 1993), aff'd, 107 F.3d 1328 (9th Cir. 1997)

Valley Telecasting Co. v. FCC, 118 U.S.App.D.C. 410, 336 F.2d 914 (1964)

Valley Telecasting Co. v. FCC, 119 U.S.App.D.C. 169, 338 F.2d 278 (1964)

Valley Vision, Inc. v. FCC, 127 U.S.App.D.C. 291, 383 F.2d 218 (1967)

Valley Vision, Inc. v. FCC, 399 F.2d 511 (9th Cir. 1968)

ValueVision International, Inc. v. FCC, 331 U.S.App.D.C. 331, 149 F.3d 1204 (1998)

Van Curler Broadcasting Corp. v. FCC, 96 U.S.App.D.C. 184, 225 F.2d 23 (1955)

Van Curler Broadcasting Corp. v. United States, 98 U.S.App.D.C. 432, 236 F.2d 727, cert. denied, 352 U.S. 935 (1956)

Ventura Broadcasting Co. v. FCC, 246 U.S.App.D.C. 315, 765 F.2d 184 (1985)

Verizon Communications Inc. v. FCC, 535 U.S. 467, 152 L.Ed.2d 701, 122 S.Ct. 1646 (2002)

Verizon Communications Inc. v. Law Offices of Curtis V. Trinko, LLP, 540 U.S. 398, 157 L.Ed.2d 823, 124 S.Ct. 872 (2004)

Verizon Telephone Companies v. FCC, 348 U.S.App.D.C. 98, 269 F.3d 1098 (2001)

Verizon Telephone Companies v. FCC, 362 U.S.App.D.C. 404, 374 F.3d 1229 (2004)

Verizon Telephone Companies, et al. v. FCC, 292 F.3d 903 (D.C. Cir. 2002)

Vernal Enterprises, Inc. v. FCC and United States, 359 U.S.App.D.C. 355, 355 F.3d 650 (2004)

Viacom International, Inc. v. FCC, 672 F.2d 1034 (2nd Cir. 1982)

Viacom International, Inc. v. FCC, 828 F.Supp. 741 (N.D.Cal. 1993)

Victor Broadcasting, Inc. v. FCC, 232 U.S.App.D.C. 270, 722 F.2d 756 (1983)

Virgin Islands Tel. Corp. v. FCC, 300 U.S.App.D.C. 359, 989 F.2d 1231 (1993)

Virgin Islands Tel. Corp. v. FCC, 339 U.S.App.D.C. 174, 198 F.3d 921 (1999)

Virginia State Corp. Comm'n v. FCC, 737 F.2d 388 (4th Cir. 1984), rev'd, *Louisiana Public Serv. Comm'n v. FCC*, 476 U.S. 355 (1986)

Vue-Metrics, Inc. v. FCC, 199 U.S.App.D.C. 10, 615 F.2d 1369 (1980)

Wade v. FCC, 293 U.S.App.D.C. 57, 951 F.2d 1324 (1992)

Wade v. FCC, 296 U.S.App.D.C. 182, 966 F.2d 702 (1992)

Wade v. FCC, 298 U.S.App.D.C. 99, 976 F.2d 47 (1992)

Wade v. FCC, 300 U.S.App.D.C. 84, 986 F.2d 1433 (1993)

WADECO, Inc. v. FCC, 202 U.S.App.D.C. 122, 628 F.2d 122 (1980)

WAIT Radio v. FCC, 135 U.S.App.D.C. 317, 418 F.2d 1153 (1969)

WAIT Radio v. FCC, 148 U.S.App.D.C. 179, 459 F.2d 1203, cert. denied, 409 U.S. 1027 (1972)

Walker v. FCC, 200 U.S.App.D.C. 299, 627 F.2d 352 (1980)

Walton Broadcasting, Inc. v. FCC, 220 U.S.App.D.C. 86, 679 F.2d 263 (1982)

Ward v. FCC, 71 U.S.App.D.C. 166, 108 F.2d 486 (1939)

Warner v. FCC, 110 U.S.App.D.C. 266, 292 F.2d 759 (1961)

Warner v. FCC, 296 U.S.App.D.C. 357, 968 F.2d 93 (1992)

Warner v. FCC, 301 U.S.App.D.C. 108, 990 F.2d 1378 (1993)

Warren v. FCC, 244 U.S.App.D.C. 38, 755 F.2d 181 (1985)

Washington Ass'n for Television and Children v. FCC, 214 U.S.App.D.C. 446, 665 F.2d 1264 (1981)

Washington Ass'n for Television and Children v. FCC, 229 U.S.App.D.C. 363, 712 F.2d 677 (1983)

Washington Utilities & Transp. Comm'n v. FCC, 513 F.2d 1142 (9th Cir. 1975), cert. denied, 423 U.S. 836 (1975)

Waterway Communications Systems, Inc. v. FCC, 271 U.S.App.D.C. 146, 851 F.2d 401 (1988)

Way of Life Television Network, Inc. v. FCC, 193 U.S.App.D.C. 202, 593 F.2d 1356 (1979)

WBEN, Inc. v. FCC, 110 U.S.App.D.C. 200, 290 F.2d 743 (1961)

WBEN, Inc. v. FCC, 175 U.S.App.D.C. 363, 535 F.2d 1325 (1976)

WBEN, Inc. v. United States, 396 F.2d 601 (2nd Cir.), cert. denied, 393 U.S. 914 (1968)

WCCO Radio, Inc. v. FCC, 235 U.S.App.D.C. 294, 731 F.2d 996 (1984)

WCOV, Inc. v. FCC, 150 U.S.App.D.C. 303, 464 F.2d 812 (1972)

WCOV, Inc. v. FCC, 230 U.S.App.D.C. 71, 713 F.2d 865 (1983)

WCOV, Inc. v. FCC, 235 U.S.App.D.C. 294, 731 F.2d 996 (1984)

WEBR v. FCC, 136 U.S.App.D.C. 316, 420 F.2d 158 (1969)

Wentronics, Inc. v. FCC, 118 U.S.App.D.C. 36, 331 F.2d 782 (1964)

West Coast Media, Inc. v. FCC, 224 U.S.App.D.C. 423, 695 F.2d 617 (1982), cert. denied, 464 U.S. 816 (1983)

West Michigan Broadcasting Co. v. FCC, 236 U.S.App.D.C. 335, 735 F.2d 601 (1984), cert. denied, 470 U.S. 1027 (1985)

West Michigan Telecasters, Inc. v. FCC, 130 U.S.App.D.C. 39, 396 F.2d 688 (1968)

West Michigan Telecasters, Inc. v. FCC, 148 U.S.App.D.C. 375, 460 F.2d 883 (1972)

Western Broadcasting Co. v. FCC, 218 U.S.App.D.C. 201, 674 F.2d 44 (1982)

Williams v. FCC, 120 U.S.App.D.C. 385, 347 F.2d 479 (1965)

Williams v. FCC, 232 U.S.App.D.C. 263, 721 F.2d 1424 (1983)

Williams County Broadcasting Systems, Inc. v. FCC, 186 U.S.App.D.C. 330, 569 F.2d 161 (1978)

Wilson v. A.H. Belo Corp., 87 F.3d 393 (9th Cir. 1996)

Wilson & Co. v. United States, 335 F.2d 788 (7th Cir. 1964), cert. denied, 380 U.S. 951 (1965)

Winnebago Television Corp. v. United States, 103 U.S.App.D.C. 311, 258 F.2d 163 (1958)

Winter Park Communications, Inc. v. FCC, 277 U.S.App.D.C. 134, 873 F.2d 347 (1989), aff'd, *Metro Broadcasting, Inc. v. FCC*, 497 U.S. 547 (1990)

WIRL Television Co. v. United States, 102 U.S.App.D.C. 341, 253 F.2d 863, vacated, 358 U.S. 51 (1958)

WIRL Television Co. v. United States, 107 U.S.App.D.C. 21, 274 F.2d 83 (1959)

WITN-TV, Inc. v. FCC, 270 U.S.App.D.C. 392, 849 F.2d 1521 (1988)

WJG Telephone Co. v. FCC, 218 U.S.App.D.C. 367, 675 F.2d 386 (1982)

WJHG-TV, Inc. v. FCC, 162 U.S.App.D.C. 20, 495 F.2d 1076 (1974)

WJIV-TV v. FCC, 97 U.S.App.D.C. 391, 231 F.2d 725 (1956)

WJR, The Goodwill Station v. FCC, 84 U.S.App.D.C. 1, 174 F.2d 226 (1948), rev'd, 337 U.S. 265 (1949)

WJR, The Goodwill Station v. FCC, 84 U.S.App.D.C. 23, 174 F.2d 248 (1949)

WJR, The Goodwill Station v. FCC, 85 U.S.App.D.C. 392, 178 F.2d 720 (1949)

WKAT, Inc. v. FCC, 103 U.S.App.D.C. 324, 258 F.2d 418 (1958)

WKAT, Inc. v. FCC, 111 U.S.App.D.C. 253, 296 F.2d 375, cert. denied, 368 U.S. 841 (1961)

WLIL, Inc. v. FCC, 122 U.S.App.D.C. 246, 352 F.2d 722 (1965)

WLOS TV, Inc. v. FCC, 289 U.S.App.D.C. 377, 932 F.2d 993 (1991)

WLOX Broadcasting, Inc. v. FCC, 104 U.S.App.D.C. 194, 260 F.2d 712 (1958)

WLNY v. FCC, 163 F.3d 137 (1998)

WLVA, Inc. v. FCC, 148 U.S.App.D.C. 262, 459 F.2d 1286 (1972)

WMOZ, Inc. v. FCC, 120 U.S.App.D.C. 103, 344 F.2d 197 (1965)

WNCN Listeners Guild v. FCC, 197 U.S.App.D.C. 319, 610 F.2d 838 (1979), rev'd, 450 U.S. 582 (1981)

WNNE-TV, Inc. v. FCC, 227 U.S.App.D.C. 18, 702 F.2d 1206 (1983)

WOKO, Inc. v. FCC, 71 U.S.App.D.C. 228, 109 F.2d 665 (1939)

WOKO, Inc. v. FCC, 80 U.S.App.D.C. 333, 153 F.2d 623, rev'd, 329 U.S. 223 (1946)

Wold Communications, Inc. v. FCC, 237 U.S.App.D.C. 29, 735 F.2d 1465 (1984)

Wometco Enterprises, Inc. v. FCC, 114 U.S.App.D.C. 261, 314 F.2d 266 (1963)

Woodfork v. FCC, 315 U.S.App.D.C. 78, 70 F.3d 639, cert. denied, 518 U.S. 1017 (1996)

Woodland Broadcasting Co. v. FCC, 134 U.S.App.D.C. 264, 414 F.2d 1160 (1969)

Woodmen of the World Life Ins. Ass'n v. FCC, 69 U.S.App.D.C. 87, 99 F.2d 122 (1938)

Woodmen of the World Life Ins. Ass'n v. FRC, 61 U.S.App.D.C. 54, 57 F.2d 420 (1932)

Woodmen of the World Life Ins. Ass'n v. FRC, 62 U.S.App.D.C. 138, 65 F.2d 484 (1933)

Woodmen of the World Life Ins. Soc'y v. FCC, 70 U.S.App.D.C. 196, 105 F.2d 75, cert. denied, 308 U.S. 588 (1939)

WorldCom, Inc. v FCC, 345 U.S.App.D.C. 70, 238 F.3d 449 (2001)

WorldCom, Inc. v FCC, 345 U.S.App.D.C. 346, 246 F.3d 690 (2001)

WorldCom, Inc. v. FCC, 288 F.3d 429 (2002)

WorldCom, Inc. v. FCC, 308 F.3d 1 (D.C. Cir. 2002)

World Communications, Inc. v. FCC, 305 U.S.App.D.C. 282, 20 F.3d 472 (1994)

WORZ, Inc. v. FCC, 103 U.S.App.D.C. 195, 257 F.2d 199, vacated, 358 U.S. 55 (1958)

WORZ, Inc. v. FCC, 106 U.S.App.D.C. 14, 268 F.2d 889, mandamus denied, 361 U.S. 805 (1959)

WORZ, Inc. v. FCC, 116 U.S.App.D.C. 316, 323 F.2d 618 (1963), cert. denied, 376 U.S. 914 (1964)

WORZ, Inc. v. FCC, 120 U.S.App.D.C. 191, 345 F.2d 85, cert. denied, 382 U.S. 893 (1965)

Wrather-Alvarez Broadcasting, Inc. v. FCC, 101 U.S.App.D.C. 324, 248 F.2d 646 (1957)

WREC, Inc. v. FRC, 62 U.S.App.D.C. 312, 67 F.2d 578 (1933)

Writers Guild of America, West, Inc. v. American Broadcasting Cos., Inc., 609 F.2d 355 (9th Cir. 1979), cert. denied, 449 U.S. 824 (1980)

Writers Guild of America, West, Inc. v. FCC, 423 F.Supp. 1064 (C.D. Cal. 1976), vacated, 609 F.2d 355 (9th Cir. 1976), cert. denied, 449 U.S. 824 (1980)

W.S. Butterfield Theatres, Inc. v. FCC, 99 U.S.App.D.C. 71, 237 F.2d 552 (1956)

W.S. Butterfield Theatres, Inc. v. FCC, 106 U.S.App.D.C. 283, 272 F.2d 512 (1959)

WSB, Inc. v. FCC, 318 U.S.App.D.C. 129, 85 F.3d 695 (1996)

WSTE-TV, Inc. v. FCC, 185 U.S.App.D.C. 13, 566 F.2d 333 (1977)

WTSP-TV, Inc. v. FCC, 240 U.S.App.D.C. 45, 743 F.2d 45 (1984)

WWHT, Inc. v. FCC, 211 U.S.App.D.C. 218, 656 F.2d 807 (1981)

Wyszatycki v. FCC, 105 U.S.App.D.C. 399, 267 F.2d 676 (1959)

Yakima Valley Cablevision, Inc. v. FCC, 254 U.S.App.D.C. 28, 794 F.2d 737 (1986)

Yale Broadcasting Co. v. FCC, 155 U.S.App.D.C. 390, 478 F.2d 594, cert. denied, 414 U.S. 914 (1973)

Yankee Network v. FCC, 71 U.S.App.D.C. 11, 107 F.2d 212 (1939)

Yellow Freight Systems, Inc. v. FCC, 656 F.2d 600 (10th Cir. 1981)

Younts v. FCC, 301 U.S.App.D.C. 406, 995 F.2d 306 (1993)

Zenith Radio Corp. v. FCC, 93 U.S.App.D.C. 284, 211 F.2d 629 (1954)

Z-Tel Communications v. FCC, 357 U.S.App.D.C. 141, 333 F.3d 262 (2003)

APPENDIX 2

Instructions for FCC Form 303-S Application for Renewal of Broadcast Station License and FCC Form 303-S

Although the amount of paperwork required by the Commission has dropped dramatically over the last twenty years, there is still much to be done if a licensee wishes to renew. FCC Form 303-S is used to renew all broadcast licenses, including both radio and television stations. The form is instructive in that it is an excellent measure of what the Commission is concerned about and what the Commission defines as the public interest, convenience, and necessity. The form may also be informative for citizens who might wish to participate in a broadcast license renewal proceeding.

INSTRUCTIONS FOR FCC 303-S
APPLICATION FOR RENEWAL OF BROADCAST STATION LICENSE

(FCC FORM 303-S ATTACHED)

A. This form is used to apply for renewal of license of a commercial or noncommercial educational AM, FM, TV, Class A TV, FM translator, TV translator, Low Power TV or Low Power FM broadcast station. It is also to be used in seeking the joint renewal of licenses for an FM or TV translator station and its co-owned primary FM, TV or LPTV station.

B. FCC Form 303-S consists of Sections I, II, III, IV and V. Those sections which do not apply to the station license being renewed should not be submitted as part of your application. Submit relevant sections only.

   All applicants must complete and submit Sections I and II of this form. AM and FM radio applicants must also submit Section III. TV and Class A TV applicants must submit Section IV. FM Translator, TV Translator and Low Power FM applicants must also complete Section V.

   Applicants seeking to renew the licenses of both a translator (FM or TV) and a co-owned primary FM, TV or LPTV station on the same form should complete and submit Sections I, II, III, and IV of this form.

C. References to FCC Rules are made in this application form. Before filling it out, applicant should have on hand and be familiar with the current broadcast, translator, LPTV and LPFM rules, which are contained in 47 Code of Federal Regulations (C.F.R.):

   (1)   Part 0 "Commission Organization"
   (2)   Part 1 "Practice and Procedure"
   (3)   Part 17 "Construction, Marking, and Lighting of Antenna Structures"
   (4)   Part 73 "Radio Broadcast Services"
   (5)   Part 74 "Experimental, Auxiliary, and Special Broadcast and Other Program
           Distributional Services"

   FCC Rules may be purchased from the Government Printing Office. Current prices may be obtained from the GPO Customer Service Desk at (202) 512-1803. For payment by credit card, call (202) 518-1800 or 1-866-518-1800, M-F, 8 a.m. to 4 p.m. EST; facsimile orders may be placed by dialing (202) 518-2233, 24 hours a day. Payment by check may be made to the Superintendent of Documents, Attn: New Orders, P.O. Box 371954, Pittsburgh, PA 15250-7954.

D. Electronic Filing of Application Forms. The Commission is currently developing electronic versions of various broadcast station application and reporting forms, such as this application form. As each application form and report goes online, the Commission will, by Public Notice, announce its availability and the procedures to be followed for accessing and filing the application form or report electronically via the Internet. For a six-month period following issuance of this Public Notice, the subject application form or report can be filed with the Commission either electronically or in a paper format. Electronic filing will become mandatory, on a form-by-form basis, six months after each application form or report becomes available for filing electronically.

E. Applicants should provide all information requested by this application. If any portions of the application are not applicable, the applicant should so state. **Defective or incomplete applications will be returned**

without consideration. Inadvertently accepted applications are also subject to dismissal. See 47 C.F.R. Section 73.3564(b).

F. In accordance with 47 C.F.R. Section 1.65, applicants have a continuing obligation to advise the Commission, through amendments, of any substantial and material changes in the information furnished in this application. This requirement continues until the FCC action on this application is no longer subject to reconsideration by the Commission or review by any court.

G. This application requires applicants to certify compliance with many statutory and regulatory requirements. Detailed instructions and worksheets provide additional information regarding Commission rules and policies. These materials are designed to track the standards and criteria that the Commission applies to determine compliance and to increase the reliability of applicant certifications. They are not intended to be substitutes for familiarity with the Communications Act and the Commission's regulations, policies, and precedent. While applicants are required to review all application instructions and worksheets, they are not required to complete or retain any documentation created or collected to complete the application. See Section II, Item 1.

H. This application is presented primarily in a "Yes/No" certification format. However, it contains places for submitting explanations and exhibits where necessary or appropriate. Each certification constitutes a material representation. Applicants may only mark the "Yes" certification when they are certain that the response is correct. A "No" response is required if the applicant is requesting a waiver of a pertinent rule and/or policy, or where the applicant is uncertain that the application fully satisfies the pertinent rule and/or policy. Thus a "No" response to any of the certification Items **will not** cause the immediate dismissal of the application provided that an appropriate exhibit is submitted.

I. Except as specifically noted to the contrary in Form 303-S or these instructions, each certification covers the entire license term. However, if the station license was assigned or transferred during the subject license pursuant to a "long-form" application on FCC Form 314 or 315, the renewal applicant's certifications should cover only the period during which the renewal applicant held the station's license.

J. Except as specifically indicated in Section II, Item 6, below, as used in this application form, the term "party to the application" includes any individual or entity whose ownership or positional interest in the applicant is attributable. An attributable interest is an ownership interest in or relation to an applicant or licensee which will confer on its holder that degree of influence or control over the applicant or licensee sufficient to implicate the Commission's multiple ownership rules. Applicants should review the Commission's multiple ownership attribution policies and standards which are set forth in the Notes to 47 C.F.R. Section 73.3555, as revised and explained in Review of the Commission's Regulations Governing Attribution of Broadcast and Cable/MDS Interests, FCC 99-207, released August 6, 1999, on reconsideration, FCC 00-438, released January 19, 2001. See also, Report and Order in MM Docket No. 83-46, 97 FCC 2d 997 (1984), reconsideration granted in part, 58 RR 2d 604 (1985), further modified on reconsideration, 61 RR 2d 739 (1986).

Equity/Debt Plus Attribution Standard. Certain interests held by substantial investors in, or creditors of, the applicant may also be attributable and the investor reportable as a party to the application, if the interest falls within the Commission's equity/debt plus (**EDP**) attribution standard. Under the **EDP** standard, the interest held, aggregating both equity and debt, must exceed 33% of the total asset value (all equity plus all debt) of the applicant, a broadcast station licensee, cable television system, daily newspaper or other media outlet subject to the Commission's broadcast multiple ownership rules **AND** the interest holder must either also hold an attributable interest in a media outlet in the same market or supply over 15% of the total weekly broadcast programming hours of the station in which the interest is held. For example, the equity interest of an insulated limited partner in a limited partnership applicant would normally not be considered attributable.

However, under the **EDP** standard, that interest would be attributable if the limited partner's interest exceeded 33% of the applicant's total asset value **AND** the limited partner also held a 5% voting interest in a radio or television station licensee in the same market.

Additionally, "parties to the application" includes the following with respect to each of the listed applicant entities:

INDIVIDUAL APPLICANT: The natural person seeking to hold in his or her own right the authorization specified in this application.

PARTNERSHIP APPLICANT: Each partner, including all limited partners. However, a limited partner in a limited partnership is **not** considered a party to the application **IF** the limited partner is not materially involved, directly or indirectly, in the management or operation of the media-related activities of the partnership. Sufficient insulation of a limited partner for purposes of this certification would be assured if the limited partnership arrangement:

(1)   specifies that any exempt limited partner (if not a natural person, its directors, officers, partners, etc.) cannot act as an employee of the limited partnership if his or her functions, directly or indirectly, relate to the media enterprises of the company;

(2)   bars any exempt limited partner from serving, in any material capacity, as an independent contractor or agent with respect to the partnership's media enterprises;

(3)   restricts any exempted limited partner from communicating with the licensee or the general partner on matters pertaining to the day-to-day operations of its business;

(4)   empowers the general partner to veto any admissions of additional general partners admitted by vote of the exempt limited partners;

(5)   prohibits any exempt limited partner from voting on the removal of a general partner or limits this right to situations where the general partner is subject to bankruptcy proceedings, as described in Sections 402 (4)-(5) of the Revised Uniform Limited Partnership Act, is adjudicated incompetent by a court of competent jurisdiction, or is removed for cause, as determined by an independent party;

(6)   bars any exempt limited partner from performing any services to the limited partnership materially relating to its media activities, with the exception of making loans to, or acting as a surety for, the business; and

(7)   states, in express terms, that any exempt limited partner is prohibited from becoming actively involved in the management or operation of the media businesses of the partnership.

Notwithstanding conformance of the partnership agreement to these criteria, however, the requisite certification **cannot** be made **IF** the limited partner's interest is attributable under the Commission's EDP attribution standard described below; or **IF** the applicant has actual knowledge of a material involvement of a limited partner in the management or operation of the media-related businesses of the partnership. In the event that the applicant cannot certify as to the noninvolvement of a limited partner, the limited partner will be considered as a party to this application.

INSTRUCTIONS FOR SECTION I: GENERAL INFORMATION

Item 1: Legal Name of Licensee. The name of the applicant must be stated exactly in Item 1. If the applicant is a corporation, the exact corporate name; if a partnership, the name under which the partnership does business; if an unincorporated association, the name of the executive officer, his/her office, and the name of the association; and if an individual applicant, the person's full legal name.

Applicants should use only those state abbreviations approved by the U.S. Postal Service.

Facility ID Number. Radio and TV Facility ID Numbers can be obtained at the FCC's Internet Website at www.fcc.gov/mb. Once at this website, scroll down and select CDBS Public Access. You can also obtain your Facility ID Number by calling: Radio (202) 418-2700, TV (202) 418-1600. Further, the Facility ID Number is now included on all Radio and TV authorizations and postcards.

FCC Registration Number (FRN). To comply with the Debt Collection Improvement Act of 1996, the applicant must enter its FRN number, a ten-digit unique entity identifier for anyone doing business with the Commission. The FRN can be obtained through the FCC webpage at **http://www.fcc.gov** or by manually submitting FCC Form 160. FCC Form 160 is available for downloading from http://www.fcc.gov/formpage.html or by calling 1-800-418-3676. Questions concerning the FCC Registration Number can be directed to the Commission's Registration System help desk at **http://www.CORES@fcc.gov** or by calling 1-877-480-3201.

Item 2: Contact Representative. If the applicant is represented by a third party (for example, legal counsel), that person's name, firm or company, mailing address and telephone/electronic mail address may be specified in Item 2.

Item 3: Fees. By law, the Commission is required to collect charges for certain regulatory services it provides to the public. Generally, applicants seeking to renew the license for a commercial AM, FM TV, Class A TV, FM translator, TV translator or Low Power TV station is required to pay and submit a fee with the filing of FCC Form 303-S. However, government entities, which include any possession, state, city, county, town, village municipal organization or similar political organization or subpart thereof controlled by publicly elected and/or duly appointed public officials exercising sovereign direction and control over their respective communities or programs, are exempt from the payment of this fee. Also exempted from this fee are licensees of noncommercial educational radio or television broadcast stations. (This includes licensees of noncommercial educational FM and full service TV broadcast stations seeking renewal of the licenses for their translator or low power TV stations provided those stations operate on a noncommercial educational basis.) Low Power TV or TV Translator stations that rebroadcast the programming of a primary noncommercial educational station, but are not co-owned by the licensee of such a station, are required to file fees. Renewal applications that earlier obtained either a fee refund because of an NTIA facilities grant for the stations or a fee waiver because of demonstrated compliance with the eligibility and service requirements of 47 C.F.R. Section 73.503 or Section 73.621, and that continue to operate those stations on a noncommercial basis, are similarly exempted from this fee. See 47 C.F.R. Section 1.112. To avail itself of any fee exemption, the renewal applicant must indicate its eligibility by checking the appropriate box in Item 3, Section I. FCC Form 303-S applications not involving the payment of a fee must be hand-delivered or mailed to the FCC's Washington, D.C. offices. See 47 C.F.R. Section 0.401(a). Do not send fee exempt applications to Mellon Bank, because it will result in a delay in processing the application.

When filing a fee-exempt application, an applicant must complete Item 3 and provide an explanation as appropriate.

The Commission's fee collection program utilizes a U.S. Treasury lockbox bank for maximum efficiency of collection and processing. Prior to the institution of mandatory electronic filing procedures, all paper-form FCC Form 303-S applicants requiring the remittance of a fee, or for which a waiver or deferral from the fee requirement is requested, must be submitted to the appropriate post office box address. See 47 C.F.R. Section 0.401(b). A listing of the required fee and the address to which FCC Form 303-S should be mailed or otherwise delivered are also set forth in the "Media Bureau Fee Filing Guide." This document can be either obtained by writing to the Commission's Form Distribution Center, 9300 E. Hampton Drive, Capitol Heights, Maryland 20743, or by calling 1-800-418-FORM and leaving your request on the answering machine provided for this purpose. See also 47 C.F.R. Section 1.1104. The Fee Filing Guide also contains a list of the Fee Type Codes needed to complete this application.

Payment of any required fee must be made by check, bank draft, money order, or credit card. If payment is by check, bank draft, or money order, the remittance must be denominated in U.S. dollars, drawn upon a U.S. institution, and made payable to the Federal Communications Commission. No postdated, altered, or third-party checks will be accepted. **DO NOT SEND CASH**. Additionally, checks dated six months or older will not be accepted.

Procedures for payment of application fees when applications are filed electronically are available on the electronic filing system. Payment of application fees for paper-filed applications may also be made by Electronic Payment provided that prior approval has been obtained from the Commission. Applicants interested in this option must first contact the Credit and Debt Management Center at (202) 418-1995 to make the necessary arrangements.

Applicants hand-delivering FCC Forms 303-S may receive dated receipt copies by presenting copies of the applications to the acceptance clerk at the time of delivery. For mailed-in applications, a "return copy" of the application should be furnished and clearly marked as a "return copy." The applicant should attach this copy to a stamped, self-addressed envelope. Only one piece of paper per application will be stamped for receipt purposes.

For further information regarding the applicability of a fee, the amount of the fee, or the payment of the fee, applicants should consult the "Media Bureau Services Fee Filing Guide."

Item 4: Purpose of Application. This question requires that the applicant identify the purpose of the application and should identify whether a renewal is being filed or an amendment to a pending renewal is being filed.

Item 5: Facility Information. This question requires that the applicant identify whether it is licensed by the Commission as a commercial or noncommercial educational licensee. A licensee that merely elects to operate its station on a noncommercial basis is not considered to be a noncommercial educational license.

Item 6: Service and Community of License. The facility should be described by its service, call letters, and specific community of license or area as listed on the station's existing license. See 47 C.F.R. Section 74.1201(a), 74.701(a) and 74.701(f) for definition of an FM Translator, TV Translator and Low Power TV broadcast station, respectively. For purposes of Item 6a., AM, FM or TV stations, the location of the facility should be described in terms of the specific city or community to which the station is licensed. Translator and Low Power TV stations should specify the area the stations are licensed to serve.

If the applicant seeks to renew the license **only** for an individual FM or TV translator, Low Power TV, Low Power FM, or Class A TV station, the applicant should respond only to Item 6a. The applicant should identify the appropriate service and list the station's call letters, facility identification number, community of license or area, and state.

If the applicant seeks the joint renewal for an FM or TV translator station or LPTV station and its co-owned primary FM, TV, or LPTV station, the applicant should indicate "Yes" to Item 6b. and skip directly to Item 7. The applicant should provide information with regard to such translator station for which renewal is sought in response to Section V below.

Item 7: Other Authorizations. This question must be completed by a radio or television renewal applicant seeking to continue its authority to operate an FM Booster or TV Booster station in conjunction with the primary station. The FM or TV Booster station should be described in terms of its call letters and the name of the specific community which it serves.

INSTRUCTIONS FOR SECTION II: LEGAL INFORMATION

Item 1: Certification. Each applicant is responsible for the information that the application, instructions, and worksheets convey. As a key element in the Commission's streamlined licensing process, a certification that these materials have been reviewed and that each response is based on the applicant's review is required.

Items 2 and 3: Character Issues/Adverse Findings. Item 2 requires the applicant to certify that neither it nor any party to the application has had any interest in or connection with an application that was or is the subject of unresolved character issues. An applicant must disclose in response to Item 3 whether an adverse finding has been made with respect to the applicant or any party to the application regarding certain relevant non-broadcast matters. The Commission's character policies and litigation reporting requirements for broadcast applicants focus on misconduct that violates the Communications Act or a Commission rule or policy and on certain specified non-FCC misconduct. In responding to Items 2 and 3, applicants should review the Commission's character qualifications policies, which are fully set forth in Character Qualifications. 102 FCC 2d 1179 (1985), reconsideration denied, 1 FCC Rcd 421 (1986), as modified, 5 FCC Rcd 3252 (1990) and 7 FCC Rcd 6564 (1992).

Where the response to Item 2a. or 2b. is "No," the applicant must submit an exhibit that includes an identification of the party having had the interest, the call letters and location of the station or file number of the application or docket, and a description of the nature of the interest or connection, including relevant dates. The applicant should also fully explain why the unresolved character issue is not an impediment to a grant of this application.

In responding to Item 3, the applicant should consider any relevant adverse finding that occurred within the past ten years. Where that adverse finding was fully disclosed to the Commission in an application filed on behalf of this station or in another broadcast station application and the Commission, by specific ruling or by subsequent grant of the application, found the adverse finding not to be disqualifying, it need not be reported again and the assignee may respond "Yes" to this item. However, an adverse finding that has not been reported to the Commission and considered in connection with a prior application would require a "No" response.

Where the response to Item 3 is "No," the applicant must provide in an exhibit a full disclosure of the persons and matters involved, including an identification of the court or administrative body and the proceeding (by dates and file numbers), and the disposition of the litigation. Where the requisite information has been earlier disclosed in connection with another pending application, or as required by 47 C.F.R. Section 1.65(c), the applicant need only provide an identification of that previous submission by reference to the file number in the case of an application, the call letters of the station regarding which the application or Section 1.65 information was filed, and the date of filing. The assignee should also fully explain why the adverse finding is not an impediment to a grant of this application.

Item 4: FCC Violations During the Preceding License Term. Section 309(k) of the Communications Act of 1934, as amended, 47 U.S.C. Section 309(k) states that the Commission shall grant a license renewal application if it finds, with respect to that station, during the preceding license term, that: (1) the station has served the public interest, convenience, and necessity; (2) there have been no serious violations by the licensee of the Communications Act or the Commission's Rules; and (3) there have been no other violations of the Act or the Commission's rules, which, taken together, would constitute a pattern of abuse. This question asks the applicant to certify that, with respect to the station for which a renewal application is being submitted, there were no violations of the Communications Act of the Commission's Rules. If the renewal applicant has violated the Act or the Rules, it must respond "No" and submit an explanatory exhibit detailing the number and nature of the violations and any adjudication by the Commission (Notice of Violation, Forfeiture Order, etc.).

For purposes of this license renewal form only, an applicant is required to disclose only violations of the Communications Act of 1934, as amended, or the Rules of the Commission that occurred at the subject station during the license term, as preliminarily or finally determined by the Commission, staff, or a court of competent jurisdiction. This includes Notices of Violation, Notices of Apparent Liability, Forfeiture Orders, and other specific findings of Act or Rule violations. It does not include "violations" identified by the station itself or in conjunction with the station's participation in an Alternative Broadcast Inspection Program. In responding to this item, licensees should not submit any information concerning self-discovered or other "violations" that have not been identified by the Commission, staff, or court. Licensees are advised that the Commission may also consider other violations by the station that come to its attention in determining whether to grant this license renewal application.

Item 5: Alien Ownership and Control. Aliens, foreign governments and corporations, and corporations of which less than 80% of the capital stock is owned or voted by U.S. citizens are prohibited from holding a broadcast station license. Where a corporate licensee is directly or indirectly controlled by another corporation, of which less that 75% of that corporation's stock is owned by or voted by U.S. citizens, the Commission must consider whether denial of renewal would serve the public interest. Licensees are expected to employ reasonable, good faith methods to ensure the accuracy and completeness of their citizenship representations.

Item 6: Anti-Drug Abuse Act Certification. This question requires the applicant to certify that neither it nor any party to the application is subject to denial of federal benefits pursuant to the Anti-Drug Abuse Act of 1988. 21 U.S.C. Section 862.

Section 5301 of the Anti-Drug Abuse Act of 1988 provides federal and state court judges the discretion to deny federal benefits to individuals convicted of offenses consisting of the distribution or possession of controlled substances. Federal benefits within the scope of the statute include FCC authorizations. A "Yes" response to Item 6 constitutes a certification that neither the applicant nor any party to this application has been convicted of such an offense or, if it has, it is not ineligible to receive the authorization sought by this application because of Section 5301.

With respect to this question only, the term "party to the application" includes if the applicant is an individual, that individual; if the applicant is a corporation or unincorporated association, all officers, directors, or persons holding 5 percent or more of the outstanding stock or shares (voting and/or non-voting) of the applicant; all members if a membership association's and if the applicant is a partnership, all general partners and all limited partners, including both insulated and non-insulated limited partners, holding a 5 percent or more interest in the partnership.

INSTRUCTIONS FOR SECTION III: AM and FM Licensees Only

Item 1: Biennial Ownership Report. This question asks the renewal applicant to certify that it has filed with the Commission the biennial ownership reports required by 47 C.F.R. 73.3615. Each licensee of an AM, FM, and TV broadcast station shall file an Ownership Report on FCC Form 323 (commercial) or 323-E (noncommercial/educational) every two years on the anniversary of the date that its renewal application is required to be filed. Licensees owning more than one broadcast station with different anniversary dates need to file only one Report every two years on the anniversary of their choice, provided that they are not more than two years apart. A licensee with a current and unamended Report on file at the Commission may certify that it has reviewed its current Report and that it is accurate by validating electronically its previously filed report.

Note: FCC Form 323 and 323-E must be filed electronically. Paper versions of these forms will not be accepted for filing unless accompanied by an appropriate request for waiver of the electronic filing requirement. *See* 47C.F.R. Section 73.3615.

Item 2: EEO Program. Each licensee of an AM, FM and TV broadcast station is required to afford equal employment opportunity to all qualified persons and to refrain from discrimination in employment and related benefits on the basis of race, color, religion, national origin, etc. *See* 47 C.F.R. Section 73.2080. Pursuant to these requirements, a license renewal applicant whose station employs five or more full-time employees must file a report of its activities to ensure equal employment opportunity. If a station employment unit employs fewer than five full-time employees, no equal employment opportunity program information need be filed.

Additionally, each licensee must place in the station's public inspection file annually AND POST ON THE STATION'S WEBSITE, if any, a report containing lists of (1) all full-time vacancies filled during the preceding year, identified by job title; (2) for each such vacancy, the recruitment source(s) utilized to fill the vacancy, (including, if applicable, organizations entitled to notification pursuant to paragraph (c)(1)(ii) of this section, which should be separately identified), identified by name, address, contact person and telephone number; (3) the recruitment source that referred the hiree for each full-time vacancy during the preceding year; (4) data reflecting the total number of persons interviewed for full-time vacancies during the preceding year and the total number of interviewees referred by each recruitment source utilized in connection with such vacancies; and (5) a list and brief description of initiatives undertaken pursuant to Section 73.2080(c)(2) during the preceding year.

Item 3: Local Public File. Commercial and noncommercial educational AM and FM licensees must maintain certain documents pertaining to its station in a file that is to be kept at the station's main studio or other accessible place in the community of license. The file must be available for inspection by anyone during regular business hours. The documents to be maintained generally include applications for a construction permit and for license renewal, assignment or transfer of control; ownership and employment reports; and quarterly lists of the community issues most significantly addressed by the station's programming during the preceding three months. A complete listing of the required documents and their mandatory retention periods is set forth in 47 C.F.R. Sections 73.3526 and 73.3527. Applicants that have not so maintained their file should provide an exhibit identifying the items that are missing/late filed, and identifying steps taken to reconstruct missing information, and to prevent such problems in the future.

Item 4: Discontinued Operation. Section 312(g) of the Communications Act of 1934, 47 U.S.C. Section 312(g), states that if a broadcast station fails to transmit broadcast signals for any consecutive 12-month period, then the station license expires automatically, by operation of law, at the end of that 12-month period. The Commission has no discretion to reinstate a broadcast license that has expired pursuant to Section 312(g). *See OCC Acquisition, Inc.*, 17 FCC Rcd 6147 (2002). Additionally, a station that does cease broadcasting for nearly 12 months may not preserve its license by recommencing operation with unauthorized facilities. *See Letter to Idaho Broadcasting Consortium*, 16 FCC Rcd 1721 (M.M. Bur. 2001). Accordingly, this item requires the licensee to certify that the station was not silent for any consecutive 12-month period during the preceding license term. By answering "Yes" to this question, the applicant certifies that (1) it was not silent for any consecutive 12-month period during the preceding license term; and (2) if the station was silent for any period of time during the preceding license term, it resumed broadcasting *with authorized facilities* before 12 months from the date on which that station went silent. If the applicant cannot make this certification, its license renewal application will be dismissed and the Commission's data base will be amended to reflect the expiration of the station's license.

Item 5: Silent Station. The Commission will not review the license of a station that is not broadcasting. *See Birach Broadcasting Corporation*, 16 FCC Rcd 5015 (2001). "Broadcasting" means "the dissemination of radio communications intended to be received by the public." 47 U.S.C. Section 153(6). Accordingly, this item requires the applicant to certify that its commercial AM or FM broadcast station is currently transmitting signals intended to be received by the public. An application may not answer "Yes" to this question if the station is transmitting only "test signals."

Note: Noncommercial educational FM stations, while authorized for limited-time operation, are required to operate at least 36 hours per week, consisting of at least 5 hours of operation on at least 6 days of the week. Stations licensed to *educational institutions* are not required to operate on Saturday or Sunday or observe the minimum operating requirements during those days when school is not in session. 47 C.F.R. Section 73.561(a). [Licensees of noncommercial educational FM applicants adhering to these requirements may answer "Yes" to this question whether or not the station is on the air on the particular day on which the license renewal application is submitted electronically.]

Note: A noncommercial educational AM broadcast station is expected to provide continuous service except where causes beyond its control warrant interruption. Where causes beyond the control of the licensee make it impossible to continue operation, the station may discontinue operation for a period of 30 days without further authority from the FCC. However, notification of the discontinuance must be sent to the FCC in Washington, D.C. no later than 10 days after the discontinued operation. Failure to operate for a period of 30 days or more, except for causes beyond the control of the licensee, as well as the actual hours of operation during the entire license period, shall be taken into consideration in the renewal of the station's license. *See* 47 C.F.R. Section 73.1740(b).

Item 6: Environmental Effects. This question requires that the applicant either certify that its facility complies with the Commission's maximum permissible radiofrequency electromagnetic exposure limits for controlled and uncontrolled environments. Worksheet #1 includes specific subsections for RF exposure analysis. These pages are designed to facilitate and substantiate the certification. Their use is voluntary but strongly encouraged.

Note: Licensees are reminded that the Commission retains the authority to revoke any station license for a licensee's failure to satisfy the requirements of the National Environmental Policy Act, the National Historic Preservation Act, the Endangered Species Act, or other environmental statute, regulation, or directive at the time it sought authorization for the original construction or modification of its broadcast facilities. 47 U.S.C. Sections 312(a)(2) (authorizing the revocation of a station license "because of conditions coming to the attention of the Commission which would warrant it in refusing to grant a license or permit on an original application . . . .") See also FCC Form 301 Instructions, Page 11, "General Environmental" Worksheet.

RF Exposure Requirements. In 1996, the Commission adopted guidelines and procedures for evaluating environmental effects of RF emissions. All applications subject to environmental processing filed on or after October 15, 1997 must demonstrate compliance with these requirements. These guidelines incorporate two tiers of exposure limits:

> **General population/uncontrolled** exposure limits apply to situations in which the general public may be exposed or in which persons who are exposed as a consequence of their employment may not be made fully aware of the potential for exposure or cannot exercise control over their exposure. Members of the general public are always considered under this category when exposure is not employment-related.

> **Occupational/controlled** exposure limits apply to human exposure to RF fields when persons are exposed as a consequence of their employment and in which those persons who are exposed have been made fully aware of the potential for exposure and can exercise control over their exposure. These limits also apply where exposure is of a transient nature as a result of incidental passage through a location where exposure levels may be above the general populations/uncontrolled limits as long as the exposed person has been made fully aware of the potential for exposure and can exercise control over his or her exposure by leaving the area or some other appropriate means.

The guidelines are explained in more detail in OET Bulletin 65, entitled <u>Evaluating Compliance with FCC Guidelines for Human Exposure to Radiofrequency Electromagnetic Fields</u>, Edition 97-01, released August, 1997, and <u>Supplement A: Additional Information for Radio and Television Broadcast Stations</u> (referred to here as "OET Bulletin 65" and "Supplement A," respectively). Both OET Bulletin 65 and Supplement A can be viewed and/or downloaded from the FCC Internet site at http://www/fcc.gov/oet/rfsafety. Copies can also be purchased from the Commission's duplicating/research contractor, Qualex International, Room CY-B402, 445 12th Street, SW, Washington, D.C. 20554 (telephone: (202) 863-2893. Additional information may be obtained from the RF Safety Group at rfsafety@fcc.gov or (202) 418-2464 or from the FCC Call Center at 1-888-CALL FCC (225-5322).

The RF worksheets and tables appended to Worksheet #1 below will enable certain categories of stations to determine whether or not the proposed facility will have a significant environmental impact as defined by Section 1.1307. Some, but not all, stations will be able to use the RF worksheets. Generally, the RF worksheets can only be used in the following situations: (1) single use tower; (2) single tower with several FM/FM translators; or (3) a multiple tower AM array with no other user co-located within the array. Additionally, the RF worksheets can be used in regard to an AM station only if access to the AM station is restricted by a fence or other barrier that will preclude casual or inadvertent access to the site and warning signs are posted at appropriate intervals describing the potential for RF exposure. *See* "RF Exposure Compliance Worksheet Instructions" for more detail on eligibility.

If after using the worksheets the applicant finds that levels will exceed the RF guidelines, levels may still be acceptable based on a more detailed evaluation of a number of variables (*e.g.*, antenna radiation patterns or measurement data). In that case, the applicant must submit an exhibit to the application that explains why the proposed facility does not exceed the RF radiation exposure guidelines at locations where humans are likely to be present, or describing measures or circumstances which will prevent or discourage humans from entering those areas where the RF exposure exceeds the guidelines (*e.g.*, fencing or remote location). The guidelines are explained in more detail in OET Bulletin 65.

If the applicant is not eligible to use the worksheets, it is not an indication that the proposed facility will cause excessive exposure. Generally, applicants that are not able to use the worksheets will need to utilize more complex calculations or measurements to demonstrate compliance. For this reason, applicants who are not eligible to use the worksheets should consider seeking the assistance of a qualified consulting engineer in determining whether the proposed facility will meet the RF exposure guidelines.

WORKSHEET #1: ENVIRONMENTAL

Some, but not all, applicants for AM and FM facilities will be able to use the RF worksheets. Generally, an AM or FM applicant can use the RF worksheets if: (1) it is the only user on its tower; (2) its station is one of several FM/FM translator stations located on a single tower; or (3) its station uses a multiple-tower AM array but no other user is co-located within the array. Additionally, the RF worksheets can be used in regard to an AM station only if access to the AM station is restricted by use of a fence or other barrier that will preclude casual or inadvertent access to the site and warning signs are posted at appropriate intervals describing the potential for RF exposure.

If an applicant cannot use the RF worksheets, it may show its compliance with RF guidelines in other ways, as detailed in OET Bulletin 65.

If the worksheets indicate that an applicant exceeds acceptable RF levels, it does not necessarily mean that the proposed station does not or cannot meet the Commission's RF requirements. The worksheets are based on generalized "worst case" presumptions. It may be that a more individualized evaluation of the proposed station (possibly with the help of a consulting engineer) will demonstrate that RF levels are acceptable. Among the individual factors that may be relevant are antenna radiation patterns, actual RF measurements, barriers/precautions that prevent access to high RF areas, etc. These factors are also explained in OET Bulletin 65.

Applicants satisfying the RF requirements on the basis of such non-worksheet factors should submit a detailed explanation demonstrating their compliance. Otherwise, applicants should submit an Environmental Assessment, as explained in 47 C.F.R. Section 1.1311, explaining the environmental consequences of the proposed operation.

RF EXPOSURE COMPLIANCE WORKSHEET/INSTRUCTIONS

Who may use these worksheets?

1. A directional AM station (i.e., one using a multiple tower array) that does not share its towers with any other non-excluded RF sources (including, but not limited to FM or TV transmitting antennas) and is located more than 315 meters (1.034 feet) from any other tower or non-excluded RF radiation sources; or

2. A non-directional AM station located on a single-use tower more that 315 meters (1,034 feet) from any other tower or other non-excluded RF radiation sources; or

3. An FM station on a single tower that may or may not support other FM stations (including FM translators and boosters) and that is more than 315 meters (1,034 feet) from any other tower or non-excluded RF sources.

4. An FM translator on a single tower that may or may not support other FM stations (including FM translators and boosters) that is more than 315 meters (1,034 feet) from any other tower or other non-excluded RF sources.

Ineligible Sites.

Please note that the applicant cannot use these worksheets if any of the following apply:

1. The application is for a television or digital television facility;

2. There are other towers or supporting structures with non-excluded RF sources within 315 meters of the tower; *See* 47 C.F.R. Section 1.1307(b)

3. There are TV antennas and/or other RF sources on the tower other than AM or FM antennas that are not categorically excluded from environmental processing by 47 C.F.R. Section 1.1307;

4. There is an FM, TV or other non-excluded RF source co-located within a multiple tower AM array;

5. The tower is located at a site where the terrain or a building or other inhabited structure (other than a transmitter building) within a 315 meter radius is higher than the level of the terrain at the base of the tower. **(Note:** Sites with transmitter buildings at the base of the tower are considered "eligible" provided that procedures are established in accordance with the methods described in OET Bulletin 65 to protect persons with access to such buildings from RF exposure in excess of the FCC-adopted limits.); or

6. AM towers where access is not restricted by fencing or other barrier that preclude casual or inadvertent access to the site and warning signs are not included at appropriate intervals describing the potential for RF exposure.

The above categories have been excluded from the RF worksheets not because of a propensity to cause excessive RF radiation, but because a determination of their compliance involves more complex calculations and measurements. If you are not eligible to use the RF worksheets, or elect not to use them, before reaching a determination with respect to your facilities you should review **OET Bulletin 65 and Supplement A** in order to properly evaluate your facility for compliance with the RF guidelines. The bulletin provides information and assistance on the RF guidelines, prediction methods, measurement procedures and instrumentation, methods for controlling exposure, and reference material. It will instruct the applicant on the type of data which may demonstrate compliance with the Commission's RF guidelines in support of your response. If you continue to have trouble evaluating your site after consulting the Bulletin, you may want to seek the assistance of a qualified engineer in determining whether these facilities meet the FCC RF exposure guidelines.

Other Evaluations

These worksheets represent "worst case" calculations, and as such, should be used in your initial attempt to determine compliance. If use of the worksheet indicates that you exceed the RF guidelines, levels may still be acceptable based on more detailed evaluation of variables such as antenna type and vertical radiation patterns. In this case you may submit a statement explaining why your facilities do not exceed the RF exposure guidelines at locations where humans are likely to be present, or describing those measures or circumstances which will prevent or discourage humans from entering those areas where the RF levels exceed the guidelines or which will otherwise control access in accordance with the time-averaging limits described in the guidelines. See OET Bulletin 65 and Supplement A. This statement may include:

(i)   antenna radiation patterns showing that the site complies with the guidelines described in OET Bulletin 65;

(ii)   measurements that show the site to comply with the FCC-adopted guidelines;

(iii)   a description of what warning signs, fences or other barriers preclude excessive RF exposure;

(iv)   any other statement necessary to demonstrate compliance with the RF guidelines.

Federal Communications Commission
Washington, D.C. 20554

Approved by OMB
3060-0110

How to Use RF Worksheets

Attached are:

Worksheet #1 – FM, FM translator & FM booster
Worksheet #1A-Multiple FM User Tower
Worksheet #2 – AM
Worksheet #2A – Multiple Tower AM Array
AM Fence Distance Tables

FM Contributors:

a.   **Single Use FM or FM translator tower** – Use **Worksheet #1** to determine compliance with the FCC RF exposure limits.

b.   **Multiple – use FM (including translator & booster)** – Use **Worksheet #1A for each FM facility on the tower to obtain an approximate power and antenna height** and **complete Worksheet #1 as above.**

AM Contributors:

a.   **Single Tower Site:** Use **Worksheet #2** to determine if the distance to the fence or other restrictive barrier provides adequate protection to the general public pursuant to FCC guidelines.

b.   **Multiple Tower Site** – Use **Worksheet #2 for each tower in the array** to determine if the tower is adequately distanced from the fence (or other restrictive barrier). This determination may be made by either of the following methods:

i.   a "worst case" prediction could be made by assuming that all transmitted power is radiated from each tower. Use **Worksheet #2A** to list the power and fence distance for each tower. Then use **Worksheet #2** for each tower to determine compliance with the FCC guidelines for the single tower.

ii.   use the actual transmitted power for each tower. Use **Worksheet #2A** to list transmitted powers and restriction distances for each tower. Then, use **Worksheet #2** for each tower to determine compliance with the FCC guidelines for the single tower.

If any single tower is not adequately distanced from the fence or restrictive barrier, you may not continue to use these worksheets.

CAUTION: Even if you conclude from the use of these worksheets that human exposure to RF electromagnetic fields is consistent with our guidelines, be aware that each site user must also meet requirements with respect to "on-tower" or other exposure by workers at the site (including RF exposure on one tower caused by sources on another tower or towers). These requirements include, but are not limited to the reduction or cessation of transmitter power when persons have access to the site, tower, or antenna. Such procedures must be coordinated among all tower users. **See OET Bulletin 65 for further details.**

RF Worksheet #1 – FM (including translators & boosters)

PLEASE COPY BEFORE USING. THE DETERMINATION OF COMPLIANCE MAY INVOLVE REPEATED CALCULATIONS. IF LOCATED ON A MULTIPLE FM USER TOWER, PLEASE COMPLETE RF WORKSHEET 1A BEFORE PROCEEDING.

EFFECTIVE RADIATION CENTER HEIGHT

Enter proposed "height of radiation center above ground" OR as listed in Line 1 _____ m (1)
of Worksheet 1A.

Is antenna supporting structure located on the roof of a building? (check one)

☐ Yes   ☐ No   (2)

If Line 2 is "Yes" enter the building height measured at the base of the antenna
supporting structure in Line 3
If Line 2 is "No" enter "0" in Line 3...……..........._____ m   (3)
Subtract Line (3) from Line (1)...……. ...._____ m   (4)
Subtract the value 2.0 from Line (4)...................................... ...._____ m   (5)

TOTAL EFFECTIVE RADIATED POWER
(If "beam tilt" is utilized, list maximum values)

List Effective Radiated Power in the Horizontal Plane.............................…..……...._____ kW (6)
List Effective Radiated Power in the Vertical Plane...............................….……..._____ kW (7)
Add Lines (6) and (7) OR list value from Line 2 in Worksheet 1A…….....…..._____ kW (8)

PERCENTAGE OF FCC RF LIMIT(S) FOR MAXIMUM PERMISSIBLE EXPOSURE
Multiply Line (8) by 33.41 ...._____ (9)
Multiply the value listed in Line (5) by itself...............................…....…….._____ (10)
Divide Line (9) by Line (10) ....….._____ (11)
Multiply Line (11) by (100) ....…….......….._____ (12)

DETERMINATION OF COMPLIANCE WITH CONTROLLED/OCCUPATIONAL LIMIT

Does Line (12) exceed 100%..   ☐ Yes ☐ No (13)

IF YOU ANSWERED "YES" IN LINE (13), THE WORKSHEETS MAY NOT BE USED IN THIS CASE.*

IF YOU ANSWERED "NO" IN LINE (13), THEN THE SITE SHOULD COMPLY WITH THE FCC'S CONTROLLED/OCCUPATIONAL RF EXPOSURE LIMITS FOR GROUND LEVEL EXPOSURE

*In this case, you may need to prepare an Environmental Assessment. See Instructions for Section III-C FCC Form 301.

DETERMINATION OF COMPLIANCE WITH THE UNCONTROLLED/GENERAL POPULATION LIMIT
Does Line (12) exceed 20%.. ☐ Yes ☐ No (14)

IF YOU ANSWERED "NO" IN LINE (14), THEN THE SITE SHOULD COMPLY WITH THE FCC'S UNCONTROLLED/GENERAL POPULATION RF EXPOSURE LIMITS FOR GROUND LEVEL EXPOSURE. NO FURTHER STUDY REQUIRED.

IF YOU ANSWERED "YES" IN LINE (14), CONTINUE.

ROOFTOP WITH RESTRICTED ACCESS.

If you answered "YES" in Line (14) and "YES" in Line (2) (indicating that the tower is located on the roof of a building), and the general public is not allowed access to the rooftop level, repeat lines 5 through 12, entering the value in Line (1) directly in Line (4). (If Multiple FM Use tower, recalculations should be in accordance with instructions on Worksheet #1A.) **Otherwise, go to the next section.**

Upon recalculation, does Line (12) exceed 20%... ☐ Yes ☐ No (15)

IF YOU ANSWERED "YES" IN LINE (15), THE WORKSHEETS MAY NOT BE USED IN THIS CASE. *

IF YOU ANSWERED "NO" IN LINE (15), THEN THE AREA AT GROUND LEVEL SHOULD COMPLY WITH THE FCC'S UNCONTROLLED/GENERAL POPULATION EXPOSURE LIMIT. NO FURTHER STUDY REQUIRED.

ACCESS TO BASE OF TOWER RESTRICTED BY FENCING.

If the tower is not located on the roof of a building, is the base of the tower surrounded by fencing or other restrictive barrier and are appropriate warning signs posted on the fence that adequately detail the nature of the RF exposure environment contained therein?........

☐ Yes ☐ No (16)

IF YOU ANSWERED "NO" IN LINE (16), THE WORKSHEET MAY NOT BE USED IN THIS CASE.*

If you answered "Yes" in Line (16), what is the distance from the base

of the tower to the fence or barrier at its nearest point............... .... _____ m (17)
Multiply Line (9) (as calculated previously) by 5............................….. _____ (18)
Subtract Line (10) (as calculated previously) from Line (18).................. _____ (19)
Take the square root of Line (19)..….. _____ m (20)

Is Line (20) less than or equal to Line (17)................................…....... ☐ Yes ☐ No (21)

IF YOU ANSWERED "YES" IN LINE (21), THEN THE RF FIELD OUTSIDE THE FENCE COMPLIES WITH THE FCC'S UNCONTROLLED/GENERAL POPULATION EXPOSURE LIMIT. NO FURTHER STUDY REQUIRED.

IF YOU ANSWERED "NO" IN LINE (21), THE WORKSHEETS MAY NOT BE USED IN THIS CASE.*

* In this case, you may need to prepare an Environmental Assessment. See instructions for Section III-C of FCC Form 301.

Federal Communications Commission
Washington, DC 20554

Approved by OMB
3060-0110

RF WORKSHEET #1A –Multiple FM Use Tower

The procedure below will allow for a "worst-case" determination to be made in situations where several FM stations share a common tower. This determination is based upon the "worst case" assumption that all RF energy is emanating from a single antenna located at the same height (i.e., antenna center of radiation above ground level) as the lowest user on the tower.

Complete for all call signs.

For each call sign, **the total** of the Horizontal and the Vertical ERP's must be used. If "beam tilt" is utilized, list maximum values.

COLUMN 1 CALL SIGN	COLUMN 2 HEIGHT OF ANTENNA RADIATION CENTER ABOVE GROUND LEVEL	COLUMN 3 TOTAL EFFECTIVE RADIATED POWER (HORIZONTAL AND VERTICAL)
	meters	kilowatts
	meters	kilowatts
	meters	kilowatts
	meters	kilowatts
	meters	kilowatts
	meters	kilowatts

List the smallest value in Column 2……………………………………....._____   m (1)
List the total of all values in Column 3………………………………….._____   kW (2)

The value listed in line (1) above must be used in line (1) on Worksheet 1.
The value listed in line (2) above must be used in line (8) on Worksheet 1.

Now complete worksheet 1 (except for lines 6 and 7).

311

RF WORKSHEET #2: AM

PLEASE COPY THIS WORKSHEET PRIOR TO USING. IN THE CASE OF A MULTIPLE TOWER ARRAY, A COPY IS NECESSARY FOR EACH TOWER LISTED IN RF WORKSHEET #2A. See AM Instruction b. to "How to Use RF worksheets" on page 5 of Appendix A.

SINGLE TOWER

Enter the transmitted power...……..…………._____ kW (1)
Enter the distance from the tower to the nearest point of the fence or other
   restrictive barrier enclosing the tower………………………. ………………...……._____ m (2)

DETERMINATION OF WAVELENGTH

Method 1: Electrical Height

The tower height in wavelength may be obtained from the electrical height in degrees of the radiator.

Electrical height of the radiator………………………………………………._____ degrees (3a)
Divide Line 3(a) by 360 degrees………………....…….…………………….._____ wavelength (3b)

Method 2: Physical Height

Alternatively, the wavelength may be obtained from the physical height of the radiator above the tower base and the frequency of the station.

Overall height of the radiator above the tower base…………………………....._____ m (4a)
List the station's frequency………………………….…….………………......_____ kHz (4b)
Divide 300,000 by Line (4b)…………………………………………….…....._____ m (4c)
Divide Line (4a) by Line 4(c) ……….… …………………………..………......_____ wavelength (4d)

REQUIRED RESTRICTION DISTANCE

Use the appropriate AM fence distance table based on the wavelength determined in either Line (3b) or Line (4d) above. If the transmitted power is not listed in the table, use next highest valu e (e.g., if the transmitted power is 2.5 kW, use the fence value in the 5 kW column).

List the fence distance obtained from the appropriate table…………………..._____ m (5)

Is the value listed in Line (5) less than or equal to the value listed in Line (2)? ☐ Yes   ☐ No   (6)

If line (6) is "Yes," are warning signs posted at appropriate intervals which
describe the nature of the potential hazard? ☐ Yes   ☐ No   (7)

IF EITHER LINE (6) OR LINE (7) WAS ANSWERED "NO", you may need to prepare an Environmental Assessment. However, in order to determine the need for such an Assessment please see the **NOTE** on page 5 of Appendix A. If after consideration of such factors as the antenna radiation pattern, measurement data and the barriers which restrict access you conclude that an Environmental Assessment is required, please see Section I of the instructions to this worksheet entitled "Environmental Assessment."

IF BOTH LINE (6) AND LINE (7) WERE ANSWERED "YES", it appears that this tower complies with the FCC guidelines with respect to the general public. Please be aware, that each site user must also meet requirements with respect to "on-tower" or other exposure by workers at the site (including RF fields caused by other facilities on the tower, or RF fields caused by facilities on another tower or towers). These requirements include, but are not limited to the reduction or cessation of transmitter power when persons have access to the site, tower, or antenna. **See OET Bulletin 65 for more details**.

RF WORKSHEET #2A Multiple Tower AM Array

Do not use this table if there are FM, TV or other non-excluded RF sources on any single tower of the array.

Tower Number	Transmitted Power (kW)	Distance to Fence (meters)
1		
2		
3		
4		
5		
6		
7		
8		
9		
10		
11		
12		

If each tower listed above meets the distance requirements of the worksheet #2, it appears this tower complies with the FCC guidelines with respect to the general public. Please be aware, that each site user must also meet requirements with respect to "on-tower" or other exposure by workers at the site. These requirements include, but are not limited to the reduction or cessation of transmitter power when persons have access to the site, tower, or antenna. **See OET Bulletin 65 for more details.**

If the distance from the base of the tower to the fence is less than the value listed above, you may need to prepare an Environmental Assessment. However, in order to determine the need for such an Assessment please see the **NOTE** on page 5 of Appendix A. If after consideration of such factors as the antenna radiation pattern, measurement data and the barriers which restrict access you conclude that an Environmental Assessment is required, please see Section I of the instructions to this worksheet entitled "Environmental Assessment."

AM FENCE DISTANCE TABLES

TABLE 1. Predicted Distances for Compliance with FCC Limits: 0.1-0.2 Wavelength

Frequency (kHz)	Transmitter Power (kW)			
	50	10	5	1
	Predicted Distance for Compliance with FCC Limits (meters)			
535-740	13	7	6	3
750-940	12	7	5	3
950-1140	11	6	5	3
1150-1340	10	6	5	3
1350-1540	10	6	5	3
1550-1705	10	6	5	3

TABLE 2. Predicted Distances for Compliance with FCC Limits: 0.21-0.4 Wavelength

Frequency (kHz)	Transmitter Power (kW)			
	50	10	5	1
	Predicted Distance for Compliance with FCC Limits (meters)			
535-740	4	2	2	1
750-940	4	2	2	1
950-1140	4	2	2	1
1150-1340	4	2	2	1
1350-1540	4	2	2	1
1550-1705	5	2	2	1

TABLE 3. Predicted Distances for Compliance with FCC Limits: 0.41-0.55 Wavelength

Frequency (kHz)	Transmitter Power (kW)			
	50	10	5	1
	Predicted Distance for Compliance with FCC Limits (meters)			
535-740	4	3	2	2
750-940	4	2	2	2
950-1140	4	2	2	1
1150-1340	4	2	2	2
1350-1540	4	2	2	2
1550-1705	4	3	2	1

TABLE 4. Predicted Distances for Compliance with FCC Limits: 0.56-6255 Wavelength

Frequency (kHz)	Transmitter Power (kW)			
	50	10	5	1
	Predicted Distance for Compliance with FCC Limits (meters)			
535-740	4	3	2	1
750-940	4	2	2	1
950-1140	4	2	2	1
1150-1340	4	2	2	1
1350-1540	4	2	2	1
1550-1705	4	2	2	2

Approved by OMB
3060-0110

INSTRUCTIONS FOR SECTION IV – To be Completed by TV and Class A TV licensees only.

Item 1: Biennial Ownership Report. This question asks the renewal applicant to certify that it has filed with the Commission the biennial ownership reports required by 47 C.F.R. 73.3615. Each licensee of an AM, FM, and TV broadcast station shall file an Ownership Report on FCC Form 323 (commercial) or 323-E (noncommercial/educational) every two years on the anniversary of the date that its renewal application is required to be filed. Licensees owning more than one broadcast station with different anniversary dates need to file only one Report every two years on the anniversary of their choice, provided that they are not more than two years apart. A licensee with a current and unamended Report on file at the Commission may certify that it has reviewed its current Report and that it is accurate by validating electronically its previously filed report.

Note: FCC Form 323 and 323-E must be filed electronically. Paper versions of these forms will not be accepted for filing unless accompanied by an appropriate request for waiver of the electronic filing requirement.

Item 2: EEO Program. Each licensee of an AM, FM and TV broadcast station is required to afford equal employment opportunity to all qualified persons and to refrain from discrimination in employment and related benefits on the basis of race, color, religion, national origin, etc. *See* 47 C.F.R. Section 73.2080. Pursuant to these requirements, a license renewal applicant whose station employs five or more full-time employees must file a report of its activities to ensure equal employment opportunity. If a station employment unit employs fewer than five full-time employees, no equal employment opportunity program information need be filed.

Additionally, each licensee must place in the station's public inspection file annually AND POST ON THE STATION'S WEBSITE, if any, a report containing lists of (1) all full-time vacancies filled during the preceding year, identified by job title; (2) for each such vacancy, the recruitment source(s) utilized to fill the vacancy, (including, if applicable, organizations entitled to notification pursuant to paragraph (c)(1)(ii) of this section, which should be separately identified), identified by name, address, contact person and telephone number; (3) the recruitment source that referred the hiree for each full-time vacancy during the preceding year; (4) data reflecting the total number of persons interviewed for full-time vacancies during the preceding year and the total number of interviewees referred by each recruitment source utilized in connection with such vacancies; and (5) a list and brief description of initiatives undertaken pursuant to Section 73.2080(c)(2) during the preceding year.

Item 3: Local Public File. Commercial and noncommercial educational AM and FM licensees must maintain certain documents pertaining to its station in a file that is to be kept at the station's main studio. The file must be available for inspection by anyone during regular business hours. The documents to be maintained generally include applications for a construction permit and for license renewal, assignment or transfer of control; ownership and employment reports; and quarterly lists of the community issues most significantly addressed by the station's programming during the preceding three months. A complete listing of the required documents and their mandatory retention periods is set forth in 47 C.F.R. Sections 73.3526 and 73.3527. Applicants that have not so maintained their file should provide an exhibit identifying the Items that are missing/late filed, and identifying steps taken to reconstruct missing information, and to prevent such problems in the future.

Item 4: Violent Programming. This question should be completed by commercial TV and Class A TV applicants. On February 8, 1996 the Telecommunications Act of 1996, Pub. L. No. 104-104, 110 Stat. 56 (1996) was approved. That legislation, among other things, amended Section 308 of the Communications Act of 1934 to require television broadcast station renewal applicants to submit a summary of complaints received from the public regarding violent programming aired by their stations. Licensee certifies that no written comments or suggestions have been received from the public that comment on its station's programming and characterize that programming as constituting violent programming.

Item 5: Children's Programming Commercial Limitations. Commercial TV and Class A commercial television licensees must limit the amount of commercial matter in "children's programming", which is defined for this purpose as programming originally produced and broadcast primarily for an audience of children 12 years of age and under. The children's programming commercial limitations are no more than 12 minutes of commercial matter per hour on weekdays, and no more than 10.5 minutes of commercials on weekends. The limits also apply *pro rata* to children's programs which are 5 minutes or more and which are not part of a longer block of children's programming. There are no restrictions on how commercials within the limits are configured within an hour's block of children's programming, *i.e.,* it is not necessary to prorate the commercial limits for separate children's programs within the hour.

Item 6: Children's Programming. Each commercial TV and Class A TV licensee is required to describe in its renewal application its efforts to serve the educational and information needs of children. Programming directed to the educational and informational needs of children is an identifiable unit of program material that is not a commercial or promotional announcement, that is originally produced and broadcast for an audience of children 16 years of age and under, and that furthers the positive development of the child in any respect, including, but not limited to, the child's cognitive/intellectual or emotional/social needs.

Each year, on a quarterly basis, each commercial TV and Class A TV licensee is required to prepare and electronically file a Children's Television Programming Report (FCC Form 398), setting forth the efforts made by the licensee during the quarter, as well as efforts planned for the next quarter, to serve the educational and informational needs of the children. FCC Form 398 is required to be filed with the Commission and a copy placed in the station's public inspection file by the tenth day of the preceding calendar quarter (*i.e.,* by April 10 for the first quarterly report; by July 10 for the second quarterly report; by October 10 for the third quarterly report; and by January 10 for the fourth quarterly report). Incorporating by reference previously filed FCC Form 398s satisfies the children's program information thought to be elicited by the FCC Form 303-S.

Item 7: CORE Programming. CORE Programming is defined as programming that is specifically designed to serve the educational and informational needs of children and that also satisfies each of the following criteria:

(1) the program has serving the educational and informational needs of children ages 16 and under as a significant purpose;
(2) the program is aired between the hours of 7:00 a.m. and 10 p.m.;
(3) the program is a regularly scheduled weekly program;
(4) the program is at least 30 minutes in length;
(5) the educational and information objective of the program and the target child audience are specified in writing in the licensee's Children's Television Programming Report, as described in 47 C.F.R. Section 73.3526(a)(8)(iii); and
(6) instructions for listing the program as educational and informational, including an indication of the age group for which the program is intended, are provided to publishers of program guides.

When the licensee has broadcasted three hours per week (averaged over a six-month period) of CORE Programming, it will be deemed to have satisfied its obligation to meet the educational and informational needs of children. A licensee will also be deemed to have satisfied this obligation (and be similarly eligible for Commission staff approval of its children's programming showing), where the licensee sets forth in an exhibit that it has aired an assortment of different types of educational and informational programming that, while somewhat less than three hours per week of CORE Programming, demonstrates a level of commitment to educating and informing children that it is at least equivalent to airing three hours per week of CORE Programming.

Items 8, 9, and 10: To assist parents in planning and selecting programs for their children to watch, the Commission has established various public information initiatives. In accord with these initiatives, a licensee is required to identify CORE Programming at the time those programs are aired in a form that is at the sole discretion of the licensee; to disseminate information identifying the station's CORE Programming to publishers of program guides and listings; and to publicize the existence and location where the public can access information regarding the station's informational and educational children's programming efforts.

Item 11: An applicant may provide any other comments or information it wishes the Commission to consider in evaluating whether the licensee has met its obligations under the Children's Television Act and the Commission's rules. This may include, but is not limited to, information on any non-CORE educational and informational programming that the station plans to air, as well as information on any existing or proposed non-broadcast activities that the licensee believes enhance the educational and informational value to children of the licensee's educational programming.

Item 12: Continued Class A Eligibility. On November 29, 1999, the Community Broadcasters Protection Act of 1999 was signed into law. That legislation provides that a low power television licensee may convert the secondary status of its station to the new Class A status, provided it can satisfy certain statutorily-established criteria. To become eligible for a Class A certificate of eligibility, the licensee's station must, during the 90-day period ending November 28, 1999, have: (1) broadcast a minimum of 18 hours per day; (2) broadcast an average of at least three hours per week of programming produced within the market area served by the station or by a group of commonly-controlled low power television stations; and (3) been in compliance with the Commission's regulations applicable to the low power television service. The legislation also provided that a licensee obtaining Class A designation shall continue to be accorded primary status as a television broadcaster, as long as its station continues to meet the requirements of (1) and (2) above.

Item 13: Discontinued Operations. Section 312(g) of the Communications Act of 1934, 47 U.S.C. Section 312(g), states that if a broadcast station fails to transmit broadcast signals for any consecutive 12-month period, then the station license expires automatically, by operation of law, at the end of that 12-month period. The Commission has no discretion to reinstate a broadcast license that has expired pursuant to Section 312(g). *See OCC Acquisition, Inc.*, 17 FCC Rcd 6147 (2002). Additionally, a station that does cease broadcasting for nearly 12 months may not preserve its license by recommencing operation with unauthorized facilities. *See Letter to Idaho Broadcasting Consortium*. 16 FCC Rcd 1721 (M.M. Bur. 2001). Accordingly, this Item requires the licensee to certify that the station was not silent for any consecutive 12-month period during the preceding license term. By answering "Yes" to this question, the applicant is considered to be certifying that: (1) it was not silent for any consecutive 12-month period during the preceding license term; and (2) if the station was silent for any period of time during the preceding license term, it resumed broadcasting *with authorized facilities* before 12 months from the date on which that station went silent. If the applicant cannot make this certification, its license renewal application will be dismissed and the Commission's data base will be amended to reflect the expiration of the station's license.

Item 14: Silent Station. The Commission will not review the license of a station that is not broadcasting. *See Birach Broadcasting Corporation*, 16 FCC Rcd 5015 (2001). "Broadcasting" means "the dissemination of radio communications intended to be received by the public." 47 C.F.R. 153(6). Accordingly, this Item requires the applicant to certify that its commercial TV or Class A TV broadcast station is currently transmitting signals intended to be received by the public. An application may not answer "Yes" to this question if the station is transmitting only "test signals."

Note: A noncommercial educational TV broadcast station is expected to provide continuous service, except where causes beyond its control warrant interruption. Where causes beyond the control of the licensee make it impossible to continue operation, the station may discontinue operation for a period of 30 days without further authority from the FCC. However, notification of the discontinuance must be sent to the FCC in Washington, D.C. no later than 10 days after the discontinued operation. Failure to operate for a period of 30 days or more, except for causes beyond the control of the licensee, as well as the actual hours of operation during the entire license period, shall be taken into consideration in the renewal of the station's license. *See* 47 C.F.R. Section 73.1740(b).

Item 15: Environmental Effects. TV and Class A TV renewal applications must review the instructions for Section III, Item 5, of this form before completing this item.

Item 16: Local TV Ownership Waiver. Section 73.3555(b) of the Commission Rules limits the number of full-power commercial television broadcast stations in the same Nielsen Designated Market Area (DMA) in which a licensee may have a cognizable interest. That rule, however, may be waived by the Commission in cases where the station is "failing." The Commission presumes a waiver is in the public interest where the licensee has demonstrated that the station to be acquired has had a low all-day audience share, its financial condition is poor, and its acquisition will produce public interest benefits. In DMA's with 11 or fewer full-power commercial and noncommercial educational stations, the Commission will also consider waiver of its proscription of the common ownership of more than one of the four top-ranked commercial television stations in the market for "marginal" – but not yet "failing" stations. At renewal time, the licensee must briefly describe the "failing" or "marginal" station waiver granted by the Commission and submit a specific, factual showing of the program-related benefits that have accrued to the public as a result of that waiver.

INSTRUCTIONS FOR SECTION V: To Be Completed By FM and TV Translator and Low Power TV Licensees Only

Item 1. Station Information. The equipment should identify the FM and TV translator and LPTV station(s) for which license renewal is requested. Licensees must specify the station's community of license, call letters, and facility identifier.

Item 2. Operational Status. A FM, TV translator, or LPTV station is expected to provide continuous service, except where causes beyond its control warrant interruption. Where causes beyond the control of the licensee make it impossible to continue operation, the station may discontinue operation for a period of 30 days without further authority from the FCC. However, notification of the discontinuance must be sent to the FCC no later than 10 days after the discontinued operation. Failure to operate for a period of 30 days or more, except for causes beyond the control of the licensee, shall be deemed evidence of discontinuation of operation and the licensee of the translator or LPTV station may be cancelled at the discretion of the FCC. See 47 C.F.R. Sections 74.763 and 74.1263. Item 2 requires licensee to certify that it is on the air.

Section 325(a) of the Communications Act of 1934, as amended, prohibits the rebroadcast of the programs of a broadcast station without the express authority of the originating station. Where the renewal applicant is not the licensee of the originating station, written authority must be obtained prior to any rebroadcasting. Also, where the licensee has changed the station being rebroadcast, written notification must be made to the Commission in accordance with 47 C.F.R. Section 74.784 or 74.1251.

Item 2(a). Requires an FM Translator, TV Translator and LPTV licensee to certify compliance with this requirement. When the primary station is co-owned, the applicant also should answer "Yes" to this Item.

Item 3a. The provisions of 47 C.F.R Section 74.1232(d) provide that an authorization for an other area FM translator (*i.e.,* **FM translator** station whose coverage contour extends beyond the protected contour of the commercial primary station) will not be granted to the licensee of a commercial FM radio broadcast station, or to any person or entity having any interest or connection with the primary FM station. For the purposes of this rule, interested and connected parties extend to group owners, corporate parents, shareholders, officers, directors, employees, general and limited partners, family members and business associates.

Item 3b. The provisions of 47 C.F.R. Section 74.2132(e) provide that an authorization for an other area FM translator (*i.e.,* **FM translator** station whose coverage contour extends beyond the protected contour of the commercial primary station) shall not receive any support, before, during or after construction, either directly or indirectly, from the commercial primary FM radio broadcast station, or from any person or entity having any interest or connection with the primary FM station. For the purposes of this rule, interested and connected parties extend to group owners, corporate parents, shareholders, officers, directors, employees, general and limited partners, family members, business associates, and advertisers.

Item 4. Each licensee of an LPTV broadcast station is required to afford equal employment opportunity to all qualified persons and to refrain from discrimination in employment and related benefits on the basis of race, color, religion, national origin, etc. *See* 47 C.F.R. Section 73.2080. Pursuant to these requirements, a license renewal applicant whose station employs five or more full-time employees must file a report of its activities to ensure equal employment opportunity. If a station employment unit employs fewer than five full-time employees, no equal employment opportunity program information need be filed. Additionally, each licensee must maintain with its station's records, AND POST ON THE STATION'S WEBSITE, if any, an annual report containing lists of (1) all full-time vacancies filled during the preceding year, identified by job title, (2) for each such vacancy, the recruitment source(s) utilized to fill the vacancy, (including, if applicable, organizations entitled to notification pursuant to paragraph (c)(1)(ii) of this section, which should be separately identified), identified by name, address, contact person and telephone number; (3) the recruitment source that referred the hiree for each full-time vacancy during the preceding year; (4) data reflecting the total number of persons interviewed for full-time vacancies during the preceding year and the total number of interviewees referred by each recruitment source utilized in connection with such vacancies; and (5) a list and brief description of initiatives undertaken pursuant to Section 73.2080(c)(2) during the preceding year.

Item 5.   Environmental Effects. FM and TV translator and LPTV renewal applicants must review the Instructions to Section III, Item 6, of this form before completing this item.

FCC NOTICE TO INDIVIDUALS REQUIRED BY THE PRIVACY ACT AND THE PAPERWORK REDUCTION ACT

The FCC is authorized under the Communications Act of 1934, as amended, to collect the personal information we request in this form. We will use the information provided in the application to determine whether approving this application is in the public interest. If we believe there may be a violation or potential violation of a FCC statute, regulation, rule or order, your application may be referred to the Federal, state or local agency responsible for investigating, prosecuting, enforcing or implementing the statute, rule, regulation or order. In certain cases, the information in your application may be disclosed to the Department of Justice or a court or adjudicative body when (a) the FCC; (b) any employee of the FCC; or (c) the United States Government is a party to a proceeding before the body or has an interest in the proceeding. In addition, all information provided in this form will be available for public inspection.

If you owe a past due debt to the federal government, any information you provide may also be disclosed to the Department of Treasury Financial Management Service, other federal agencies and/or your employer to offset your salary, IRS tax refund or other payments to collect that debt. The FCC may also provide this information to these agencies through the matching of computer records when authorized.

If you do not provide the information requested on this form, the application may be returned without action having been taken upon it or its processing may be delayed while a request is made to provide the missing information. Your response is required to obtain the requested authorization.

We have estimated that each response to this collection of information will take from 37 hours to 119 hours. Our estimate includes the time to read the instructions, look through existing records, gather and maintain the required data, and actually complete and review the form or response. If you have any comments on this estimate, or on how we can improve the collection and reduce the burden it causes you, please write the Federal Communications Commission, AMD-PERM, Paperwork Reduction Project (3060-0027), Washington, DC 20554. We will also accept your comments via the Internet if your send them to Judith-B.Herman@fcc.gov. Please DO NOT SEND COMPLETED APPLICATIONS TO THIS ADDRESS. Remember - you are not required to respond to a collection of information sponsored by the Federal government, and the government may not conduct or sponsor this collection, unless it displays a currently valid OMB control number or if we fail to provide you with this notice. This collection has been assigned an OMB control number of 3060-0027.

THE FOREGOING NOTICE IS REQUIRED BY THE PRIVACY ACT OF 1974, P.L. 93-579, DECEMBER 31, 1974, 5 U.S.C. 552a(e)(3), AND THE PAPERWORK REDUCTION ACT OF 1995, P.L. 104-13, OCTOBER 1, 1995, 44 U.S.C. 3507.

Federal Communications Commission
Washington, D. C. 20554

OMB 3060-0110
July 2004

FOR FCC USE ONLY	

FCC 303-S

APPLICATION FOR
RENEWAL OF BROADCAST STATION
LICENSE

FOR COMMISSION USE ONLY	
FILE NO.	

Section I - General Information- TO BE COMPLETED BY ALL APPLICANTS

1.

Legal Name of Licensee		
Mailing Address		
City	State or Country (if foreign address)	ZIP Code
Telephone Number (include area code)	E-Mail Address (if available)	
FCC Registration Number	Call Sign	Facility Identifier

2.

Contact Representative	Firm or Company Name	
Mailing Address		
City	State or Country (if foreign address)	ZIP Code
Telephone Number (include area code)	E-Mail Address (if available)	

3. If this application has been submitted without a fee, indicate reason for fee exemption (see 47 C.F.R. Section 1.1114):

☐ Governmental Entity   ☐ Noncommercial Educational Licensee   ☐ Other _____

323

4.   **Purpose of Application.**

☐   Renewal of license

☐   Amendment to pending renewal application
    If an amendment, submit as an exhibit a listing by Section and Item
    Number the portions of the pending application that are being revised.

Exhibit

5.   **Facility Information**:   ☐ Commercial   ☐ Noncommercial Educational

6.   **Service and Community of License**

a.   ☐ AM   ☐ FM   ☐ TV   ☐ FM Translator   ☐ LPFM

     ☐ TV Translator   ☐ Low Power TV   ☐ Class A TV

Community of License/Area to be Served	
City	State

b.   Does this application include one or more FM translator station(s), or TV translator
     station(s), LPTV station(s), in addition to the station listed in Section I, Question 1?
     (The callsign(s) of any associated FM translators, TV translators or LPTVs will be
     requested in Section V).
     ☐ Yes   ☐ No

7.   **Other Authorizations.** List call signs, facility identifiers and location(s) of any FM
     booster or TV booster station(s) for which renewal of license is also requested.

Exhibit No.	☐ N/A

NOTE: **In addition to the information called for in Sections II, III, IV and V, an explanatory exhibit providing full particulars must be submitted for each item for which a "No" response is provided.**

Section II - Legal -TO BE COMPLETED BY ALL APPLICANTS

1. **Certification.** Licensee certifies that it has answered each question in this application based on its review of the application instructions and worksheets. Licensee further certifies that where it has made an affirmative certification below, this certification constitutes its representation that the application satisfies each of the pertinent standards and criteria set forth in the application, instructions, and worksheets.

☐ Yes ☐ No

2. **Character Issues.** Licensee certifies that neither the licensee nor any party to the application has or has had any interest in, or connection with:

   a. any broadcast application in any proceeding where character issues were left unresolved or were resolved adversely against the applicant or any party to the application; or

   ☐ Yes ☐ No   See Explanation in Exhibit No.

   b. any pending broadcast application in which character issues have been raised.

   ☐ Yes ☐ No   See Explanation in Exhibit No.

3. **Adverse Findings.** Licensee certifies that, with respect to the licensee and each party to the application, no adverse finding has been made, nor has an adverse final action been taken by any court or administrative body in a civil or criminal proceeding brought under the provisions of any laws related to the following: any felony; mass media-related antitrust or unfair competition; fraudulent statements to another governmental unit; or discrimination.

☐ Yes ☐ No   See Explanation in Exhibit No.

4. **FCC Violations during the Preceding License Term**. Licensee certifies that, with respect to the station(s) for which renewal is requested, there have been no violations by the licensee of the Communications Act of 1934, as amended, or the rules or regulations of the   Commission during the preceding license term. If No, the licensee must submit an explanatory exhibit providing complete descriptions of all violations.

☐ Yes ☐ No   See Explanation in Exhibit No.

5. **Alien Ownership and Control.** Licensee certifies that it complies with the provisions of Section 310 of the Communications Act of 1934, as amended, relating to interests of aliens and foreign governments.

☐ Yes ☐ No   See Explanation in Exhibit No.

6. **Anti-Drug Abuse Act Certification.** Licensee certifies that neither licensee nor any party to the application is subject to denial of federal benefits pursuant to Section 5301 of the Anti-Drug Abuse Act of 1988, 21 U.S.C. Section 862.

☐ Yes ☐ No

I certify that the statements in this application are true, complete, and correct to the best of my knowledge and belief, and are made in good faith. I acknowledge that all certifications and attached Exhibits are considered material representations. I hereby waive any claim to the use of any particular frequency as against the regulatory power of the United States because of the previous use of the same, whether by license or otherwise, and request an authorization in accordance with this application. (See Section 304 of the Communications Act of 1934, as amended.)

Typed or Printed Name of Person Signing	Typed or Printed Title of Person Signing
Signature	Date

WILLFUL FALSE STATEMENTS ON THIS FORM ARE PUNISHABLE BY FINE AND/OR IMPRISONMENT (U.S. CODE, TITLE 18, SECTION 1001), AND/OR REVOCATION OF ANY STATION LICENSE OR CONSTRUCTION PERMIT (U.S. CODE, TITLE 47, SECTION 312(a)(1)), AND/OR FORFEITURE (U.S. CODE, TITLE 47, SECTION 503).

Section III - TO BE COMPLETED BY AM and FM LICENSEES ONLY

1. **Biennial Ownership Report:** Licensee certifies that the station's Biennial Ownership Report (FCC Form 323 or 323-E) has been filed with the Commission as required by 47 C.F.R. Section 73.3615.

   ☐ Yes ☐ No

   See Explanation in Exhibit No.

2. **EEO Program:** Licensee certifies that:
   a. The station's Broadcast EEO Program Report (FCC Form 396) has been filed with the Commission, as required by 47 C.F.R. Section 73.2080(f)(1).

   ☐ Yes ☐ No

   See Explanation in Exhibit No.

   Specify FCC Form 396 File Number [   ]

   b. The station has posted its most recent Broadcast EEO Public File Report on the station's website, as required by 47 C.F.R. Section 73.2080(c)(6).

   ☐ Yes ☐ No

   ☐ N/A

   See Explanation in Exhibit No.

3. **Local Public File.** Licensee certifies that the documentation, required by 47 C.F.R. Sections 73.3526 or 73.3527, as applicable, has been placed in the station's public inspection file at the appropriate times.

   ☐ Yes ☐ No

   See Explanation in Exhibit No.

4. **Discontinued Operations.** Licensee certifies that during the preceding license term the station has not been silent for any consecutive 12-month period.

   ☐ Yes ☐ No

   See Explanation in Exhibit No.

5. **Silent Station.** Licensee certifies that the station is currently on the air broadcasting programming intended to be received by the public.

   ☐ Yes ☐ No

6. **Environmental Effects.** Licensee certifies that the specified facility complies with the maximum permissible radiofrequency electromagnetic exposure limits for controlled and uncontrolled environments. Unless the licensee can determine compliance through the use of the RF worksheets in the Instructions to this Form, **an Exhibit is required.**

   ☐ Yes ☐ No

   See Explanation in Exhibit No.

   By checking "Yes" above, the licensee also certifies that it, in coordination with other users of the site, will reduce power or cease operation as necessary to protect persons having access to the site, tower, or antenna from radiofrequency electromagnetic exposure in excess of FCC guidelines.

Section IV - TO BE COMPLETED BY TV AND CLASS A LICENSEES ONLY

1. **Biennial Ownership Report.** Licensee certifies that the station's Biennial Ownership Report (FCC Form 323 or 323-E) has been filed with the Commission, as required by 47 C.F.R. Section 73.3615.

   ☐ Yes ☐ No | See Explanation in Exhibit No.

2. **EEO Program.** Licensee certifies that:
   a. The station's Broadcast EEO Program Report (FCC Form 396), has been filed with the Commission, as required by 47 C.F.R. Section 73.2080(f)(1).

   ☐ Yes ☐ No | See Explanation in Exhibit No.

   Specify FCC Form 396 File Number [   ]

   b. The station has posted its most recent Broadcast EEO Public File Report on the station's website, as required by 47 C.F.R. Section 73.2080(c)(6).

   ☐ Yes ☐ No ☐ N/A | See Explanation in Exhibit No.

3. **Local Public File.** Licensee certifies that the documentation required by 47 C.F.R. Sections 73.3526 or 73.3527, as applicable, has been placed in its station's inspection file at the appropriate times.

   ☐ Yes ☐ No

4. **Violent Programming.** Licensee certifies that no written comments or suggestions have been received from the public that comment on its station's programming and characterize that programming as constituting violent programming.

   ☐ Yes ☐ No ☐ N/A

   If No, **submit as an Exhibit** a summary of those written comments and suggestions received from the public.

   See Explanation in Exhibit No.

5. **Children's Programming Commercial Limitations.** For the period of time covered by this application, the licensee certifies that it has complied with the limits on commercial matter as set forth in 47 C.F.R. Section 73.670. (The limits are no more than 12 minutes of commercial matter per hour during children's programming on weekdays, and no more than 10.5 minutes of commercial matter per hour during children's programming on weekends. The limits also apply pro rata to children's programs which are 5 minutes or more and which are not part of a longer block of children's programming.

   ☐ Yes ☐ No

   See Explanation in Exhibit No.

   If No, **submit as an Exhibit** a list of each segment of programming 5 minutes or more in duration designed for children 12 years and under and broadcast during the license period which contained commercial matter in excess of the limits. For each programming segment so listed, indicate the length of the segment, the amount of commercial matter contained therein, and an explanation of why the limits were exceeded.

6. For the period of time covered by this applicant, the licensee certifies that it has filed with the Commission, **and incorporated by reference,** the Children's Television Programming Reports (FCC Form 398) as described in 47 C.F.R. Section 73.3526.

   ☐ Yes ☐ No

   See Explanation in Exhibit No.

7. For the period of time covered by this application, the licensee certifies that the average number of hours of CORE Programming per week broadcast by the station totalled 3 hours or more (averaged over a six-month period).

☐ Yes ☐ No

Exhibit No.

8. The licensee certifies that it identifies each CORE Program aired at the beginning of the airing of each program as required by 47 C.F.R. Section 73.673.

☐ Yes ☐ No

If No, **submit as an Exhibit** a statement of explanation.

Exhibit No.

9. The licensee certifies that it provides information identifying each CORE Program aired on its station, including an indication of the target child audience, to publishers of program guides as required by 47 C.F.R. Section 73.673.

☐ Yes ☐ No

If No, **submit as an Exhibit** a statement of explanation.

Exhibit No.

10. The licensee certifies that it publicizes the existence and location of the station's Children's Television Programming Reports (FCC Form 398) as required by 47 C.F.R. Section 73.3526(e)(11)(iii).

☐ Yes ☐ No

If No, **submit as an Exhibit** a statement of explanation, including the specific steps the applicant intends to implement to ensure compliance in the future.

Exhibit No.

11. The licensee may include as an exhibit any other comments or information it wants the Commision to consider in evaluating compliance with the Children's Television Act. This may include information on any other non-core educational and informational programming that the applicant aired or plans to air, or any existing or proposed non-broadcast efforts that will enhance the educational and informational value of such programming to children. See 47 C.F.R. Section 73.671, NOTE 2.

Exhibit No.

12. **Continued Class A Eligibility.** Licensee certifies that its station does, and will continue to, broadcast: (a) a minimum of 18 hours per day; and (b) an average of at least 3 hours per week of programming each quarter produced within the market area served by the station, or by a group of commonly controlled low power or Class A stations whose predicted Grade B contours are contiguous.

☐ Yes ☐ No | See Explanation in Exhibit No.

13. **Discontinued Operations.** Licensee certifies that during the preceding license term, the station has not been silent for any consecutive 12-month period.

☐ Yes ☐ No | See Explanation in Exhibit No.

14. **Silent Station.** Licensee certifies that the station is currently on the air broadcasting programming intended to be received by the public.

☐ Yes ☐ No

15. **Environmental Effects.** Licensee certifies that the specified facility complies with the maximum permissible radiofrequency electronicmagnetic exposure limits for controlled and uncontrolled environments.

☐ Yes ☐ No

See Explanation in Exhibit No.

By checking "Yes" above, the licensee also certifies that it, in coordination with other users of the site, will reduce power or cease operation as necessary to protect persons having access to the site, tower or antenna from radiofrequency electromagnetic exposure in excess of FCC guidelines.

16. **Local TV Ownership Waiver.** Has the licensee been granted a "failing" or "marginal" station waiver of 47 C.F.R. Section 73.3555(b)?

☐ Yes ☐ No

If Yes, **submit as an Exhibit** a specific factual showing of the program-related benefits that have accrued to the public as a result of that waiver.

Exhibit No.

Section V - TO BE COMPLETED BY FM AND TV TRANSLATOR AND LOW POWER TV LICENSEES ONLY

1. **Station Information:**

Call Sign	Facility Identifier	Area Licensed to Serve	
		City	State

2. **Operational Status:**

   a. **Silent station**: Licensee certifies that the station is currently on the air. ☐ Yes ☐ No | See explanation in Exhibit No.

   b. **Rebroadcast Status**. Licensee certifies that the station is currently rebroadcasting the signal of an FM, TV, or LPTV station. ☐ Yes ☐ No ☐ N/A

   See explanation in Exhibit No.

   If Yes, identify the station being broadcast:

Call sign	Facility Identifier	Area Licensed to Serve	
		City	State

   c. **Rebroadcast Consent**. Licensee certifies that it has obtained written authority from the licensee of the primary station identified above for retransmitting the primary station's programming. ☐ Yes ☐ No ☐ N/A

   See explanation in Exhibit No.

3. **For FM Translator Applicants Only:**

   a. Licensee certifies that it is in compliance with 47 C.F.R. Section 74.1232(d) which prohibits the common ownership of a commercial primary station and a FM translator station whose coverage contour extends beyond the coverage contour of the commercial primary station being rebroadcast. This restriction also applies to any person or entity having any interest in, or any connection with, the primary FM station. ☐ Yes ☐ No

   See explanation in Exhibit No.

   b. Licensee certifies that it is in compliance with 47 C.F.R. Section 74.1232(e) which prohibits an FM translator station whose coverage extends beyond the protected contour of the commercial primary station being rebroadcast from receiving any support (except for specified technical assistance), before, during, or after construction, directly or indirectly, from the primary station, or any person or entity having any interest in, or any connection with, the primary station. ☐ Yes ☐ No ☐ N/A

   See explanation in Exhibit No.

330

4. **For Low Power TV Applicants Only.** Licensee certifies that it has filed with the Commission, the station's Broadcast EEO Program Report (FCC Form 396) and has posted the most recent Public File Report on the station's website, as required by 47 C.F.R. Section 73.2080(f)(1).

☐ Yes ☐ No ☐ N/A

See explanation in Exhibit No.

5. **Environmental Effects.** Licensee certifies that the specified facility complies with the maximum permissible radiofrequency electromagnetic exposure limits for controlled and uncontrolled environments.

☐ Yes ☐ No

See explanation in Exhibit No.

By checking "Yes" above, the licensee also certifies that, in coordination with other users of the site, will reduce power or cease operation as necessary to protect persons having access to the site, tower, or antenna from radiofrequency eletromagnetic exposure in excess of FCC guidelines.

APPENDIX 3

Policy Statement
In the Matter of Industry Guidance on the Commission's Case Law Interpreting 18 U.S.C. Sect. 1464 and Enforcement Policies Regarding Broadcast Indecency

File No. EB-00-IH-0089

This FCC document was released in 2001, as the Commission began to more rigorously enforce the broadcast indecency regulations. The Policy Statement is interesting in a number of ways. First, it demonstrates how FCC policy is presented to the public. It also shows how complicated the regulation of indecency actually is and how fine a line the FCC must walk in censoring content. Finally, the concurring and dissenting statements by the various commissioners highlights debate that happens among commissioners over policy.

The examples of indecent broadcasts have not been included here. An unexpurgated version can be found at http://www.fcc.gov/eb/Orders/2001/fcc01090.doc.

Before the
Federal Communications Commission
Washington, D.C. 20554

In the Matter of	)
	)
Industry Guidance On the Commission's	) File No. EB-00-IH-0089
Case Law Interpreting 18 U.S.C. § 1464	)
and Enforcement Policies Regarding	)
Broadcast Indecency	)
	)

POLICY STATEMENT

Adopted: March 14, 2001   **Released:** April 6, 2001

By the Commission: Commissioners Ness and Furchtgott-Roth issuing separate statements; Commissioner Tristani dissenting and issuing a statement.

I.   INTRODUCTION

1.   The Commission issues this Policy Statement to provide guidance to the broadcast industry regarding our case law interpreting 18 U.S.C. § 1464 and our enforcement policies with respect to broadcast indecency. This document is divided into five parts. Section I gives an overview of this document. Section II provides the statutory basis for indecency regulation and discusses the judicial history of such regulation. Section III describes the analytical approach the Commission uses in making indecency determinations. This section also presents a comparison of selected rulings intended to illustrate the various factors that have proved significant in resolving indecency complaints. The cited material refers only to broadcast indecency actions and does not include any discussion of case law concerning indecency enforcement actions in other services regulated by this agency such as cable, telephone, or amateur radio. Section IV describes the Commission's broadcast indecency enforcement process. Section V is the conclusion.

II.   STATUTORY BASIS/JUDICIAL HISTORY

2.   It is a violation of federal law to broadcast obscene or indecent programming. Specifically, Title 18 of the United States Code, Section 1464 (18 U.S.C. § 1464), prohibits the utterance of "any obscene, indecent, or profane language by means of radio communication."[1] Congress has given the Federal Communications Commission the responsibility for administratively enforcing 18 U.S.C. § 1464. In doing so, the Commission may revoke a station license, impose a monetary forfeiture, or issue a warning for the broadcast of indecent material.[2] *See* 47 U.S.C. Sections 312(a)(6) and 503(b)(1)(D).

---

[1] Obscene and profane language and depictions are not within the scope of this Policy Statement.

[2] Although Section 1464 is a criminal statutue, the Commission has authority to impose civil penalties for the broadcast of indecent material without regard to the criminal nature of the statute. *FCC v. Pacifica Foundation*, 438 U.S. 726, 739, n. 13 (1978); *see also Action for Children's Television v. FCC*, 852 F.2d 1332, 1335 (D.C.Cir. 1988) (continued....)

3.   The FCC's enforcement policy under Section 1464 has been shaped by a number of judicial and legislative decisions. In particular, because the Supreme Court has determined that obscene speech is not entitled to First Amendment protection, obscene speech cannot be broadcast at any time. [3] In contrast, indecent speech is protected by the First Amendment, and thus, the government must both identify a compelling interest for any regulation it may impose on indecent speech and choose the least restrictive means to further that interest. [4] Even under this restrictive standard, the courts have consistently upheld the Commission's authority to regulate indecent speech, albeit with certain limitations.

4.   *FCC v. Pacifica Foundation,* 438 U.S. 726 (1978), provides the judicial foundation for FCC indecency enforcement. In that case, the Supreme Court held that the government could constitutionally regulate indecent broadcasts.[5] In addition, the Court quoted the Commission's definition of indecency with apparent approval.[6] The definition, "language or material that, in context, depicts or describes, in terms patently offensive as measured by contemporary community standards for the broadcast medium, sexual or excretory activities or organs," has remained substantially unchanged since the time of the *Pacifica* decision.[7] Moreover, the definition has been specifically upheld against constitutional challenges in the *Action for Children's Television (ACT)* cases in the D.C. Circuit Court of Appeals.[8] Further, in *Reno v. ACLU,* 521 U.S. 844 (1997), the U.S. Supreme Court struck down an indecency standard for the Internet but did not question the constitutionality of our broadcast indecency standard. Rather, the Court recognized the "special justifications for regulation of the broadcast media that are not applicable to other speakers." *Reno v. ACLU,* 521 U.S. at 868.[9]

(Continued from previous page) ———————————————————

(see n. 8 for full case history) (Commission has authority to sanction licensees for broadcast of indecent material). The Department of Justice is responsible for prosecution of criminal violations of the statute.

[3] *See Miller v. California,* 413 U.S. 15 (1973), *reh'g. denied,* 414 U.S. 881 (1973); *Sable Communications of California, Inc. v. FCC,* 492 U.S. 115 (1989); 47 C.F.R. § 73. 3999(a). Obscene speech is defined by a three-part test: (1) an average person, applying contemporary community standards, must find that the material, as a whole, appeals to the prurient interest; (2) the material must depict or describe, in a patently offensive way, sexual conduct specifically defined by applicable law; and (3) the material, taken as a whole, must lack serious literary, artistic, political, or scientific value. *Miller v. California,* 413 U.S. at 24.

[4] *Sable v. FCC,* 492 U.S. at 126.

[5] *Id.* at 748-50 (upholding Commission declaratory order that afternoon broadcast of a recording of a 12 minute monologue entitled "Filthy Words" was indecent as broadcast); *see also* 742-47 (Stevens, J.) and 757-61 (Powell, J.).

[6] *Id.* at 732.

[7] *Enforcement of Prohibitions Against Broadcast Indecency in 18 U.S.C. § 1464, 8 FCC Rcd 704, n. 10 (1993). See also Action for Children's Television v. FCC,* 852 F.2d 1332, 1338 (D.C.Cir. 1988) and *Action for Children's Television v. FCC,* 58 F.3d 654, 657 (D.C. Cir. 1995) (see n. 8 for full case history).

[8] *Action for Children's Television v. FCC,* 852 F.2d 1332, 1339 (D.C.Cir. 1988) (*"ACT I"*); *Action for Children's Television v. FCC,* 932 F.2d 1504, 1508 (D.C. Cir. 1991*), cert. denied,* 112 S. Ct. 1282 (1992) (*"ACT II"*); *Action for Children's Television v. FCC,* 58 F.3d 654, 657 (D.C. Cir. 1995*), cert. denied, 116 S. Ct. 701 (1996)* (*"ACT III"*).

[9] These special justifications included the history of extensive government regulation of the broadcast medium, the scarcity of available frequencies at its inception, and broadcast's "invasive" nature. *Id. See also Commission's* (continued....)

5.   Although the D.C. Circuit approved the FCC's definition of indecency in the *ACT* cases, it also established several restrictive parameters on FCC enforcement. The court's decisions made clear that the FCC had to identify the compelling government interests that warranted regulation and also explain how the regulations were narrowly tailored to further those interests. In *ACT I*, the court rejected as inadequately supported the Commission's determination that it could reach and regulate indecent material aired as late as 11:00 p.m., and remanded the cases involved to the Commission for proceedings to ascertain the proper scope of the "safe harbor" period, that is, the time during which indecent speech may be legally broadcast. Before the Commission could comply with the court's remand order, however, Congress intervened and instructed the Commission to adopt rules that enforced the provisions of 18 U.S.C. § 1464 on a "24 hour per day basis."[10] The rule adopted to implement this legislative mandate was stayed and was ultimately vacated by the court in *ACT II* as unconstitutional. In 1992, responding to the decision in *ACT II*, Congress directed the Commission to adopt a new "safe harbor" – generally 12 midnight to 6:00 a.m., but 10:00 p.m. to 6:00 a.m. for certain noncommercial stations. The Commission implemented this statutory scheme in January 1993.[11] Before this rule could become effective, however, the court stayed it pending judicial review. In 1995, the D.C. Circuit, *en banc*, held in *ACT III* that there was not a sufficient justification in the record to support a preferential "safe harbor" period for noncommercial stations and that the more restrictive midnight to 6:00 a.m. "safe harbor" for commercial stations was therefore unconstitutional. The court concluded, however, that the less restrictive 10:00 p.m. to 6:00 a.m. "safe harbor" had been justified as a properly tailored means of vindicating the government's compelling interest in the welfare of children and remanded the case to the Commission "with instructions to limit its ban on the broadcasting of indecent programs to the period from 6:00 a.m. to 10:00 p.m." *ACT III*, 58 F.3d at 669-70. The Commission implemented the court's instructions by appropriately conforming Section 73.3999 of its rules.[12] These changes became effective on August 28, 1995.[13]

6.   Thus, outside the 10:00 p.m. to 6:00 a.m. safe harbor, the courts have approved regulation of broadcast indecency to further the compelling government interests in supporting parental supervision of children and more generally its concern for children's well being. *Act III*, 58 F.3d at 661 (and cases cited therein).[14] The principles of enforcement articulated below are intended to further these interests.

(Continued from previous page) ————————————
Forfeiture Policy Statement and Amendment of Section 1.80 of the Rules to Incorporate the Forfeiture Guidelines, 15 FCC Rcd 303, 305-06 (1999) ("courts have repeatedly upheld the Commission's indecency standard").

[10] *Making Appropriations for the Departments of Commerce, Justice, and State, the Judiciary and Related Agencies for the Fiscal Year Ending September 30, 1989, and for Other Purposes*, Pub. L. No. 100-459, Section 608, 102 Stat. 2186, 2228 (1988).

[11] *Public Telecommunications Act of 1992*, Pub. L. No. 102-356, § 16(a), 106 Stat. 949, 954 (1992); *Enforcement of Prohibitions Against Broadcast Indecency in 18 U.S.C. § 1464, Report and Order*, 8 FCC Rcd 704 (1993).

[12] *Enforcement of Prohibitions Against Broadcast Indecency in 18 U.S.C. § 1464, Memorandum Opinion and Order*, 10 FCC Rcd 10558 (1995).

[13] 60 FR 44439 (August 28, 1995).

[14] The Commission has also identified "protection of the home against intrusion by offensive broadcasts" as a compelling government interest. The court did not address the validity of that interest. *ACT III*, 58 F.3d at 660-61. The Supreme Court has noted, however, that the "uniquely pervasive presence" of the broadcast media, with the audience continually tuning in and out, so as to make content warnings less effectual, is a reason for affording (continued....)

III.   INDECENCY DETERMINATIONS

A.   <u>Analytical Approach</u>

7.   Indecency findings involve at least two fundamental determinations. First, the material alleged to be indecent must fall within the subject matter scope of our indecency definition – that is, the material must describe or depict sexual or excretory organs or activities. *WPBN/WTOM License Subsidiary, Inc. (WPBN-TV and WTOM-TV)*, 15 FCC Rcd 1838, 1840-41 (2000).

8.   Second, the broadcast must be *patently offensive* as measured by contemporary community standards for the broadcast medium. In applying the "community standards for the broadcast medium" criterion, the Commission has stated:

> The determination as to whether certain programming is patently offensive is not a local one and does not encompass any particular geographic area. Rather, the standard is that of an average broadcast viewer or listener and not the sensibilities of any individual complainant.

WPBN/WTOM License Subsidiary, Inc., 15 FCC Rcd at 1841.[15]

9.   In determining whether material is patently offensive, the *full context* in which the material appeared is critically important.[16] It is not sufficient, for example, to know that explicit sexual terms or descriptions were used, just as it is not sufficient to know only that no such terms or descriptions were used. Explicit language in the context of a *bona fide* newscast might not be patently offensive,[17] while sexual innuendo that persists and is sufficiently clear to make the sexual meaning inescapable might

---

(Continued from previous page) ———————————————

broadcast media more limited First Amendment protections as compared to other forms of communications. *FCC v. Pacifica Foundation*, 438 U.S. at 748-49.

[15] The Commission's interpretation of the term "contemporary community standards" flows from its analysis of the definition of that term set forth in the Supreme Court's decision in *Hamling v. United States*, 418 U.S. 87 (1974), *reh'g denied*, 419 U.S. 885 (1974). In *Infinity Broadcasting Corporation of Pennsylvania (WYSP(FM))*, 3 FCC Rcd 930 (1987) (subsequent history omitted), the commission observed that in *Hamling*, which involved obscenity, "the Court explained that the purpose of 'contemporary community standards' was to ensure that material is judged neither on the basis of a decisionmaker's personal opinion, nor by its effect on a particularly sensitive or insensitive person or group." 3 FCC Rcd at 933, *citing* 418 U.S. at 107. The Commission also relied on the fact that the Court in *Hamling* indicated that decisionmakers need not use any precise geographic area in evaluating material. 3 FCC Rcd at 933, *citing* 418 U.S. at 104-05. Consistent with *Hamling*, the Commission concluded that its evaluation of allegedly indecent material is "not one based on a local standard, but one based on a broader standard for broadcasting generally." 3 FCC Rcd at 933.

[16] *WPBN/WTOM License Subsidiary, Inc.*, 15 FCC Rcd at 1841; *Infinity Broadcasting Corp.*, 3 FCC Rcd 930, 931-32 (1987), *aff'd in part, vacated in part, remanded sub nom. Act I*, 852 F.2d 1332 (D.C. Cir. 1988) (subsequent history omitted).

[17] *Peter Branton*, 6 FCC Rcd 610 (1991), *aff'd sub nom. Branton v. FCC*, 993 F.2d 906 (D.C. Cir. 1993), *cert. denied 511 U.S. 1052* (1994).

be.[18] Moreover, contextual determinations are necessarily highly fact-specific, making it difficult to catalog comprehensively all of the possible contextual factors that might exacerbate or mitigate the patent offensiveness of particular material.[19] An analysis of Commission case law reveals that various factors have been consistently considered relevant in indecency determinations. By comparing cases with analogous analytical structures, but different outcomes, we hope to highlight how these factors are applied in varying circumstances and the impact of these variables on a finding of patent offensiveness.

B.   Case Comparisons

10.   The principal factors that have proved significant in our decisions to date are: (1) the *explicitness or graphic nature* of the description or depiction of sexual or excretory organs or activities; (2) whether the material *dwells on or repeats at length* descriptions of sexual or excretory organs or activities; (3) *whether the material appears to pander or is used to titillate*, or *whether the material appears to have been presented for its shock value.* In assessing all of the factors, and particularly the third factor, the overall context of the broadcast in which the disputed material appeared is critical. Each indecency case presents its own particular mix of these, and possibly other, factors, which must be balanced to ultimately determine whether the material is patently offensive and therefore indecent. No single factor generally provides the basis for an indecency finding. To illustrate the noted factors, however, and to provide a sense of the weight these considerations have carried in specific factual contexts, a comparison of cases has been organized to provide examples of decisions in which each of these factors has played a particularly significant role, whether exacerbating or mitigating, in the indecency determination made.

11.   It should be noted that the brief descriptions and excerpts from broadcasts that are reproduced in this document are intended only as a research tool and should not be taken as a meaningful selection of words and phrases to be evaluated for indecency purposes without the fuller context that the tapes or transcripts provide. The excerpts from broadcasts used in this section have often been shortened or compressed. In order to make the excerpts more readable, however, we have frequently omitted any indication of these ellipses from the text. Moreover, in cases where material was included in a complaint but not specifically cited in the decision based on the complaint, we caution against relying on the omission as if it were of decisional significance. For example, if portions of a voluminous transcript are the object of an enforcement action, those portions not included are not necessarily deemed not indecent. The omissions may be the result of an editing process that attempted to highlight the most significant material within its context. No inference should be drawn regarding the material deleted.

1.   Explicitness/Graphic Description Versus Indirectness/Implication

12.   The more explicit or graphic the description or depiction, the greater the likelihood that the material will be considered patently offensive. Merely because the material consists of double entendre or innuendo, however, does not preclude an indecency finding if the sexual or excretory import is unmistakable.

---

[18] *See Great American Television and Radio Company, Inc. (WFBQ(FM)),* 6 FCC Rcd 3692 (MMB 1990) ("Candy Wrapper").

[19] *See e.g., Infinity Broadcasting Corp.,* 3 FCC Rcd 930, 931-32 (1987), *aff'd in part, vacated in part on other grounds, remanded sub nom. Act I,* 852 F.2d 1332 (D.C. Cir. 1988) (subsequent history omitted*).*

13. Following are examples of decisions where the explicit/graphic nature of the description of sexual or excretory organs or activities played a central role in the determination that the broadcast was indecent.

EXAMPLES OF BROADCASTS THAT HAVE GARNERED COMPLAINTS HAVE BEEN DELETED BECAUSE OF EXPLICIT LANGUAGE. THE FULL FCC DOCUMENT CAN BE FOUND AT http://www.fcc.gov/eb/Orders/2001/fcc01090.doc.

IV. ENFORCEMENT PROCESS

24. The Commission does not independently monitor broadcasts for indecent material. Its enforcement actions are based on documented complaints of indecent broadcasting received from the public. Given the sensitive nature of these cases and the critical role of context in an indecency determination, it is important that the Commission be afforded as full a record as possible to evaluate allegations of indecent programming. In order for a complaint to be considered, our practice is that it must generally include: (1) a full or partial tape or transcript or significant excerpts of the program;[20] (2) the date and time of the broadcast; and (3) the call sign of the station involved. Any tapes or other documentation of the programming supplied by the complainant, of necessity, become part of the Commission's records and cannot be returned. Documented complaints should be directed to the FCC, Investigations and Hearings Division, Enforcement Bureau, 445 Twelfth Street, S.W., Washington, D.C. 20554.

25. If a complaint does not contain the supporting material described above, or if it indicates that a broadcast occurred during "safe harbor" hours or the material cited does not fall within the subject matter scope of our indecency definition, it is usually dismissed by a letter to the complainant advising of the deficiency. In many of these cases, the station may not be aware that a complaint has been filed.

26. If, however, the staff determines that a documented complaint meets the subject matter requirements of the indecency definition and the material complained of was aired outside "safe harbor" hours, then the broadcast at issue is evaluated for patent offensiveness. Where the staff determines that the broadcast is not patently offensive, the complaint will be denied. If, however, the staff determines that further enforcement action might be warranted,[21] the Enforcement Bureau, in conjunction with other Commission offices, examines the material and decides upon an appropriate disposition, which might include any of the following: (1) denial of the complaint by staff letter based upon a finding that the material, in context, is not patently offensive and therefore not indecent; (2) issuance of a Letter of Inquiry (LOI) to the licensee seeking further information concerning or an explanation of the circumstances surrounding the broadcast; (3) issuance of a Notice of Apparent Liability (NAL) for monetary forfeiture; and (4) formal referral of the case to the full Commission for its consideration and

---

[20] *See Citicasters Co., licensee of Station KSJO(FM), San Jose, California,* 15 FCC Rcd 19095 (EB 2000) (forfeiture paid) ("While the complainant did not provide us with an exact transcript of the broadcast, we find that she has provided us with sufficient context to make the determination that the broadcast was indecent.").

[21] In *Act IV*, the court rejected a facial challenge to the Commission's procedures for imposing forfeitures for the broadcast of indecent materials. *Action for Children's Television v. FCC,* 59 F.3d 1249 (D.C. Cir. 1995), *cert. denied,* 116 S. Ct. 773 (1996) ("*Act IV*").

action.[22] Generally, the last of these alternatives is taken in cases where issues beyond straightforward indecency violations may be involved or where the potential sanction for the indecent programming exceeds the Bureau's delegated forfeiture authority of $25,000 (47 C.F.R. § 0.311).

27.   Where an LOI is issued, the licensee's comments are generally sought concerning the allegedly indecent broadcast to assist in determining whether the material is actionable and whether a sanction is warranted. If it is determined that no further action is warranted, the licensee and the complainant will be so advised. Where a *preliminary* determination is made that the material was aired and was indecent, an NAL is issued. If the Commission previously determined that the broadcast of the same material was indecent, the subsequent broadcast constitutes egregious misconduct and a higher forfeiture amount is warranted. *KGB, Inc. (KGB-FM)*, 13 FCC Rcd 16396 (1998) ("higher degree of culpability for the subsequent broadcast of material previously determined by the Commission to be indecent").

28.   The licensee is afforded an opportunity to respond to the NAL, a step which is required by statute. 47 U.S.C. § 503(b). Once the Commission or its staff has considered any response by the licensee, it may order payment of a monetary penalty by issuing a Forfeiture Order. Alternatively, if the preliminary finding of violation in the NAL is successfully rebutted by the licensee, the NAL may be rescinded. If a Forfeiture Order is issued, the monetary penalty assessed may either be the same as specified in the NAL or it may be a lesser amount if the licensee has demonstrated that mitigating factors warrant a reduction in forfeiture.

29.   A Forfeiture Order may be appealed by the licensee through the administrative process under several different provisions of the Commission's rules. The licensee also has the legal right to refuse to pay the fine. In such a case, the Commission may refer the matter to the U.S. Department of Justice, which can initiate a trial *de novo* in a U.S. District Court. The trial court may start anew to evaluate the allegations of indecency.

V.   CONCLUSION

30.   The Commission issues this Policy Statement to provide guidance to broadcast licensees regarding compliance with the Commission's indecency regulations.[23] By summarizing the regulations and explaining the Commission's analytical approach to reviewing allegedly indecent material, the Commission provides a framework by which broadcast licensees can assess the legality of airing

---

[22] This section discusses the typical process. The Commission also has authority to send forfeiture cases to a hearing, in which case the procedures discussed here differ. *See* 47 U.S.C. § 503(b)(3). *See also* 47 U.S.C. § 312(b) (revocation hearing for violation of 18 U.S.C. § 1464).

[23] This Policy Statement addresses the February 22, 1994, Agreement for Settlement and Dismissal with Prejudice between the United States of America, by and through the Department of Justice and Federal Communications Commission, and Evergreen Media Corporation of Chicago, AM, Licensee of Radio Station WLUP(AM). Specifically, in paragraph 2(b) of the settlement agreement, the Commission agreed to "publish industry guidance relating to its caselaw interpreting 18 U.S.C. § 1464 and the FCC's enforcement policies with respect to broadcast indecency." *United States v. Evergreen Media Corp.*, Civ. No. 92 C 5600 (N.D. Ill., E. Div. 1994). The settlement agreement also provides that the forfeiture order imposed in *Evergreen Media Corporation of Chicago AM WLUP(AM)*, 6 FCC Rcd 502 (MMB 1991), is null and void and expunged from the record. It further specifies that the Notice of Apparent Liability issued to WLUP on February 25, 1993, *Evergreen Media Corporation of Chicago AM (WLUP(AM))*, 8 FCC Rcd 1266 (1993), became null and void and expunged from the record six months from the date of the agreement. Accordingly, those decisions are officially vacated.

potentially indecent material. Numerous examples are provided in this document in an effort to assist broadcast licensees. However, this document is not intended to be an all-inclusive summary of every indecency finding issued by the Commission and it should not be relied upon as such. There are many additional cases that could have been cited. Further, as discussed above, the excerpts from broadcasts quoted in this document are intended only as a research tool. A complete understanding of the material, and the Commission's analysis thereof, requires review of the tapes or transcripts and the Commission's rulings thereon.

VI.   ORDERING CLAUSE

31.   Accordingly, it is ORDERED that this Policy Statement is ADOPTED.

FEDERAL COMMUNICATIONS COMMISSION

Magalie Roman Salas
32.   Secretary

Separate Statement of Commissioner Susan Ness

In Re: Industry Guidance on the Commission's Case Law Interpreting 18 U.S.C. 1464 and Enforcement Policies Regarding Broadcast Indecency

Our enforcement of the broadcast indecency statute compels the FCC to reconcile two competing fundamental obligations: (1) to ensure that the airwaves are free of indecent programming material during prescribed hours when children are most likely to be in the audience; and (2) to respect the First Amendment rights of broadcasters regarding program content.

Understandably, the public is outraged by the increasingly coarse content aired on radio and television at all hours of the day, including times when children are likely to be listening or watching. The flood of letters and e-mails we receive reflect a high degree of anger. As a parent, I share the public's frustration. Many parents feel that they cannot enjoy watching daytime or primetime television with their children for fear that their youngsters will be exposed to indecent material – content that just a few years ago would have been unimaginable on broadcast television.

Despite an onslaught of on-air smut, the Commission necessarily walks a delicate line when addressing content issues, and must be careful not to tread on the First Amendment -- the constitutional bulwark of our free society. Even words that might be construed as indecent are subject to some constitutional protection against government regulation.[1]

That said, the Supreme Court has seen fit, despite declining broadcast audience shares, to reaffirm the FCC's broadcast indecency enforcement role, given the "pervasive" and "invasive" characteristics of the free over the air broadcast medium.[2] Our Policy Statement on indecency reconciles our statutory mandate and constitutional obligation by providing helpful guidance to broadcasters and the public alike. The guidance we offer – a restatement of existing statutory, regulatory, and judicial law – establishes a measure of clarity in an inherently subjective area.

Recommended Procedural Improvements

We should strive to make our complaint procedures as user-friendly as possible.[3] I believe that our complaint process could be improved if, prior to acting on an indecency complaint, the Commission routinely forwarded the complaint to the licensee in question. The Policy Statement concedes that in "many [indecency] cases, the station may not be aware that a complaint has been filed."[4] Moreover, many consumers feel that the Commission mechanically dismisses their

---

[1] *FCC v. Pacifica Foundation*, 438 U.S. 726, 746 (1978) (while offensive words might "ordinarily lack literary, political, or scientific value, they are not entirely outside the protection of the First Amendment), *cf. id.* at 745 ("obscenity may be wholly prohibited").

[2] See, *Reno v. ACLU*, 521 U.S. 844, 868 (1997).

[3] The Policy Statement is careful to point out that complaints need not be letter perfect, *see, e.g.,* n. 20 (citing Bureau decision that an inexact transcript may be sufficient to meet procedural requirements).

[4] Policy Statement at para. 24.

complaints. I do not believe that broadcasters' First Amendment rights would be threatened if we were to send broadcasters a courtesy copy of complaints filed with the FCC. Indeed, most broadcasters *want* to be made aware of audience complaints. And consumers would be reassured that their views were being treated seriously.

Broadcasters Are Part of a National Community

Release of this Policy Statement alone will not solve the festering problem of indecency on the airwaves. However, it is entirely within the power of broadcasters to address it -- and to do so *without government intrusion*. It is not a violation of the First Amendment for broadcasters on their own to take responsibility for the programming they air, and to exercise that power in a manner that celebrates rather than debases humankind.

It is time for broadcasters to consider reinstating a voluntary code of conduct. I encourage broadcasters, the Bush Administration, and Congress swiftly to resolve any antitrust impediments to such action and move ahead.

We all are part of a National Community. As stewards of the airwaves, broadcasters play a vital leadership role in setting the cultural tone of our society. They can choose to raise the standard or to lower it. I hope that broadcasters will rise to the occasion by reaffirming the unique role of broadcasting as a family friendly medium. The public deserves no less.

33.

34. **Separate Statement of Commissioner Harold W. Furchtgott-Roth**
35.
36. **In the Matter of Guidance on the Commission's Case Law Interpreting**
37. **18 U.S.C. Section 1464 and Enforcement Policies Regarding Broadcast Indecency**

The Commission is obliged, under a settlement agreement, to issue guidance on its broadcast indecency policies. As the courts have noted, there is a certain "vagueness inherent in [this] subject matter."[1] I find that the policy statement establishes necessary boundaries for this elusive and highly subjective area of the law.

I must note, however, that Commission action to enforce the indecency guidelines would set the stage for a new constitutional challenge regarding our authority to regulate content. To be sure, *Red Lion v. FCC*[2] and its progeny, *FCC v. Pacifica*,[3] have not yet been overruled. Nevertheless, their continuing validity is highly doubtful from both an empirical and jurisprudential point of view.[4]

If rules regulating broadcast content were ever a justifiable infringement of speech, it was because of the relative dominance of that medium in the communications marketplace of the past.[5] As the Commission has long recognized, the facts underlying this justification are no longer true.[6]

---

[1]*Action for Children's Television v. FCC*, 852 F.2d 1332, 1338 (1998) (internal quotation and citation omitted).

[2]395 U.S. 367 (1969).

[3]438 U.S. 726 (1978).

[4]Since *Pacifica*, the Courts have repeatedly struck down indecency regulations and other content-based restrictions. *See, e.g., United States v. Playboy Entertainment Group, Inc.*, 120 S.Ct. 1878 (2000) (striking down statutory adult cable channel scrambling requirements); *Greater New Orleans Broadcasting Ass'n v. U.S.*, 527 U.S. 173 (1999) (striking down the statutory and regulatory bans on casino advertising for broadcast stations); *Reno v. ACLU*, 117 S.Ct. 2329 (1997) (striking down statutory internet indecency requirements); *Denver Area Educ. Telecomms. Consortium, Inc. v. FCC*, 518 U.S. 727 (1996) (striking down certain statutory indecency requirements for commercial leased access and public access channels on cable television systems); and *Sable Communications v. FCC*, 492 U.S. 115 (1989) (striking down a ban on indecent telephone messages). *See also, Time Warner Entertainment Co. v. FCC*, __ F.3d. __ (D.C. Cir. 2001) (striking down FCC cable ownership cap and channel occupancy limits); and *Charter Communications v. County of Santa Cruz*, __ F.Supp. __ (N.D. Cal. 2001) (striking down local cable franchise transfer requirements).

[5]*See, e.g., FCC v. Pottsville Broadcasting Co.*, 309 U.S. 134, 137 (1940) (ownership rules justified by "a widespread fear that in the absence of governmental control the public interest might be subordinated to monopolistic domination"); *see also Red Lion Broadcasting Co. v. FCC*, 395 U.S. 367 (1969) (justifying, at that point in history, a "less rigorous standard of First Amendment scrutiny" on the basis of "spectrum scarcity").

[6]*See 1985 Fairness Report*, 102 FCC 2d 145, 198-221 (1985); *Syracuse Peace Council*, 2 FCC Rcd 5043, 5053 (1985).

Today, the video marketplace is rife with an abundance of programming,[7] distributed by several types of content providers.[8] A competitive radio marketplace is evolving as well, with dynamic new outlets for speech on the horizon.[9] Because of these market transformations, the ability of the broadcast industry to corral content and control information flow has greatly diminished.[10] In my judgment, as alternative sources of programming and distribution increase, broadcast content restrictions must be eliminated.

For these reasons, I believe that the lenient constitutional standard for reviewing broadcast speech, formally announced in *Red Lion*, rests on a shaky empirical foundation.[11] Technology, especially digital communications, has advanced to the point where broadcast deregulation is not only warranted, but long overdue. In my view, the bases for challenging broadcast indecency has been well laid, and the issue is ripe for court review.[12]

I must note my amazement that it has taken over seven years for the Commission to fulfill its obligation to issue this item. While broadcast indecency is a delicate issue to discuss, it has not benefited the industry or the Commission to ignore the matter. I commend the Chairman for taking the initiative to move this item. Norm Goldstein and others staff members deserve special credit for crafting a document that makes the best of a difficult situation for the Commission.

---

[7]There are well over two hundred channels of video programming developed by the cable and broadcast industries. In addition, hyper-localized programming, produced by public, educational and governmental entities, is now available on cable systems throughout the United States. Also, dozens of pay-per-view programming options exist for cable and satellite subscribers. Finally, internet users have access to tens of thousands of audio programming sources and streaming video technology will soon advance to the point that broadcast quality television will be available to anyone connected to the world wide web.

[8]Cable operators, cable overbuilders, OVS operators, internet service providers, wireless video systems, SMATV, common carriers, and satellite carriers are just some of the possible outlets for distributing video content. The promise of multiplexed digital television signals, available to everyone over-the-air, adds even more video programming choices for the American public.

[9]Satellite radio will debut soon and digital audio broadcasting holds out much promise for the future of terrestrial radio transmission. Both types of services will offer listeners more channels of programming at higher quality levels than is available today. Moreover, hundreds of radio stations are currently streaming content over the internet, with thousands of more to follow.

[10]*See* Joint Statement of Commissioners Powell and Furchtgott-Roth, *In re Personal Attack and Political Editorial Rules*, FCC Gen. Docket No. 83-484, at 5 and n. 15 (citing statistics on boom in communications outlets).

[11]It is ironic that streaming video or audio content from a television or radio station would likely receive more constitutional protection, *see Reno*, than would the same exact content broadcast over-the-air. A more interesting First Amendment question will soon arise when digital television stations begin offering subscription services over-the-air. Will intermediate scrutiny apply because the pay service is akin to cable television or will a lesser standard apply because it is available over-the-air? The same inquiries attach to radio signals delivered to listeners on a subscription basis via satellite.

[12]Dissenting Statement of Commissioner Harold W. Furchtgott-Roth, *In the Matter of 1998 Biennial Regulatory Review: Review of the Commission's Broadcast Ownership Rules and Other Rules Adopted Pursuant to Section 202 of the Communications Act* (rel. June 20, 2000).

With these observations in mind, I vote to adopt this policy statement.

38.

39.

40.

Dissenting Statement of Commissioner Gloria Tristani

41. IN THE MATTER OF INDUSTRY GUIDANCE ON THE COMMISSION'S CASE LAW INTERPRETING
42. 18 U.S.C. §1464 AND ENFORCEMENT POLICIES REGARDING BROADCAST INDECENCY, EB

43. FILE NO. 00-IH-0089

I dissent from the issuance of this "Policy Statement" (hereinafter "Statement") for three reasons. First, the Statement creates a false impression that it satisfies an obligation assumed by the Commission in 1994. Second, the Statement perpetuates the myth that broadcast indecency standards are too vague and compliance so difficult that a Policy Statement is necessary to provide further guidance. Most importantly, this Statement diverts this Agency's attention and resources away from the ongoing problem of lax enforcement, which is a pressing concern of America's citizens.

The Statement notes that on February 22, 1994 the Commission entered into a Settlement Agreement with Evergreen Media Corporation (hereinafter "Agreement").[1] At fn 23 the Statement cites the terms of the Agreement as the source of our obligation to produce this Statement:

> Specifically, in paragraph 2(b) of the settlement agreement, the Commission agreed to "publish industry guidance relating to its caselaw interpreting 18 U.S.C. § 1464 and the FCCs enforcement policies with respect to broadcast indecency."[2]

The Agreement actually imposed a significantly more restricted obligation.

> *Within nine months of the date of this Agreement*, the FCC shall publish industry guidance relating to its caselaw interpreting 18 U.S.C. § 1464 and the FCCs enforcement policies with respect to broadcast indecency.[3]

Six and one half years later, it is clear the FCC did not observe the terms of the Agreement. While I cannot support the FCC's failure to comply with the timeline set forth in the original Agreement, the record does not disclose a single effort by Evergreen to seek specific performance under the Agreement. It is well settled that "equity aids the vigilant, not those who slumber on their rights," and doctrines such as laches are designed to promote diligence and prevent enforcement of stale claims.[4] The public interest is not served by permitting Evergreen to sit silently on the sidelines while Commission after

---

[1] *See United States v. Evergreen Media Corp.*, Civ. No. 92 C 5600 (N.D. Ill., E. Div. 1994).

[2] *See Policy Statement* at p. 17-18, n.23.

[3] *See Settlement Agreement* at p. 3.

[4] *See e.g. Powell v. Zuckert*, 366 F.2d 634, 636 (D.C.Cir.1966).

Commission failed to act. Even if the FCC shirked its duty under the Agreement, as long as Evergreen retained the benefit of dismissal of indecency cases against it as set out in the Agreement, a strong case exists that Evergreen ratified this agency's inaction for almost 7 years.[5] If Evergreen Media Corporation had an enforceable interest in the Agreement, it has long since been waived.

Moreover, the obligation to issue the Statement was subject to several conditions precedent that bound Evergreen Media.[6] The Statement itself does not disclose whether Evergreen complied with its obligations, and with the exception of noting payment of $10,000 forfeiture, the record on file at the Commission is silent on the same point. FCC Mass Media Bureau records disclose that Evergreen Media no longer owns the license to which the Agreement's terms attached. Finally, the Agreement does not bind the Commission to provide to Evergreen's assigns the relief set forth in the Agreement.[7] In the absence of the party executing the Agreement, and no successor to accede to those interests, it appears there is no extant legal duty or enforceable right upon which the issuance of the Statement can be based.

I turn next to the underpinnings of the need for this statement. The Statement provides:

> The Commission issues this Policy Statement to provide guidance to the broadcast industry regarding our case law interpreting 18 U.S.C. § 1464 and our enforcement policies with respect to broadcast indecency.[8]

First, settlement of a case involving a single licensee should not compel the FCC to adopt our most significant industry-wide Policy Statement on this subject, particularly when doing so does not serve the public interest. Second, there is nothing in the record demonstrating that Evergreen Media failed to understand the FCC's, or the U.S. Supreme Court's, cases on broadcast indecency. In fact Evergreen agreed to issue to its employees a "policy statement" that was to be based upon "the FCC's definition of broadcast indecency."[9] It his difficult to understand how Evergreen could both issue a policy statement containing the FCC's definition of indecency to its employees *and* simultaneously be unable to understand the FCC's definition. But leaving that quirk aside, there is simply no proof that broadcast licensees are in need of this Policy

---

[5] *See e.g., Buffum v. Peter Barceloux Co.*, 289 U.S. 227, 234 (1933).

[6] The Agreement provides the parties exchanged "consideration and mutual promises hereinafter stated." *See Settlement Agreement* at p. 2 The Agreement describes, at Para. 3, several actions to be undertaken by Evergreen. The Agreement is a form of an executory contract the terms of which require timely satisfaction to constitute compliance. Failure by either party to perform would make the Agreement voidable or unenforceable.

[7] *See Settlement Agreement* at p. 4.

[8] *See Statement* at p.1.

[9] *See Settlement Agreement,* at p. 3.

Statement. No factual basis exists for concluding that confusion about the standards or overreaching enforcement by the FCC requires this Statement.

Moreover, I am aware of no rush of inquiries by broadcast licensees seeking to learn whether their programs comply with our indecency caselaw. In the absence of such requests, this Policy Statement will likely become instead a "how-to" manual for those licensees who wish to tread the line drawn by our cases. It likely may lead to responses to future enforcement actions that cite the Statement as establishing false safe harbors. In the absence of proof that the Statement addresses concerns supported by the FCC's history of enforcement, or the record of the Evergreen case, the Statement is nothing more than a remedy in search of a problem. It would better serve the public if the FCC got serious about enforcing the broadcast indecency standards. For these reasons, I dissent.

Annotated Bibliography

This list of selected references contains both works used in the preparation of this manuscript and works to assist the reader in future research on the FCC and communications policy. It is by no means comprehensive. The books were located through a thorough keyword search of the Library of Congress catalog and the articles were identified through keyword searches of the EBSCO Host electronic databases.

BOOKS

American Bar Association. *Turner Broadcasting v. FCC: Exploring the Regulatory and Constitutional Ramifications.* Chicago, IL: American Bar Association, 1995.
   A legal analysis of a major case relating to the First Amendment rights of cable television operators.

Aufderheide, Patricia. *Communications Policy and the Public Interest: The Telecommunications Act of 1996.* New York: Guilford Press, 1999.
   A well-written and accessible overview of the political debate surrounding the passage of the Telecommunications Act of 1996.

Bagdikian, Ben H. *The New Media Monopoly.* Boston: Beacon Press, 2004.
   A classic treatment of the problems associated with media concentration.

Barnouw, Erik. *A Tower in Babel: A History of Broadcasting in the United States to 1933.* New York: Oxford University Press, 1966.
   The first volume in Barnouw's history of U.S. broadcasting.

———. *The Golden Web: A History of Broadcasting in the United States from 1933 to 1953.* New York: Oxford University Press, 1968.
   The second volume in Barnouw's history of U.S. broadcasting.

———. *The Image Empire: A History of Broadcasting in the United States from 1953.* New York: Oxford University Press, 1970.
   The third volume in Barnouw's history of U.S. broadcasting.

Baughman, James L. *Television's Guardians: The FCC and the Politics of Programming, 1958–1967*. Knoxville: University of Tennessee Press, 1985.

A good narrative of the FCC's regulation of television programming during the heyday of the "public interest" standard.

Bensman, Marvin R. *Broadcast Regulation: Selected Cases and Decisions*, 2nd ed. Lanham, MD: University Press of America, 1985.

A thorough though dated annotated list of federal court cases relating to the broadcasting industry.

———. *Broadcast/Cable Regulation*. Lanham, MD: University Press of America, 1990.

Bensman's updated version of the "broadcasting" cases list, this time with cable decisions included.

———. *The Beginning of Broadcast Regulation in the Twentieth Century*. Jefferson, NC: McFarland & Co., 2000.

A thoroughly researched and documented history of federal regulation of the radio industry leading up to the passage of the Radio Act of 1927.

Berner, Richard O. *Constraints on the Regulatory Process: A Case Study of Regulation of Cable Television*. Cambridge, MA: Ballinger, 1976.

A case study of cable television regulation during its early years.

Besen, Stanley M. *Misregulating Television: Network Dominance and the FCC*. Chicago: University of Chicago Press, 1984.

A critique of FCC television regulation by an economic analyst.

Besen, Stanley M., and Leland L. Johnson. *Regulation of Media Ownership by the Federal Communications Commission: An Assessment*. Santa Monica, CA: Rand, 1984.

A RAND study of media ownership, primarily from an economic perspective.

Besen, Stanley M., and Bridger M. Mitchell. *Economic Analysis and Television Regulation: A Review*. Santa Monica, CA: Rand, 1973.

A somewhat dated albeit interesting look at economic analysis as it relates to television regulation.

Bolter, Walter G. *The Transition to Competition: Telecommunications Policy for the 1980s*. Englewood Cliffs, NJ: Prentice Hall, 1984.

An analysis of U.S. telecommunications policy undertaken by a prominent economist at the time of the breakup of AT&T.

Bolter, Walter G., James W. McConnaughey, and Fred J. Kelsey. *Telecommunications Policy for the 1990s and Beyond*. Armonk, NY: M.E. Sharpe, 1990.

An insightful look at some of the history of telecommunications policy accompanied by a discussion of future prospects for change.

Botein, Michael, and Douglas H. Ginsburg. *Regulation of the Electronic Mass Media: Law and Policy for Radio, Television, Cable, and the New Video Technologies*, 3rd ed. St. Paul, MN: West Group, 1998.

A legal text cataloging the major legal issues pertaining to mass media regulation.

Braun, Mark J. *AM Stereo and the FCC: Case Study of a Marketplace Shibboleth.* Norwood, NJ: Ablex, 1994.
> A study of FCC radio regulation based in part on interviews with agency insiders.

Brenner, Daniel L. *Law and Regulation of Common Carriers in the Communications Industry.* Boulder, CO: Westview Press, 1992.
> An excellent collection of primary sources and commentary on the history of common carrier regulation in the United States.

Brenner, Daniel L., Monroe E. Price, and Michael Meyerson. *Cable Television and Other Nonbroadcast Video: Law and Policy.* Eagan, MN: Thomson/West, 2003.
> A recent text dealing with the law and policy of nonbroadcast video programming.

Brenner, Daniel L., and William L. Rivers. *Free But Regulated: Conflicting Traditions in Media Law: Collected Essays with Commentary,* 1st ed. Ames: Iowa State University Press, 1982.
> A collection of essays by various authors on issues pertaining to media law and regulation.

Brinson, Susan L. *Personal and Public Interests: Frieda B. Hennock and the Federal Communications Commission.* Westport, CT: Praeger, 2002.
> The culmination of Dr. Brinson's research on FCC commissioner Frieda Hennock.

———. *The Red Scare, Politics, and the Federal Communications Commission, 1941–1960.* Westport, CT: Praeger, 2004.
> This book is the culmination of Dr. Brinson's research on FCC activities during the red scare.

Brock, Gerald W. *The Telecommunications Industry: The Dynamics of Market Structure.* Cambridge, MA: Harvard University Press, 1981.
> An accessible study of the economic and politics of the telecommunications industry and federal telecommunications policy prior to the breakup of AT&T.

———. *Telecommunication Policy for the Information Age: From Monopoly to Competition.* Cambridge, MA: Harvard University Press, 1994.
> Dr. Brock, former FCC common carrier bureau chief, traces the history of telephone regulation through the lenses of his "decentralized policy process" theory.

Cave, Martin, and Robert W. Crandall. *Telecommunications Liberalization on Two Sides of the Atlantic.* Washington, DC: AEI-Brookings Joint Center for Regulatory Studies, 2001.
> A recent study of telecommunications deregulation in the United States and Europe.

Cherington, Paul W., Leon V. Hirsch, and Robert Brandwein. *Television Station Ownership: A Case Study of Federal Agency Regulation.* New York: Hastings House, 1971.
> A study of the FCC and station ownership prior to the 1970s.

Cohen, Jeffrey E. *The Politics of Telecommunications Regulation: The States and the Divestiture of AT&T.* Armonk, NY: M.E. Sharpe, 1992.

    An interesting study of the activities of state regulators following the break up of AT&T.

Cole, Barry G. *After the Breakup: Assessing the New Post-AT&T Divestiture Era.* New York: Columbia University Press, 1991.

    An edited volume containing articles assessing the development of competition in the telecommunications industry following the breakup of AT&T.

Cole, Barry G., and Mal Oettinger. *Reluctant Regulators: The FCC and the Broadcast Audience.* Reading, MA: Addison-Wesley, 1978.

    A study of broadcast regulation at the FCC prior to the late 1970s.

Cowan, Geoffrey. *See No Evil: The Backstage Battle over Sex and Violence on Television,* 1st ed. New York: Simon and Schuster, 1980.

    A popular account the role of the FCC and the broadcast industry in television programming during the 1970s.

Crandall, Robert W. *After the Breakup: U.S. Telecommunications in a More Competitive Era.* Washington, DC: Brookings Institution, 1991.

    A look at competition in the telecommunications industry from the standpoint of an economic analyst.

————. *Competition and Chaos: U.S. Telecommunications Since the 1996 Telecom Act.* Washington, DC: Brookings Institution, 2005.

    An up-to-date analysis of the economic impact of the Telecommunications Act of 1996 on the telecommunications industry. The book also explores the role of regulators in the implementation of the act.

Crandall, Robert W., and James H. Alleman. *Broadband: Should We Regulate High-Speed Internet Access?* Washington, DC: AEI-Brookings Joint Center for Regulatory Studies, 2002.

    An economic study of the prospect of regulating internet access.

Crandall, Robert W., and Kenneth Flamm. *Changing the Rules: Technological Change, International Competition, and Regulation in Communications.* Washington, DC: Brookings Institution, 1989.

    An edited volume that addresses such issues as technological change and international competition in the telecommunications industry before and after the breakup of AT&T.

Crandall, Robert W., and Harold W. Furchtgott-Roth. *Cable TV: Regulation or Competition?* Washington, DC: Brookings Institution, 1996.

    An economic analysis of cable television regulation by a Brookings Institution economist and a soon-to-be FCC commissioner.

Crandall, Robert W., and Leonard Waverman. *Talk Is Cheap: The Promise of Regulatory Reform in North American Telecommunications.* Washington, DC: Brookings Institution, 1995.

    A study of the economics and politics of telecommunications regulation on the eve of the passage of the Telecommunications Act of 1996.

———. *Who Pays for Universal Service? When Telephone Subsidies Become Transparent.* Washington, DC: Brookings Institution Press, 2000.

An economic study of the distribution of costs associated with providing universal telephone service.

Davis, Stephen B. *The Law of Radio Communication,* 1st ed. New York: McGraw-Hill, 1927.

A legal and policy study of radio regulation prior to and including the Radio Act of 1927 by a former solicitor general for the Department of Commerce.

Diamond, Edwin, Norman Sandler, and Milton Mueller. *Telecommunications in Crisis: The First Amendment, Technology, and Deregulation.* Washington, DC: Cato Institute, 1983.

A study of telecommunications deregulation that explores its implications for freedom of the press.

Dill, Clarence C. *Radio Law, Practice and Procedure.* Washington, DC: National Law Book Company, 1938.

A study of radio law and regulation by a senator involved in the writing of the Radio Act of 1927.

Einstein, Mara. *Media Diversity: Economics, Ownership, and the FCC.* Mahwah, NJ: Erlbaum, 2004.

A recent study of the impact of FCC deregulation on television diversity.

Eisenach, Jeffrey A., and Randolph J. May. *Communications Deregulation and FCC Reform: Finishing the Job.* Boston: Kluwer Academic Publishers, 2001.

A collection of articles urging the further deregulation of the telecommunications industry.

Emeritz, Robert E. *Pike & Fischer's FCC Organization & Procedures.* Bethesda, MD: Pike & Fisher, 1994.

A breakdown of the FCC's administrative processes published by a leading publisher in the field of communications law.

———, ed. *The Telecommunications Act of 1996: Law and Legislative History.* Bethesda, MD: Pike & Fischer, Inc., 1996.

This volume contains the full text of the Communications Act of 1934 as amended through 1996. It also contains key documents from the legislative history of the Telecommunications Act of 1996.

Emery, Walter B. *Broadcasting and Government: Responsibilities and Regulations.* East Lansing: Michigan State University Press, 1961.

A thorough and informative discussion of communications law and FCC organization and procedures as they existed prior to 1961.

Erickson, Don V. *Armstrong's Fight for FM Broadcasting: One Man vs. Big Business and Bureaucracy.* Tuscaloosa: University of Alabama Press, 1973.

This book is a study of the role of Edwin H. Armstrong in the development of FM broadcasting.

Faulhaber, Gerald R. *Telecommunications in Turmoil: Technology and Public Policy.* Cambridge, MA: Ballinger, 1987.

This book provides some interesting insights into the reorganization of the telecommunications industry during the years surrounding the breakup of AT&T.

Flannery, Gerald V., ed. *Commissioners of the FCC, 1927–1994.* Lanham, MD: University Press of America, 1995.

This book contains some interesting biographical information about former commissioners of the FCC and FRC.

Fleissner, Jennifer. *The Federal Communications Commission.* New York: Chelsea House Publishers, 1992.

A brief but insightful historical introduction to the FCC intended for high school and college audiences.

Fly, James L. *Chain Broadcasting Regulations and Free Speech.* Washington, DC: Federal Communications Commission, 1942.

A discussion of the First Amendment implications of the FCC's chain broadcasting rules by the controversial chairman who oversaw their development.

Geller, Henry. *A Modest Proposal to Reform the Federal Communications Commission.* Santa Monica, CA: Rand Corp., 1974.

A proposal for reform of the FCC by the former chief counsel of the Agency.

Gerbner, George, Larry P. Gross, and William H. Melody. *Communications Technology and Social Policy: Understanding the New "Cultural Revolution."* New York: Wiley, 1973.

An edited volume containing essays that explore the impact of communications technology on society.

Ginsburg, Douglas H. *Regulation of Broadcasting: Law and Policy towards Radio, Television, and Cable Communications.* St. Paul, MN: West Publishing, 1979.

A legal text on the regulation of broadcasting by a professor and former assistant attorney general.

Graham, James M., and Victor H. Kramer. *Appointments to the Regulatory Agencies: The Federal Communications Commission and the Federal Trade Commission, 1949–1974.* Washington, DC: U.S. Government Printing Office, 1976.

A government document that provides biographical information about commissioners who served at the FCC between 1949 and 1976.

Guimary, Donald L. *Citizens' Groups and Broadcasting.* New York: Praeger, 1975.

A study of the role played by citizen groups in the regulation of broadcasting.

Haight, Timothy R. *Telecommunications Policy and the Citizen: Public Interest Perspectives on the Communications Act Rewrite.* New York: Praeger, 1979.

A volume of essays that explore the efforts in Congress to rewrite the Communications Act of 1934 to introduce greater competition into the communication industry.

Havick, John J. *Communications Policy and the Political Process*. Westport, CT: Greenwood Press, 1983.

An edited volume containing essays on the politics of communications policy right around the time of the breakup of AT&T.

Henck, Fred W., and Bernard Strassburg. *A Slippery Slope: The Long Road to the Breakup of AT&T*. Westport, CT: Greenwood Press, 1988.

An insightful overview of the history of telephone regulation at the FCC that covers the period from the 1940s to the breakup of AT&T. The second author was a former common carrier bureau chief at the FCC.

Hendershot, Heather. *Saturday Morning Censors: Television Regulation Before the V-chip*. Durham, NC: Duke University Press, 1998.

A look at the regulation of television content prior to the mid-1990s.

Herring, James M., and Gerald C. Gross. *Telecommunications: Economics and Regulation*, 1st ed. New York/London: McGraw-Hill, 1936.

A classic, early textbook on the regulation of the telecommunications industry that covers both broadcast and common carrier issues. The second author was an FCC official at the time.

Higgins, Richard S., and Paul H. Rubin. *Deregulating Telecommunications: The Baby Bells Case for Competition*. New York: Wiley, 1995.

A study exploring the need for increased competition in the telecommunications industry in the mid-1990s.

Hilliard, Robert L. *The Federal Communications Commission: A Primer*. Boston: Focal Press, 1991.

A brief and informative, albeit dated, overview of the FCC's statutory authority, organization, and procedures.

Horwitz, Robert B. *The Irony of Regulatory Reform: The Deregulation of American Telecommunications*. New York: Oxford University Press, 1989.

A thorough and lengthy exploration of the political evolution of communications regulation and the forces that led to deregulation.

Huber, Peter W. *Law and Disorder in Cyberspace: Abolish the FCC and Let Common Law Rule the Telecosm*. New York: Oxford University Press, 1997.

A treatise on communications regulation by a prominent advocate of deregulation.

Hudson, Heather E. *Global Connections: International Telecommunications Infrastructure and Policy*. New York: Van Nostrand Reinhold, 1997.

A study examining the directions being taken in telecommunications policy by various nations in the 1990s.

Hughes, Gordon, and David Vines. *Deregulation and the Future of Commercial Television*. Aberdeen, Scotland: Aberdeen University Press, 1989.

A study exploring the impact of deregulation on the television industry.

Johnson, Leland L. *Competition and Cross-Subsidization in the Telephone Industry*. Santa Monica, CA: Rand Corp., 1982.

A study of the economics of the telephone industry by a prominent economist.

Jung, Donald J. *The Federal Communications Commission, the Broadcast Industry, and the Fairness Doctrine, 1981–1987.* Lanham, MD: University Press of America, 1996.
  An interesting look at the highly contentious debates over continuing the use of the Fairness Doctrine during the Reagan years.

———. *Implications of Deregulation on the Public Administration of the Federal Communications Commission, 1981–1987: An Annotated Bibliography.* Monticello, IL: Vance Bibliographies, 1989.
  A bibliography of sources dealing with the FCC and deregulation during the 1980s.

Jussawalla, Meheroo. *Global Telecommunications Policies: The Challenge of Change.* Westport, CT: Greenwood Press, 1993.
  A volume of essays on the telecommunications policies of various nations edited by an economist.

Kinsley, Michael E. *Outer Space and Inner Sanctums: Government, Business, and Satellite Communication.* New York: Wiley, 1976.
  A study focused on the Communications Satellite Corporation and the role of government in shaping satellite communication in the United States.

Kittross, John M. *Administration of American Telecommunications Policy.* New York: Arno Press, 1980.
  An overview of the history of U.S. telecommunications policy prior to the breakup of AT&T.

Korsching, Peter F., Patricia C. Hipple, and Eric Abbott. *Having All the Right Connections: Telecommunications and Rural Viability.* Westport, CT: Praeger, 2000.
  This volume focuses on key issues relating to the extension of telecommunications services to rural areas.

Krasnow, Erwin G., Lawrence D. Longley, and Herbert A. Terry. *The Politics of Broadcast Regulation,* 3rd ed. New York: St. Martin's Press, 1982.
  One of the classic books on the politics of broadcast regulation by two communications scholars and a political scientist. In this volume, Krasnow, Longley, and Terry develop their "systems model" of broadcast regulation.

Kuhn, Raymond. *The Politics of Broadcasting.* New York: St. Martin's Press, 1985.
  An edited volume containing essays on the policies and politics of broadcast regulation in the United States.

Labunski, Richard E. *The First Amendment Under Siege: The Politics of Broadcast Regulation.* Westport, CT: Greenwood Press, 1981.
  A study of the impact of broadcast regulation on the First Amendment rights of broadcasters.

Lamberton, D. M. *Beyond Competition: The Future of Telecommunications.* Amsterdam/New York: Elsevier Science, 1995.

An edited volume containing articles on contemporary issues relating to telecommunications policy around the world.

———. *The New Research Frontiers of Communications Policy*. Amsterdam/New York: Elsevier, 1997.
An edited volume containing essays that provide an overview of the kinds of economic and social research that are being done on telecommunications and information issues.

Langtry, Bruce. *All Connected: Universal Service in Telecommunications*. Carlton South, Vic., Australia: Melbourne University Press, 1998.
A study of the ethical issues surrounding universal service in telecommunications policy.

Largo, Martha P., ed. *The Federal Communications Commission: What Role?* New York: Nova Science Publishers, 2004.
A recent edited volume containing essays that call for further deregulation of the telecommunications industry.

LeDue, Don R. *Cable Television and the FCC: A Crisis in Media Control*. Philadelphia: Temple University Press, 1973.
One of the major studies of the FCC's efforts to develop a regulatory regime for cable television in the 1960s and early 1970s.

———. *Beyond Broadcasting: Patterns in Policy and Law*. New York: Longman, 1987.
A good overview of the law and policies of broadcast regulation as of 1987.

Levin, Harvey J. *Fact and Fancy in Television Regulation: An Economic Study of Policy Alternatives*. New York: Russell Sage Foundation, 1980.
A study of television regulation alternatives by a prominent economist.

———. *The Invisible Resource: Use and Regulation of the Radio Spectrum*. Baltimore: Johns Hopkins Press, 1971.
A thorough study of the economic, engineering, and public policy aspects of the electromagnetic spectrum.

Levy, Brian, and Pablo T. Spiller. *Regulations, Institutions, and Commitment: Comparative Studies of Telecommunications*. New York: Cambridge University Press, 1996.
A comparative study of telecommunications regulation across several nations.

Lewin, Leonard, ed. *Telecommunications in the U.S.: Trends and Policies*. Dedham, MA: Artech, 1981.
An edited volume of key issues of telecommunications policy and FCC regulation up to the early 1980s.

Lipschultz, Jeremy H. *Broadcast Indecency: F.C.C. Regulation and the First Amendment*. Boston: Focal Press, 1997.
A study of FCC indecency regulation and its implications for freedom of speech and press.

Loomis, David G., and Lester D. Taylor. *Forecasting the Internet: Understanding the Explosive Growth of Data Communications*. Boston: Kluwer Academic Publishers, 2002.

> An economic study of the internet that focuses on pricing and demand.

MacAvoy, Paul W. *Deregulation of Cable Television*. Washington, DC: American Enterprise Institute for Public Policy Research, 1977.

> A study by a prominent economist on the need for deregulation of the cable television industry.

Magnant, Robert S. *Domestic Satellite: An FCC Giant Step: Toward Competitive Telecommunications Policy*. Boulder, CO: Westview, 1977.

> A study of FCC policymaking toward satellite communications.

McChesney, Robert W. *Telecommunications, Mass Media, and Democracy: The Battle For the Control of US Broadcasting, 1928–1935*. New York: Oxford University Press, 1993.

> A major work in the field of broadcast history. This book details the struggle between commercial and noncommercial broadcasters to gain control of the airwaves in the years leading up to the passage of the Communications Act of 1934.

McMahon, Robert S. *Federal Regulation of the Radio and Television Broadcast Industry in the United States, 1927–1959: With Special Reference to the Establishment and Operation of Workable Administrative Standards*. New York: Arno Press, 1979.

> A good historical overview of the development of administrative standards at the FRC and FCC.

Mills, Kay. *Changing Channels: The Civil Rights Case That Transformed Television*. Jackson: University Press of Mississippi, 2004.

> The story of legal challenge to a southern station that refused to provide fair coverage of civil rights issues.

Minow, Newton N., and Walter Millis. *Bureaucracy Is Not Muddling Through*. Santa Barbara, CA: Center for the Study of Democratic Institutions, 1963.

> A critical look at the FCC by a former chairman.

Mosco, Vincent. *The Regulation of Broadcasting in the United States: A Comparative Analysis*. Cambridge, MA: Harvard University, Program on Information Technologies and Public Policy, 1975.

> A somewhat dated but informative look at the communications laws and FCC regulation of broadcasting.

Mueller, Milton. *Telephone Companies in Paradise: A Case Study in Telecommunications Deregulation*. New Brunswick, NJ: Transaction Publishers, 1993.

> A case study of state-level deregulation of telephone service in the late 1980s.

———. *Universal Service: Competition, Interconnection, and Monopoly in the Making of the American Telephone System*. Cambridge, MA: MIT Press; Washington, DC: AEI Press, 1997.

> An informative and historical look at the concept of universal service as it developed for telephone regulation.

————. *Ruling the Root: Internet Governance and the Taming of Cyberspace*. Cambridge, MA: MIT Press, 2002.

A recent treatment of the challenges that confront those who seek to regulate the internet.

Napoli, Philip M. *Foundations of Communications Policy: Principles and Process in the Regulation of Electronic Media*. Cresskill, NJ: Hampton Press, 2001.

A good general overview of the basic features of communications policy in the United States.

Newberg, Paula R., ed. *New Directions in Telecommunications Policy*. Durham, NC: Duke University Press, 1989.

Two edited volumes containing chapters dealing with contemporary issues of communications regulation by scholars in various fields.

Noam, Eli M., and Gerard Pogorel. *Asymmetric Deregulation: The Dynamics of Telecommunications Policy in Europe and the United States*. Norwood, NJ: Ablex, 1994.

A comparative study of the development of competition in the telecommunications industry from an economic standpoint.

Noll, Roger G., Merton J. Peck, and John J. McGowan. *Economic Aspects of Television Regulation*. Washington, DC: Brookings Institution, 1973.

A major study of the economics of television by leading economists.

Olufs, Dick. *The Making of Telecommunications Policy*. Boulder, CO: Lynne Rienner Publishers, 1999.

A somewhat theoretical political science study of the telecommunications policy process.

Paglin, Max D. *A Legislative History of the Communications Act of 1934*. New York: Oxford University Press, 1989.

A collection of essays and primary sources that trace the development of the Communications Act of 1934.

Palmer, Michael, and Jeremy Tunstall. *Liberating Communications: Policy-Making in France and Britain*. Oxford, UK/Cambridge, MA: Basil Blackwell, 1990.

A prominent study of communications deregulation in Western European nations.

Park, Rolla E. *Audience Diversion Due to Cable Television: Data for Response to Industry Comments*. Santa Monica, CA: Rand, 1979.

A study of audience trends in the video programming industry during the late 1970s.

————. *The Exclusivity Provisions of the Federal Communications Commission's Cable Television Regulations*. Santa Monica, CA: Rand, 1972.

A RAND study of FCC cable television policy in the early 1970s.

Pike & Fischer, Inc. *Communications Regulation: Current Service*. Bethesda, MD: Pike & Fischer, 1995.

A reference volume on communications regulation issues by a leading publisher of communications law and reference books.

Pool, Ithiel de Sola. *Technologies of Freedom*. Cambridge, MA: Belknap Press, 1983.
A leading study of the free speech issues associated with telecommunications technologies.

———, ed. *The Social Impact of the Telephone*. Cambridge, MA: MIT Press, 1977.
An edited volume containing essays that explore the impact of telephone technology.

Pool, Ithiel de Sola, and Eli M. Noam. *Technologies without Boundaries: On Telecommunications in a Global Age*. Cambridge, MA: Harvard University Press, 1990.
A look at the future of telecommunications technologies by two leading scholars.

Powe, Lucas A. *American Broadcasting and the First Amendment*. Berkeley: University of California Press, 1987.
A good study that analyzes why broadcasting receives somewhat different treatment under the First Amendment than other media.

Ray, William B. *FCC: The Ups and Downs of Radio-TV Regulation*, 1st ed. Ames: Iowa State University Press, 1990.
A good look at the political relationship between the FCC, interest groups, and the other branches of government as the Commission has gone about the business of regulating broadcasting over several decades.

Ricks, Jay E., and Richard E. Wiley. *The Cable Communications Policy Act of 1984*. New York: Law & Business/Harcourt Brace Jovanovich, 1985.
A breakdown of the 1984 Cable Act coauthored by a former FCC chairman.

Rosen, Philip T. *The Modern Stentors: Radio Broadcasters and the Federal Government, 1920–1934*. Westport, CT: Greenwood Press, 1980.
A well-researched look at the politics behind the development of radio regulation during its formative years.

Sapronov, Walter, and William H. Read, eds. *Telecommunications: Law, Regulation, and Policy*. Stamford, CT: Ablex, 1998.
An edited volume of essays dealing with issues of relatively current interest in telecommunications regulation.

Schmeckebrier, Laurence F. *The Federal Radio Commission: Its History, Activities and Organization*. Washington, DC: The Brookings Institution, 1932.
This volume provides an informative overview of the history of radio regulation prior to 1932.

Sewell, Stephen F. *The Federal Communications Commission and the Supreme Court*. United States: S.F. Sewell, 1995.
A look at key FCC legal and regulatory issues that have come before the U.S. Supreme Court.

Shipan, Charles R. *Designing Judicial Review: Interest Groups, Congress, and Communications Policy*. Ann Arbor: University of Michigan Press, 1997.

A theoretical political science study that explores the political choices that went into creating the judicial review provisions of the Radio Act of 1927 and the Communications Act of 1934.

Shooshan, Harry M. *Disconnecting Bell: The Impact of the AT&T Divestiture.* New York: Pergamon Press, 1984.
A collection of issues exploring the history and likely results of the breakup of AT&T.

Slotten, Hugh R. *Radio and Television Regulation: Broadcast Technology in the United States, 1920–1960.* Baltimore: Johns Hopkins University Press, 2000.
A good historical study of radio and television regulation that discusses the early legislative debates as well as issues before the FCC over several decades.

Socolow, A. W. *The Law of Radio Broadcasting.* New York: Baker, Voorhis & Co., 1939.
An early treatise on the radio laws.

Steinfield, Charles W., Johannes M. Bauer, and Laurence Caby. *Telecommunications in Transition: Policies, Services, and Technologies in the European Community.* Thousand Oaks, CA: Sage Publications, 1994.
Another good comparative study of recent trends in telecommunications regulation.

Stern, Robert H. *The Federal Communications Commission and Television: The Regulatory Process in an Environment of Rapid Technical Innovation.* New York: Arno Press, 1979.
A study of the FCC's regulatory responses to television technology.

Stone, Alan. *How America Got On-Line: Politics, Markets, and the Revolution in Telecommunications.* Armonk, NY: M.E. Sharpe, 1997.
An updated presentation of Stone's earlier research on the development of telephone regulation in the United States.

————. *Public Service Liberalism: Telecommunications and Transitions in Public Policy.* Princeton, NJ: Princeton University Press, 1991.
A historical study that looks at the legal treatment of public services industries prior to the late nineteenth century and how these doctrines were adapted and eventually perverted in the era of regulation.

————. *Wrong Number: The Breakup of AT&T.* New York: Basic Books, 1989.
A thoroughly researched account of the major regulatory decisions leading up to the breakup of AT&T. A good source for those seeking an in-depth policy history.

Temin, Peter, and Louis Galambos. *The Fall of the Bell System: A Study in Prices and Politics.* New York: Cambridge University Press, 1987.
A very well-researched study of the policy decisions, people, and politics in the decades leading up to the breakup of AT&T. The authors are two prominent historians who employ a combination of personal interviews and archival research.

Teske, Paul E. *After Divestiture: The Political Economy of State Telecommunications Regulation.* Albany: State University of New York Press, 1990.

A study of state-level telecommunications regulation in the 1980s by a leading political scientist.

———. *American Regulatory Federalism and Telecommunications Infrastructure.* Hillsdale, NJ: Erlbaum, 1995.

A volume of essays that explore state-level innovations in telecommunications regulation.

Ulloth, Dana R. *The Supreme Court: A Judicial Review of the Federal Communications Commission.* New York: Arno Press, 1979.

A study of Supreme Court decisions that have impacted FCC regulation.

U.S. Congress. House. Committee on Interstate and Foreign Commerce. Special Subcommittee on Legislative Oversight. *Digest of Cases Remanded to Federal Communications Commission by the Appellate Courts, and Report as to Adequacy of Statutory Provisions Pertaining to Such Remands.* Washington, DC: U.S. Government Printing Office, 1958.

A government document that profiles some of the major early federal court cases involving the FCC.

———. *Regulation of Broadcasting: Half a Century of Government Regulation of Broadcasting and the Need for Further Legislative Action.* Washington, DC: U.S. Government Printing Office, 1958.

A government document prepared for a congressional committee that traces the development of broadcast regulation up through 1958.

Vogelsang, Ingo, and Benjamin M. Compaine. *The Internet Upheaval: Raising Questions, Seeking Answers in Communications Policy.* Cambridge, MA: MIT Press, 2000.

This volume explores some of the public policy challenges presented by the internet.

Weinhaus, Carol L., and Anthony G. Oettinger. *Behind the Telephone Debates.* Norwood, NJ: Ablex, 1988.

A study that provides an analysis of the choices that are made by telecommunications firms in the regulatory process.

Weiss, Leonard W., and Michael W. Klass, eds. *Regulatory Reform: What Actually Happened.* Boston: Little, Brown, 1986.

An edited volume containing a series of essays on the deregulation of various industries in the late 1970s and early 1980s.

Zarkin, Kimberly A. *Anti-Indecency Groups and the Federal Communications Commission: A Study in the Politics of Broadcast Regulation.* Lewiston, NY: Edwin Mellen Press, 2003.

A study that profiles the impact of two anti-indecency groups on FCC decisionmaking through their participation in FCC dockets, complaints, and congressional hearings.

Zarkin, Michael J. *Social Learning and the History of U.S. Telecommunications Policy, 1900–1996: Creating the Telecommunications Act of 1996.* Lewiston, NY: Edwin Mellen Press, 2003.

A political science study of congressional and FCC decisionmaking in the area of telephone regulation throughout much of the twentieth century. The author takes the position that telecommunications policy change is best viewed as a process of "social learning." This volume also provides a fairly complete legislative history of the Telecommunications Act of 1996.

JOURNAL ARTICLES

Abernathy, Kathleen Q. "The Role of the Federal Communications Commission on the Path from Vast Wasteland to Fertile Plain." *Federal Communications Law Journal* 55 (2003): 435.

A discussion of the FCC's role in the regulation of broadcast programming from the standpoint of a commissioner.

Blackman, Colin R. "Convergence between Telecommunications and Other Media." *Telecommunications Policy* 22 (1998): 163.

An examination of the regulatory issues surrounding technological convergence of different sectors of the communications industry.

Botein, Michael. "Cable TV in the U.S.A: The Legal and Regulatory Environment." *Journal of Media Law and Practice* 3 (1982): 320.

An interesting look at the legal environment surrounding cable television regulation.

Brand, Keith. "The Rebirth of Low-Power FM Broadcasting in the U.S." *Journal of Radio Studies* 11 (2004): 153.

A study examining the impact of low-power FM on ownership diversity in broadcasting since 2000.

Brenner, Daniel L. "The Regulation of Radio and Television in the United States." *Journal of Media Law and Practice* 11 (1990): 60.

An article on radio and television regulation by a former assistant to FCC Chairman Mark Fowler.

Brinson, Susan L. "Epilogue to the Quiz Show Scandal: A Case Study of the FCC and Corporate Favoritism." *Journal of Broadcasting and Electronic Media* 47 (2003): 276.

A look at the FCC's application of its "character" requirements for broadcast licensees in the wake of the 1950s quiz show scandal.

———. "Missed Opportunities: FCC Commissioner Frieda Hennock and the UHF Debate." *Journal of Broadcasting and Electronic Media* 44 (2000): 248.

A study focusing on the role of Frieda Hennock, the first female FCC Commissioner, in the early development of UHF television.

———. "War on the Homefront: The FCC and the House Un-American Activities Committee." *Historical Journal of Film, Radio, and Television* 21 (2001): 63.

A historical study of the FCC's role in policing the media industry during the Red Scare of the 1950s.

———. "Reds Need Not Apply: Communism and the FCC, 1940–1960." *Communication Law and Policy* 7 (2002): 107.

A look at the impact of the Red Scare on the actions of the FCC over two decades.

Calabrese, Andrew. "Stealth Regulation: Moral Meltdown and Political Radicalism at the FCC." *New Media and Society* 6 (2004): 106.

A commentary on the development of the communications industry since the passage of the Telecommunications Act of 1996.

Campbell, Heather E., and Marianne Barrett. "Cable Television and Telephony in the Telecommunications Act of 1996: Economics, Law, Regulation, and Politics." *Communication Law and Policy* 2 (1997): 477.

An article that calls into question exactly how much "deregulation" the Telecommunications Act of 1996 introduced into the telephone and cable television industries.

Canon, Bradley C. "Voting Behavior on the FCC." *Midwest Journal of Political Science* 13 (1969): 587.

An interesting, although somewhat dated, political science study of FCC commissioner voting patterns.

Clark, Naeemah. "The Birth of an Advocacy Group." *Journalism History* 30 (2004): 66.

This article presents a case study of Action for Children's Television, a citizen group that actively lobbies the FCC over issues relating to broadcast programming content.

Coase, Ronald H. "The Federal Communications Commission." *Journal of Law and Economics* 2 (1959): 1.

A classic article on the FCC's regulation of broadcasting by an eminent economist. In this piece, Coase advances the idea of spectrum auctions as an alternative to the traditional public interest approach to broadcast licensing.

Cohen, Jeffrey E. "The Dynamics of the Revolving Door on the FCC." *American Journal of Political Science* 30 (1986): 689.

A political science study testing the hypothesis that FCC commissioners with a history of employment in the media industry will be more supportive of the industry in their voting patterns.

———. "The Telephone Problem and the Road to Telephone Regulation in the United States, 1876–1917." *Journal of Policy History* 6 (1991): 42.

A historical study of early telephone regulation in the United States by a political scientist employing "public choice" theory.

Coopman, Ted M. "FCC Enforcement Difficulties with Unlicensed Micro Radio." *Journal of Broadcasting and Electronic Media* 43 (1999): 582.

An article detailing some of the regulatory and enforcement strategies used by the FCC to deal with unlicensed micro radio.

Devins, Neal. "Congress, the FCC and the Search for the Public Trustee." *Law and Contemporary Problems* 56 (1993): 145.

This article looks at the constitutional issues surrounding the efforts of the FCC to retrench from policies protecting media diversity, such as the Fairness Doctrine.

Donnerstein, Edward, Barbara Wilson, and Daniel Linz. "On the Regulation of Broadcast Incedency to Protect Children." *Journal of Broadcasting and Electronic Media* 36 (1992): 111.

An article by several authors whose research is aimed at understanding the impact of media indecency and violence on children and the prospects of regulation as a solution.

Edwardson, Mickie. "James Lawrence Fly's Report on Chain Broadcasting (1941) and the Regulation of Monopoly in America." *Historical Journal of Film, Radio, and Television* 22 (2002): 397.

Presents a discussion of the FCC's 1941 Report on Chain Broadcasting and the specific steps it outlined for the prevention of radio concentration in the United States.

Fowler, Mark, and Daniel Brenner. "A Marketplace Approach to Broadcast Regulation." *Texas Law Review* 60 (1982): 207.

This is a classis law review by another controversial former FCC chairman. In the article, Fowler and his legal assistant make the case for a policy of deregulation in the broadcasting industry.

Garcia-Murillo, Martha A., and Ian MacInnes. "FCC Organizational Structure and Regulatory Convergence." *Telecommunications Policy* 25 (2001): 431.

The article presents a systematic analysis of FCC decisionmaking to demonstrate that the agency's current system of organization, based largely around distinct industry sectors, has become obsolete in the face of technological convergence.

Glasser, Theodore L., and Harvey Jassem. "Indecent Broadcasts and the Listener's Right of Privacy." *Journal of Broadcasting* 24 (1980): 285.

This article explores some key issues associated with broadcast indecency shortly after the Supreme Court's *Pacifica* decision.

Godfrey, Donald G. "The 1927 Radio Act: People and Politics." *Journalism History* 4 (1977): 74.

This is a good overview of the personalities and political considerations involved in the making of the Radio Act.

Goodman, Mark, and Mark Gring. "The Ideological Fight over Creation of the Federal Radio Commission in 1927." *Journalism History* 26 (2000): 117.

Presents an analysis of how the contrasting regulatory philosophies of Herbert Hoover, Senator Clarence Dill, and Representative Wallace White shaped the creation of the Federal Radio Commission.

Gormley, William T. "A Test of the Revolving Door Hypothesis at the FCC." *American Journal of Political Science* 23 (1979): 665.

A political science article that looks at the relationship between the votes of FCC commissioners and their work history prior to joining the Commission.

Hazlett, Thomas. "The Rationality of U.S. Regulation of the Broadcast Spectrum." *Journal of Law and Economics* 33 (1990): 133.

This is a classic article by an eminent economist that characterizes the Radio Act of 1927 as a rational political bargain between legislators and the broadcast industry.

Holman, JoAnne, and Michael A. McGregor. "'Thank You for Taking the Time to Read This': Public Participation via New Communication Technologies at the FCC." *Journalism and Communication Monographs* 2 (2001): 159.

A study that explores the extent to which e-mail comments are considered by the FCC in decisionmaking.

Horwitz, Robert B. "Broadcast Reform Revisited: Reverend Everett C. Parker and the 'Standing' Case." *The Communications Review* 2, no. 3 (1997): 311.

An interesting study of the U.S. Appeals Court Case in which citizens gained standing to challenge broadcast license renewals before the FCC.

Huff, W.A.K. "FCC Standard-Setting with Regard to FM Stereo and AM Stereo." *Journalism Quarterly* 68 (1991): 483.

Compares the development of the FCC's decisionmaking surrounding the setting of standards for both FM and AM stereo. The article notes the consequences of the FCC's decision to allow the marketplace to determine AM standards early on.

Kim, Haeryon. "Congressional Influence on the FCC: An Analysis of Confirmation Hearings for Commission Chairmen, 1969–1989." *Communications and the Law* 15 (1993): 37.

An interesting overview of the political issues discussed in the confirmation hearings of FCC chairmen.

———. "The Politics of Deregulation: Public Participation in the FCC Rulemaking Process for DBS." *Telecommunications Policy* 19 (1995): 51.

A study of the politics of public participation in a major FCC rulemaking.

Klopfenstein, Bruce C., and David Sedman. "Technical Standards and the Marketplace: The Case of AM Stereo." *Journal of Broadcasting and Electronic Media* 34 (1990): 171.

A study of the FCC's decision to let the marketplace determine technical standards for AM stereo.

Lichty, Lawrence W. "The Impact of FRC and FCC Commissioners' Backgrounds on the Regulation of Broadcasting." *Journal of Broadcasting* 6 (1962): 97.

Lichty provides biographical sketches of FRC and FCC commissioners up through 1960.

Lipschultz, Jeremy H. "Conceptual Problems of Broadcast Indecency Policy and Application." *Communications and the Law* 14 (1992): 3.

Lipschultz provides a compelling social science analysis of broadcast indecency policy.

Longley, Lawrence D., Erwin G. Krasnow, and Herbert A. Terry. "The Courts in Broadcast Regulatory Policy-Making." *Hastings Comm/Ent Law Journal* 4 (1982): 377.

A study of the role played by the federal courts in shaping the countours of broadcast regulation.

Longley, Lawrence D., Herbert A. Terry, and Erwin G. Krasnow. "Citizens Groups in Broadcast Regulatory Policy-Making." *Policy Studies Journal* 12 (1983): 258.

A study exploring the impact and relative strength of citizens groups in the making of broadcast policy.

Mason, Laurie, Christine M. Bachen, and Stephanie L. Craft. "Support for FCC Minority Ownership Policy: How Broadcast Station Owner Race or Ethnicity Affects News and Public Affairs Programming Diversity." *Communication Law and Policy* 6 (2001): 37.

Details the results of a study in which broadcast stations were surveyed to determine whether the race/ethnicity of the owner impacts diversity in news coverage.

McChesney, Robert W. "Franklin Roosevelt, His Administration, and the Communications Act of 1934." *American Journalism* 5, no. 4 (1988): 204.

A well-researched look at the influence of FDR in shaping the Communications Act.

———. "Media Policy Goes to Main Street: The Uprising of 2003." *Communication Review* 7, no. 3 (2004): 223.

In this article, McChesney analyzes the public opposition to the efforts of the FCC to increase media consolidation in 2003.

McGregor, Michael A. "The FCC's Use of Informal Comments in Rule-Making Proceedings." *Journal of Broadcasting and Electronic Media* 30 (1986): 413.

An interesting look at the FCC's rulemaking practices.

Moss, David A., and Michael R. Fein. "Radio Regulation Revisited: Coase, the FCC, and the Public Interest." *Journal of Policy History* 15 (2003): 389.

A very good recent article by two authors who argue that, contrary to the arguments of many political economists, the authors of the Radio Act of 1927 were truly interested in the "public interest."

Napoli, Philip M. "Government Assessment of the FCC." *Telecommunications Policy* 22 (1998): 409.

A study of assessments that have been made of FCC activities by the other branches of government.

———. "The Marketplace of Ideas Metaphor in Communications Regulation." *Journal of Communication* 49, no. 4 (1999): 151.

Presents an analysis of the FCC's use of the marketplace of ideas metaphor as a rhetorical strategy used in the justification of deregulatory policies.

———. "The Federal Communications Commission and Broadcast Policy-Making, 1966–1995: A Logistic Regression Analysis of Interest Group Influence." *Communication Law and Policy* 5 (2000): 203.

A quantitative study of interest group participation in broadcast policy decisionmaking over several decades.

————. "The Public Interest Obligations Initiative: Lost in the Digital Television Shuffle." *Journal of Broadcasting and Electronic Media* 47 (2003): 153.

An article focusing on issues related to the public interest obligations of digital broadcasters in the United States.

Nord, David P. "The FCC, Educational Broadcasting, and Political Interest Group Activity." *Journal of Broadcasting* 22 (1978): 321.

A study of the role played by citizen groups in matters pertaining to educational broadcasting before the FCC.

Raphael, Chad. "The FCC's Broadcast News Distortion Rules: Regulation by Drooping Eyelid." *Communications Law and Policy* 6 (2001): 485.

The article presents an analysis of the FCC's long-standing broadcast news distortion rules and ultimately concludes that the policy is mainly symbolic in its current form.

Rivera-Sanchez, Milagros. "Developing and Indecency Standard: The Federal Communications Commission and the Regulation of Offensive Speech, 1927–1964." *Journalism History* 20 (1993): 3.

One of the best historical works on the development of the FCC's indecency standard.

————. "The Origins of the Ban on 'Obscene, Indecent, or Profane' Language of the Radio Act of 1927." *Journalism and Communication Monographs* no. 149 (1995): 1.

A monograph that chronicles the origins of the regulation of broadcast indecency as stipulated in section 29 of the Radio Act of 1927.

Rivera-Sanchez, Milagros, and Michelle Ballard. "A Decade of Indecency Enforcement: A Study of How the Federal Communications Commission Assesses Indecency Fines, 1987–1997." *Journalism and Mass Communication Quarterly* 50 (1998): 637.

A look at the FCC's indecency regulatory activities during a time when these issues have become more politically prominent.

Rosston, Gregory L. "The Long and Winding Road: The FCC Paves the Path with Good Intentions." *Telecommunications Policy* 27 (2003): 501.

An article that profiles some of the problems that the FCC is encountering in moving toward a market-based spectrum policy.

Rowland, William D., Jr. "The Meaning of 'The Public Interest' in Communications Policy, Part I: Its Origins in State and Federal Regulation." *Communication Law and Policy* 2 (1997): 309.

Presents an examination of the legal meaning of the concept of public interest prior to the inception of broadcast regulation.

————. "The Meaning of 'The Public Interest' in Communications Policy, Part II: Its Implementation in Early Broadcast Law and Regulation." *Communication Law and Policy* 2 (1997): 363.

Provides a discussion of the development of the public interest standard during the early years of radio law.

Samoriski, Jan H., John L. Huffman, and Denise M. Trauth. "The V-Chip and Cyber Cops: Technology vs. Regulation." *Communication Law and Policy* 2 (1997): 143.
Provides an analysis of the interests at stake in regulating television violence and indecency on the internet and why they might be better served by requiring the use of filtering technology rather than employing other regulatory measures.

Smith, F. Leslie. "Quelling Radio's Quacks: The FCC's First Public-Interest Programming Campaign." *Journalism Quarterly* 71 (1994): 594.
An article that examines the FCC's first campaign to ensure that broadcasters programmed in the public interest.

Socolow, Michael J. "Questioning Advertising's Influence over American Radio: The Blue Book Controversy of 1945–1947." *Journal of Radio Studies* 9 (2002): 282.
This article presents an analysis of the political controversy surrounding the FCC's 1946 *Blue Book*.

Steel, Peter B. "Who Wants DTV?" *Journal of Broadcasting and Electronic Media* 47 (2003): 149.
This article examines some of the regulatory problems that the FCC has faced in the transition from analog to digital television.

Sullivan, John L., and Amy B. Jordan. "Playing by the Rules: Impact and Implementation of Children's Educational Television Regulations among Local Broadcasters." *Communication Law and Policy* 4 (1999): 483.
A study examining the implementation of the FCC's 1997 regulations on educational programming for children.

Timmer, Joel. "Broadcast, Cable and Digital Must Carry: The Other Digital Divide." *Communication Law and Policy* 9, no. 1 (2004): 101.
An article analyzing how the law of must carry will apply to cable television providers as the transition is made from analog to digital television.

———. "Incrementalism and Policymaking on Television Violence." *Communication Law and Policy* 9 (2004): 351.
In this article, a theoretical explanation is offered for why Congress switched to a more proactive approach to regulating television violence in the 1990s.

Wenmouth, Williams. "Impact of Commissioner Background on FCC Decisions, 1962–1975." *Journal of Broadcasting* 20 (1976): 239.
A study of backgrounds and policy preferences of FCC Commissioners.

Wiley, Richard E., and Lawrence W. Secrest. "Recent Developments in Program Content Regulation." *Federal Communications Law Journal* 57 (2005): 235.
This article presents a discussion of recent developments in the FCC's regulation of broadcast indecency.

Zarkin, Kimberly A., and Michael J. Zarkin. "Entrepreneurial Politics and Civil Liberties Policy: The Case of Communications Decency Legislation." *International Social Science Review* 77, no. 3/4 (2002): 191.

A policy study that offers an explanation for why Congress passes communications decency laws, even when it seems apparent that they will be ruled unconstitutional by the courts.

Zarkin, Michael J. "Telecommunications Policy Learning: The Case of the FCC's Computer Inquiries." *Telecommunications Policy* 27 (2003): 283.

This article provides a historical progression through the FCC's three computer inquiries between 1966 and 1986. The article concludes that in each of these inquiries, the FCC learned from experience.

———. "Drawing Lessons from Across the Pond: The Fungibility of US and British Telephone Regulation." *Policy and Politics* 33 (2005): 191.

A study that explores how FCC learned from the experiences of the British in the formulation of price caps regulation in the late 1980s.

Index

About the Authors

KIMBERLY A. ZARKIN is Assistant Professor of Communications at Westminster College in Salt Lake City, UT. She is author of *Anti-Indecency Groups and the Federal Communications Commission: A Study in the Politics of Broadcast Regulation* (2003).

MICHAEL J. ZARKIN is Assistant Professor of Political Science at Westminster College in Salt Lake City, UT. He is author of *Social Learning and the History of U.S. Telecommunications Policy, 1900–1996* (2003).